# LONDON MATHEMATICAL SOCIETY LECTURE NOTE SERIES

Managing Editor: Professor Endre Süli, Mathematical Institute, University of Oxford,
Woodstock Road, Oxford OX2 6GG, United Kingdom

The titles below are available from booksellers, or from Cambridge University Press at
www.cambridge.org/mathematics

"In this book, Jeffrey Shallit gives combinatorics on words enthusiasts access to new and exciting tools to compute examples and test conjectures. Far from a mere user's manual, the text fully introduces the reader to the interactions of logic and words, proving basic theorems like the decidability of Presburger arithmetic. It will be of great use to students and researchers, as well as the source of many future developments."

— Dominique Perrin, Université Gustave Eiffel

"This book focuses on a decision procedure, which is rather easy to implement as a computer program and allows one to prove many results, classical and new, in combinatorics on words. It addresses decision problems and enumeration problems on sequences that are expressible in first-order logic. The reader will appreciate the style, which is relaxed and pleasant to read, and the numerous examples and exercises. This book is a useful complement to the previous monograph, *Automatic Sequences*, co-authored by Shallit and Allouche."

— Yann Bugeaud, University of Strasbourg

"This is a marvelous book with a very fresh approach to the decidability and structural analysis of combinatorics on words. It combines three different mathematical research topics: first-order logic, automatic sequences, and combinatorics on words. More precisely, it interprets infinite morphic words as automatic sequences via $k$-automata and expresses properties (of words) in first-order logic. Due to the decidability of such logic, decision results and structural properties of combinatorics on words are established. A crucial role in this approach is to employ a powerful software package called `Walnut`. The author illustrates the power of his approach by giving a huge number of results obtained by this method. Not only are old and new results proved, but even some errors in previous ones are corrected. Anybody interested in, or curious about, this topic should be enthusiastic about this masterpiece."

— Juhani Karhumäki, University of Turku (Emeritus)

London Mathematical Society Lecture Note Series: 482

# The Logical Approach
# to Automatic Sequences
## Exploring Combinatorics on Words with Walnut

JEFFREY SHALLIT

*University of Waterloo*

CAMBRIDGE
UNIVERSITY PRESS

# CAMBRIDGE
## UNIVERSITY PRESS

University Printing House, Cambridge CB2 8BS, United Kingdom

One Liberty Plaza, 20th Floor, New York, NY 10006, USA

477 Williamstown Road, Port Melbourne, VIC 3207, Australia

314–321, 3rd Floor, Plot 3, Splendor Forum, Jasola District Centre,
New Delhi – 110025, India

103 Penang Road, #05–06/07, Visioncrest Commercial, Singapore 238467

Cambridge University Press is part of the University of Cambridge.

It furthers the University's mission by disseminating knowledge in the pursuit of
education, learning, and research at the highest international levels of excellence.

www.cambridge.org
Information on this title: www.cambridge.org/9781108745246
DOI: 10.1017/9781108775267

© Jeffrey Shallit 2023

First published 2023

A catalogue record for this publication is available from the British Library.

ISBN 978-1-108-74524-6 Paperback

# Contents

# Preface

To summarize, this is what you'll learn from this book.

1 A decision procedure for *proving* theorems about a large class of interesting sequences exists (and handles many famous sequences such as Thue-Morse, Rudin-Shapiro, etc.), based on first-order logic.

2 Many properties that have long been studied in combinatorics on words can be phrased in first-order logic (including some for which this is not so obvious!) and hence are amenable to this procedure.

3 The decision procedure is relatively easy to implement as a computer program, and often runs remarkably quickly, despite its formidable worst-case complexity—and there is an implementation that is free and publicly available, called Walnut.

4 The existence of this decision procedure allows one to very simply prove many results on the kinds of sequences in its domain, the *automatic* sequences. This gives a "logical approach" to the topic of automatic sequences that has not received enough attention.

5 The method can also be used to not simply decide, but also *enumerate*, many aspects of sequences.

6 Many results already in the literature (in dozens of papers and Ph.D. theses) can be reproved by Walnut in a matter of seconds (including fixing at least two that were wrong!).

7 Many new results can be proved, such as avoidability of the pattern $xxx^R$—see Section 8.5.18.

8 However, there are some well-defined limits to what we can do with the method because either

- the property is not expressible in first-order logic.
- the underlying sequence leads to undecidability.

The book can be useful to you even if you don't want to know all the details about how Walnut works. If you're looking to verify a certain property of a sequence, the 80 or so examples in Chapter 8 can be used as templates to help find the appropriate Walnut code to test the property. Similarly, the examples in Chapters 9 and 10 can be used as templates to solve enumeration problems.

# About the book

The title of this book is a bit of a pun. On the one hand, the book is devoted to looking at automatic sequences through the lens of first-order logic. On the other hand, my book with Allouche on automatic sequences published in 2003 [16] almost entirely omitted mention of the logical approach, which is powerful and fundamental, and so it seems "logical" to revisit automatic sequences from this different viewpoint. In this latter sense, this book is a companion to [16]. In this book, we take a fresh look at some of the results in [16] and reprove them in a much simpler manner. (For an example, see Section 8.11.2.)

The basic ideas of this "logical" approach to automatic sequences go back to J. Richard Büchi, in a famous 1962 paper. Since then, his work has been corrected and extended by many people, including Véronique Bruyère, Georges Hansel, Christian Michaux, Roger Villemaire, and others. This book is based on their work, for which I am very grateful.

This book is based on many papers by me and my co-authors; for example, [54, 12, 77, 347, 64, 324, 168, 174, 173, 175, 78, 169, 171, 325, 280, 170, 348, 127, 279, 36, 28, 337, 349, 350, 352, 354, 355, 356, 357]. Sometimes I've taken text verbatim from these papers. In other cases you may want to look at the papers for more details.

My philosophy in the book is not to prove everything in detail. When proofs are omitted, they can almost always be found in the references provided. Many of the details we omit can be found in [16] or the books of Michel Rigo [317, 318].

Throughout the book there are exercises to help understand the material. I encourage you to try them. There are also open problems; if you solve any of them, please let me know! Similarly, if you find new uses for Walnut, please let me know.

In this book I could cover only a small number of the possible applications of the decision procedure to combinatorics on words. I maintain a web page

https://cs.uwaterloo.ca/~shallit/walnut.html

that tries to list all of the papers that have used `Walnut` in one form or another to do useful computations.

If you or someone you know has written a relevant paper not on this list, please contact me so that I can add it. Similarly, if you discover any errors in the text, please inform me at `shallit@uwaterloo.ca`. The URL above is also the place to learn about new versions of `Walnut`.

# Acknowledgments

I am very grateful to Hamoon Mousavi, Narad Rampersad, Jean-Paul Allouche, James Currie, Lucas Mol, Jason Bell, Émilie Charlier, Luke Schaeffer, Michel Rigo, Pascal Ochem, Aseem Raj Baranwal, and Christoph Haase for valuable discussions over the last ten years.

I thank Jason Bell, Émilie Charlier, Daniel Gabric, Judah Koslowe, Lucas Mol, Narad Rampersad, Michel Rigo, Luke Schaeffer, Thomas Stoll, Arthur Wesley, and Anatoly Zavyalov for pointing out a variety of typos and errors in the manuscript. Of course, all errors that remain are my responsibility. Everyone should be grateful to Hamoon Mousavi, for creating the wonderful software called `Walnut` and making it available free to the world. In addition, thanks are due to to Aseem Raj Baranwal, who modified `Walnut` to allow Ostrowski numeration systems, and to Laindon C. Burnett, Kai Hsiang Yang, and Anatoly Zavyalov, who added many useful features to `Walnut`.

A preliminary implementation of some of the ideas here was carried out previously by Daniel Goč and Dane Henshall.

I am grateful to Sarah Routledge, Clare Dennison, and Kaitlin Leach at Cambridge University Press for their expert assistance in getting this book published.

This work benefited from the use of the CrySP RIPPLE Facility at the University of Waterloo. Thanks to Ian Goldberg for allowing me to run computations on this machine.

# Permissions

Material from Chapter 2 is reprinted by permission from Cambridge University Press. Shallit, J. (2008). *A Second Course in Formal Languages and Automata Theory.*

Material from Sections 3.5, 5.4–5.5, and Chapter 9 is reprinted by permission from Cambridge University Press. Allouche, J., Shallit, J. (2003). *Automatic Sequences: Theory, Applications, Generalizations.*

The material from Sections 8.5.7–8.5.8, 8.6.3, 8.6.12 and Theorem 8.6.6 is reprinted by permission from EDP Sciences. Mousavi H., Schaeffer L., Shallit J. Decision Algorithms for Fibonacci-Automatic Words, I: Basic Results. In *RAIRO–Theor. Inf. Appl.* Volume 50, Number 1.

Material from Section 8.5.21 is reprinted by permission from EDP Sciences. Shallit J., Zarifi R. Circular critical exponents for Thue–Morse factors. In *RAIRO–Theor. Inf. Appl.* Volume 53, Number 1–2.

Material from Section 8.6.13 is reprinted by permission from Springer Nature. Goč D., Henshall D., Shallit J. (2012) Automatic Theorem-Proving in Combinatorics on Words. In: Moreira N., Reis R. (eds) *Implementation and Application of Automata.* CIAA 2012. Lecture Notes in Computer Science, vol. 7381. Springer, Berlin, Heidelberg.

Material from Section 8.8.2 is reprinted by permission from Springer Nature. Goč D., Saari K., Shallit J. (2013) Primitive Words and Lyndon Words in Automatic and Linearly Recurrent Sequences. In: Dediu AH., Martín-Vide C., Truthe B. (eds) *Language and Automata Theory and Applications. LATA 2013.* Lecture Notes in Computer Science, vol. 7810. Springer, Berlin, Heidelberg.

Material from Sections 8.8.3, 8.8.5, and 8.8.8 is reprinted by permission from [336].

Material from Section 8.10.1 is reprinted by permission from Taylor & Francis Group. Kaplan C., Shallit J. (2021) A Frameless 2-Coloring of the Plane Lattice, *Mathematics Magazine.*

Material from Sections 9.11.6 and 9.11.7 is reprinted by permission from World Scientific Press. Du C., Mousavi H., Schaeffer L., Shallit J. (2016) Decision Algorithms for Fibonacci-Automatic Words, III: Enumeration and Abelian Properties. In: *International Journal of Foundations of Computer Science*, Vol. 27, No. 08, pp. 943–963.

Material from Chapter 10 is reprinted by permission from Springer Nature. Shallit J. (2021) Synchronized Sequences. In: Springer, *WORDS 2021: Combinatorics on Words*, by Lecroq T., Puzynina S. (eds).

Material from Section 10.8.19 is reprinted by permission from Springer Nature. Goč D., Schaeffer L., Shallit J. (2013) Subword Complexity and *k*-

Synchronization. In: Béal MP., Carton O. (eds) *Developments in Language Theory. DLT 2013.* Lecture Notes in Computer Science, vol. 7907. Springer, Berlin, Heidelberg.

Material from Section 10.11 is reprinted by permission from Springer Nature. Baranwal A.R., Shallit J. (2019) Critical Exponent of Infinite Balanced Words via the Pell Number System. In: Mercaş R., Reidenbach D. (eds) *Combinatorics on Words. WORDS 2019.* Lecture Notes in Computer Science, vol. 11682. Springer, Cham.

Material from Section 11.5 is reprinted by permission from Springer Nature. Bell J.P., Lidbetter T.F., Shallit J. (2018) Additive Number Theory via Approximation by Regular Languages. In: Hoshi M., Seki S. (eds) *Developments in Language Theory. DLT 2018.* Lecture Notes in Computer Science, vol. 11088. Springer, Cham.

Material from Chapter 12 is reprinted by permission from Springer Nature. Goč D., Mousavi H., Schaeffer L., Shallit J. (2015) A New Approach to the Paperfolding Sequences. In: Beckmann A., Mitrana V., Soskova M. (eds) *Evolving Computability. CiE 2015.* Lecture Notes in Computer Science, vol. 9136. Springer, Cham.

# 1

# Introduction

Sequences abound in the mathematical literature! To name just a few, there are the Fibonacci numbers [376]

$$0, 1, 1, 2, 3, 5, 8, 13, \ldots$$

defined by $F_0 = 0$, $F_1 = 1$, and $F_n = F_{n-1} + F_{n-2}$ for $n \geq 2$; the Pell numbers

$$0, 1, 2, 5, 12, 29, 70, 169, 408, \ldots$$

defined by $P_0 = 0$, $P_1 = 1$, and $P_n = 2P_{n-1} + P_{n-2}$ for $n \geq 2$; Propp's sequence

$$0, 2, 3, 6, 7, 8, 9, 12, 15, 18, 19, 20, \ldots,$$

the unique strictly increasing sequence satisfying $s(s(n)) = 3n$, and so forth. These are examples of sequences with domain and codomain $\mathbb{N} = \{0, 1, 2, \ldots\}$, the natural numbers; all have been widely studied. If these three sequences are not enough for you, you can explore more than 350,000 sequences at the remarkable OEIS (*On-Line Encyclopedia of Integer Sequences*), available at https://oeis.org .

We'll return to sequences taking their values in $\mathbb{N}$ in Section 2.5 and Chapter 9, but for the moment let's start with some simpler sequences: sequences $(a_n)_{n \geq 0}$ taking their values[1] in a *finite alphabet* of symbols $\Sigma$, such as $\Sigma_2 = \{0, 1\}$. There are, of course, uncountably many such sequences, but only countably many that can be computed by a Turing machine (in the sense that the Turing machine starts with a representation of $n$ on its tape and ends with $a_n$ on the tape). Sequences of this kind are also called *infinite words*, and we will use the terms interchangeably in this book.

Here's an example of the kind of sequence we will study. The so-called

---

[1] Sometimes we write $a_n$ for the $n$th term of a sequence, and sometimes we write $a(n)$. They almost always represent the same thing, and the choice depends on what is typographically nicest.

1

*Thue-Morse sequence* **t** is a celebrated binary sequence named after the Norwegian mathematician Axel Thue [373, 374, 45], who discovered it in 1912, and Marston Morse, who independently discovered it in 1921 [275]. It also appears if one reads "between the lines" in an 1851 paper of Étienne Prouhet [303], and it has since been rediscovered many times (e.g., [140]). For more information about **t**, see the survey [15].

The Thue-Morse sequence is given by

$$\mathbf{t} = (t_n)_{n \geq 0} = t_0 t_1 t_2 \cdots = 0110100110010110100010110 \cdots ,$$

and can be defined in several different ways, as follows:

(a) $t_n$ is the parity of the number of 1s in the binary representation of $n$: 1 if there are an odd number of 1s, and 0 if there are an even number.

(b) $t_n$ satisfies the identities $t_{2n} = t_n$ and $t_{2n+1} = 1 - t_n$ for $n \geq 0$.

(c) Define the morphism $\mu$ as follows: $\mu(0) = 01$ and $\mu(1) = 10$. It obeys the rule $\mu(xy) = \mu(x)\mu(y)$ for finite words $x, y$. Now iterate $\mu$ on 0, writing $\mu^0$ for the identity map, $\mu^1 = \mu$, $\mu^2(0) = \mu(\mu(0)) = 0110$, $\mu^3(0) = \mu(\mu(\mu(0))) = 01101001$, etc. Then **t** is the unique infinite word of which all the $\mu^n(0)$ are prefixes; we write this as $\mathbf{t} = \lim_{n \to \infty} \mu^n(0)$.

(d) Define a sequence of finite words as follows: $Z_0 = 0$, and $Z_n = Z_{n-1}\overline{Z_{n-1}}$ for $n \geq 1$, where the overline denotes binary complement: it maps 0 to 1 and 1 to 0. Thus $Z_1 = 01$, $Z_2 = 0110$, etc. Then $\mathbf{t} = \lim_{n \to \infty} Z_n$.

(e) Consider a simple computing model: the finite automaton. Starting in the state labeled 0, feed the automaton in Figure 1.1 with the base-2 representation of $n$ as input, following the labeled arrows as each bit of the input is read, and output the name of the state reached after all the bits have been processed. The result is $t_n$.

*Exercise* 1　Prove the equivalence of these five definitions. Hint: start by proving that $Z_n = \mu^n(0)$.

The word **t** has been studied for a long time and has many amazing properties [15]. In this book, we show how we can "automatically" study the properties of infinite words like **t** and their generalizations, using the language of first-order logic to state conjectures and a theorem-prover to prove them.

First, let's talk about factors and periods of words.

## 1.1 Powers, factors, periods, exponents

Words are finite or infinite strings of symbols, and concatenation is the basic operation on words. We write $w \cdot x$ or just $wx$ for the concatenation of $w$ and

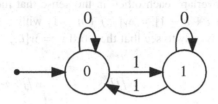

Figure 1.1 Automaton for the Thue-Morse sequence **t**.

$x$. Thus, for example, house · boat = houseboat. In analogy with ordinary multiplication, we write

$$w^n = \overbrace{ww\cdots w}^{n}$$

for the $n$th power of a word. Thus, for example, (hots)$^2$ = hotshots.

We usually index finite words starting from position 1. If $w = a_1 a_2 \cdots a_n$, with each $a_i$ a single symbol, we write $w[i] = a_i$. The expression $w[i..j]$ denotes the block $a_i a_{i+1} \cdots a_j$. If $i > j$, then $w[i..j]$ denotes the empty word $\epsilon$. The *length* of a finite word $w = a_1 \cdots a_n$ is written with absolute value signs: $|w| = n$.

In contrast, we usually index infinite words starting from position 0. If $\mathbf{w} = a_0 a_1 a_2 \cdots$, then again we write $\mathbf{w}[i] = a_i$ and $\mathbf{w}[i..j] = a_i a_{i+1} \cdots a_j$.

A *factor* of a word $x$ is a contiguous block sitting inside $x$. For example, bank is a factor of embankment.

We say a finite nonempty word $w$ of length $n$ has *period* $p$, for $1 \le p \le n$, if $w[i] = w[i + p]$ for $1 \le i \le n - p$. (Similarly, an infinite word $\mathbf{x}$ has period $p$ if $x[i] = x[i+p]$ for all $i \ge 0$.) For example, the word entente has three periods: 3, 6, and 7. The smallest period of a word is sometimes called *the* period, and we denote it by per($w$).

A word like murmur is called a *square*, because it can be written in the form $xx = x^2$ for a nonempty word $x$. There is also a special term for a word that is just slightly more than a square. A word of length $2n + 1$ and period $n$, for $n \ge 1$, is called an *overlap*. For example, the word entente is an overlap: it has length 7 and period 3. An equivalent way to express an overlap is as a word of the form $axaxa$, where $a$ is a single letter, and $x$ is a possibly empty word.

(By the way, here is where the name "overlap" comes from. Suppose we have two occurrences of a word $x = x[1..n]$ inside a larger word $w$, and these two occurrences "overlap" each other, in the sense that there are indices $i, j$ such that $x = w[i..i + n - 1] = w[j..j + n - 1]$ with $i < j < i + n$. See Figure 1.2. Then it is easy to see that the word $v := w[i..j + n - 1]$ has period

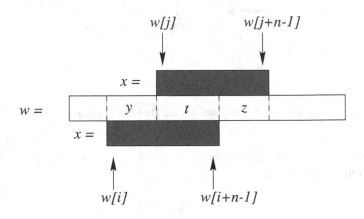

Figure 1.2 Overlapping occurrences in a word. Reprinted from [159] with permission from Elsevier.

$p = j - i$. Since $i + n > j$, by adding $j - 2i$ to both sides of this inequality, we get $|v| = j + n - i > 2(j - i)$. So the first $2(j - i) + 1$ symbols of $v$ form an overlap.)

*Exercise 2*   Find some squares and overlaps in your native language. If you find any good ones not listed at

>    https://cs.uwaterloo.ca/~shallit/repetitions.html ,

please tell me about them!

Thue proved in 1912 that the infinite Thue-Morse sequence **t** has an amazing property: it is *overlap-free*; that is, it contains no factor that is an overlap [374]. No really completely trivial proof of this fact is known; even the shortest proofs take about a page and require some case analysis.

*Exercise 3*   Try to prove that **t** is overlap-free. It is not so easy!

Thue's result was among the very earliest in the subfield of discrete mathematics called *combinatorics on words*. This is the study of words, both finite and infinite, and their properties, and involves combinatorics, algebra, number theory, and logic. Although it can be said to start with Thue, combinatorics on words took off in the 1980s and continues to be very active today. For example, there is a biannual conference on the topic, called (not surprisingly) WORDS; it attracts researchers from all over the world.

One important subtopic in combinatorics on words is the study of *pattern avoidance*. Here we are given a set $S$ of *forbidden factors*, and we want to know if there exists an infinite word *avoiding* $S$: that is, containing no element of $S$ as a factor. Alternatively, we might be given a set of *forbidden patterns*. For example, the pattern $xx$ represents a square, $xxx$ represents a cube, and so forth. A pattern represents an infinite set of words obtained by replacing each letter in the pattern with a nonempty word over some alphabet $\Sigma$. So the pattern $xx$ represents the set $\{xx \ : \ x$ is a nonempty word over $\Sigma\}$.

*Exercise* 4    Show that avoiding overlaps is the same as avoiding the two patterns $xxx$ and $xyxyx$ simultaneously.

In addition to the existence of an infinite word avoiding $S$, we are also often interested in enumerating the number of length-$n$ finite words avoiding $S$. For the avoidance of powers, see the survey of Shur [362].

## 1.2  A decision procedure

We want to explore the properties of words. Now, wouldn't it be nice if there were some sort of decision procedure—an algorithm or computer program—that could take a definition of an infinite word like **t**, and the property we want to prove about it (in this case, overlap-freeness), and *automatically* determine whether the property holds, without significant human intervention? We could use this hypothetical procedure to prove properties of sequences that we have guessed empirically, or to check claims in the literature, or to explore large numbers of sequences to look for one having a particular property that we want.

The goal of this book is to show that such a decision procedure exists and can be used for dozens of results in combinatorics on words! I will first discuss the kinds of sequences it works on, and the kinds of properties that can be tested. In the heart of the book—Chapters 8, 9, and 10—we'll explore a large number of examples of how the procedure can be used to solve problems in combinatorics on words. With it, we can easily rediscover and prove existing results, find the right statement for incorrect results that have been published, and obtain many new results—often with little effort. No more long induction proofs or proofs by enumeration of cases! Typically, a property can be stated in one line or just a few lines, and proved in seconds. The drudgery of long case analysis (which nobody wanted to read, anyway!) can now be replaced by a machine computation.

Not only does such a decision procedure exist, it has been implemented in free software, and is readily available for everyone to use. It is called `Walnut`, and was originally designed by Hamoon Mousavi. To solve problems with `Walnut`, all we have to do is

(a) find a certain kind of representation for the sequence—an automaton.

(b) express the property we want to test as a formula in first-order logic.

(c) type the formula into `Walnut` and examine the results.

Furthermore, we can use the same sorts of ideas to solve the kinds of problems that combinatorialists truly love: *enumeration problems*. For example, we can "automatically" find formulas for the number of length-$n$ words appearing in a sequence that have certain properties (such as being a square). In many cases, we can also find asymptotic estimates for the number of such words. The resulting sequences, taking values in $\mathbb{N}$, appear in two different families— called *regular* or *synchronized*—and include sequences like $(s_2(n))_{n \geq 0}$ (the total number of $1$s in the binary expansion of $n$) and $(v_2(n))_{n \geq 1}$ (the exponent of the highest power of 2 dividing $n$).

In the next section we will see some examples of the kinds of things we can do.

## 1.3 Two simple examples

Let's start with an extremely simple example—in fact, one of the first theorems that was "automatically" proved by computers, back in 1954 by Martin Davis [111]: *the sum of two even numbers is even*.

We can express the assertion "$m$ is even" in first-order logic, where the underlying domain is $\mathbb{N}$, as follows: $\text{EVEN}(m) := \exists k \; m = 2k$. Then a logical formulation of "the sum of two even numbers is even" is as follows:

$$\forall m, n \; (\text{EVEN}(m) \wedge \text{EVEN}(n)) \implies \text{EVEN}(m + n).$$

Here, as usual, the symbol $\exists$ is the existential quantifier, and should be read as "there exists". The symbol $\forall$ is the universal quantifier, and should be read as "for all".

This can be translated into `Walnut` as follows:

```
def even "Ek m=2*k":
eval davisthm "Am,n ($even(m) & $even(n)) => $even(m+n)":
```

which returns TRUE. The theorem is proved!

You will notice that the Walnut commands are almost exactly the same as the first-order logic formulas, with some very minor differences. First, Walnut uses E to represent the existential quantifier ∃, and it uses A to represent the universal quantifier ∀. Second, the & sign represents conjunction (AND) and the two symbols => represent logical implication.

Next, let's try to verify a much less trivial theorem: that the Thue-Morse sequence **t** is overlap-free. The first step is to express the property "having a factor that is an overlap" more precisely, so it can be translated into first-order logic.

We saw above that an overlap is a word of length $2n + 1$ and period $n$, for $n \geq 1$. Then such an overlap occurring at position $i$ would be characterized by the equalities $\mathbf{t}[i + j] = \mathbf{t}[i + j + n]$ for $0 \leq j \leq n$. We can therefore write a first-order logic formula asserting that **t** has an overlap as follows:

$$\exists i, n \, (n \geq 1) \wedge \forall j \, (j \geq 0 \wedge j \leq n) \implies \mathbf{t}[i + j] = \mathbf{t}[i + j + n].$$

This can be written in Walnut as follows:

```
eval test "Ei,n (n >=1) & Aj (j<=n) => T[i+j] = T[i+j+n]";
```

Here T is Walnut's way of representing the Thue-Morse sequence **t** via an automaton. Since by default Walnut assumes all variables take non-negative integer values, we do not need to specify the $j \geq 0$ clause.

In general, Walnut uses capital letters for infinite words represented by automata, and lower-case letters for variable names. Some important sequences, such as **t**, are built-in to Walnut in this way; others you'll have to define yourself. In our example, the name test specifies the filename where results are stored.

Now all we have to do is type the command above, asserting that **t** has an overlap, into Walnut. And here is what we get:

```
FALSE
```

This means there is no overlap in **t**. We have therefore reproved the following classic result of Thue from 1912 [374]:

**Theorem 1.3.1** *The Thue-Morse sequence is overlap-free.*

But Walnut can do much more than just get yes/no answers to questions. For example, it's easy to see that **t** contains squares: in just the first 17 symbols of **t** we find the squares 00, 11, 1010, 0101, 101101, and 10011001. For a square $x^2 = xx$, let's call $|x|$ the *order* of the square $xx$. A natural question is, which orders of squares occur in **t**?

We can answer this question with our decision procedure. When we write a formula with some free variables, the decision procedure produces an automaton that accepts, as inputs, the values of those free variables that make the formula true. (Here a variable is "bound" if it has a quantifier associated with it, and "free" otherwise.)

Let's write a formula for the orders of squares in **t**: $n$ is the order of a square if and only if the logical formula

$$\exists i \; \forall j \, (j < n) \implies \mathbf{t}[i + j] = \mathbf{t}[i + j + n]$$

is true. Translated to `Walnut`, this gives

```
eval thuesquare "n>=1 & Ei Aj (j<n) => T[i+j]=T[i+j+n]":
```

As a result we get the automaton depicted in Figure 1.3, which recognizes the base-2 representation of all numbers corresponding to orders of squares in **t**.

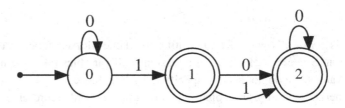

Figure 1.3 Automaton accepting the base-2 representation of orders of squares in the Thue-Morse sequence **t**.

Here is how to understand the automaton. Starting at the initial state labeled 0, and given a binary word as input, we follow the corresponding arrows, when possible. If we successfully arrive at either state 1 or 2, labeled with a double circle, the input is said to be accepted.

When we examine the automaton in Figure 1.3, we see that the words accepted are of the form $1 \overbrace{00 \cdots 0}^{i}$ and $11 \overbrace{00 \cdots 0}^{i}$ for $i \geq 0$. Interpreting these as numbers in base 2, we have now reproved an old theorem of Thue [374]:

**Theorem 1.3.2** *The orders of squares occurring in* **t** *are precisely*

$$\{2^n : n \geq 0\} \cup \{3 \cdot 2^n : n \geq 0\}.$$

So we have now seen the good news: many properties of certain kinds of sequences are easy to discover and prove with very little effort! All we have to do is translate the property into the appropriate first-order logic formula, and run `Walnut` on it.

`Walnut` can prove or disprove results that you conjecture, as we saw in the case of **t** being overlap-free. And, in some cases, it can even *produce the statement* of the theorem you're looking for, in addition to proving it, as we saw in the case of the orders of squares in **t**.

This magic is in the spirit of other kinds of constructive mathematics. For example, computer algebra systems like `Maple` and `Mathematica` can "automatically" compute integrals and solve equations. Gosper's algorithm and the Wilf-Zeilberger method can be used to automatically prove identities involving binomial coefficients and hypergeometric sums [298]. SAT solvers are now routinely used to solve combinatorial problems [193].

But I don't want to engage in the sin of false advertising. There are also three bits of bad news.

First, the proofs that the method constructs consist, essentially, of the computations of `Walnut` themselves. Unlike the case of problems in the class NP— such as satisfiability—there is no "short certificate" we can produce that would allow someone else to independently verify the answer that is produced. The only provable verification we currently know is to run the decision procedure again, perhaps on a different machine and with a different implementation.

Second, the *worst-case* running time of the decision procedure is quite bad (exactly how bad will have to wait until Chapter 6). Nevertheless, the reader will see, after consulting all the examples given in this book, that the procedure is still practical for a very wide range of problems. It seems that "most" examples that people care about *don't* result in the worst-case behavior. Why this is so is still unknown.

Third, we can't handle every kind of property and every kind of sequence. `Walnut` is limited to handling first-order statements about *automatic sequences*: that is, sequences that are generated in a simple way by finite automata.

Even with all these caveats, we can handle a diverse number of applications in combinatorics on words with these tools, as you will see.

If you haven't understood everything so far, don't worry! The basics are explained in Chapters 2–7. So now I invite you to join me on this journey of exploration through combinatorics on words, accompanied by our spectacular software tool called `Walnut`.

# 2

# Words and sequences

In this chapter we discuss words and infinite words (sequences) in more detail, giving complete definitions. A small amount of this material is repeated from the previous chapter.

## 2.1 Finite words

A good source for the material in this section are the books of Lothaire [245], Hopcroft and Ullman [203], or my own book [346].

We will be working a lot with words. A *word* is an ordered string of symbols, and may be finite or infinite. Generally speaking, we write the symbols of a word in the tt font, like this.

Let's start with finite words. A finite word can be viewed as a map from $\{1, 2, \ldots, n\}$ (or sometimes $\{0, 1, \ldots, n-1\}$) to a finite set of symbols $\Sigma$, called an alphabet. The set of all finite words over an alphabet $\Sigma$ is written $\Sigma^*$. The set of all finite nonempty words is written $\Sigma^+$. By $\Sigma_k$ we mean the alphabet $\{0, 1, \ldots, k-1\}$ of cardinality $k$.

Every finite word $x$ has a length associated with it, which is the total number of symbols it contains; it is written $|x|$. Thus, for example, $|\text{five}| = 4$. The empty word $\epsilon$ is a distinguished word of length 0.

In this book, we typically use the letters $a, b, c, d$ as variables representing single letters, and the letters $p, q, r, s, t, u, v, w, x, y, z$ as variables representing finite words.

As we saw before, words can be joined together, or *concatenated*. The set of all finite words over $\Sigma$ forms a monoid under the concatenation operation, with the identity element being the empty word $\epsilon$. Concatenation of words is expressed syntactically like multiplication: both $xy$ and $x \cdot y$ denote the concatenation of $x$ and $y$, although we'll usually omit the dot. Note that concatenation is, not, in general, commutative: (book)(case) $\neq$ (case)(book). We define powers of a word as follows: $x^0 = \epsilon$, and $x^n = x \cdot x^{n-1}$ for $n \geq 1$.

*Exercise 5* Prove that for all natural numbers $m, n$ and finite words $x$ we have $x^{m+n} = x^m x^n$.

We can combine two equal-length words over different alphabets to form a compound word over a larger alphabet. If $w = a_1 \cdots a_n \in \Delta^*$ and $x = b_1 \cdots b_n \in \Sigma^*$, then by $w \times x$ we mean the word $[a_1, b_1] \cdots [a_n, b_n]$ defined over the alphabet $\Delta \times \Sigma$. For example, clip $\times$ aloe = [c,a][l,l][i,o][p,e].

If $w = xyz$ for (possibly empty) words $w, x, y, z$, we say that $x$ is a *prefix* of $w$, that $z$ is a *suffix* of $w$, and that $y$ is a *factor*[1] of $w$. The set of all prefixes of $x$ is Pref($x$), the set of all suffixes of $x$ is Suff($x$), and the set of all factors of $x$ is Fac($x$). A prefix $x$ of $w$ is called *proper* if $x \neq w$, and similarly for suffix and factor. By $|x|_a$ we mean the number of occurrences of the letter $a$ as a factor of $x$. This is generalized to $|x|_w$, which is the number of (possibly overlapping) occurrences of the word $w$ in $x$. For example, $|\text{confrontation}|_{\text{on}} = 3$ and $|\text{entente}|_{\text{ente}} = 2$. The number of distinct length-$n$ factors of a finite or infinite word $x$ is known as its *subword complexity* or *factor complexity*, and is denoted $\rho_x(n)$.

It is sometimes important to distinguish between *factors* and *occurrences* of factors. A factor is a word, but an occurrence refers to a certain starting position and length where that factor occurs within another word. The same factor may have many different occurrences.

By $x^R$ we mean the reversal (sometimes called mirror image) of the word $x$. Thus, for example, (drawer)$^R$ = reward. We can define $x^R$ more formally as follows: $\epsilon^R = \epsilon$, and for $x$ a word and $a$ a single letter we have $(xa)^R = a \cdot x^R$.

*Exercise 6* Show that for words $x, y$ we have $(xy)^R = y^R x^R$.

If $w$ can be obtained from $x$ by striking out 0 or more letters, we say that $w$ is a *subsequence* of $x$.[2] For example, the word seen is a subsequence of subsequence.

We now mention a number of different kinds of words. All have been studied extensively in the literature (see, e.g., [245, 246]).

As we already saw above, a nonempty word $x$ is a *power* if it can be written in the form $x = w^e$ for an integer $e \geq 2$. If $e = 2$, it is called a *square*. If $e = 3$, it is called a *cube*, and so forth. A nonempty word that is not a power is called *primitive*. Given a nonempty word $z$, there is a unique way to write it as $y^i$,

---

[1] The term "factor" is sometimes called "subword" or "substring" in the literature.

[2] There is real potential for confusion here, since this concept is also sometimes called "(scattered) subword" or "substring" in the literature.

where $y$ is primitive and $i$ is an integer $\geq 1$; this $y$ is called the *primitive root* of $z$. Thus, for example, the primitive root of `murmur` is `mur`.

We use "free" as a suffix to indicate that a word contains no occurrences of a given pattern. Thus a *squarefree* word contains no squares, an *overlap-free* word contains no overlaps, and so forth.

As we saw before, a *period* of a finite word $x = x[1..n]$ is an integer $p$, $1 \leq p \leq n$, such that $x[i] = x[i + p]$ for $1 \leq i \leq n - p$. For example, `alfalfa` has periods 3, 6, and 7. The least period of a word is sometimes called *the* period. In the literature, the word "period" sometimes also refers to the prefix of the word of the given period length. So we might say that the word `alf` is a period of the word `alfalfa`. Hopefully these two conflicting usages will not be too confusing.

A generalization of integer power of a word is rational power. If $q$ divides $|x|$, then by $x^{p/q}$ we mean the prefix of length $(p/q)|x|$ of $x^\omega = xxx\cdots$. For example, $(\text{ent})^{7/3} = $ `entente`. When we speak about a word $w$ being a $(p/q)$th power, its *order* is defined to be $(q/p)|w|$. Thus, for example, the order of a square $xx$ is $|x|$. Caution: for rational exponents $e, f$, it is no longer necessarily true that $x^{e+f} = x^e x^f$. A word $w$ of length $p$ and smallest period $q$ has exponent $p/q$, and we write $\exp(w) = p/q$.

A word having no factor that is an $\alpha$-power for $\alpha \geq \beta$ is called $\beta$-power-free. If it has no factor that is an $\alpha$-power for $\alpha > \beta$, it is called $\beta^+$-power-free. The *critical exponent* $ce(w)$ of a finite or infinite word $w$ is defined to be the supremum, over all finite nonempty factors of $w$, of $\exp(w)$. Of course, this supremum is attained for finite words, but may not be attained for infinite words.

A *morphism* is a map $h : \Sigma^* \to \Sigma^*$ that obeys the identity $h(xy) = h(x)h(y)$ for finite words. (A morphism is sometimes called a *substitution* in the literature.) A morphism can be defined by its action on each letter of $\Sigma$. If there is some $k \geq 1$ such that $|h(a)| = k$ for all $a \in \Sigma$, then we say that $h$ is *k-uniform* (or just uniform). A 1-uniform morphism is also called a *coding*. Sometimes we define a coding in an abbreviated fashion by writing $\tau(a_1 a_2 \cdots a_t) = b_1 b_2 \cdots b_t$; here the intended meaning is $\tau(a_i) = b_i$ for $1 \leq i \leq t$. A morphism $h$ can be applied to an infinite word in the obvious way: if it is applied to the word $a_0 a_1 a_2 \cdots$, the result is $h(a_0)h(a_1)h(a_2)\cdots$.

The *Parikh map* $\psi$ has domain $\Sigma^*$ and range $\mathbb{N}^k$, where $k = |\Sigma|$. Assuming that $\Sigma = \Sigma_k$, it is defined by $\psi(x) = (|x|_0, |x|_1, \ldots, |x|_{k-1})$. That is, the Parikh map (sometimes called the abelianization) counts the number of occurrences of each letter of the alphabet in the word $x$. Two finite words $w, x$ are *abelian equivalent* if one is a permutation of the other; in other words, if $\psi(w) = \psi(x)$. For example, the English words `night` and `thing` are abelian equivalent.

Erdős defined the notion of abelian power in 1961 [139]. A word $w$ is an *abelian square* if $w = x'x''$ where $\psi(x') = \psi(x'')$. For example, the English word `reappear` is an abelian square (and you might say the first half reappears in the second half). More generally, a word $w$ is an abelian $n$th power, for $n \geq 2$ an integer, if $w = x_1 x_2 \cdots x_n$ where $\psi(x_1) = \psi(x_j)$ for $2 \leq j \leq n$.

There are at least two different notions of antipower in the literature. For example, over a binary alphabet, an *antisquare* is a word of the form $x\bar{x}$, where the bar is the binary complement map defined by $\bar{0} = 1$, $\bar{1} = 0$. Another, incompatible definition of $n$-antipower is that it is $n$ consecutive blocks of the same length, no two of which are the same [147]. Similarly, there is a notion of $n$-antipower in the abelian sense [146].

Two words $x, y$ are called *conjugates* if one is a cyclic shift of the other; that is, if there exist possibly empty words $u, v$ such that $x = uv$ and $y = vu$. For example, the English words `spectre` and `respect` are conjugates. The set of all conjugates of a word $x$ (including the word itself) is written Conj($x$). Thus, for example, Conj(`eat`) = {`eat`, `tea`, `ate`}.

*Exercise 7*  Prove that every conjugate of a power of a word $x$ is a power of a conjugate of $x$.

There are two basic theorems about periodicities in words, called the Lyndon-Schützenberger theorems. For proofs, see [252, 346]:

**Theorem 2.1.1**  *Let $x, y \in \Sigma^+$. Then the following nine conditions are equivalent:*

*(1) There exist $z \in \Sigma^+$ and integers $k, \ell > 0$ such that $x = z^k$ and $y = z^\ell$.*
*(2) $x^\omega = y^\omega$.*
*(3) There exist integers $i, j > 0$ such that $x^i = y^j$.*
*(4) $xy = yx$.*
*(5) $x^m y^n = y^n x^m$ for all integers $m, n \geq 0$.*
*(6) There exist integers $r, s > 0$ such that $x^r y^s = y^s x^r$.*
*(7) Define the morphism $h : \{a, b\}^* \to \Sigma^*$ by $h(a) = x$ and $h(b) = y$. Then there exist two distinct words $u, v \in \{a, b\}^*$ such that $h(u) = h(v)$.*
*(8) $x\{x, y\}^* \cap y\{x, y\}^* \neq \emptyset$.*
*(9) $x\{x, y\}^\omega \cap y\{x, y\}^\omega \neq \emptyset$.*

**Theorem 2.1.2**  *Let $y \in \Sigma^+$. Then the following six conditions are equivalent:*

*(1) There exists a nonempty word $p$ such that $p$ is both a proper prefix and suffix of $y$.*
*(2) There exist $u \in \Sigma^+$ and $v \in \Sigma^*$ and an integer $e \geq 1$ such that $y = (uv)^e u$.*
*(3) There exist $s \in \Sigma^+$ and $t \in \Sigma^*$ such that $y = sts$.*

*(4) There exist $u \in \Sigma^+$ and $v \in \Sigma^*$ such that $uv$ is a proper prefix of $y$, and $uvy = yvu$.*

*(5) There exist a nonempty proper prefix $x$ of $y$ and a possibly empty word $z$ and an integer $i \geq 2$ such that $yz = x^i$.*

*(6) There exist a nonempty proper suffix $r$ of $y$ and a possibly empty word $w$ and an integer $j \geq 2$ such that $wy = r^j$.*

A factor $w$ of $x$ is said to be *right-special* if both $wa$ and $wb$ are factors of $x$, for two distinct letters $a$ and $b$. For example, the English word `bananas` has the right-special factor `na`, which can be followed by both n and s. There is a corresponding notion of *left-special*. A factor that is both right- and left-special is said to be *bispecial*.

A word $x$ is a *palindrome* if $x = x^R$. Examples of palindromes in English include `radar` and `redivider`.

*Exercise* 8   Find some palindromes in your native language.

Droubay, Justin, and Pirillo [124] proved that every word of length $n$ contains at most $n + 1$ distinct palindromic factors (including the empty word). A word is called *rich* if it contains exactly this many. For example, the English words `logology` and `Mississippi` are both rich, with `Mississippi` having the following distinct nonempty palindromic factors:

M, i, s, p, ss, pp, sis, issi, ippi, ssiss, ississi.

For more about rich words, see [166, 248, 59, 57].

Over a binary alphabet, an *antipalindrome* is a word of the form $x\,\overline{x^R}$.

A nonempty word $w$ is a *border* of a word $x$ if $w \neq x$ is both a prefix and a suffix of $x$. A word $x$ is *bordered* if it has a border, and *unbordered* otherwise. For example, the English word `entanglement` is bordered with border `ent`. A word $x$ is called *closed* (aka "complete first return") if it is of length $\leq 1$, or if it has a border $w$ with $|x|_w = 2$. For example, `abracadabra` is closed because of the border `abra`, while `alfalfa` is closed because of the border `alfa`. The latter example shows that, in the definition, the prefix and suffix are allowed to overlap. For more about closed words, see [24].

A word $x$ is called *privileged* if it is of length $\leq 1$, or it has a border $w$ with $|x|_w = 2$ that is itself privileged. Clearly every privileged word is closed, but `mama` is an example of an English word that is closed but not privileged. For more about privileged words, see [221, 295, 296, 154].

A word $x$ is called *trapezoidal* if it has, for each $n \geq 0$, at most $n + 1$ distinct factors of length $n$. Since for $n = 1$ the definition requires at most 2 distinct factors, this means that every trapezoidal word can be defined over an alphabet

of at most 2 letters. An example of a trapezoidal word in English is the word
deeded. See, for example, [247, 107, 248, 58].

A word $x$ is called *balanced* if the inequality $||y|_a - |z|_a| \leq 1$ holds for all
identical-length factors $y, z$ of $x$ and all letters $a$ of the alphabet. Otherwise it
is *unbalanced*. An example of a balanced word in English is banana.

*Open Question* 2.1.3   Inspired by a question of Jacques Sakarovitch, consider
those words $x$ over the finite alphabet $\Sigma_k = \{0, 1, \ldots, k - 1\}$ with the property
that for all factors $y, z$ of $x$ of the same length, we have $|\Sigma y - \Sigma z| < M$. (Here $\Sigma y$
means the sum of all the symbols in the word, understood as integers.) In the
case where $k = M = 2$, these are just the balanced words, and are enumerated
by Sloane's sequence A005598, and by the formula $1 + \sum_{1 \leq i \leq n} (n - i + 1)\varphi(i)$,
where $\varphi$ is Euler's phi-function. How about for other cases, such as $(k, M) =$
$(3, 2)$ or $(2, 3)$?

If the alphabet $\Sigma$ is ordered (as is the case, for example, for $\Sigma_k$, where $0 <$
$1 < \cdots < k - 1$), then we can extend this total order from letters to words. We
write $w <_d x$ if either one of the following holds:

(a) $w$ is a proper prefix of $x$.
(b) there exist words $y, z, z'$ and letters $a < b$ such that $w = yaz$ and $x = ybz'$.

For example, using the usual ordering of the alphabet, we have

$$\text{common} <_d \text{con} <_d \text{conjugate} <_d \text{cotton}.$$

This is called *lexicographic* or *dictionary* order. We write $w \leq_d x$ if either
$w <_d x$ or $w = x$.

An alternative order is *radix order*. Here we write $w <_r x$ if either one of the
following holds:

(a) $|w| < |x|$.
(b) $|w| = |x|$ and $w <_d x$.

In this ordering we have con $<_r$ common $<_r$ cotton $<_r$ conjugate. Again,
we write $w \leq_r x$ if either $w <_r x$ or $w = x$. The radix order is the one typically
used when listing words.

A nonempty word $x$ is a *Lyndon word* if it is primitive and lexicographically
less than all of its nonempty proper suffixes.[3] Thus the word academy is Lyndon, while googol and googoo are not. We call the lexicographically least
conjugate of the primitive root of $x$ the *Lyndon root* of $x$. Lyndon words have
received a great deal of attention in the combinatorics on words literature (e.g.,
see [132]).

---

[3] There is also a version where "suffixes" is replaced by "prefixes".

*Exercise* 9   Show that one can test whether a word is primitive in linear time. Hint: use the Knuth-Morris-Pratt algorithm [225].

A famous theorem states that every finite word has a unique factorization as a product of Lyndon words, in which the successive terms are lexicographically (not necessarily strictly) decreasing; see, e.g., [261].

If $w, x$ are two words of the same length, say $w = a_1 a_2 \cdots a_n$ and $x = b_1 b_2 \cdots b_n$ then their *perfect shuffle* is defined by $w \amalg x = a_1 b_1 \cdots a_n b_n$. For example, term $\amalg$ hoes = theorems.

## 2.2 Infinite words (sequences)

A good source for this material is the book of Perrin and Pin [297].

A one-sided infinite word (or infinite sequence—we use these terms interchangeably) is a map from $\mathbb{N}$ (or sometimes $\mathbb{N}_{>0}$) to $\Sigma$. A two-sided infinite word is a map from $\mathbb{Z}$ to $\Sigma$. In this book, names of infinite words are typically given in the **bold** font. The set of all one-sided infinite words is written $\Sigma^\omega$ or $\Sigma^{\mathbb{N}}$; the set of all two-sided infinite words is written $^\omega \Sigma^\omega$ or $\Sigma^{\mathbb{Z}}$. We'll focus almost entirely on one-sided infinite words in this book. Unless otherwise indicated, infinite words are typically indexed starting at position 0. If $\mathbf{x} = a_0 a_1 a_2 \cdots$ is an infinite word, with each $a_i$ a single letter, then by $\mathbf{x}[i..j]$ for $j \geq i - 1$ we mean the finite word $a_i a_{i+1} \cdots a_j$. By $[i..j]$ we mean the set $\{i, i + 1, \ldots, j\}$.

One of the easiest ways to make a binary infinite sequence (or infinite word) is to start with a subset $S \subseteq \mathbb{N}$ of the natural numbers, and define

$$\chi_S(n) = \begin{cases} 1, & \text{if } n \in S; \\ 0, & \text{if } n \notin S. \end{cases}$$

The sequence $(\chi_S(n))_{n \geq 0}$ is called the *characteristic sequence* of the set $S$.

Most of the properties we have discussed for finite words have their analogues for infinite words. For example, (one-sided) infinite words have finite prefixes and finite factors, but do not have finite suffixes.

We can extend the definition of lexicographic order to right-infinite words in the obvious way. Similarly, we can extend the definition of Lyndon words to right-infinite words as follows: an infinite word $\mathbf{x}$ is Lyndon if it is lexicographically less than all of its suffixes.

If $x$ is a finite nonempty word, then by $x^\omega$ we mean the right-infinite word $xxx \cdots$. An infinite word $\mathbf{y}$ is *purely periodic* if there is a finite word $x$ such that $\mathbf{y} = x^\omega$. It is *ultimately periodic* if it is of the form $\mathbf{y} = zx^\omega$ for finite words $x, z$. In this case the word $z$ is sometimes called the *preperiod*.

A finite factor $w$ of an infinite word $\mathbf{x}$ is said to be *recurrent* if it occurs infinitely often in $\mathbf{x}$. The word $\mathbf{x}$ is recurrent if every factor that occurs at least once is a recurrent factor. A factor $w$ is *uniformly recurrent* if there exists a map $s(w)$ such that two consecutive occurrences of $w$ in $\mathbf{x}$ are always separated by at most $s(w)$ positions. (Here, by separation, we mean the absolute difference of the starting positions of the factors.) If all factors are uniformly recurrent, then the word $\mathbf{x}$ itself is said to be uniformly recurrent. Let $S_{\mathbf{x}}(n)$ be the minimum possible constant $s(w)$ over all length-$n$ words $w$. Then $\mathbf{x}$ is said to be *linearly recurrent* if it is uniformly recurrent, and $S_{\mathbf{x}}(n) = O(n)$. If $\mathbf{x}$ is linearly recurrent, then two quantities are of interest, both sometimes referred to as the recurrence constant or recurrence quotient: $\sup_{n \geq 1} S_{\mathbf{x}}(n)/n$ and $\limsup_{n \geq 1} S_{\mathbf{x}}(n)/n$.

Alternatively, the infinite word $\mathbf{x}$ is uniformly recurrent if there is a function $r : \mathbb{N} \to \mathbb{N}$ such that every length-$r(n)$ factor contains all length-$n$ factors in it. We define $R_{\mathbf{x}}(n)$ to be the optimal bound $r(n)$ for all $n$. The two functions $R_{\mathbf{x}}(n)$ and $S_{\mathbf{x}}(n)$ are closely related, as the following exercise shows.

*Exercise 10* Prove that $R_{\mathbf{x}}(n) = S_{\mathbf{x}}(n) + n - 1$.

The *orbit* of a one-sided infinite word $\mathbf{a} = a_0 a_1 a_2 \cdots$ is the set of all its shifts:

$$\{a_j a_{j+1} a_{j+2} \cdots : j \geq 0\}.$$

The *orbit closure* of an infinite word $\mathbf{a}$ is the closure (in the topological sense) of the orbit: it is the set of all infinite words $\mathbf{b} = b_0 b_1 b_2 \cdots$ such that all finite prefixes of $\mathbf{b}$ occur as factors of $\mathbf{a}$.

Siromoney et al. [364] proved that every infinite word $\mathbf{x} = a_0 a_1 a_2 \cdots$ has a unique Lyndon factorization; namely, exactly one of the following two cases holds:

(a) $\mathbf{x} = w_1 w_2 w_3 \cdots$ where each $w_i$ is a finite Lyndon word and $w_1 \geq w_2 \geq w_3 \cdots$; or

(b) $\mathbf{x} = w_1 w_2 w_3 \cdots w_r \mathbf{w}$ where $w_i$ is a finite Lyndon word for $1 \leq i \leq r$, and $\mathbf{w}$ is an infinite Lyndon word, and $w_1 \geq w_2 \geq \cdots \geq w_r \geq \mathbf{w}$.

If (a) holds we say that the Lyndon factorization of $\mathbf{x}$ is infinite; otherwise we say it is finite.

The definition of perfect shuffle is extended to infinite words as follows: if $\mathbf{w} = a_0 a_1 a_2 \cdots$ and $\mathbf{x} = b_0 b_1 b_2 \cdots$ then $\mathbf{w} \amalg \mathbf{x} = a_0 b_0 a_1 b_1 \cdots$.

We have already seen the definition of the critical exponent $\mathrm{ce}(\mathbf{x})$: it is $\sup\{\exp(w) : w \in \mathrm{Fac}(\mathbf{x})\}$. For infinite words the critical exponent could be attained by some finite factor, or not attained. Of course, if the critical exponent is an irrational number, then it is not attained by any finite factor. There are also some interesting variations on this concept. The *initial critical exponent*, ice($\mathbf{x}$), is restricted to prefixes; it is defined to be sup$\{\exp(w) \ : \ w \in \mathrm{Pref}(\mathbf{x})\}$. The *asymptotic critical exponent*, ace($\mathbf{x}$), considers exponents of arbitrarily large factors; it is defined to be

$$\sup\{\alpha \ : \ \text{there exist arbitrarily long } w \in \mathrm{Fac}(\mathbf{x}) \text{ with } \exp(w) \geq \alpha\}.$$

## 2.3 Morphisms and morphic words

One basic mechanism for generating infinite words is the *iterated morphism*.

If there is a letter $a$ such that $h(a) = ax$ for a word $x$, and further $h^i(x) \neq \epsilon$ for all $i \geq 0$, then we say that $h$ is *prolongable* on $a$. We can iterate a morphism, letting $h^0$ be the identity map, $h^1 = h$, $h^2 = h \circ h$, and so forth. It is now easy to see that if $h$ is prolongable on $a$, say $h(a) = ax$, then

$$h^n(a) = a\,x\,h(x)\,h^2(x) \cdots h^{n-1}(x)$$

for all $n \geq 0$. Clearly each $h^n(a)$ is a prefix of a unique infinite word, which we denote by $h^\omega(a)$. Note that $h^\omega(a)$ is a *fixed point* of $h$, in the sense that $h(h^\omega(a)) = h^\omega(a)$.

If an infinite word can be written as $h^\omega(a)$ for a prolongable morphism $h$, then we say it is *pure morphic*. If a word is the image, under a coding, of a pure morphic word, then we say it is *morphic*. Morphic and pure morphic words form a very interesting and widely-studied class of sequences over a finite alphabet.

If an infinite word $\mathbf{x}$ can be written as the image, under a coding, of a prolongable morphism that is $k$-uniform, then we say $\mathbf{x}$ is $k$-*automatic*.

We will see many examples of morphic sequences in the following sections.

## 2.4 Some famous sequences

In this section we introduce several very famous sequences that have been studied for decades in the combinatorics on words literature. These sequences will reappear throughout the book. All are *automatic*, in the sense we will discuss in Chapter 5.

### 2.4.1 The Thue-Morse sequence

We already talked about the celebrated *Thue-Morse sequence* $\mathbf{t} = t_0 t_1 t_2 \cdots = $ 01101001 $\cdots$ in Chapter 1. As we saw, it can be defined by the relations $t_0 = $

$0$, $t_{2n} = t_n$, and $t_{2n+1} = 1 - t_n$ for $n \geq 0$. It is also expressible as the fixed point, starting with $0$, of the morphism $\mu : 0 \to 01, 1 \to 10$.

The Thue-Morse sequence appears in many different areas of mathematics; see the survey [15]. It is sequence A010060 in the OEIS. Here is one teaser, the amazing Woods-Robbins identity:

**Theorem 2.4.1** *We have*

$$\prod_{i \geq 0} \left( \frac{2i + 1}{2i + 2} \right)^{(-1)^{t_i}} = \frac{\sqrt{2}}{2}.$$

*Exercise* 11 Try to prove Theorem 2.4.1. Hint: break the infinite product up into odd- and even-indexed terms.

*Open Question* 2.4.2 Is there a simple closed form for the real number

$$\sum_{n \geq 0} (-1)^{t_n} / (n + 1) \ ?$$

It is about $0.39876108810841881240743054440027306033680891 5467$. Is it irrational? Transcendental?

### 2.4.2 The twisted Thue-Morse sequence

Another version of the Thue-Morse sequence is the sequence

**ttm** $= (t'_n)_{n \geq 0} = 0010011010010110011010011001011 \cdots$,

where we count the number of $0$s, modulo 2, in the base-2 representation of $n$. (Here $t'_0 = 0$ because $(0)_2 = \epsilon$.) It is called the *twisted Thue-Morse sequence* and is sequence A059448 in the OEIS.

Another representation of this sequence is as the image, under the coding $0, 1 \to 0$ and $2 \to 1$, of the fixed point of the morphism sending $0 \to 01$, $1 \to 21, 2 \to 12$.

### 2.4.3 The ternary Thue-Morse sequence

Thue introduced a variation on his sequence that is sometimes called the *ternary Thue-Morse sequence*, and abbreviated **vtm** (the "v" stands for "variant"). It is sequence A036577 in the OEIS. We have **vtm** $= 210201 \cdots$. It can be defined in a number of different ways, all of which are equivalent.

(a) It is the infinite fixed point, starting with $2$, of the morphism defined by $2 \to 210, 1 \to 20$, and $0 \to 1$.

(b) It is the image, under the coding $\tau$ defined by $\tau(0123) = 2101$, of the fixed point of the morphism $g$ defined by $g(0) = 01$, $g(1) = 20$, $g(2) = 23$, and $g(3) = 02$.

(c) It is the sequence that counts the number of consecutive 0s between each pair of consecutive 1s in **t**.

(d) It is (up to renaming of the letters) the sequence obtained by taking the first difference of **t**.

For more about **vtm**, see [42].

### 2.4.4 Characteristic sequence of powers of 2

This sequence $\mathbf{p}_2 = 011010001000000010\cdots$ is defined by $\mathbf{p}_2[n] = 1$ if $n$ is a power of 2, and 0 otherwise. It is sequence A209229 in the OEIS. More generally, we can consider the analogous word $\mathbf{p}_k$ for integers $k \geq 2$.

### 2.4.5 The second-bit sequence

This sequence $\mathbf{sb} = 000100110000111000000001\cdots$ consists of the second bit in the base-2 representation of $n$ (starting with the most significant digit). It is sequence A079944 in the OEIS. Alternatively, it is given by the image, under the coding that sends $0, 1, 2 \to 0$ and $3 \to 1$, of the fixed point, starting with 0, of the morphism $0 \to 01$, $1 \to 23$, $2 \to 22$, $3 \to 33$.

### 2.4.6 The Cantor sequence

The *Cantor integers* are those integers whose base-3 representation contains no 1:

$$C = \{0, 2, 6, 8, 18, 20, 24, 26, \ldots\}.$$

The *Cantor sequence* $\mathbf{ca} = 101000101000000000\cdots$ is the characteristic sequence $(\chi_C(n))_{n\geq 0}$. It is sequence A088917 in the OEIS.

It is the fixed point, starting with 1, of the morphism sending $0 \to 000$ and $1 \to 101$.

*Exercise* 12    The *central Delannoy numbers* are defined by $d(n) = \sum_{0 \leq i \leq n} \binom{n}{i} 2^i$. Show that $\chi_C(n) = d(n) \bmod 3$.

### 2.4.7 The Rudin-Shapiro sequence

Recall that $|(n)_k|_w$ denotes the number of (possibly overlapping) occurrences of the word $w$ in the base-$k$ representation of $n$. The *Rudin-Shapiro sequence* $\mathbf{r} =$

$r_0 r_1 r_2 \cdots = 00010010 \cdots$ is then defined by the relation $\mathbf{r}[n] = |(n)_2|_{11} \bmod 2$.
It is sequence A020987 in the OEIS.[4] The first few terms are as follows:

| $n$ | 0 | 1 | 2 | 3 | 4 | 5 | 6 | 7 | 8 | 9 | 10 | 11 |
|---|---|---|---|---|---|---|---|---|---|---|---|---|
| $|(n)_2|_{11}$ | 0 | 0 | 0 | 1 | 0 | 0 | 1 | 2 | 0 | 0 | 0 | 1 |
| $r_n$ | 0 | 0 | 0 | 1 | 0 | 0 | 1 | 0 | 0 | 0 | 0 | 1 |

The Rudin-Shapiro sequence $\mathbf{r}$ has a truly *amazing* pseudorandomness property; namely, that for all integers $c \geq 1$ we have

$$\sum_{0 \leq n < N} [r_n = r_{n+c}] = \frac{N}{2} + o(N),$$

where the implied error term in the $o(N)$ can depend on $c$. (Here $[x = y]$ is the so-called *Iverson bracket*, defined to be 1 if $x = y$ and 0 otherwise.) In other words, there is basically no correlation between $\mathbf{r}$ and each of its shifts. In this respect, $\mathbf{r}$ behaves just like a truly random sequence! See [199].

In Figure 2.1 we depict the difference $(\sum_{0 \leq n < N} [r_n = r_{n+1}]) - \frac{N}{2}$ for $N = 0, 1, \ldots, 2^{14} - 1$.

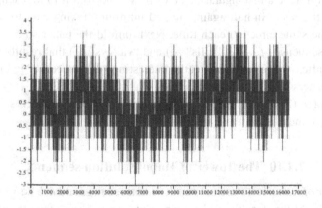

Figure 2.1 Pseudorandomness of the Rudin-Shapiro sequence.

---

[4] Actually, this sequence was first discovered by Golay [176, 177]; then again, independently, by Shapiro [360]; and finally, popularized by Rudin [327].

### 2.4.8 The Baum-Sweet sequence

The *Baum-Sweet sequence* **bs** = 11011001010010011001000001001···
arises in the continued fraction expansion of a certain formal power series [3, 31]. It is sequence A086747 in the OEIS, and is defined as follows: **bs**$[n]$ = 1 if the base-2 representation of $n$ contains no run of 0s of odd length, and 0 otherwise. (Since the base-2 representation of 0 is defined to be $\epsilon$, the empty word, we have **bs**[0] = 1.) Here by a "run" we mean a maximal block of consecutive identical letters, one that cannot be extended to the left or right. For example, the word 1100010000 has two runs of 0s, one of length 3 and one of length 4.

### 2.4.9 The regular paperfolding sequence

The *regular paperfolding sequence* **p** = $p_1 p_2 \cdots$ = 00100110··· is defined by the relations $p_{2n} = p_n$, $p_{4n+1} = 0$, and $p_{4n+3} = 1$ for $n \geq 0$. See [119]. It is sequence A014707 in the OEIS. By convention we set **p**$[n]$ = $p_{n+1}$, so there is an "off-by-one" issue in the definition. For another description, see Example 5.4.2. The variant **zp** of the paperfolding sequence is obtained from **p** by concatenating a 0 at the front to make the indexing consistent: **zp** := 0**p**.

The name "paperfolding sequence" arises from an interesting geometric construction: take a rectangular piece of paper and fold it in half lengthwise, then fold the result in half again, etc., ad infinitum, taking care to make the folds in the same direction each time. Next, unfold the paper so all folds are 90°. The sequence $(f_i)_{i \geq 1}$ of "hills" (0) and "valleys" (1) that results is **p**. For example, after twelve folds, we get the interesting "dragon curve" in Figure 2.2 (where corners have been rounded off for clarity).

In Chapter 12, we will encounter **p** again, but this time recoded so that 0 is written as 1 and 1 is written as −1.

### 2.4.10 The Tower of Hanoi solution sequence

The *Tower of Hanoi* is a classical puzzle with three pegs and $n$ disks of differing sizes [197]. At the start, the disks are placed on peg 1 with the smallest at the top and the largest at the bottom. The goal is to move the disks to one of the other pegs, subject to the rule that a larger disk may never be placed on top of a smaller disk.

Let us encode the possible moves as follows:

- 0 means 'move a disk from peg 1 to peg 2'.
- 1 means 'move a disk from peg 2 to peg 1'.

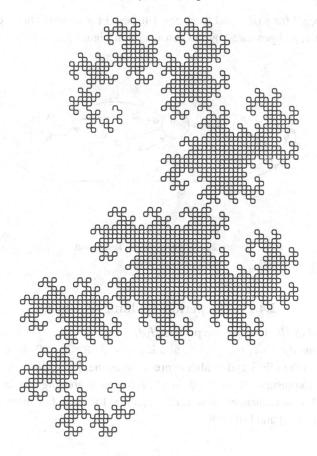

Figure 2.2 Building the regular paperfolding sequence: twelve folds.

- 2 means 'move a disk from peg 3 to peg 1'.
- 3 means 'move a disk from peg 1 to peg 3'.
- 4 means 'move a disk from peg 2 to peg 3'.
- 5 means 'move a disk from peg 3 to peg 2'.

Then it can be shown [5] that there is a unique infinite sequence

$$\mathbf{th} = 03402503412403402502412503402503\cdots$$

that solves the Tower of Hanoi problem, using the smallest possible number of moves, for all numbers of disks: the first $2^n - 1$ symbols move $n$ disks from peg 1 to peg 2 for $n$ odd, and from peg 1 to peg 3 for $n$ even. This sequence is 2-automatic, and generated by the automaton in Figure 2.3.

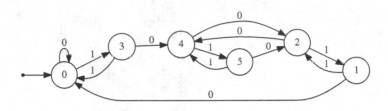

Figure 2.3 Tower of Hanoi automaton.

### 2.4.11 The period-doubling sequence

The *period-doubling sequence* **pd** $= d_0d_1d_2\cdots = 10111010\cdots$ is defined by the relations $d_{2n} = 1$, $d_{4n+1} = 0$, and $d_{4n+3} = d_n$ for $n \geq 0$. It is sequence A035263 in the OEIS and is also expressible as the fixed point, starting with 1, of the morphism $\delta : 1 \to 10$, $0 \to 11$. It has an interesting connection with the Thue-Morse sequence: namely, $d_i = |t_{i+1} - t_i|$ for $i \geq 0$. For more about **pd**, see [181, p. 176] and [40, 108].

### 2.4.12 The Mephisto Waltz sequence

The Mephisto Waltz sequence **mw** $= 001001110\cdots$ is given by the fixed point of the morphism $0 \to 001$, $1 \to 110$ starting with 0; see [214, pp. 105–106 and p. 215]. Another definition is **mw**$[n] = |(n)_3|_2$ mod 2: the number of 2s in the base-3 representation of $n$, taken modulo 2. This is one representative of a large class of sequences with similar properties; see [149].

### 2.4.13 Stewart's choral sequence

Stewart's choral sequence **sc** $= 001001011\cdots$ is given by the fixed point of the morphism $0 \to 001$, $1 \to 011$; see [367, Chap. 6] and [285]. Alternatively, we have **sc**$[n] = 1$ if and only if the base-3 representation of $n$ ends in a word of the form $21\cdots1$ for some non-negative number of 1s. It is sequence A116178 in the OEIS.

This is one of a family of eight very similar binary sequences studied by Noche [286, 287].

### 2.4.14 Leech's word

Leech's word **le** $= 012102120121012021\cdots$ is the fixed point, starting with 0, of the 13-uniform morphism

$$0 \to 0121021201210$$
$$1 \to 1202102012021$$
$$2 \to 2010210120102 .$$

It is sequence A337005 in the OEIS. Like **vtm**, Leech's word is squarefree. See [236].

### 2.4.15 Dejean's word

Dejean's word **dej** $= 0120212012102120210120102\cdots$ is the fixed point, starting with 0, of the 19-uniform morphism

$$0 \to 0120212012102120210$$
$$1 \to 1201020120210201021$$
$$2 \to 2012101201021012102 .$$

Dejean's word has the property that it avoids the smallest rational power avoidable over a ternary alphabet. See [117].

### 2.4.16 The infinite Fibonacci word

The infinite *Fibonacci word* $\mathbf{f} = f_0 f_1 f_2 \cdots = 01001010 \cdots$ is the fixed point, starting with 0, of the morphism $\varphi : 0 \to 01, 1 \to 0$. It is one of a large class of similar words, called *Sturmian sequences*. See, for example, [44]. It has many equivalent definitions, and we mention three below:

(a) Let $\tau = (3 - \sqrt{5})/2$. Then $f_i = \lfloor (i + 2)\tau \rfloor - \lfloor (i + 1)\tau \rfloor$ for $i \geq 0$.
(b) Define the finite Fibonacci words $X_i$ as follows: $X_1 = 1$, $X_2 = 0$, and $X_i = X_{i-1} X_{i-2}$ for $n \geq 3$. Then $\mathbf{f} = \lim_{n \to \infty} X_i$. Notice that $|X_i| = F_i$ for $i \geq 1$; this connection with the Fibonacci sequence explains the name.
(c) Consider the set $S = \{\lfloor \gamma n \rfloor - 1 : n \geq 0\}$ for $\gamma = (3 + \sqrt{5})/2$. Then $\mathbf{f}$ is the characteristic sequence of $S$.

It is sequence A003849 in the OEIS.

## 2.4.17 The Rote-Fibonacci word

The *Rote-Fibonacci word*

**rf** = 00100110110110010011011011001001001101100100100110 · · ·

is an infinite binary word defined to be $\tau(g^\omega(a))$, where $g$ is the morphism sending

$$0 \to 01; \qquad 1 \to 2; \qquad 2 \to 34; \qquad 3 \to 56$$
$$4 \to 3; \qquad 5 \to 27; \qquad 6 \to 0; \qquad 7 \to 5$$

and the coding $\tau$ satisfies $\tau(01234567) = 00100111$. It is sequence A273129 in the OEIS. We will see in Section 8.5.18 that **rf** avoids the pattern $xxx^R$.

## 2.4.18 The Fibonacci-Thue-Morse sequence

This is a binary sequence **ftm** = 011101001000110001011 · · · that is an analogue of the Thue-Morse sequence for Fibonacci representation: **ftm**$[n]$ = 1 if the sum of the bits in the Fibonacci representation of $n$ is odd, and 0 otherwise; see Section 3.2. It is sequence A095076 in the OEIS. Alternatively, it is the image, under the coding $\tau(n) = n \bmod 2$, of the fixed point (starting with 0) of the morphism

$$0 \to 01; \quad 1 \to 3; \quad 2 \to 0; \quad 3 \to 32.$$

## 2.4.19 The Tribonacci word

The *Tribonacci sequence* or *Tribonacci word*

$$\textbf{tr} = 0102010010201010201001020102010100102 \cdots$$

is the fixed point, starting with 0, of the morphism $0 \to 01$, $1 \to 02$, and $2 \to 0$. See, for example, [81, 372]. It is sequence A080843 in the OEIS.

An alternate definition involves the finite Tribonacci words: define $Y_1 = 0$, $Y_2 = 01$, $Y_3 = 0102$, and $Y_n = Y_{n-1}Y_{n-2}Y_{n-3}$ for $n \geq 4$. Then **tr** $= \lim_{n \to \infty} Y_n$.

## 2.4.20 The Hilbert space-filling curve

Hilbert [196] invented a continuous curve, built iteratively, that fills the unit square. Instead, we may consider it as a curve that visits all the lattice points $(x, y)$ with non-negative integer coordinates, and each point exactly once. To draw it, we start at $(0,0)$ and follow a sequence of steps of unit length, described as follows:

$$\mathbf{hc} = 0121103010332300\cdots,$$

where 0 represents $(0,1)$, 1 represents $(1,0)$, 2 represents $(0,-1)$, and 3 represents $(-1,0)$.

The sequence **hc** can be described as the image, under the coding $\tau$ defined by $\tau(01234567) = 01213032$, of the fixed point of the morphism $h$ defined as follows:

$$0 \to 0123; \qquad 1 \to 1045; \qquad 2 \to 1046; \qquad 3 \to 7650;$$
$$4 \to 0127; \qquad 5 \to 6731; \qquad 6 \to 6732; \qquad 7 \to 7654.$$

For example, the first three generations are depicted in Figure 2.4.

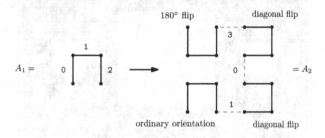

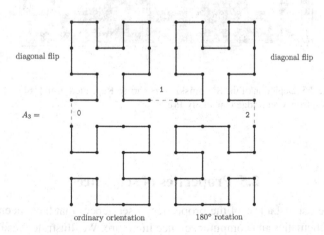

Figure 2.4 First three generations of the Hilbert curve. Reprinted from [355] by permission from Springer Nature.

### 2.4.21 The Sierpiński carpet array

It is also possible to study two-dimensional sequences, also called *tables*, *matrices*, or *arrays*. For example, the Sierpiński carpet array is defined as follows: $\mathbf{sca}[i, j] = 0$ if $(i)_3$ and $(j)_3$ have at least one $1$ occurring in the same position, and $1$ otherwise. The first 243 rows and columns of $\mathbf{sca}$ are depicted in Figure 2.5, where we have drawn a black square if a position of $\mathbf{sca}$ is $1$ and a white square if it is $0$. Similarly, one can study arrays of higher dimension.

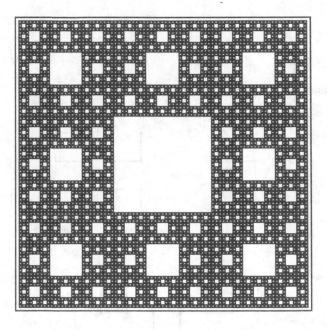

Figure 2.5 Depiction of the Sierpiński carpet array. Reprinted from [16] with permission from Cambridge University Press.

## 2.5 Properties of sequences

Below we list just a few of the properties of sequences that have been studied in the mathematics and computer science literature. We illustrate these with the specific example of the Thue-Morse sequence. This will serve as a roadmap to the kinds of things we will study in this book. For each property, we point to the section in the book where it is discussed in more detail.

Recall that by the term *factor* we mean a contiguous block of symbols inside another word.

1 **t** is not ultimately periodic (see Section 8.4.1).

2 **t** contains no factor that is an *overlap*, that is, a word of the form $axaxa$, where $a$ is a single letter and $x$ is an arbitrary finite word [373, 374, 45]. See Section 8.5.5.

3 **t** contains infinitely many distinct palindromic factors and infinitely many distinct antipalindromic factors. See Section 8.6.3.

4 The number $p(n)$ of distinct palindromic factors of length $n$ in **t** is given by

$$p(n) = \begin{cases} 0, & \text{if } n \text{ odd and } n \geq 5; \\ 1, & \text{if } n = 0; \\ 2, & \text{if } 1 \leq n \leq 4, \text{ or } n \text{ even and } 3 \cdot 4^k + 2 \leq n \leq 4^{k+1} \text{ for } k \geq 1; \\ 4, & \text{if } n \text{ even and } 4^k + 2 \leq n \leq 3 \cdot 4^k \text{ for } k \geq 1; \end{cases}$$

see [50]. A similar expression exists for the number $p'(n)$ of distinct antipalindromic factors of length $n$. See Section 9.11.3.

5 **t** contains infinitely many distinct square factors $xx$, but for each such factor we have $|x| = 2^n$ or $3 \cdot 2^n$, for $n \geq 1$. See Section 8.5.

6 **t** is *mirror invariant*: if $x$ is a finite factor of **t**, then so is its reverse $x^R$. See Section 8.6.6.

7 **t** is *recurrent*, that is, every factor that occurs, occurs infinitely often [275]. See Section 8.7.1.

8 **t** is *uniformly recurrent*, that is, for all factors $x$ occurring in **t**, there is a constant $c(x)$ such that two consecutive occurrences of $x$ are separated by at most $c(x)$ symbols [276, pp. 834 et seq.]. See Section 8.7.2.

9 **t** is *linearly recurrent*, that is, it is uniformly recurrent and furthermore there is a constant $C$ such that $c(x) \leq C|x|$ for all factors $x$ [276, pp. 834 et seq.]. In fact, the optimal bound is given by $c(1) = 3$, $c(2) = 8$, and $c(n) = 9 \cdot 2^e$ for $n \geq 3$, where $e = \lfloor \log_2(n-2) \rfloor$. See Section 8.7.3.

10 The lexicographically least sequence in the orbit closure of **t** is $\overline{t_1}\,\overline{t_2}\,\overline{t_3}\cdots$, which is also 2-automatic [10]. See Section 8.11.1.

11 The *subword complexity* $\rho(n)$ of **t**, which is the function counting the number of distinct factors of **t**, is given by

$$\rho(n) = \begin{cases} 2^n, & \text{if } 0 \leq n \leq 2; \\ 2n + 2^{t+2} - 2, & \text{if } 3 \cdot 2^t \leq n \leq 2^{t+2} + 1; \\ 4n - 2^t - 4, & \text{if } 2^t + 1 \leq n \leq 3 \cdot 2^{t-1}; \end{cases}$$

see [53, 250]. See Sections 8.8.6, 9.11.1, and 10.8.19.

12 **t** has an unbordered factor of length $n$ if $n \not\equiv 1 \pmod 6$ [105]. (Here by an *unbordered* word $y$ we mean one with no expression in the form $y = uvu$ for words $u, v$ with $u$ nonempty.) See Section 8.6.13.

## 2.6 Proving properties of words through exhaustive search

Frequently in combinatorics on words we are trying to either prove or disprove the existence of an infinite word with a given property, such as being overlap-free, squarefree, avoiding squares of order $\geq 3$, containing at most three distinct squares, and so forth. In some cases this can be done through exhaustive search.

This is particularly true when the desired property $P$ is *hereditary* (every factor of a word with property $P$ has property $P$) and we want to establish that no infinite word has property $P$. In this case we can exhaustively search the tree of possibilities, using either depth-first or breadth-first search. Conceptually this amounts to visiting the vertices of the (potentially) infinite tree $T$ whose root is labeled with $\epsilon$, and every node of $T$ labeled $x$ has children labeled $xa$ for each $a \in \Sigma$, the alphabet. When a node labeled $x$ is visited, we check to see whether all its suffixes have property $P$. If not, then there is no need to explore $x$ further. If so, then we eventually explore all of $x$'s children.

In *breadth-first search* we maintain a queue of vertices on the frontier between vertices already visited in $T$ and those yet to be explored. If all of the suffixes of $x$ have property $P$, for each $a \in \Sigma$ we add $xa$ to the queue of vertices to explore later. This amounts to visiting the vertices of $T$ level by level: words of length $n$ are explored before those of length $n + 1$, etc. Breadth-first search may consume a lot of space, because of the need to maintain the queue.

In *depth-first search* we search as deeply as possible in the tree until we can no longer go deeper; then we *backtrack* to previous levels and explore other paths. This is more space-efficient, but somewhat trickier to program.

In both cases, if only finitely many words have property $P$, the search terminates, and this constitutes a proof that no infinite word has the given property. Furthermore, the search can tell us what the longest finite word with the property is.

Various tricks can be used to speed up searches like this. For example, if the property $P$ is invariant under permutations of the alphabet, then we can assume that the word starts with a specific letter. Furthermore, if the alphabet is $\Sigma_k = \{0, 1, \ldots, k - 1\}$, we can assume that the word is *orderly*: this means the first occurrence of each letter $i$ precedes the first occurrence of $i + 1$ for $0 \le i \le k - 2$.

*Exercise* 13   Show that no infinite word over $\{0, 1, 2\}$ exists that is both squarefree, and contains at most 9 distinct factors of length 3. What is the longest such word?

In the case that there *is* an infinite word having property $P$, then the corresponding search will not terminate. However, in this case, breadth-first search can be used to identify promising ways to construct an infinite word with the given property, as we will see in Section 8.5.3.

## 2.7 Languages

Sometimes we have to deal with finite or infinite collections of words. A *language* $L$ is a set of words over the alphabet $\Sigma$; in other words, it is a subset of $\Sigma^*$.

Since a language is a set, we can use all the usual boolean operations on languages, such as union ($L_1 \cup L_2$), intersection ($L_1 \cap L_2$), complement with respect to $\Sigma^*$ ($\overline{L} = \Sigma^* - L$), and so forth.

Languages also have other kinds of operations. A basic one is concatenation:

$$L_1 L_2 = \{xy \,:\, x \in L_1, y \in L_2\}.$$

Once we have concatenation, we can also get powers: $L^n = \overbrace{LL\cdots L}^{n}$. More precisely, we define $L^0 = \{\epsilon\}$ and $L^n = L \cdot L^{n-1}$ for $n \ge 1$.

By $L^*$, the *Kleene closure* of $L$, we mean the language defined by $\bigcup_{i \ge 0} L^i$. This language is the set of all finite words obtainable by concatenating 0 or more words of $L$, in any order. Note that $L^*$ always contains $\epsilon$, by definition.

# 3

# Number representations and numeration systems

## 3.1 Base-$k$ representation

Let $k \geq 2$ be an integer. The usual base-$k$ representation uses the digits in $\Sigma_k = \{0, 1, \ldots, k - 1\}$ to represent natural numbers. We recall the following familiar result:

**Theorem 3.1.1** *Every natural number $n$ has a unique canonical representation*

$$n = \sum_{1 \leq i \leq t} a_i k^{t-i},$$

*where $t \geq 0$ and $0 \leq a_i < k$ for $1 \leq i \leq t$, and $a_t \neq 0$.*

*Exercise* 14  Prove Theorem 3.1.1.

The canonical base-$k$ representation of $n$ can be viewed as a word $a_1 a_2 \cdots a_t$, and we write $(n)_k = a_1 a_2 \cdots a_t$. Thus, for example, we have $(43)_2 = 101011$. Our convention is that the canonical representation for 0 is $\epsilon$, the empty word—this differs from the usual convention, which is to use 0. The set of all canonical base-$k$ representations is written $C_k$. For example,

$$C_2 = \{\epsilon, 1, 10, 11, 100, 101, 110, 111, \ldots\}.$$

There are, of course, other possible base-$k$ representations for a natural number $n$, resulting from an arbitrary number of leading zeros. The set of all possible base-$k$ representations for $n$ is $\{0^i (n)_k : i \geq 0\}$.[1]

We generalize the notation $(n)_k$ to sets: if $S \subseteq \mathbb{N}$, then $(S)_k = \{(n)_k : n \in S\}$.

If $w$ is a word over $\Sigma_k$ (possibly with leading zeros), then $[w]_k$ denotes the

---

[1] Let us recall here that the notation $0^i$ means $\overbrace{00 \cdots 0}^{i}$. There is a possible source of confusion between powers of words and powers of integers, but the context should make things clear.

integer represented by $w$ in base $k$. Thus $[0101011]_2 = 43$. More generally, if $w = a_1 \cdots a_t$ for $a_i \in \mathbb{Z}$, then we define $[w]_k = \sum_{1 \le i \le t} a_i k^{t-i}$.

We will also need to generalize all this to allow encoding pairs (or triples, quadruples, etc.) of integers in base $k$. We handle pairs by first padding the representation of the smaller integer with leading zeros, so it has the same length as the larger one, and then coding the pair as a word over $\Sigma_k^2 = \Sigma_k \times \Sigma_k$. This gives the *canonical representation* of a pair $(m, n)$, and is denoted $(m, n)_k$. Note that the canonical representation of a pair never begins with the symbol $[0, 0]$. For example, the canonical representation of the pair $(20, 13)$ in base 2 is

$$w = [1,0] [0,1] [1,1] [0,0] [0,1],$$

where the first components spell out $10100$ and the second components spell out $01101$. Again, the set of all possible base-$k$ representations for the pair $(m, n)$ is given by the language $\{ [0,0]^i (m,n)_k : i \ge 0 \}$.

Given a finite word $x \in (\Sigma_k^j)^*$, we define the *projections* $\pi_i(x)$ $(i = 1, 2, \ldots, j)$ onto the $i$th coordinate. Thus, for example, $\pi_1(w)$ for the word $w$ above is $10100$ and $\pi_2(w) = 01101$.

The convention in this book is that by default we assume that all base-$k$ representations are written with the most significant digit first (msd). In some cases, however, it is easier to deal with the reversed representations, where the least significant digit (lsd) appears first (and shorter representations, if necessary, are padded with *trailing* zeros).

In some cases we want to encode the elements of pairs (or triples, etc.) in *different* bases. We write $(m, n)_{k,\ell}$ to denote the word over the alphabet $\Sigma_k \times \Sigma_\ell$ where the first component is the base-$k$ representation of $m$ and the second component is the base-$\ell$ representation of $n$ (and the shorter, if necessary, is padded with leading zeros). For example,

$$(17, 43)_{2,3} = [1,0] [0,1] [0,1] [0,2] [1,1].$$

## 3.2 Fibonacci representation

Let the Fibonacci numbers be defined, as usual, by $F_0 = 0$, $F_1 = 1$, and $F_n = F_{n-1} + F_{n-2}$ for $n \ge 2$. (We caution the reader that some authors use a different indexing for these numbers, although they really shouldn't.)

It is well known, and goes back to Ostrowski [290], Lekkerkerker [238], and Zeckendorf [383], that every non-negative integer can be represented as

| $n$ | $(n)_F$ | $n$ | $(n)_F$ |
|---|---|---|---|
| 0 | $\epsilon$ | 10 | 10010 |
| 1 | 1 | 11 | 10100 |
| 2 | 10 | 12 | 10101 |
| 3 | 100 | 13 | 100000 |
| 4 | 101 | 14 | 100001 |
| 5 | 1000 | 15 | 100010 |
| 6 | 1001 | 16 | 100100 |
| 7 | 1010 | 17 | 100101 |
| 8 | 10000 | 18 | 101000 |
| 9 | 10001 | 19 | 101001 |

Table 3.1 *Fibonacci representation of the integers* $\{0, 1, \ldots, 19\}$.

a sum of Fibonacci numbers $(F_i)_{i \geq 2}$. This makes Fibonacci representation a strong analogue of base-2 representation. However, to ensure uniqueness of the representation, we have to add the constraint that *no two consecutive Fibonacci numbers are used*. For example, $43 = F_9 + F_6 + F_2 = F_9 + F_5 + F_4 + F_2$, but the second representation uses two consecutive Fibonacci numbers, so it is not valid. Also see [66, 155].

A Fibonacci representation is generally written as a binary word $a_1 a_2 \cdots a_t$ representing the integer $\sum_{1 \leq i \leq t} a_i F_{t+2-i}$. The binary word 10010001, for example, is the Fibonacci representation of 43. By $(n)_F$ we mean the *canonical* Fibonacci representation for the integer $n$, having no leading zeros or consecutive 1s. As you might guess, we say that $(0)_F = \epsilon$, the empty word.

For $w = a_1 a_2 \cdots a_t$, a word over $\mathbb{Z}$, we define $[w]_F := \sum_{1 \leq i \leq t} a_i F_{t+2-i}$. Table 3.1 gives the Fibonacci representation of the first few natural numbers.

*Exercise 15*   The *Lucas numbers* $L_n$ are defined by $L_0 = 2$, $L_1 = 1$, and $L_n = L_{n-1} + L_{n-2}$. What is the Fibonacci representation of $L_n$?

*Exercise 16*   Let $w, x$ be binary words. Prove that $[w]_F = [x]_F$ iff $[w0]_F = [x0]_F$. Also show, by means of a counterexample, that the result is no longer true if $w$ is over a larger alphabet such as $\{0, 1, 2\}$.

## 3.3 Tribonacci representation

Let the Tribonacci numbers be defined, as usual, by the linear recurrence $T_n = T_{n-1} + T_{n-2} + T_{n-3}$ for $n \geq 3$ with initial values $T_0 = 0$, $T_1 = 1$, $T_2 = 1$. (We caution the reader that some authors use a different indexing for these numbers.) Table 3.2 gives the first few Tribonacci numbers. From the theory

| $n$ | 0 | 1 | 2 | 3 | 4 | 5 | 6 | 7 | 8 | 9 | 10 | 11 | 12 | 13 |
|---|---|---|---|---|---|---|---|---|---|---|---|---|---|---|
| $T_n$ | 0 | 1 | 1 | 2 | 4 | 7 | 13 | 24 | 44 | 81 | 149 | 274 | 504 | 927 |

Table 3.2 *The first few Tribonacci numbers.*

of linear recurrences we know that

$$T_n = c_1\alpha^n + c_2\beta^n + c_3\gamma^n$$

where $\alpha, \beta, \gamma$ are the zeros of the polynomial $x^3 - x^2 - x - 1$. The only real zero is $\alpha \doteq 1.83928675521416113$; the other two zeros are complex and are of magnitude $< 3/4$. Solving for the constants, we find that

$$c_1 \doteq 0.336228116994941094225,$$

the real zero of the polynomial $44x^3 - 2x - 1 = 0$. It follows that $T_n = c_1\alpha^n + O(.75^n)$. In particular $T_n/T_{n-1} = \alpha + O(.41^n)$.

It is well known that every non-negative integer can be represented, in an essentially unique way, as a sum of Tribonacci numbers $(T_i)_{i\geq 2}$, subject to the constraint that no three consecutive Tribonacci numbers are used [68]. For example, $43 = T_7 + T_6 + T_4 + T_3$.

Such a representation can be written as a binary word $a_1 a_2 \cdots a_t$ representing the integer $\sum_{1\leq i\leq t} a_i T_{t+2-i}$. For example, the binary word 110110 is the Tribonacci representation of 43. By $(n)_T$ we mean the *canonical* Tribonacci representation for the integer $n$, having no leading zeros or occurrences of 111. Note that $(0)_T = \epsilon$, the empty word.

Let $\Sigma_2 = \{0, 1\}$. For $w = a_1 a_2 \cdots a_t \in \mathbb{N}^t$, we define $[w]_T := \sum_{1\leq i\leq t} a_i T_{t+2-i}$, even if $w$ has leading zeros or occurrences of the word 111.

Table 3.3 gives the Tribonacci representation of the first few natural numbers.

## 3.4 Pell representation

Define the *Pell numbers* as follows: $P_0 = 0$, $P_1 = 1$, and $P_n = 2P_{n-1} + P_{n-2}$ for $n \geq 2$. Table 3.4 gives the first few Pell numbers.

**Theorem 3.4.1** *Up to leading zeros, every non-negative integer has a unique representation in the form* $\sum_{1\leq i\leq t} a_i P_{t+1-i}$, *subject to the restrictions*

(a) $a_i \in \{0, 1, 2\}$ *for* $i \geq 2$.
(b) $a_1 \in \{0, 1\}$.

| $n$ | $(n)_T$ | $n$ | $(n)_T$ |
|---|---|---|---|
| 0 | $\epsilon$ | 10 | 1011 |
| 1 | 1 | 11 | 1100 |
| 2 | 10 | 12 | 1101 |
| 3 | 11 | 13 | 10000 |
| 4 | 100 | 14 | 10001 |
| 5 | 101 | 15 | 10010 |
| 6 | 110 | 16 | 10011 |
| 7 | 1000 | 17 | 10100 |
| 8 | 1001 | 18 | 10101 |
| 9 | 1010 | 19 | 10110 |

Table 3.3 *Tribonacci representation of the integers* $\{0, 1, \ldots, 19\}$.

| $n$ | 0 | 1 | 2 | 3 | 4 | 5 | 6 | 7 | 8 | 9 | 10 | 11 |
|---|---|---|---|---|---|---|---|---|---|---|---|---|
| $P_n$ | 0 | 1 | 2 | 5 | 12 | 29 | 70 | 169 | 408 | 985 | 2378 | 5741 |

Table 3.4 *The first few Pell numbers.*

*(c) If $a_i = 2$, then $a_{i-1} = 0$.*

For example, $43 = P_5 + P_4 + P_2$.

By $[x]_P$, for $x = a_1 \cdots a_t \in \Sigma_3^*$, we mean the integer $\sum_{1 \leq i \leq t} a_i P_{t-i}$. If $n = \sum_{1 \leq i \leq t} a_i P_i$ is an expression for $n$ with the $a_i$ satisfying the three conditions above, then the canonical Pell representation of $n$ is $a_t \cdots a_1$, and is denoted $(n)_P$. Thus $(43)_P = 11010$.

*Exercise* 17   Show that the set of all canonical representations in the Pell system is given by the regular expression $\epsilon \cup \{1, 20\}\{0, 1, 20\}^*$.

## 3.5 Ostrowski representation

A good reference on this topic is the chapter on Sturmian words in [246].

Let $\theta, \rho$ be real numbers with $0 < \theta, \rho < 1$. For $n \geq 1$ define

$$s_n = \lfloor (n + 1)\theta + \rho \rfloor - \lfloor n\theta + \rho \rfloor$$
$$s_n' = \lceil (n + 1)\theta + \rho \rceil - \lceil n\theta + \rho \rceil$$

for $n \geq 1$. The words $(s_n)_{n \geq 1}$ and $(s_n')_{n \geq 1}$ are called the *Sturmian words* of *slope* $\theta$ and *intercept* $\rho$. Notice that $s_n \in \{0, 1\}$.

A special case of $(s_n)_{n \geq 1}$ is where $\rho = 0$, and is easiest to work with. These are called the *Sturmian characteristic words*, and are written as $\mathbf{f}_\theta$.

**Example 3.5.1**    Take $\theta = (\sqrt{5} - 1)/2 = 0.61803 \cdots$. Then

$$\mathbf{f}_\theta := f_\theta(1) f_\theta(2) \cdots = 10110101 \cdots$$

We will see later that this is (up to renaming of the letters) the infinite Fibonacci word discussed previously.

Recall the coding defined by $\overline{0} = 1$ and $\overline{1} = 0$.

**Theorem 3.5.2**    *If $0 < \theta < 1$ is an irrational real, then $\mathbf{f}_{1-\theta} = \overline{\mathbf{f}_\theta}$.*

*Proof*  We have

$$f_\theta(n) = \lfloor (n + 1)\theta \rfloor - \lfloor n\theta \rfloor$$

and

$$\begin{aligned}
f_{1-\theta}(n) &= \lfloor (n + 1)(1 - \theta) \rfloor - \lfloor n(1 - \theta) \rfloor \\
&= \lfloor -(n + 1)\theta \rfloor + n + 1 - \lfloor -n\theta \rfloor - n \\
&= \lfloor -(n + 1)\theta \rfloor - \lfloor -n\theta \rfloor + 1.
\end{aligned}$$

So if we set $x = (n + 1)\theta$ and $y = n\theta$, then

$$\begin{aligned}
f_\theta(n) + f_{1-\theta}(n) &= \lfloor (n + 1)\theta \rfloor + \lfloor -(n + 1)\theta \rfloor - \lfloor n\theta \rfloor - \lfloor -n\theta \rfloor + 1 \\
&= \lfloor x \rfloor + \lfloor -x \rfloor - (\lfloor y \rfloor + \lfloor -y \rfloor) + 1 \\
&= (-1) - (-1) + 1 \\
&= 1,
\end{aligned}$$

because $x$ and $y$ are irrational. The result follows. $\qquad\square$

We now introduce a related infinite word:

$$\mathbf{g}_\alpha := g_\alpha(1) g_\alpha(2) \cdots$$

$$g_\alpha(n) = \begin{cases} 1, & \text{if } n = \lfloor k\alpha \rfloor \text{ for some } k, \\ 0, & \text{otherwise.} \end{cases}$$

**Theorem 3.5.3**    *Let $\alpha > 1$ be an irrational real number. Then*

$$\mathbf{g}_\alpha = \mathbf{f}_{1/\alpha}.$$

*Proof*

$$g_\alpha(n) = 1 \iff \exists k \text{ such that } n = \lfloor k\alpha \rfloor$$
$$\iff \exists k \text{ such that } n \le k\alpha < n + 1$$
$$\iff \exists k \text{ such that } n/\alpha \le k < (n + 1)/\alpha$$
$$\iff \exists k \text{ such that } \lfloor n/\alpha \rfloor = k - 1 \text{ and } \lfloor (n + 1)/\alpha \rfloor = k$$
$$\iff \lfloor (n + 1)/\alpha \rfloor - \lfloor n/\alpha \rfloor = 1$$
$$\iff f_{1/\alpha}(n) = 1.$$

□

We now define the *Sturmian characteristic morphisms* $h_n : \{0, 1\}^* \to \{0, 1\}^*$ for $n \ge 1$, as follows:

$$h_n(0) = 0^{n-1}1 \tag{3.1}$$
$$h_n(1) = 0^{n-1}10.$$

**Theorem 3.5.4**  *Let $\alpha$ be an irrational real, $0 < \alpha < 1$, and let $k \ge 1$ be an integer. Then $h_k(\mathbf{f}_\alpha) = \mathbf{f}_{1/(k+\alpha)}$.*

*Proof*  Define $d_i = h_k(f_\alpha(i))$ for $i \ge 1$. So

$$h_k(\mathbf{f}_\alpha) = d_1 d_2 d_3 \cdots .$$

Let $n$ be the position of the $m$th 1 in $h_k(\mathbf{f}_\alpha)$. Each $d_i$ contains exactly one 1, so this means we are interested in the 1 appearing in $d_m$. Then

$$|d_1 d_2 \cdots d_{m-1}| = (m - 1)k + f_\alpha(1) + \cdots + f_\alpha(m - 1)$$
$$= (m - 1)k + (\lfloor 2\alpha \rfloor - \lfloor \alpha \rfloor) + \cdots + (\lfloor m\alpha \rfloor - \lfloor (m - 1)\alpha \rfloor)$$
$$= (m - 1)k + \lfloor m\alpha \rfloor - \lfloor \alpha \rfloor$$
$$= (m - 1)k + \lfloor m\alpha \rfloor.$$

Hence

$$n = |d_1 d_2 \cdots d_{m-1}| + k = (m - 1)k + \lfloor m\alpha \rfloor + k = \lfloor m(k + \alpha) \rfloor.$$

And so

$$(h_k(\mathbf{f}_\alpha))(n) = 1 \iff \exists m \text{ such that } n = \lfloor m(k + \alpha) \rfloor$$
$$\iff g_{k+\alpha}(n) = 1$$
$$\iff f_{1/(k+\alpha)}(n) = 1.$$

□

We now give the relationship between the Ostrowski system and continued fractions. A (simple) continued fraction is an expression of the form

$$a_0 + \cfrac{1}{a_1 + \cfrac{1}{a_2 + \cfrac{1}{a_3 + \cdots}}} \tag{3.2}$$

which we abbreviate as $[a_0, a_1, a_2, a_3, \ldots]$. It may be finite or infinite. For real numbers, this expression is essentially unique provided $a_i \in \mathbb{Z}$ for all $i$, and $a_i \geq 1$ for $i \geq 1$. We say "essentially" because in the case of finite continued fractions, there is the small ambiguity that a continued fraction can end in either $a$ or $a - 1, 1$ for $a \geq 2$. For more information about continued fractions, see, for example [188].

**Example 3.5.5** Here are the continued fraction expansions for four numbers:

$$\frac{157}{68} = [2, 3, 4, 5]$$

$$\frac{1 + \sqrt{5}}{2} = [1, 1, 1, 1, \ldots]$$

$$e = [2, 1, 2, 1, 1, 4, 1, 1, 6, 1, 1, 8, \ldots]$$

$$\pi = [3, 7, 15, 1, 292, 1, 1, 1, 2, 1, 3, 1, 14, 2, 1, 1, 2, 2, \ldots].$$

The first expansion is finite, the second periodic, the third "pseudo-periodic" (consisting of blocks of the form $1, 2k, 1$), and the fourth has no obvious simple pattern.

The following lemma lets us compute the values of truncated continued fractions $[a_0, a_1, \ldots, a_n]$ in a left-to-right manner.

**Lemma 3.5.6** *Define the convergents $p_n/q_n$ as follows:*

$$p_{-2} = 0 \qquad\qquad q_{-2} = 1$$
$$p_{-1} = 1 \qquad\qquad q_{-1} = 0$$
$$p_k = a_k p_{k-1} + p_{k-2} \qquad\qquad q_k = a_k q_{k-1} + q_{k-2},$$

*for $k \geq 0$. Then*

$$\frac{p_n}{q_n} = [a_0, a_1, \ldots, a_n].$$

*Proof*  By induction on $n$. The base cases $n = 0, 1$ are easily checked. Otherwise we have

$$[a_0, a_1, \ldots, a_{n-1}, a_n, a_{n+1}] = [a_0, a_1, \ldots, a_{n-1}, a_n + 1/a_{n+1}]$$

$$= \frac{(a_n + \frac{1}{a_{n+1}})p_{n-1} + p_{n-2}}{(a_n + \frac{1}{a_{n+1}})q_{n-1} + q_{n-2}} \quad \text{(by induction)}$$

$$= \frac{(a_{n+1}a_n + 1)p_{n-1} + a_{n+1}p_{n-2}}{(a_{n+1}a_n + 1)q_{n-1} + a_{n+1}q_{n-2}}$$

$$= \frac{a_{n+1}(a_n p_{n-1} + p_{n-2}) + p_{n-1}}{a_{n+1}(a_n q_{n-1} + q_{n-2}) + q_{n-1}}$$

$$= \frac{a_{n+1}p_n + p_{n-1}}{a_{n+1}q_n + q_{n-1}}.$$

□

We can now reinterpret this in terms of products of $2 \times 2$ matrices:

**Corollary 3.5.7**  *We have*

$$\begin{bmatrix} a_0 & 1 \\ 1 & 0 \end{bmatrix} \begin{bmatrix} a_1 & 1 \\ 1 & 0 \end{bmatrix} \cdots \begin{bmatrix} a_n & 1 \\ 1 & 0 \end{bmatrix} = \begin{bmatrix} p_n & p_{n-1} \\ q_n & q_{n-1} \end{bmatrix}, \quad (3.3)$$

This is a really useful and fundamental result. From it we can obtain many other standard results on continued fractions. For example:

**Corollary 3.5.8**

(a) $(-1)^{n+1} = p_n q_{n-1} - p_{n-1} q_n.$

(b)

$$\begin{bmatrix} a_n & 1 \\ 1 & 0 \end{bmatrix} \begin{bmatrix} a_{n-1} & 1 \\ 1 & 0 \end{bmatrix} \cdots \begin{bmatrix} a_0 & 1 \\ 1 & 0 \end{bmatrix} = \begin{bmatrix} p_n & q_n \\ p_{n-1} & q_{n-1} \end{bmatrix}. \quad (3.4)$$

*Proof*

(a) Take the determinant of both sides of (3.3).

(b) Take the transpose of both sides of (3.3).

□

Given a real number $x$, we can expand it as a continued fraction as follows:

```
CFE(x) { returns continued fraction of x}
while (x ≠ ∞) do
    output(⌊x⌋)
    x := 1/(x − ⌊x⌋)
```

For example, on input $x = \pi$ we first get an output of $\lfloor \pi \rfloor = 3$. Then $x$ is set to $x_1 = 1/(\pi - 3) = 7.06251\cdots$ and the output is 7. Then $x$ is set to $1/(x_1 - 7) = 15.99659\cdots$ and the output is 15, and so forth. This gives

$$\pi = [3, 7, 15, 1, 292, \ldots].$$

There are two entirely different meanings for the symbol $[a_0, a_1, \ldots, a_n]$ in the number theory literature. The first meaning (and the one we typically intend) is a rational function in the $n + 1$ variables $a_0, a_1, \ldots, a_n$. In this interpretation, the $a_i$ could lie in any field at all and do not need to be integers. For example, if $X$ is an indeterminate, then $[X, -X, X] = (X^3 - 2X)/(X^2 - 1)$. The other meaning of $x = [a_0, a_1, \ldots]$ is that we apply the algorithm CFE to $x$ and the algorithm outputs $a_0, a_1, \ldots$. In this case, typically (but not always) we assume $x$ is a real number. In the number theory literature these two meanings are often conflated, so be careful.

Now an easy induction proves

**Theorem 3.5.9** *Let $\alpha$, $0 < \alpha < 1$ have continued fraction expansion $\alpha = [0, a_1, a_2, \ldots]$. Define $\beta_n = [0, a_n, a_{n+1}, \ldots]$ for $n \geq 1$. Then*

$$\mathbf{f}_\alpha = (h_{a_1} \circ h_{a_2} \circ \cdots \circ h_{a_n})(\mathbf{f}_{\beta_{n+1}}).$$

**Corollary 3.5.10** *If $\alpha = [0, a_1, a_2, \ldots, a_n, a_1, a_2, \ldots, a_n, a_1, a_2, \ldots]$ is a periodic continued fraction, then $\mathbf{f}_\alpha$ is a fixed point of $h_{a_1} \circ h_{a_2} \circ \cdots \circ h_{a_n}$.*

**Example 3.5.11** Take $\alpha = [0, 1, 1, 1, \ldots] = \frac{\sqrt{5}-1}{2}$. Then $\mathbf{f}_\alpha = 10110\cdots$ is a fixed point of the morphism $1 \to 10$ and $0 \to 1$.

Let $\alpha = [0, a_1, a_2, \ldots]$ be a real number. The *Sturmian characteristic words* are defined by

$$X_n = (h_{a_1} \circ h_{a_2} \circ \cdots \circ h_{a_n})(0)$$
$$Y_n = (h_{a_1} \circ h_{a_2} \circ \cdots \circ h_{a_n})(1).$$

**Proposition 3.5.12** *For $n \geq 1$ we have $Y_n = X_n X_{n-1}$.*

*Proof*   We have

$$Y_n = (h_{a_1} \circ h_{a_2} \circ \cdots \circ h_{a_n})(1)$$
$$= (h_{a_1} \circ h_{a_2} \circ \cdots \circ h_{a_{n-1}})(h_{a_n}(1))$$
$$= (h_{a_1} \circ h_{a_2} \circ \cdots \circ h_{a_{n-1}})(h_{a_n}(0)0)$$
$$= (h_{a_1} \circ h_{a_2} \circ \cdots \circ h_{a_{n-1}})(h_{a_n}(0))(h_{a_1} \circ h_{a_2} \circ \cdots \circ h_{a_{n-1}})(0)$$
$$= (h_{a_1} \circ h_{a_2} \circ \cdots \circ h_{a_n})(0)(h_{a_1} \circ h_{a_2} \circ \cdots \circ h_{a_{n-1}})(0)$$
$$= X_n X_{n-1}.$$

□

**Theorem 3.5.13**   *We have*

$$X_n = \begin{cases} 0, & \text{if } n = 0; \\ 0^{a_1-1}1, & \text{if } n = 1; \\ X_{n-1}^{a_n} X_{n-2}, & \text{if } n \geq 2. \end{cases}$$

*Proof*   By induction on $n$. It is easy to check for $n = 0, 1$. Now assume the result is true for $n' < n$ for $n \geq 2$. We prove it for $n$. We have

$$X_n = (h_{a_1} \circ h_{a_2} \circ \cdots \circ h_{a_n})(0)$$
$$= (h_{a_1} \circ h_{a_2} \circ \cdots \circ h_{a_{n-1}})(h_{a_n}(0))$$
$$= (h_{a_1} \circ h_{a_2} \circ \cdots \circ h_{a_{n-1}})(0^{a_n-1}1)$$
$$= (h_{a_1} \circ h_{a_2} \circ \cdots \circ h_{a_{n-1}})(0^{a_n-1})(h_{a_1} \circ h_{a_2} \circ \cdots \circ h_{a_{n-1}})(1)$$
$$= ((h_{a_1} \circ h_{a_2} \circ \cdots \circ h_{a_{n-1}})(0))^{a_n-1}(h_{a_1} \circ h_{a_2} \circ \cdots \circ h_{a_{n-1}})(1)$$
$$= X_{n-1}^{a_n-1} X_{n-1} X_{n-2} \quad \text{(by Prop. (3.5.12))}$$
$$= X_{n-1}^{a_n} X_{n-2}.$$

□

By comparing this recursion for $X_n$ with the recursions for the convergents in Lemma 3.5.6, we see that we have found an analogue, in words, of continued fractions!

**Example 3.5.14**   Start with the number $(3 - \sqrt{5})/2$ with continued fraction

$$[0, 2, 1, 1, \ldots].$$

Then Theorem 3.5.2 applied to Example 3.5.11 implies that the associated Sturmian characteristic word is the limit of the words $X_0 = 0$, $X_1 = 01$, and $X_n = X_{n-1}X_{n-2}$. This is, modulo a shift of indices, the defining recursion for the finite Fibonacci words. Hence the associated Sturmian characteristic word is **f**.

**Example 3.5.15** We have

$$e^{-1} = [0, 2, 1, 2, 1, 1, 4, \ldots],$$

and so the convergents are as in Table 3.5. We find

$$X_0 = 0$$
$$X_1 = 01$$
$$X_2 = 010$$
$$X_3 = 01001001$$
$$X_4 = 01001001010$$
$$X_5 = 0100100101001001001,$$

etc.

| $n$ | $-2$ | $-1$ | 0 | 1 | 2 | 3 | 4 | 5 | 6 |
|-----|------|------|---|---|---|---|---|---|---|
| $a_n$ | | | 0 | 2 | 1 | 2 | 1 | 1 | 4 |
| $p_n$ | 0 | 1 | 0 | 1 | 1 | 3 | 4 | 7 | 32 |
| $q_n$ | 1 | 0 | 1 | 2 | 3 | 8 | 11 | 19 | 87 |

Table 3.5 *Convergents to $e^{-1}$.*

**Theorem 3.5.16** *For $n \geq 0$ we have*

*(a)* $|X_n| = q_n$ *and* $|X_n|_1 = p_n$.
*(b)* $|Y_n| = q_n + q_{n-1}$ *and* $|Y_n|_1 = p_n + p_{n-1}$.

*Proof* By Proposition 3.5.12 it suffices to prove (a). This is an easy induction on $n$ (omitted). □

**Theorem 3.5.17** *For $n \geq 1$ the word $X_n$ is the prefix of $f_\alpha$ of length $q_n$.*

*Proof* From Theorem 3.5.9 we know that

$$\mathbf{f}_\alpha = (h_{a_1} \circ \cdots \circ h_{a_n})(\mathbf{f}_{\beta_{n+1}}).$$

So $\mathbf{f}_\alpha$ has a prefix of either

$$X_n = (h_{a_1} \circ h_{a_2} \circ \cdots \circ h_{a_n})(0)$$

or

$$Y_n = (h_{a_1} \circ h_{a_2} \circ \cdots \circ h_{a_n})(1).$$

But $Y_n = X_n X_{n-1}$. So $X_n$ is a prefix of $\mathbf{f}_\alpha$ and by Theorem 3.5.16 we have $|X_n| = q_n$. □

The next theorem proves the "almost-commutative" property of Sturmian characteristic words. Define $c(w) = w'ba$ if $w = w'ab$ for letters $a, b$.

**Theorem 3.5.18**   *For* $n \geq 1$ *we have* $X_n X_{n-1} = c(X_{n-1} X_n)$.

*Proof*   By induction on $n$. For $n = 1$ we have

$$X_1 X_0 = 0^{a_1-1}10 = c(0^{a_1-1}01) = c(0\ 0^{a_1-1}1) = c(X_0 X_1).$$

Assume the result is true for $n' < n$. Then

$$
\begin{aligned}
X_n X_{n-1} &= (X_{n-1}^{a_n} X_{n-2}) X_{n-1} \\
&= X_{n-1}^{a_n} c(X_{n-1} X_{n-2}) \quad \text{(by induction)} \\
&= c(X_{n-1}^{a_n} X_{n-1} X_{n-2}) \\
&= c(X_{n-1} X_{n-1}^{a_n} X_{n-2}) \\
&= c(X_{n-1} X_n).
\end{aligned}
$$

$\square$

We now state the fundamental theorem of Ostrowski representation.

**Theorem 3.5.19**   *Given a positive real irrational number* $\alpha = [a_0, a_1, \ldots,]$ *with continued fraction convergents* $p_n/q_n = [a_0, a_1, \ldots, a_n]$, *we can write every integer* $N \geq 0$ *uniquely as* $N = \sum_{0 \leq i \leq j} b_i q_i$ *where the digits* $(b_i)$ *satisfy the conditions*

(a) $0 \leq b_0 < a_1$.
(b) $0 \leq b_i \leq a_{i+1}$, *for* $i \geq 1$.
(c) *For* $i \geq 1$, *if* $b_i = a_{i+1}$, *then* $b_{i-1} = 0$.

For a proof, see [290] or [16, §3.9].

**Example 3.5.20**   Let $\alpha = \sqrt{2} = [1, 2, 2, 2, \ldots]$. Then Table 3.6 gives the first few convergents.

| $n$   | $-2$ | $-1$ | 0 | 1 | 2 | 3 | 4 | 5 |
|-------|------|------|---|---|---|----|----|----|
| $a_n$ |      |      | 1 | 2 | 2 | 2 | 2 | 2 |
| $p_n$ | 0    | 1    | 1 | 3 | 7 | 17 | 41 | 99 |
| $q_n$ | 1    | 0    | 1 | 2 | 5 | 12 | 29 | 70 |

Table 3.6 *First few convergents to* $\sqrt{2}$.

The Ostrowski numeration system corresponding to these $(q_n)$ is the Pell numeration system we mentioned previously.

We can use the Ostrowski numeration system to obtain the factorization of the prefix of length $m$ of $\mathbf{f}_\alpha$.

**Theorem 3.5.21** *Let $0 < \alpha < 1$ be an irrational real number with continued fraction expansion $[0, a_1, a_2, \ldots]$. Let $m \geq 0$ and let $b_s b_{s-1} \cdots b_0$ be the Ostrowski representation of $m$, msd first. Then*

$$f_\alpha(1)f_\alpha(2) \cdots f_\alpha(m) = X_s^{b_s} X_{s-1}^{b_{s-1}} \cdots X_0^{b_0}. \tag{3.5}$$

*Proof* By induction on $m$. For $m = 0$ both sides are $\epsilon$. If $0 < m < q_1 = a_1$, then $b_0 = m$, $X_0 = 0$, and

$$f_\alpha(1)f_\alpha(2) \cdots f_\alpha(q_1) = 0^{a_1-1}1,$$

so $f_\alpha(1)f_\alpha(2) \cdots f_\alpha(m) = X_0^{b_0}$.

Now let $s \geq 1$. Suppose Eq. (3.5) holds for all $m < q_s$. We prove it for $m < q_{s+1}$. Suppose $q_s \leq m < q_{s+1}$. Write $m = b_s q_s + r$, where $1 \leq b_s \leq a_{s+1}$, $0 \leq r < q_s$. By induction we have

$$r = \sum_{0 \leq i < s} b_i q_i$$

$$f_\alpha(1)f_\alpha(2) \cdots f_\alpha(r) = X_{s-1}^{b_{s-1}} \cdots X_0^{b_0}.$$

*Case 1: $b_s < a_{s+1}$.* Then $f_\alpha(1)f_\alpha(2) \cdots f_\alpha(m)$ is a prefix of $X_{s+1} = X_s^{a_{s+1}} X_{s-1}$. But $m = b_s q_s + r$, so $m < q_{s+1}$. Hence $f_\alpha(1)f_\alpha(2) \cdots f_\alpha(m)$ is a prefix of $X_s^{b_s+1} = X_s^{b_s} X_s$. Then

$$f_\alpha(1)f_\alpha(2) \cdots f_\alpha(m) = X_s^{b_s} f_\alpha(1)f_\alpha(2) \cdots f_\alpha(r)$$
$$= X_s^{b_s} X_{s-1}^{b_{s-1}} \cdots X_0^{b_0}.$$

*Case 2: $b_s = a_{s+1}$.* We have $m < q_{s+1}$ and so $m = b_s q_s + r = a_{s+1} q_s + r < q_{s+1}$. Thus $r < q_{s-1}$. Hence $f_\alpha(1)f_\alpha(2) \cdots f_\alpha(r)$ is a prefix of $X_{s-1}$. But $f_\alpha(1)f_\alpha(2) \cdots f_\alpha(m)$ is a prefix of $X_{s+1} = X_s^{a_{s+1}} X_{s-1}$. So

$$f_\alpha(1)f_\alpha(2) \cdots f_\alpha(m) = X_s^{a_{s+1}} f_\alpha(1)f_\alpha(2) \cdots f_\alpha(r)$$
$$= X_s^{b_s} X_{s-1}^{b_{s-1}} \cdots X_0^{b_0}.$$

$\square$

We can now characterize when $f_\alpha(n) = 1$, in terms of the Ostrowski representation of $n$.

**Theorem 3.5.22**   $f_\alpha(n) = 1$ *iff* $b_s b_{s-1} \cdots b_0$, *the Ostrowski representation of n, ends in an odd number of zeros.*

*Proof*   We have

$$f_\alpha(q_r) = \text{last symbol of } X_r$$

$$= \begin{cases} 1, & \text{if } r \text{ is odd}; \\ 0, & \text{if } r \text{ is even}. \end{cases}$$

Let $r$ be the least index for which $b_r > 0$. Then from Theorem 3.5.21 we see that $f_\alpha(n)$ is the last symbol of $X_r$, which is the last symbol of $f_\alpha(q_r)$, which is 1 iff $r$ is odd, iff $b_{r-1} \cdots b_0 = 0^r$ is an odd number of 0s.   □

# 4

# Automata

We will need finite automata, both with and without output. For more information about automata, see [203, 16, 346].

## 4.1 Basics of automata

A finite automaton can be viewed as a very simple computer. The basic model is as follows. First, there is a finite nonempty input alphabet, usually denoted by $\Sigma$. We use the abbreviation $\Sigma_k = \{0, 1, \ldots, k - 1\}$ for integers $k \geq 2$. Next, there is a finite, nonempty set of states, often denoted by $Q$. A distinguished state, usually written as $q_0$, is called the "start" or "initial" state. Certain states are called "final" or "accepting"; these are specified by giving a subset $F \subseteq Q$. Finally, there is a transition function that describes how inputs change the state: $\delta : Q \times \Sigma \to Q$, which is extended to the domain $Q \times \Sigma^*$ in the obvious way: $\delta(q, \epsilon) = q$ for all $q \in Q$ and $\delta(q, xa) = \delta(\delta(q, x), a)$ for all $q \in Q$, $x \in \Sigma^*$ and $a \in \Sigma$. A deterministic finite automaton (DFA) is then a quintuple consisting of all of these pieces: $M = (Q, \Sigma, \delta, q_0, F)$.

Automata are often depicted in a *transition diagram*, where states are displayed as circles or ovals with their names inside, and transitions are displayed as labeled arrows. Final states are denoted by double circles, and the initial state is given by a single arrow going in. See Figure 4.1.

A word $x$ is said to be *accepted* by $M$ if reading $x$, starting in $q_0$, leads to a final state; that is, if $\delta(q_0, x) \in F$. The set of all accepted words

$$\{x \in \Sigma^* : \delta(q_0, x) \in F\}$$

is said to be the *language recognized* by $M$, and is written $L(M)$. A language is said to be *regular* if it is recognized by some DFA $M$.

A basic result about finite automata is the so-called pumping lemma:

47

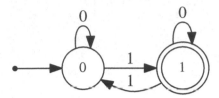

Figure 4.1 Finite automaton accepting those binary words having an odd number of 1s.

**Lemma 4.1.1**  *If L is a regular language, then there is a constant $n = n(L)$ such that for all $z \in L$ with $|z| \geq n$, there exists a decomposition $z = uvw$ with $|uv| \leq n$ and $|v| \geq 1$ such that $uv^i w \in L$ for all $i \geq 0$.*

*Proof*  If $L$ is regular, then it is recognized by a DFA $M = (Q, \Sigma, \delta, q_0, F)$ of $n$ states. This $n$ is the constant in the statement of the theorem. If $|z| \geq n$, consider the states encountered when processing the first $n$ symbols of $z$. At least $n + 1$ states are encountered, so by the pigeonhole principle, some state is repeated. This means the acceptance path in the transition diagram has a loop labeled with some nonempty word $v$. Write $z = uvw$, where $u$ is the word that precedes the loop, and $w$ the word that follows the loop. We can then go around this loop as often as we like (or not at all), and still get an acceptance path for the word $uv^i w$.                                                                    □

A state of a DFA $M = (Q, \Sigma, \delta, q_0, F)$ is called *useful* if it is part of the accepting path of some word, and *useless* otherwise. There are two different kinds of useless states: unreachable and dead. A state $q$ is *unreachable* if $\delta(q_0, x) \neq q$ for all $x \in \Sigma^*$. A state $q$ is *dead* if $\delta(q, x) \notin F$ for all $x \in \Sigma^*$.

A DFA is said to be *complete* if transitions are defined for each state and input symbol. Useless states, both unreachable and dead, can be safely removed from a DFA without changing the language recognized. Removing a dead state, however, might turn a DFA into something that is technically a nondeterministic finite automaton (discussed in the next section), since the resulting transition function is no longer total. Such a DFA is sometimes called *incomplete*. In the rest of the book, we delete useless states without comment.

## 4.2 Nondeterminism

Another generalization of finite automata is based on the concept of *nondeterminism*: there are multiple transitions on a single symbol, and acceptance of an input $x$ is defined in terms of the existence of at least one accepting path labeled with the symbols of $x$.

A nondeterministic machine replaces the range of $\delta$, which was previously just a single state, with a (possibly empty) set of states. In other words, $\delta$ is now a function mapping $Q \times \Sigma$ into $2^Q$, the set of all subsets of $Q$. The interpretation of a statement like $\delta(q, a) = S$ for a set $S$ is that, in state $q$ with input $a$, the automaton can enter any one of the states of $S$. This is then extended to the domain $Q \times \Sigma^*$ as follows: $\delta(q, \epsilon) = \{q\}$ and $\delta(q, xa) = \bigcup_{p \in \delta(q,x)} \delta(p, a)$. This gives a nondeterministic finite automaton, or NFA for short. The acceptance criterion is replaced by "$x$ is accepted if $\delta(q_0, x) \cap F \neq \emptyset$", which corresponds to the claim that at least one acceptance path leads to a state of $F$. Another small generalization is to allow the initial state $q_0$ to be a *set* of initial states.

Finally, one more generalization of NFA is the NFA-$\epsilon$: this is a nondeterministic finite automaton that allows the machine to spontaneously transition from one state to another without reading any symbols of the input. This is denoted by reading $\epsilon$, the empty word, and is carried out by extending the transition function's domain from $Q \times \Sigma$ to $Q \times (\Sigma \cup \{\epsilon\})$.

A basic theorem of automata theory is that every NFA (or NFA-$\epsilon$) can be simulated by a DFA, using something called the *subset construction*. The simulation takes place by constructing a DFA with state-set corresponding to all sets of states of the NFA. In the worst case, an NFA of $n$ states can require $2^n$ states in the smallest equivalent DFA (that is, one recognizing the same language). In practice, however, most NFAs require far fewer states to be simulated by DFAs.

*Open Question* 4.2.1   Develop a good model for the distribution of states in the smallest DFA simulating an NFA with $n$ states. (It is known there are exponentially many requiring exponentially many states, but a detailed model of the distribution is unknown.)

## 4.3 Regular expressions

Another way to represent regular languages is through *regular expressions*. These provide a shorthand for writing down regular languages over an alphabet $\Sigma$ in terms of three basic operations—union, concatenation, and Kleene closure—starting from the empty set $\emptyset$, the singleton sets $\{a\}$, and the empty word $\epsilon$.

We use the symbol $\emptyset$ for the empty set, $\epsilon$ for the set $\{\epsilon\}$, and a for the set $\{a\}$.

The union operation is the ordinary union of sets, and is denoted $L_1 \cup L_2$. In regular expressions, we often omit the braces usually employed for sets. The concatenation of languages is denoted by juxtaposition, and is defined by $L_1 L_2 = \{xy : x \in L_1, y \in L_2\}$. To define Kleene closure, we must first define powers of languages. We write $L^0 = \{\epsilon\}$, $L^1 = L$, and for $i \geq 1$ we define $L^i = L^{i-1} L$. Then the Kleene closure of $L$, written $L^*$, is defined by $\bigcup_{i \geq 0} L^i$. Note that $\emptyset^* = \{\epsilon\}$. Positive closure, denoted by $L^+$, is defined to be $\bigcup_{i \geq 1} L^i$, and is also sometimes used in regular expressions.

To understand how to evaluate a regular expression, we need the notion of precedence. Parentheses can alter the order of evaluation. Kleene $*$ is done before concatenation, which is done before union. For example, an expression like a $\cup$ bc$^*$ means a $\cup$ (b(c$^*$)) and represents the language $\{a\} \cup \{b\}\{c\}^*$.

Regular expressions do not have to be "unambiguous"; the same word can be obtained by different paths through the regular expression. For example, (0 $\cup$ 1)$^*$ $\cup$ 11 is a legitimate regular expression where 11 is specified in two different ways.

Study the following examples to get an appreciation for what regular expressions can do.

| | |
|---|---|
| (0 $\cup$ 1)$^*$010 | binary words ending in 010 |
| (0 $\cup$ 1)$^*$010(0 $\cup$ 1)$^*$ | binary words containing the factor 010 |
| (1 $\cup$ $\epsilon$)(0 $\cup$ 01)$^*$ | all binary words not containing the factor 11 |
| (0 $\cup$ $\epsilon$)(1+10)$^*$(1 $\cup$ $\epsilon$) | all binary words not containing the factor 00 |
| 0$^*$1$^*$2$^*$ | all 0s (if any) precede 1s, which precede 2s |
| 0$^+$1$^*$2$^*$ $\cup$ 1$^+$2$^*$ $\cup$ 2$^+$ | as in previous line, but not $\epsilon$ |
| 0$^*$(10$^*$10$^*$)$^*$ | binary words with an even number of 1s |

It is relatively easy to "compile" a regular expression into an equivalent NFA-$\epsilon$ of roughly the same size. The converse transformation, from an automaton (DFA, NFA, or NFA-$\epsilon$) is more complicated, however, and can result in exponential blowups in size. For standard constructions, see [203, 346].

## 4.4 Operations on automata

We will frequently need to take two automata $M_1$ and $M_2$, defined over an alphabet $\Sigma$, recognizing languages $L_1$ and $L_2$, and construct an automaton $M$

for the intersection $L_1 \cap L_2$, union $L_1 \cup L_2$, complement $\overline{L_1} = \Sigma^* - L_1$, and set difference $L_1 - L_2 = L_1 \cap \overline{L_2}$.

For these we can use a standard construction on automata called the *product* construction. Let $M_1 = (Q_1, \Sigma, \delta_1, q_1, F_1)$ and $M_2 = (Q_2, \Sigma, \delta_2, q_2, F_2)$. Define $M = (Q_1 \times Q_2, \Sigma, \delta, [q_1, q_2], F)$, where $\delta([r, s], a) = [\delta_1(r, a), \delta_2(s, a)]$. The idea is that on input $x$, the automaton $M$ simulates the behavior of $M_1$ and $M_2$ simultaneously, with $M_1$ being simulated in the first component, and $M_2$ in the second component.

If we take $F = F_1 \times F_2$, then $L(M) = L(M_1) \cap L(M_2)$. On the other hand, if we take $F = (F_1 \times Q_2) \cup (Q_1 \times F_2)$, then $L(M) = L(M_1) \cup L(M_2)$. If the original languages are recognized by machines with $m$ and $n$ states, respectively, then their union and intersection are recognized by machines with at most $mn$ states. Sometimes even fewer states are needed; some efficiency is created by starting with the initial state $[q_1, q_2]$ and then only including those states reachable from it. This can be accomplished by a kind of breadth-first search, where we use a queue to contain the states whose outgoing transitions have yet to be explored.

For the operations of intersection and union, the product construction works for both NFAs and DFAs.

Next, we need a construction for the complement language $\Sigma^* - L$. This is easy for complete DFAs: we simply change each accepting state to nonaccepting, and vice versa. If the DFA is not complete, we first complete it by adding one additional nonaccepting state and the needed transitions.

However, this idea does not work for NFAs, because there can be multiple accepting paths. (Here by a *path* we mean the sequence of states and transitions taken on an input $x$; a path is *accepting* if it ends at an accepting state.) In fact, there is no efficient complementation algorithm for NFAs, because (as mentioned before) there exist languages recognized by $n$-state NFAs for which the smallest equivalent DFA has $2^n$ states.

*Exercise 18* Give an example of an NFA $M$ where the complement language $\overline{L(M)}$ is *not* obtained by changing accepting states to nonaccepting and vice versa.

*Exercise 19* Show how to compute the symmetric difference of two regular languages, $(L_1 - L_2) \cup (L_2 - L_1)$ by manipulating the corresponding DFAs.

Another useful operation on automata we will need is reversal: given an NFA or DFA accepting the language $L$, we can create an NFA accepting $L^R$ by exchanging the set of initial states with the set of final states, and turning around the direction of the transitions: if $p \in \delta(q, a)$ in the original automaton, then the automaton for $L^R$ has $q \in \delta(p, a)$. The resulting NFA can then be converted to a DFA by the subset construction.

Finally, given a DFA $M$ recognizing $L$, we can also find a DFA for $h(L)$, where $h$ is a coding. To do so, we apply $h$ to each transition of $M$. The resulting automaton has the same number of states, but may now be an NFA. To convert it to an equivalent DFA, we use the subset construction.

Each of these constructions gives us a bound on the *state complexity* of the resulting operation; that is, the number of states needed to express it, in the worst case. We can summarize this for DFAs $M_1$ and $M_2$, with $m$ and $n$ states respectively, in Table 4.1. Here $L_1 = L(M_1)$ and $L_2 = L(M_2)$, and $h$ is a coding.

| Operation | Upper bound on state complexity |
|:---:|:---:|
| $L_1 \cup L_2$ | $mn$ |
| $L_1 \cap L_2$ | $mn$ |
| $\overline{L_1}$ | $m$ |
| $L_1^R$ | $2^m$ |
| $h(L_1)$ | $2^m$ |

Table 4.1 *State complexity of operations on DFAs.*

## 4.5 Minimization

A classical theorem from automata theory states that every DFA $M$ has a unique minimal equivalent DFA $M'$. Here "equivalent" means that $L(M) = L(M')$, "minimal" means having the smallest possible number of states [203, Thm. 3.10], and "unique" means up to renaming of the states. Furthermore, there are efficient algorithms to compute this minimal automaton of $M'$ from $M$; the fastest runs in time $O(n \log n)$ where $n$ is the number of states [202, 180, 226]. Complete and efficient C++ code for minimization is provided in a paper of Valmari [377].

No efficient algorithm for NFA minimization is known, and the minimal NFA is not unique. In fact, NFA minimization is PSPACE-complete [215], so an efficient algorithm is not likely to be found anytime soon. However, there are some heuristics known; see [291, 1, 208, 209, 163]. These have not been implemented in `Walnut` thus far.

## 4.6 Automata with output

A slightly more general model of deterministic finite automaton is called the *deterministic finite automaton with output* (DFAO). In this case, the set of final states $F$ is replaced with an output alphabet $\Delta$ and an output function $\tau : Q \to \Delta$. The output on input $x$ is then $\tau(\delta(q_0, x))$. Note that the output depends only on the *last state* reached on reading $x$. A DFAO is called a $k$-DFAO (or $k$-automaton) if its input alphabet is $\Sigma_k$.

When a DFAO is depicted, states are shown as circles or ovals. A state labeled $q/a$ means the state is called $q$ and its output is $a$. (Sometimes the state name is omitted.) Transitions on letters are depicted by arrows. The initial state is denoted by a single arrow pointing in. Figure 4.2 illustrates a 2-DFAO.

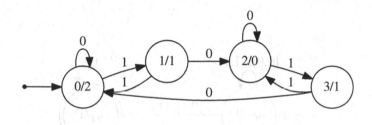

Figure 4.2 A 2-DFAO.

If a function $f : \Sigma^* \to \Delta$ is computed by a DFAO, we say it is a *finite-state function*. DFAOs can be minimized using essentially the same algorithm that is used for DFAs.

Given a finite-state function $f : \Sigma^* \to \Delta$, we may consider its reversal $f^R$ by $f^R(x) = f(x^R)$.

**Theorem 4.6.1**  *If $f$ is a finite-state function, so is its reversal $f^R$.*

*Proof*  See [16, Theorem 4.3.3, p. 139].                                □

For the state complexity of reversal of DFAOs, see [110].

## 4.7 Automata with multiple inputs

Often we will need to run automata with multiple inputs. To do so, we read the inputs *in parallel* and not in series. For example, suppose there are two inputs $x$ and $y$, with the first lying in $\Sigma^*$ and the second in $\Delta^*$, for some alphabets $\Sigma, \Delta$. In order to read these inputs in parallel, symbol-by-symbol, we need each input to have the same length. We can either require this as a condition, or pad all inputs with special symbols on the right or left, if necessary, to be as long as the longest input. First we read the first symbol of each input as a composite symbol over the cross-product of the underlying alphabets, then the second symbol, and so forth. This evidently generalizes to the case of multiple inputs.

As an example, let $\Sigma = \Delta = \{0, 1\}$, and consider the automaton in Figure 4.3, which reads two input words $x, y \in \Sigma^*$ of the same length, and accepts if and only if $x$ differs from $y$ in exactly one position. Omitted transitions go to a dead state that is nonaccepting and loops to itself on all inputs. Consider

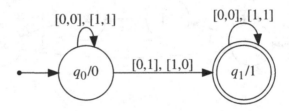

Figure 4.3 Automata accepting two inputs that differ by one bit.

the accepted word $[0,0][0,1][0,0]$. This represents an input of the pair $(000, 010)$, which is obtained by considering the first element (resp., the second element) of each pair.

*Exercise* 20 Find a regular expression for the language recognized by the DFA in Figure 4.3.

## 4.8 Combining multiple DFAs into a DFAO

Sometimes we have $t$ different DFAs $M_1, M_2, \ldots, M_t$, with the same input alphabet, whose languages are pairwise disjoint, and we would like to combine them into a *single* DFAO $M$ whose output on input $x$ is 0 if $x \notin L(M_i)$ for all $i$, and otherwise the unique index $i$ such that $x \in M_i$.

We can do this using a product construction, as follows. Let the automata be defined by $M_i = (Q_i, \Sigma, \delta_i, q_i, F_i)$ for $1 \le i \le t$, and define $M = (Q, \Sigma, \Delta, \delta, q_0, \tau)$ as follows:

- $Q = Q_1 \times Q_2 \times \cdots \times Q_t$.
- $\Delta = \{0, 1, \ldots, t\}$.
- $\delta([p_1, p_2, \ldots, p_t], a) = [\delta_1(p_1, a), \delta_2(p_2, a), \ldots, \delta(p_t, a)]$.
- $q_0 = [q_1, q_2, \ldots, q_t]$.
- $\tau([p_1, p_2, \ldots, p_t]) = i$ if $p_i \in F$, and 0 otherwise.

If each of the $M_i$ are minimal DFAs, then the resulting DFA $M$, provided unreachable states are removed, will also be minimal [359]. In practice, to construct $M$, it is easiest to start with the initial state $q_0 = [q_1, q_2, \ldots, q_t]$ and via a queue-based algorithm, include only those states reachable starting from $q_0$.

In a generalization of the construction above, we could weaken the pairwise disjoint hypothesis on the $L(M_i)$, and instead output the largest index $i$ such that $p_i \in F$, or 0 if there is none. In this case, the resulting DFAO may not be minimal.

Similarly, on input $x$ we could output the set $\{i : \delta_i(q_i, x) \in F_i\}$. Again, the resulting DFAO may not be minimal.

## 4.9 Enumeration of paths in a DFA

In this section we show how to count paths in automata.

Suppose we have a $t$-state DFA $(Q, \Delta \times \Sigma, \delta, q_0, F)$ that takes two inputs in parallel, with the first component of each input letter chosen from an alphabet $\Delta$, and the second component chosen from $\Sigma$. Our goal is to count $A : \Sigma^* \to \mathbb{N}$, the number of acceptance paths in this DFA where the second coordinate is labeled with $x \in \Sigma^*$.

We start by counting the number $N(x, i, j)$ of paths from state $q_i$ to state $q_j$ in this DFA where the second coordinate equals a given word $x$. More formally, if $|x| = n$, define

$$N(x, i, j) = |\{w \in \Delta^n : \delta(p_i, w \times x) = p_j\}|.$$

Note that $N(\epsilon, i, j) = 1$ if $i = j$ and 0 otherwise. Furthermore, note that for a single letter $b$ we have

$$N(xb, i, j) = \sum_k N(x, i, k)N(b, k, j), \tag{4.1}$$

because every path from $q_i$ to $q_j$ labeled with $xb$ in the second coordinate corresponds to some path from $q_i$ to $q_k$ (for some $k$) labeled $x$ in the second coordinate, followed by some path from $q_k$ to $q_j$ labeled $b$ in the second coordinate.

The following theorem shows how to compute $N(x, i, j)$:

**Theorem 4.9.1**  *Define the matrix-valued morphism* $\gamma : \Sigma^* \to \mathbb{N}^{t \times t}$ *as follows:*

$$[\gamma(b)]_{i,j} = N(b, i, j) = |\{a \in \Delta \: : \: \delta(p_i, [a, b]) = p_j\}| \tag{4.2}$$

*for each* $b \in \Sigma$ *and* $0 \le i, j < t$. *Then* $N(x, i, j) = [\gamma(x)]_{i,j}$.

*Proof*  By induction on $n = |x|$. The base case is $n = 0$ and is easily verified.

Now assume the result is true for $|x| < n$; we prove it for $|x| = n$. Write $x = x'b$ for a single letter $b$. Then

$$
\begin{aligned}
[\gamma(x)]_{i,j} &= [\gamma(x'b)]_{i,j} \\
&= ([\gamma(x')] \cdot [\gamma(b)])_{i,j} \\
&= \sum_k [\gamma(x')]_{i,k}[\gamma(b)]_{k,j} \quad \text{(by the definition of matrix multiplication)} \\
&= \sum_k N(x', i, k)N(b, k, j) \quad \text{(by induction and (4.2))} \\
&= N(x'b, i, j) \quad \text{(by (4.1))} \\
&= N(x, i, j).
\end{aligned}
$$

$\square$

As a corollary we get an expression for $A(x)$.

**Corollary 4.9.2**  *Let $M$ be a $t$-state DFA* $(Q, \Delta \times \Sigma, \delta, q_0, F)$ *and $\gamma$ the matrix-valued morphism defined above. Let* $v = \begin{bmatrix} 1 & 0 & 0 & \cdots & 0 \end{bmatrix}$ *and $w$ be the boolean vector with a 1 in position $i$ if $q_i \in F$, and 0 elsewhere. Then $A(x) = v\gamma(x)w$ is the number of acceptance paths for inputs of the form $y \times x$, where $y \in \Delta^*$.*

This is a very well-known result, and part of the "folklore", and can be found, for example, in [294].

## 4.10 Formal series and linear representations

We can view an NFA $M$ as follows: each input letter $a$ induces a map on the states, which can be represented by a Boolean matrix $M_a$: we have $M_a[i, j] = 1$ if and only if $q_j \in \delta(q_i, a)$. Define the matrix-valued morphism $\gamma(a) = M_a$. Then an easy induction on $|x|$ gives that $\gamma(x)[i, j] = 1$ for words $x$ if and only if $q_j \in \delta(q_i, x)$. (Here in the multiplication of vectors and matrices we use *Boolean matrix multiplication*, where $\wedge$ (AND) replaces scalar multiplication and $\vee$ (OR) replaces scalar addition.) Hence, if we define $v = [1 \ 0 \ 0 \cdots \ 0]$ and $w$ to be the column vector with 1s corresponding to the final states and 0s elsewhere, then $v\gamma(x)w = 1$ if and only if $x \in L(M)$.

We can generalize this as follows: let $K$ be a semiring and $\Sigma$ a finite alphabet. Typical examples include $K = \mathbb{N}, \mathbb{Z}$, or $\mathbb{R}$. A *formal series* is a map $S : \Sigma^* \to K$. A formal series $S$ is called *K-recognizable* or just *recognizable* if there exists a matrix-valued morphism $\gamma$, and vectors $v, w$ of the appropriate size, such that $S(x) = v\gamma(x)w$ for all $x \in \Sigma^*$. In this case, the triple $(v, \gamma, w)$ is called a *K-linear representation* or just a *linear representation* for $S$. The *rank* of such a representation is the dimension of $v$.

The results of the previous section can now be rephrased as follows: Given a DFA $(Q, \Delta \times \Sigma, \delta, q_0, F)$ that takes two inputs in parallel, with the first component of each input letter chosen from an alphabet $\Delta$, and the second component chosen from $\Sigma$, the number of acceptance paths in this DFA where the second coordinate is labeled with $x \in \Sigma^*$ is an $\mathbb{N}$-recognizable series.

**Example 4.10.1** Consider the automaton in Figure 4.4. It is a "normalizer" for base-2 representations using the digits 0, 1, 2. For example, the word 0212 represents the integer $[0212]_2 = 12 = [1100]_2$. It takes two identical-length inputs $w$ and $x$ in parallel, where $w \in \{0, 1, 2\}^*$ and $x \in \{0, 1\}^*$ and accepts if $x$ is the canonical base-2 representation of the number represented by $w$. Thus, the number of paths from $q_0$ to either $q_0$ or $q_1$, with $x$ labeling the second components, is the number of such representations that evaluate to $[x]_2$.

The corresponding linear representation is then

$$v = [1 \ \ 0 \ \ 0]; \quad \gamma(0) = \begin{bmatrix} 0 & 0 & 0 \\ 0 & 1 & 0 \\ 0 & 1 & 1 \end{bmatrix}; \quad \gamma(1) = \begin{bmatrix} 0 & 1 & 1 \\ 0 & 1 & 1 \\ 0 & 0 & 1 \end{bmatrix}; \quad w = \begin{bmatrix} 1 \\ 1 \\ 0 \end{bmatrix}.$$

We can consider this linear representaton as computing a function $s(n)$ from $\mathbb{N} \to \mathbb{N}$ as follows: $s(n) = v\gamma((n)_k)w$. This turns out to be *Stern's diatomic series*, and is sequence A002487 in the OEIS.

There is an algorithm that takes a linear representation and finds an equiva-

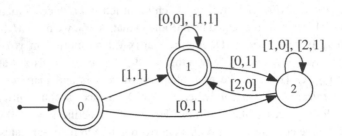

Figure 4.4 Automaton for normalizing base-2 representation using digits 0, 1, 2.

lent linear representation (that is, one computing the same function) of small-est rank; see [47, Chap. 2]. An implementation in `Maple` is available from the author. Note that if the original linear representation has integer entries, the minimized one may not.

This minimization algorithm does give us an easy way to test whether two given linear representations are equivalent (that is, determine the same func-tion). Given two linear representations, say $(v, \gamma, w)$ for $f$ and $(v', \gamma', w')$ for $g$, we can decide if $f = g$ as follows: create a new linear representation $(v'', \gamma'', w'')$ for $f - g$ as follows:

$$v'' = \begin{bmatrix} [v] & [-v'] \end{bmatrix} \qquad \gamma''(a) = \begin{bmatrix} [\gamma(a)] & 0 \\ 0 & [\gamma'(a)] \end{bmatrix} \qquad w'' = \begin{bmatrix} [w] \\ [w'] \end{bmatrix}.$$

**Theorem 4.10.2**   *The resulting minimized representation has rank* 0 *iff* $f - g =$ 0 *iff* $f = g$.

For a thorough introduction to linear representations, including algorithms for their minimization, see [47].

## 4.11  The semigroup trick

Suppose we are given a linear representation $(v, \gamma, w)$ for a function $f : \Sigma^* \to$ $\mathbb{N}$, where all the entries in the matrices and vectors are natural numbers. (This is the type of linear representation that arises from counting paths, as in Theo-rem 4.9.1.) Suppose we suspect that $f$ takes on only finite many values. How could we prove that?

One way to do it is with the so-called "semigroup trick": we explore the tree of possibilities for the vectors $v\gamma(x)$ for $x \in \Sigma^*$ using breadth-first search, until no new vectors are generated. If the search halts, the semigroup $\{v\gamma(x) : x \in \Sigma^*\}$ is finite. Furthermore, we can now construct a DFAO computing $f$, by letting the states be the set of distinct vectors that are reachable, the initial state be $v$, and the output function associated with each vector $t$ be $tw$.

More formally, the algorithm is as follows. If the algorithm halts, it has generated the DFAO $(S, \Sigma, \Delta, \delta, q_0, \tau)$ computing $f$, where $\Delta$ is some finite set.

---

Semigroup Trick $(v, \gamma, w)$

$q_0 := v$
$S := \{v\}$
$\tau(v) := vw$
Enqueue$(Q, v)$

while $Q$ nonempty do
    $t := $ Dequeue$(Q)$
    for each element $a \in \Sigma$ do
        $s := t\gamma(a)$
        $\delta(t, a) := s$
        $\tau(s) := tw$
        if $s \notin S$ then
            $S := S \cup \{s\}$
            $\tau(s) := tw$
            Enqueue$(Q, s)$

---

The algorithm will, of course, run forever if the semigroup is not finite, so in practice one can place a limit on the size of the queue.

**Example 4.11.1** Define

$$v = [0\,1\,2]; \quad \gamma(0) = \begin{bmatrix} 1 & 0 & 0 \\ 0 & 1 & 0 \\ 0 & 0 & 1 \end{bmatrix}; \quad \gamma(1) = \begin{bmatrix} 0 & 0 & -1 \\ 1 & 0 & 0 \\ 0 & 1 & 0 \end{bmatrix}; \quad \gamma(2) = \begin{bmatrix} 0 & 0 & -1 \\ 0 & 0 & 0 \\ 1 & 0 & 1 \end{bmatrix}; \quad w = \begin{bmatrix} 1 \\ 0 \\ 0 \end{bmatrix}.$$

Then the semigroup trick algorithm shows that $\{v\gamma(x) : x \in \Sigma_3^*\}$ is of cardinality 55. Furthermore $\{v\gamma(x)w : x \in \Sigma_3^*\} = \{-3, -2, -1, 0, 1, 2, 3\}$.

We observe that the trick can also be used in the other direction: instead of accumulating products of the form $v\gamma(x)$ (which generates an msd-first DFAO), one could accumulate products of the form $\gamma(x)w$. This will generate an lsd-first DFAO.

Another point is that this technique is sufficient, but not necessary, to show that the sequence $v\gamma((n)_k)w$ is bounded. It is certainly possible that the sequence could be bounded, and yet the semigroup $v\gamma(x)$ is infinite. This is because the final product by $w$, for example, could end up canceling two entries whose absolute value is large. However, by a known result [47, Corollary 2.3], if we start with a minimized linear representation, then the sequence is bounded if and only if the semigroup is finite.

## 4.12 Transducers

Finally, we will also need the notion of finite-state transducer. This is like a DFAO, except that outputs are now associated with transitions rather than states, and an output comes with each transition performed. More formally, a finite-state transducer is a machine

$$T = (Q, \Sigma, \delta, q_0, \Delta, \lambda)$$

where all quantities are as before, except that $\lambda : Q \times \Sigma \to \Delta^*$ is the output function. If $|\lambda(q, a)| = r$ for all $q \in Q, a \in \Sigma$, then the transducer is called $r$-uniform. If such an $r$ exists, it is called uniform. The *transduction* of a sequence $(a_n)_{n \geq 0}$ is the concatenation of the outputs of the transducer on the input $a_0 a_1 a_2 \cdots$. There is also a nondeterministic version of these transducers.

**Example 4.12.1** The transducer in Figure 4.5 converts the Thue-Morse sequence **t** to the period-doubling sequence **pd**.

*Open Question* 4.12.2 The separating words problem: one of my favorite open problems. I offer US $100 for any nontrivial progress.

Let $x, y$ be binary words. Let $D(x, y)$ be the number of states in the smallest DFA that accepts exactly one of $\{x, y\}$, and define $d(n) = \max_{x, y \in \{0,1\}^n} D(x, y)$. Give good upper and lower bounds on $d(n)$. It is known that there are constants $c, c'$ so that $d(n) \geq c \log n$ infinitely often and $d(n) \leq c' n^{2/5} (\log n)^{3/5}$. For more information, see [178, 322, 323, 121]. More recently, Chase [79, 80] improved the upper bound to approximately $n^{1/3}$.

*Open Question* 4.12.3 Another great open problem: for two infinite words **x** and **y**, define a partial order $\mathbf{x} \leq \mathbf{y}$ if there is a deterministic finite-state transducer that maps **y** to **x**. Write $\mathbf{x} \equiv \mathbf{y}$ if both $\mathbf{x} \leq \mathbf{y}$ and $\mathbf{y} \leq \mathbf{x}$. Observe that if **x** is an ultimately periodic sequence, then $\mathbf{x} \leq \mathbf{y}$ for all infinite sequences **y**. We say that an infinite sequence **y** is *prime* if $\mathbf{x} \leq \mathbf{y}$ implies that either **x** is

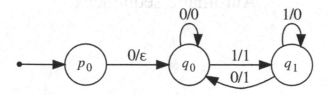

Figure 4.5 Transducer mapping **t** to **pd**.

ultimately periodic or $\mathbf{x} \equiv \mathbf{y}$. Is the Thue-Morse sequence prime? I offer US $100 for a solution. For more information, see [136, 137, 135, 366, 138].

*Open Question* 4.12.4   Michael Wehar asks if the following problem is decidable: given a finite automaton $M$, does $M$ accept the base-2 representation of at least one perfect square? Here by "decidable" we mean that there is an algorithm to solve the problem that is guaranteed to always halt and produce the right answer.

*Open Question* 4.12.5   Boris Adamczewski asks if the following problem is decidable: given a finite automaton $M$, does $M$ accept the base-2 representation of at least one prime number? The answer is not known even in the special case where $M$ recognizes a language of the form $uv^*w$, where $u, v, w$ are finite words.

An algorithm to solve this problem would resolve the question of the existence of infinitely many Fermat primes.

# 5

# Automatic sequences

In this chapter we introduce the main subject of the book, which is *automatic sequences*. Roughly speaking, an automatic sequence is a sequence over a finite alphabet whose $n$th term can be computed by a finite automaton reading a representation for $n$ in a regular numeration system (Section 6.4).

This representation could be, for example, any of the representations discussed in Chapter 3: base-$k$ representation, Fibonacci representation, Tribonacci representation, Pell representation, or Ostrowski representation. The important common feature linking these different systems is that a finite automaton can check the addition relation $x = y + z$ for representations in the system.

Let us start with $k$-automatic sequences. A reference for the material in this chapter is [16].

## 5.1 Definitions and examples

A *k-automatic sequence* is a sequence $(a_n)_{n \geq 0}$ over a finite alphabet $\Delta$ that is computable in the following way: there is a DFAO $(Q, \Sigma_k, \delta, q_0, \Delta, \tau)$ that, when given as input any base-$k$ representation of $n$, reaches a state with output $a_n$ [91, 16]. These sequences are sometimes called $k$-recognizable or uniform tag sequences.

The canonical example of this kind of sequence is the Thue-Morse sequence

$$\mathbf{t} = t_0 t_1 t_2 \cdots = 011010011001 \cdots,$$

which is generated by the automaton in Figure 5.1. Recall that a state labeled $q/a$ means the state is called $q$ and its output is $a$. The input is $n$ (here expressed in base 2), and the result for a given input is the output associated with the last state reached. Compare this DFAO with the DFA in Figure 4.1.

We now address two minor technical points about automatic sequences. The

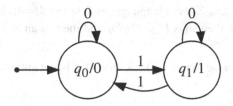

Figure 5.1 DFAO generating **t**.

first concerns the order of reading the input. *We will nearly always assume that representations are read starting with the most significant digit (msd-first).* However, this is not a real restriction. As mentioned in Section 4.4, if a $k$-DFAO exists for the msd-first convention, then another $k$-DFAO exists reading in the least-significant-digit first (lsd-first) convention. Furthermore, it is possible to computably convert from one kind of representation to the other. The only drawback is that for some kinds of sequences, the conversion between the two possibilities may cause the number of states to blow up exponentially.

*Exercise* 21   Show that any DFAO generating the $k$-automatic sequence $(a_n)_{n \geq 0}$ that takes the value 1 if $e_d = 1$ when $(n)_2 = e_t e_{t-1} \cdots e_1 e_0$, and 0 otherwise, needs $\Omega(2^d)$ states in the msd-first representation, but can be done with a DFAO of $O(d)$ states in the lsd-first representation.

*Exercise* 22   Design a 2-DFAO generating the characteristic sequence of the set $\{2^n - 2^i : 0 \leq i < n \text{ and } n \geq 0\}$.

The second issue concerns leading zeros. The DFAO in Figure 5.1 *also* produces the correct answer if the base-2 representation of the input $n$ contains any number of leading zeros. For technical reasons, we will always assume that if *some* representation of $n$ is accepted (resp., rejected), then all representations involving deleting or adding leading zeros are accepted (resp., rejected).

Even further, we can always assume $\delta(q_0, 0) = q_0$. For we can easily modify $M$ to have the property at the cost of introducing at most one additional state. To see this, introduce a new initial state $q_0'$ with transitions $\delta(q_0', 0) = q_0'$ and $\delta(q_0', i) = \delta(q_0, i)$ for $i \neq 0$, and output $\tau(q_0') = \tau(q_0)$. The general philosophy throughout is that leading zeros in any msd-first representation (or trailing zeros in any lsd-first representation) must not affect the value of the result pro-

duced. Thus when we talk about automata we can more easily focus on the set
of integers recognized, instead of their representations.

*Exercise* 23    Let $L \subseteq \Sigma_k^*$ be a language, and define $S = \{[x]_k : x \in L\}$. Show
that if $L$ is regular, then so is $L' = 0^*(S)_k$ and there is an algorithm to produce
$L'$ from $L$.

For techniques used to prove that a sequence is *not* automatic, see [18].

## 5.2  DFAOs for other famous sequences

In Figures 5.2–5.4 we display DFAOs for three other famous sequences.

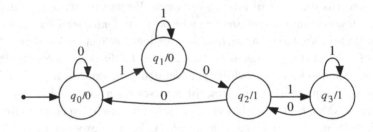

Figure 5.2  Finite automaton generating the paperfolding sequence **p**.

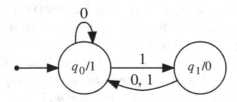

Figure 5.3  Finite automaton generating the period-doubling sequence **pd**.

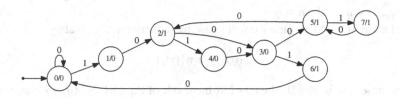

Figure 5.4 The Rote-Fibonacci automaton, generating the sequence **rf**.

## 5.3 Automatic sets

Every DFA $M = (Q, \Sigma_k, \delta, q_0, F)$ can be viewed as a DFAO with outputs in $\{0, 1\}$. Here, an output of $1$ corresponds to a final state, while an output of $0$ corresponds to a non-final state. In either case, $M$ can be viewed as recognizing a subset $S$ of $\mathbb{N}$. In this case, we say that $S$ is a $k$-*automatic set*.

Similarly, if $M$'s input alphabet is $\Sigma_k^t$, then we can view $M$ as recognizing a subset of $\mathbb{N}^t$.

From now on, if we say that $M$ recognizes a subset $S \subseteq \mathbb{N}$, then we really mean that $M$ recognizes the language $0^*(S)_k$. Similarly, if we say that $M$ recognizes a subset $S \subseteq \mathbb{N}^t$, then we really mean that $M$ recognizes the language $\overbrace{[0, 0, \ldots, 0]}^{t}{}^*(S)_k$.

## 5.4 Cobham's little theorem

We are now ready for one of the fundamental (but easy!) results about automatic sequences, which relates fixed points of uniform morphisms to automata. It is due to Cobham [91].

**Theorem 5.4.1** *Let* $\mathbf{b} = (b_n)_{n \geq 0}$ *be a sequence taking values in a finite alphabet* $\Delta$. *Then* $\mathbf{b}$ *is $k$-automatic iff there exists a finite alphabet* $\Gamma$, *a $k$-uniform morphism* $h : \Gamma^* \to \Gamma^*$ *that is prolongable on some* $a \in \Gamma$, *and a coding* $\tau : \Gamma^* \to \Delta^*$ *such that* $\mathbf{b} = \tau(h^\omega(a))$.

*Proof* $\Longrightarrow$: Suppose $\mathbf{b}$ is $k$-automatic. Then there exists a $k$-DFAO $M = (Q, \Sigma_k, \Delta, \delta, q_0, \tau)$ computing $\mathbf{b}$. Take $\Gamma = Q$. Define $h$ as follows:

$$h(q) = \delta(q, 0)\delta(q, 1) \cdots \delta(q, k-1).$$

As we have seen in Section 5.1, we can assume without loss of generality that $\delta(q_0, 0) = q_0$. Take $a = q_0$.

Define $\mathbf{w} = h^\omega(a)$. First we will show, by induction on $|y|$, that

$$\delta(q_0, y) = \mathbf{w}[[y]_k]. \tag{5.1}$$

The base case is $|y| = 0$. Then the left-hand side of Eq. (5.1) is $\delta(q_0, \epsilon) = q_0 = a$, while the right-hand side is $\mathbf{w}[0] = a$.

Now assume that Eq. (5.1) is true for all $y$ with $|y| < i$; we prove it for $|y| = i$. Write $y = xa$ for $a \in \Sigma_k$. Then

$$
\begin{aligned}
\delta(q_0, y) &= \delta(q_0, xa) \\
&= \delta(\delta(q_0, x), a) \\
&= \delta(\mathbf{w}[[x]_k], a) \quad \text{(by induction)} \\
&= (h(\mathbf{w}[[x]_k]))[a] \quad \text{(by definition of } h) \\
&= (\mathbf{w}[k[x]_k..k[x]_k + k - 1])[a] \quad \text{(since } h(\mathbf{w}) = \mathbf{w} \text{ and } h \text{ is } k\text{-uniform)} \\
&= \mathbf{w}[k[x]_k + a] \\
&= \mathbf{w}[[xa]_k] \\
&= \mathbf{w}[[y]_k],
\end{aligned}
$$

as desired.

It now follows that

$$\tau(\mathbf{w}[n]) = \tau(\mathbf{w}[(n)_k]) = \tau(\delta(q_0, (n)_k)) = b_n,$$

so $\tau(\mathbf{w}) = b_0 b_1 b_2 \cdots = \mathbf{b}$.

$\impliedby$: Suppose $\mathbf{b} = \tau(\mathbf{w})$, where $\mathbf{w} = h^\omega(a)$ for some $k$-uniform morphism $h : \Gamma^* \to \Gamma^*$ prolongable on $a$. Define the $k$-DFAO $M = (\Gamma, \Sigma_k, \Delta, \delta, q_0, \tau)$, where $q_0 = a$ and

$$\delta(q, c) := (h(q))[c] \tag{5.2}$$

for all $q \in \Gamma$ and $c \in \Sigma_k$.

We now prove that

$$\mathbf{w}[n] = \delta(q_0, (n)_k) \tag{5.3}$$

for all $n \geq 0$, by induction on $n$. For $n = 0$ we have $\delta(q_0, (0)_k) = \delta(q_0, \epsilon) = q_0 = a = \mathbf{w}[0]$.

Now assume that Eq. (5.3) holds for $n' < n$; we prove it for $n$. Write $(n)_k =$

$xa$, where $x \in \Sigma_k^*$ and $a \in \Sigma_k$. Then $n = kn' + a$ for $n' = [x]_k < n$.

$$\delta(q_0, (n)_k) = \delta(q_0, xa)$$
$$= \delta(\delta(q_0, x), a)$$
$$= \delta(\delta(q_0, (n')_k), a)$$
$$= \delta(\mathbf{w}[n'], a) \quad \text{(by induction)}$$
$$= (h(\mathbf{w}[n']))[a] \quad \text{(by Eq. (5.2))}$$
$$= \mathbf{w}[kn' + a]$$
$$= \mathbf{w}[n].$$

Hence $\tau(\delta(q_0, (n)_k)) = \tau(\mathbf{w}[n]) = \mathbf{b}[n] = b_n$. □

A consequence is that we can *trivially* convert from a $k$-DFAO computing $\mathbf{a}$ in the msd-first sense to the corresponding morphic representation $\tau(h^\omega(a))$, and vice versa, using the following correspondence:

- letters $\longleftrightarrow$ states.
- images of letters under morphism $h \longleftrightarrow$ mapping of states to other states on inputs $0, 1, \ldots, k - 1$.
- image under $\tau \longleftrightarrow$ outputs of states.

**Example 5.4.2** Let's convert from a DFAO generating a sequence to its representation as image, under a coding, of the fixed point of a morphism. Consider the DFAO in Figure 5.2. From it we construct the morphism $h$ as follows:

$$q_0 \to q_0 q_1; \quad q_1 \to q_2 q_1; \quad q_2 \to q_0 q_3; \quad q_3 \to q_2 q_3.$$

And we construct the coding $\tau : (q_0, q_1, q_2, q_3) \to 0011$. Then the paperfolding sequence $\mathbf{p}$ can be generated by $\tau(h^\omega(q_0))$.

**Example 5.4.3** Now let's do a conversion in the reverse direction. Consider the morphism defined by $g(0) = 001$ and $g(1) = 110$. Iterating $g$ gives the infinite word $001001110001001110 \cdots$, the Mephisto Waltz sequence. The corresponding 3-DFAO is depicted in Figure 5.5.

*Remark* 5.4.4 For each $k$-automatic sequence $\mathbf{b}$ there is a unique $k$-DFAO with the minimum number of states. (Uniqueness is up to renaming of the states.) Furthermore, if the states are numbered (say) $q_0, q_1, \ldots$, then there is a unique way to name the states, as follows: $q_0$ is the initial state, $q_1$ is the first state of the form $\delta(q_0, i)$ that is not equal to $q_0$, $q_2$ is either the first state of the form $\delta(q_0, j)$ unequal to $q_0$ or $q_1$ or (if there is no such state) the first state of the form $\delta(q_1, i)$ unequal to $q_0, q_1$, and so forth. This means that, given $\mathbf{b}$ and

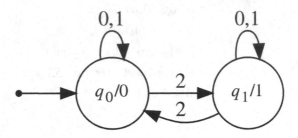

Figure 5.5  DFAO generating the Mephisto Waltz sequence.

$k$, there is a canonical $\mathbf{w} \in \Sigma_k^\omega$ and coding $\tau$ such that $\mathbf{b} = \tau(\mathbf{w})$; the sequence $\mathbf{w}$ is sometimes called the "interior sequence" of $\mathbf{b}$.

## 5.5 The $k$-kernel

Above we saw a relationship between the msd-first $k$-DFAO and a represen-tation as the image of a fixed point of a $k$-uniform morphism. This suggests trying to find a similar characterization for the lsd-first $k$-DFAO. Such a char-acterization involves a set called the $k$-kernel. This characterization, where we focus on the least significant digits of a number as opposed to the most sig-nificant digits, is particularly useful for number-theoretic considerations about automatic sequences.

Given a sequence $\mathbf{u} = (u_n)_{n \geq 0}$ its $k$-kernel is defined to be the set of se-quences

$$K_k(\mathbf{u}) = \{(u(k^i n + j))_{n \geq 0} : i \geq 0 \text{ and } 0 \leq j < k^i\}.$$

For example, for $k = 2$ this set is

$$\{(u(n))_{n \geq 0}, (u(2n))_{n \geq 0}, (u(2n+1))_{n \geq 0}, (u(4n))_{n \geq 0}, (u(4n+1))_{n \geq 0}, (u(4n+2))_{n \geq 0}, \ldots\}.$$

Notice that each sequence of the $k$-kernel arises from choosing a fixed word of length $t$, and only indexing by those $n$ having the specified trailing digits $t$ in their base-$k$ representation.

Another way to think about the kernel is that we start with a sequence and repeatedly apply the transformations

$$n \to kn$$
$$n \to kn + 1$$
$$\vdots$$
$$n \to kn + k - 1$$

to the indices. Thus, the kernel is a kind of repeated decimation of the sequence.

We are now ready to prove Eilenberg's theorem [133].

**Theorem 5.5.1** *A sequence is k-automatic iff its k-kernel is of finite cardinality.*

*Proof* $\Longrightarrow$: Suppose $(u_n)_{n\geq 0}$ is computed by a $k$-DFAO $M = (Q, \Sigma_k, \Delta, \delta, q_0, \tau)$ in msd-format. Without loss of generality, we can assume that $\delta(q_0, 0) = q_0$. Using Theorem 4.6.1, we know that there is a DFAO $M' = (Q', \Sigma_k, \Delta, \delta', q_0', \tau')$ such that $\tau(\delta(q_0, w)) = \tau'(\delta'(q_0', w^R))$. So $M'$ computes $(u_n)_{n\geq 0}$ assuming the input is given lsd-first. That is, $u(n) = \tau'(\delta'(q_0', (n)_k^R 0^i))$ for all $i \geq 0$.

Let $(u(k^e n + j))_{n\geq 0}$ be an element of the $k$-kernel. Let $w \in \Sigma_k^e$ be such that $[w]_k = j$. Let $q = \delta'(q_0', w^R)$. We claim that $(u(k^e n + j))_{n\geq 0}$ is computed (in the lsd-first sense) by the $k$-DFAO where we change the initial state of $M'$ to $q$, namely $(Q', \Sigma_k, \Delta, \delta', q, \tau')$. To see this, note that if $n \neq 0$ then

$$\delta'(q, (n)_k^R) = \delta'(\delta'(q_0', w^R), (n)_k^R)$$
$$= \delta'(q_0', w^R(n)_k^R)$$
$$= \delta'(q_0', ((n)_k w)^R)$$
$$= \delta'(q_0', (k^e n + j)_k^R),$$

and hence

$$\tau'(\delta'(q, (n)_k^R)) = \tau(\delta'(q_0', (k^e n + j)_k^R)) = u(k^e n + j).$$

On the other hand, if $n = 0$, then

$$\delta'(q, (0)_k^R)) = \delta'(q, \epsilon)$$
$$= q$$
$$= \delta'(q_0', w^R)$$
$$= \delta'(q_0', (j)_k^R 0^i) \quad \text{for some } i$$
$$= \delta'(q_0', (j)_k^R),$$

so

$$\tau'(\delta'(q,(0)_k^R)) = \tau(\delta'(q_0',(j)_k^R)) = u(j).$$

Thus we have identified each element of the $k$-kernel with some state of $M'$. It follows that the $k$-kernel is finite.

$\Longleftarrow$: Take the (finitely many) distinct elements of the $k$-kernel of $(u(n))_{n\geq0}$, and make an automaton out of them. The elements of the $k$-kernel are the states, and transitions are defined as follows: If $p = (u(k^e n + j))_{n\geq0}$, then $\delta(p,a) = q$, where $q = (u(k^e(kn + a) + j))_{n\geq0}$. The initial state is $q_0 = (u(n))_{n\geq0}$, and the output associated with $(u(k^e n + j))_{n\geq0}$ is defined to be $u(j)$.

It is now a routine exercise to see that this is consistent (that is, if $(u(k^e n + j))_{n\geq0}$ and $(u(k^f n + \ell))_{n\geq0}$ are two elements of the $k$-kernel that coincide, then on each input these two states are mapped by $\delta$ in the same way). An easy induction now shows that on input $w^R$ the automaton arrives at the state $(u(k^{|w|}n + [w]_k))_{n\geq0}$ which has output $u([w]_k)$, as desired.                                              $\square$

**Example 5.5.2**   Let $(r(n))_{n\geq0}$ be the Rudin-Shapiro sequence, as discussed in Section 2.4.7. From the definition, we can see that it satisfies the relations

$$r(2n) = r(n)$$
$$r(4n + 1) = r(n)$$
$$r(8n + 7) = r(2n + 1)$$
$$r(16n + 3) = r(8n + 3)$$
$$r(16n + 11) = r(4n + 3),$$

and hence its 2-kernel is

$$\{\,(r(n))_{n\geq0},\ (r(2n + 1))_{n\geq0},\ (r(4n + 3))_{n\geq0},\ (r(8n + 3))_{n\geq0}\,\}.$$

We can now assemble the sequence of the 2-kernel into an automaton processing its input in lsd-first order, obtaining the automaton in Figure 5.6.

*Exercise* 24   Prove that the Rudin-Shapiro sequence can be written in terms of the fixed point of a morphism acting on blocks of size 2 as if they were single letters:

$$[00] \rightarrow [00][01]$$
$$[01] \rightarrow [00][10]$$
$$[10] \rightarrow [11][01]$$
$$[11] \rightarrow [11][10].$$

This is a specific case of a more general theorem about $k$-automatic sequences:

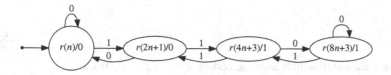

Figure 5.6 DFA computing the Rudin-Shapiro sequence.

namely, that every $k$-automatic sequence can be viewed as the fixed point of a morphism acting on blocks of size $k^r$ for some $r$. See [91, Theorem 1].

*Exercise 25*   Consider the morphism $h(\mathtt{a}) = \mathtt{aca}$, $h(\mathtt{b}) = \mathtt{bc}$, and $h(\mathtt{c}) = \mathtt{b}$. Prove that $h^i(\mathtt{a}) = \prod_{1 \le n < 2^i} (\mathtt{a} h^{\nu_2(n)}(\mathtt{c}))\mathtt{a}$, where $\nu_2$ is the 2-adic valuation. Is $h^\omega(\mathtt{a})$ an automatic sequence?

## 5.6  Using the $k$-kernel to guess a DFAO for a sequence

Frequently we have a sequence known in some way (say, by a recursion, or as the fixed point of a non-uniform morphism), and we want to determine if it is $k$-automatic for some fixed $k$. Of course, in general, this is not a decidable problem.

Nevertheless, there are heuristic procedures that can guess the automaton if the sequence is indeed $k$-automatic. The easiest way is via the $k$-kernel. Start with the sequence $(u(n))_{n \ge 0}$, as many terms that are known. The main operation compares two sequences as follows: given prefixes of two sequences in the $k$-kernel (possibly of different sizes), we can definitively say the sequences are different if one is not a prefix of the other. However, if one is a prefix of the other, we assume (possibly wrongly) they are the same. If a prefix does not match any previously computed sequence, we split it ("decimate") by computing $k$ new sequences via $n \to kn + a$ for $0 \le a < k$. If a prefix is very short, it may match multiple previously-computed sequences; in this case, the data do not allow one to uniquely determine an automaton. Otherwise, one can form an automaton out of the elements of the $k$-kernel as above.

**Example 5.6.1**   Consider the *regular paperfolding sequence* $\mathbf{p} = (p_n)_{n \ge 1}$. An alternate definition for **p** is as the limit of the words $P_n$, $n \geq 1$, where

$$P_1 = 0$$

$$P_{n+1} = P_n \, 0 \, \overline{P_n}^R \tag{5.4}$$

where the overline indicates the coding $0 \to 1$, $1 \to 0$. We find

$$P_2 = 001$$
$$P_3 = 0010011$$
$$P_4 = 001001100011011$$

$$\vdots$$

For the purpose of building an automaton it is useful to have a value defined for the index 0, so instead consider the alternate word **zp** = 0**p**, and start decimating the sequence in base 2.

$$(p_n)_{n\geq 0} = 000100110001\cdots$$
$$(p_{2n})_{n\geq 0} = 000100110001\cdots = (p_n)_{n\geq 0}$$
$$(p_{2n+1})_{n\geq 0} = 01010101\cdots$$
$$(p_{4n+1})_{n\geq 0} = 000000\cdots$$
$$(p_{4n+3})_{n\geq 0} = 111111\cdots$$
$$(p_{8n+1})_{n\geq 0} = 000000\cdots = (p_{4n+1})_{n\geq 0}$$
$$(p_{8n+5})_{n\geq 0} = 000000\cdots = (p_{4n+1})_{n\geq 0}$$
$$(p_{8n+3})_{n\geq 0} = 111111\cdots = (p_{4n+3})_{n\geq 0}$$
$$(p_{8n+7})_{n\geq 0} = 111111\cdots = (p_{4n+3})_{n\geq 0},$$

where the equalities on the right are merely conjecture on the basis of the first few terms. This gives us the (conjectured) lsd-first automaton in Figure 5.7.

*Exercise* 26   Prove that the DFAO in Figure 5.7 is correct.

Of course, for an arbitrary sequence, one cannot know with certainty whether two elements of the $k$-kernel are truly equal, by examining only finitely many terms. This could potentially lead to false conjectures.

**Example 5.6.2**   Start with the Thue-Morse sequence

$$\mathbf{t} = 0110100110010110\cdots$$

and define **s** = $(s_n)_{n\geq 0}$ to be the sequence of its run lengths (sizes of maximal

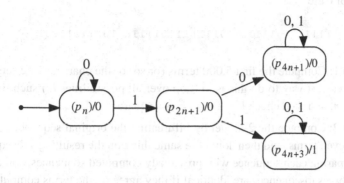

Figure 5.7 Conjectured DFAO computing the paperfolding sequence in lsd-first format.

blocks of consecutive identical elements), so

$$\mathbf{s} = 12112221121\cdots.$$

It can be shown that $\mathbf{s} = h^{\omega}(1)$, where $h(1) = 121$ and $h(2) = 12221$.

You might guess that $\mathbf{s}$ is 2-automatic—after all, it arises in a simple way from the 2-automatic sequence $\mathbf{t}$—but you would be wrong! Nevertheless, some elements of the 2-kernel can agree for many, many terms. For example, the two subsequences

$$s_{16n+1} = s_{64n+1}$$

agree for the first million terms, which might easily lead you to suspect these two elements of the 2-kernel coincide. In fact, though, the equality holds for $0 \le n \le 1864134$, but fails at $n = 1864135$.

It is an open problem to understand exactly what is going on here, and find a tight bound on the number of terms that two elements of the 2-kernel can agree on. An upper bound was given in [2].

*Open Question* 5.6.3    Explain the unusual behavior in Example 5.6.2, and find tight upper and lower bounds for the number of terms two sequences in the 2-kernel can agree.

*Exercise* 27    Use the experimental approach based on the 2-kernel to deduce an automaton for the characteristic sequence $\mathbf{c} = (c_n)_{n\ge0}$ of those non-negative integers $n$ that are the sum of three non-negative integer squares. The first few terms of **c** are

$$1111111011111110111111101111101101111111101 \cdots.$$

- Step 1: Compute the first 5,000 terms (or so) of the characteristic sequence. The easiest way to do this is to loop over all possibilities $i, j$ such that $i^2 + j^2 \leq n$, and then check if $n - i^2 - j^2$ is a square.

- Step 2: Compute the 2-kernel by bifurcating the original sequence into odd and even terms, and then doing the same thing on the resulting subsequence, comparing each sequence with previously computed sequences, and assuming two subsequences are identical if they agree on the terms computed.

- Step 3: Assemble these sequences into a least-significant-digit-first automaton.

- Step 4: Can you prove the automaton is correct?

We can also use these ideas to find a lower bound on the number of states needed by a $k$-DFAO to generate an infinite word $(a(r))_{r \geq 0}$ that starts with a known finite prefix $w$. This can be done by adapting a classical result on automata, the Myhill-Nerode theorem.

First, we explain how to do this for lsd-first DFAOs. We compute the largest prefix of each element of the $k$-kernel possible, based on our knowledge of $w$. Consider the member of the $k$-kernel $(a(k^e r + i))_{r \geq 0}$. If $w$ has length $n$, then we can determine a prefix of length $\lceil (n - i)/k^e \rceil + 1$ of this element of the $k$-kernel. Thus we can associate each element of the $k$-kernel with a finite word. Arrange these words in descending order by length, and as you encounter each new word, count it iff it is not a prefix of an earlier word in the list. The total is a lower bound on the number of states in an lsd-first DFAO generating $(a(r))_{r \geq 0}$.

For msd-first DFAOs, a modification of this idea works. Instead of an element of the $k$-kernel, we consider those values of $(a(r))_{r \geq 0}$ that correspond to $r$ having the base-$k$ representation of $r$ beginning with any fixed block.

*Exercise* 28  Let $x, w$ be two finite words, with $x$ nonempty. Define $A_0 = x$ and $A_{n+1} = A_n w A_n^R$. Show that $\mathbf{A} = \lim_{n \to \infty}$ exists, is 2-automatic, closed under reversal of factors, and uniformly recurrent. Further, find a necessary and sufficient criterion for $\mathbf{A}$ to be ultimately periodic.

*Exercise* 29  Define $a(n) = (\sum_{0 \leq i \leq n} t_i) \bmod 2$, where $\mathbf{t} = t_0 t_1 t_2 \cdots$ is the Thue-Morse sequence. Use the guessing procedure described in this section to guess a DFAO generating $(a(n))_{n \geq 0}$.

## 5.7 Another way to guess the automaton

Above we saw how to guess the automaton for a $k$-automatic sequence that was based on the $k$-kernel; in other words, it was based on looking at the subsequences defined by fixing the last few bits of the base-$k$ representation of $n$. This technique can (potentially) produce the automaton in lsd-first format.

There's a different way to handle this problem, which is based on fixing the *first* few bits instead. Here is one way to describe it. Given a sequence $\mathbf{a} = (a(n))_{n \geq 0}$, create a two-dimensional infinite array where the rows are labeled by the elements of $C_k$ in radix order, and the columns are labeled by the elements of $\Sigma_k^*$. In row $x$ and column $y$, put $a([xy]_k)$. It is now easy to show that this infinite array has only finitely many distinct rows iff $\mathbf{a}$ is $k$-automatic. Of course, we cannot compute the whole array, but we can assume two rows are identical iff they agree on the number of terms that are known. Assign a state for each distinct row, and create a transition function that, on input $a \in \Sigma_k$, maps the row labeled $x$ to the row labeled $xa$. The output of the row labeled $x$ is the value of $a([x]_k)$ corresponding to $y = \epsilon$. This creates an msd-first automaton.

**Example 5.7.1** Let us apply this technique to the characteristic sequence of the powers of 2. Suppose we know the value of this sequence for $0 \leq n \leq 15$. Then we can construct Table 5.1. From this data we would guess that there are three distinct rows, corresponding to $x = \epsilon$, $x = 1$, and $x = 11$. This gives us the 3-state msd-first 2-DFAO given in Figure 5.8.

| $x \backslash y$ | $\epsilon$ | 0 | 1 | 00 | 01 | 10 | 11 | 000 | 001 | 010 | 011 | 100 |
|---|---|---|---|---|---|---|---|---|---|---|---|---|
| $\epsilon$ | 0 | 0 | 1 | 0 | 1 | 1 | 0 | 0 | 1 | 1 | 0 | 1 |
| 1 | 1 | 1 | 0 | 1 | 0 | 0 | 0 | 1 | 0 | 0 | 0 | 0 |
| 10 | 1 | 1 | 0 | 1 | 0 | 0 | 0 | | | | | |
| 11 | 0 | 0 | 0 | 1 | 0 | 0 | 0 | | | | | |
| 000 | 0 | 0 | 1 | | | | | | | | | |
| 001 | 1 | 1 | 0 | | | | | | | | | |
| 010 | 1 | 1 | 0 | | | | | | | | | |
| 011 | 0 | 0 | 0 | | | | | | | | | |
| 100 | 1 | 1 | 0 | | | | | | | | | |
| 101 | 0 | 0 | 0 | | | | | | | | | |
| 110 | 0 | 0 | 0 | | | | | | | | | |
| 111 | 0 | 0 | 0 | | | | | | | | | |

Table 5.1 *Guessing the automaton for the characteristic sequence of the powers of 2.*

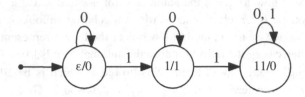

Figure 5.8 DFAO computing the characteristic sequence of powers of 2.

## 5.8 Cobham's big theorem

We can use the $k$-kernel to prove an easy, but important result about automatic sequences:

**Theorem 5.8.1** *A sequence is $k$-automatic iff it is $k^f$-automatic for some $f \geq 1$.*

*Proof* Suppose $(a(n))_{n \geq 0}$ is $k$-automatic. Then from Theorem 5.5.1 its $k$-kernel is finite. But the $k^f$-kernel of every sequence—automatic or not—is evidently a subset of the $k$-kernel, so it must also be finite.

For the converse, suppose $(a(n))_{n \geq 0}$ is $k^f$-automatic. Then its $k^f$-kernel $S$ is finite, so write

$$S = \{(a((k^f)^{e_i}n + g_i))_{n \geq 0} : 1 \leq i \leq t\}$$

for some $t$ and some $e_1, e_2, \ldots, e_t$ and $g_1, g_2, \ldots, g_t$ satisfying $0 \leq g_i < k^{fe_i}$. Define $M = \max_{1 \leq i \leq t} e_i$. Define $S' = \{(a(k^h n + \ell))_{n \geq 0} : h < f(M+1), 0 \leq \ell < k^h\}$, and note that $S'$ is finite. We claim the $k$-kernel of $(a(n))_{n \geq 0}$ is contained in $S'$.

To see this, let $(a(k^h n + \ell))_{n \geq 0}$ be an arbitrary element of the $k$-kernel. Using the division algorithm write $h = qf + r$ for some $q$ and $0 \leq r < f$. Also write $\ell = sk^{qf} + t$ for $0 \leq t < k^{qf}$. Clearly $s < k^r$. Then

$$
\begin{aligned}
a(k^h n + \ell) &= a(k^{fq}(k^r n + s) + t) \\
&= a((k^f)^q m + t) \quad \text{for } m = k^r n + s \\
&= a((k^f)^{e_i} m + g_i) \quad \text{for some } e_i, g_i, 0 \leq g_i < k^{fe_i} \\
&= a(k^{fe_i}(k^r n + s) + g_i) \\
&= a(k^{fe_i + r} n + u) \quad \text{for } u = k^{fe_i} s + g_i.
\end{aligned}
$$

Now $fe_i + r < fe_i + f < f(M+1)$, and $u = k^{fe_i} s + g_i \leq k^{fe_i}(k^r - 1) + g_i < k^{fe_i + r}$. Hence $(a(k^n + \ell))_{n\geq 0} = (a(k^{fe_i + r} n + u))_{n\geq 0} \in S'$. $\qquad\qquad\qquad\square$

One of the most fundamental results about $k$-automatic sequences is that they are essentially characterized by the integer $k$. We say positive integers $k$ and $\ell$ are *multiplicatively dependent* if there are integers $i, j > 0$ such that $k^i = \ell^j$; otherwise they are *multiplicatively independent*. Then Cobham's big theorem is

**Theorem 5.8.2** *A sequence is both $k$-automatic and $\ell$-automatic, for $k$ and $\ell$ multiplicatively independent, iff it is ultimately periodic.*

For a proof, see [91, 320, 230].

*Exercise 30* Prove that $k, \ell$ are multiplicatively independent iff $\log k$ and $\log \ell$ are linearly independent over $\mathbb{Q}$.

## 5.9 Fibonacci-automatic sequences

Up until now we have only worked with $k$-automatic sequences, based on ordinary base-$k$ numeration. However, there are other possible numeration systems that one can base sequences on. For example, the Fibonacci numeration system defined in Section 3.2 allows us to define *Fibonacci-automatic sequences*.

**Definition 5.9.1** A sequence $(a_n)_{n\geq 0}$ is said to be *Fibonacci-automatic* if there exists a DFAO $M = (Q, \Sigma_2, \Delta, \delta, q_0, \tau)$ such that $a_n = \tau(\delta(q_0, (n)_F))$ for all $n \geq 0$.

As usual, we typically insist that the DFAO compute correctly even if the input has leading 0s, and further that $\delta(q_0, 0) = q_0$. However, we do *not* insist that the DFAO compute correctly when the input violates the fundamental rule of Fibonacci representation, which is that a representation must not contain two consecutive ones. In this case the output is unspecified.

**Example 5.9.2** Recall the infinite word **ftm** introduced in Section 2.4.18: **ftm**$[n]$ is the number of 1s, computed modulo 2, in the Fibonacci representation of $n$. Then **ftm** is computed by the DFAO in Figure 5.9. The set $\{n : \text{ftm}[n] = 0\}$ forms sequence A095096 and the set $\{n : \text{ftm}[n] = 1\}$ forms sequence A020899 in the OEIS.

*Exercise 31* Consider the sequence of words defined by $Y_1 = 1, Y_2 = 0$, and $Y_n = Y_{n-2}Y_{n-1}$. Show that $Y_1, Y_3, Y_5, \ldots$ are all prefixes of some infinite word

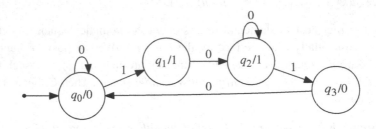

Figure 5.9 DFAO computing the Fibonacci-Thue-Morse sequence.

$\mathbf{y}_1$ and $Y_2, Y_4, Y_6, \ldots$ are all prefixes of some infinite word $\mathbf{y}_2$. Further show that both $\mathbf{y}_1$ and $\mathbf{y}_2$ are Fibonacci-automatic.

Nearly all of the results we proved for $k$-automatic sequences have natural analogues in the Fibonacci-automatic sequences. Most of these analogues are clear. For the $k$-kernel, instead of looking at subsequences of the form $(g(k^e \cdot n + f))_{n \geq 0}$, we instead look at the subsequences that result by fixing the trailing bits of the representation for $n$ to be equal to a given block.

*Exercise 32*   Let $m \geq 1$ be an integer. Show that the minimal DFA recognizing those $(n)_F$ with $n \equiv 0 \pmod{m}$ has $2m^2$ states. (This is one reason why computations in the Fibonacci numeration system can be significantly harder than in base-$k$.) For generalizations, see [76].

## 5.10  Tribonacci-automatic sequences

Another generalization of automatic sequences is to Tribonacci representation, as discussed in Section 3.3. In analogy with Definition 5.9.1 we have

**Definition 5.10.1**   A sequence $(a_n)_{n \geq 0}$ is said to be *Tribonacci-automatic* if there exists a DFAO $M = (Q, \Sigma_2, \Delta, \delta, q_0, \tau)$ such that $a_n = \tau(\delta(q_0, (n)_T))$ for all $n \geq 0$.

Again, we typically insist that the DFAO compute correctly even if the input has leading zeros, and further that $\delta(q_0, 0) = q_0$. However, we do *not* insist that the DFAO compute correctly when the input violates the fundamental rule of

Tribonacci representation, which is that a representation must not contain three consecutive 1s.

**Example 5.10.2**   Let us construct the DFAO for the Tribonacci word **tr**. It is computed by the DFAO in Figure 5.10.

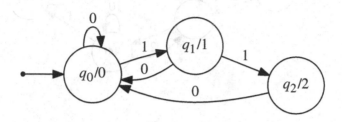

Figure 5.10  DFAO computing the Tribonacci word.

## 5.11  Pell-automatic sequences

In analogy with the Fibonacci-automatic sequences, we can define the Pell-automatic sequences, based on the Pell numeration system described in Section 3.4. For example, let us consider the sequence **pad**, defined as follows:

$$\mathbf{pad}[n] = \begin{cases} 1, & \text{if } (n)_P \text{ contains all three digits } 0, 1, 2; \\ 0, & \text{otherwise.} \end{cases}$$

Then **pad** is Pell-automatic, and is generated by the Pell DFAO in Figure 5.11.

## 5.12  Ostrowski-automatic sequences

Given an irrational number $\alpha$, we may consider the Ostrowski numeration system based on $\alpha$. If a sequence can be generated by an automaton that takes, in parallel, the partial quotients of the continued fraction for $\alpha$ represented in

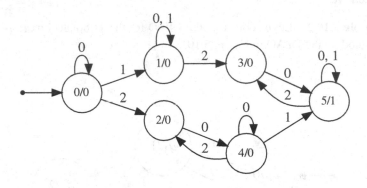

Figure 5.11 Pell DFAO generating the sequence **pad**.

some base $k$, together with the digits of the Ostrowski representation of $n$, then we say it is Ostrowski automatic.

This becomes particularly simple in the case where $\alpha$ is a quadratic irrational, when the continued fraction is ultimately periodic. In this case we do not need the partial quotients, as they can be subsumed into the automaton itself.

## 5.13  Two-dimensional sequences

We can generalize the theory of one-dimensional automatic sequences to $d$-dimensional automatic arrays. For example, for $d = 2$, a $k$-automatic infinite table can be computed by an automaton taking the row and column indices as inputs, in parallel, both expressed in base $k$, as discussed in Section 4.9.

As another example, consider the Sierpiński carpet array introduced in Section 2.4.21. We can generate this using the two-state base-3 automaton in Figure 5.12.

For $k$-automatic sequences, there is also an equivalent generalization in terms of matrix-valued morphisms. Here a symbol is mapped to a $k \times k$ matrix of symbols. For more details, see, for example, [329, 330, 331, 332]. For example, the

Sierpiński carpet array is generated as the fixed point of the morphism

$$1 \to \begin{bmatrix} 1 & 1 & 1 \\ 1 & 0 & 1 \\ 1 & 1 & 1 \end{bmatrix}; \qquad 0 \to \begin{bmatrix} 0 & 0 & 0 \\ 0 & 0 & 0 \\ 0 & 0 & 0 \end{bmatrix}.$$

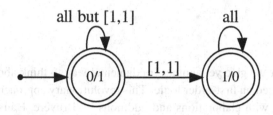

Figure 5.12 Finite automaton generating the Sierpiński carpet array.

# 6

# First-order logic and automatic sequences

In this chapter we give yet another fundamental way to think about automatic sequences, based on first-order logic. This revolutionary approach is originally due to Büchi, with elaborations and additions by Bruyère, Hansel, Michaux, and Villemaire, and their ideas form the basis for this book. A good reference for the material in this section is the wonderful survey paper by these last four authors [56].

## 6.1 First-order logic

First-order logic is a formal system with quantified variables. A *predicate* can be viewed as a function of one or more variables over a domain that, when values are substituted for the variables, evaluates to TRUE or FALSE. An example is the function GOLDBACH($n$), which evaluates to TRUE if $n$ is the sum of two prime numbers, and FALSE otherwise. A first-order *formula* is an expression involving the basic logical operations, variables, and quantification of variables. The basic operations are not ($\neg$), and ($\wedge$), or ($\vee$), logical implication ( $\implies$ ), and iff ( $\iff$ ). Quantifiers are applied to variables in a formula; the most important are the existential quantifier $\exists$ (there exists) and the universal quantifier $\forall$ (for all). Parentheses may be used for grouping.

Additional domain-specific operations, such as addition, multiplication, or equality, are often allowed.

**Example 6.1.1** If we have a predicate for primality, then GOLDBACH($n$) can be expressed as

$$\exists p, q \text{ IsPrime}(p) \wedge \text{IsPrime}(q) \wedge n = p + q.$$

**Example 6.1.2** Suppose the domain is a group $G$ with multiplication denoted by ·. Then the formula

$$\forall x \, \forall y \, x \cdot y = y \cdot x$$

asserts that $G$ is commutative (abelian).

**Example 6.1.3** Suppose the domain is a set $S$ with a binary operation $\cdot$ : $S \times S \to S$ and distinguished element $e$. Then the formula

$$(\forall x \, \forall y \, \forall z \, x \cdot (y \cdot z) = (x \cdot y) \cdot z) \land (\forall x \, (x \cdot e) = x \land (e \cdot x) = x)$$

$$\land \, (\forall x \, \exists y \, (x \cdot y = e) \land (y \cdot x) = e)$$

is the assertion that $S$ is a group under the operation $\cdot$, where the identity element is $e$.

**Example 6.1.4** Another quantifier that is sometimes used is $\exists_\infty$, meaning "there exist infinitely many". However, if the domain is the natural numbers $\mathbb{N}$, then $\exists_\infty$ can be implemented using the existing quantifiers: the formula $\exists_\infty x \, P(x)$ is logically equivalent to $\forall i \, \exists x \, (x \geq i) \land P(x)$.

In this book we are only interested in first-order logic where the domain of variables is $\mathbb{N} = \{0, 1, \ldots, \}$, the natural numbers. Here not that much is expressible unless we have a useful operation to go along with it, and the most obvious operation to include is addition.

For more about first-order logic, see, for example, [253].

## 6.2 Presburger arithmetic

*Presburger arithmetic* is the name given to $\text{Th}(\mathbb{N}, +)$, the set of all true first-order formulas over the logical structure of the natural numbers with addition.[1] Let us look at some examples of formulas over the logical structure $\langle \mathbb{N}, + \rangle$.

First, we have the basic formula $\text{IN}(i, r, s)$, which is true if and only if $i \in [r..s]$:

$$\text{IN}(i, r, s) := (i \geq r) \land (i \leq s),$$

---

[1] Sometimes Presburger arithmetic is written as $\text{Th}(\mathbb{N}, +, <, 0, 1)$, explicitly including the operation of "less than" among the other operations, and the constants 0 and 1. But this is not actually necessary for $\mathbb{N}$, since we can express the assertion $x < y$ explicitly in Presburger arithmetic by writing

$$\exists t \, (\lnot(t = 0)) \land x + t = y$$

instead. Similarly, we can express $x \leq y$ as $(x < y) \lor (x = y)$, we can express $x = 0$ as $x + x = x$ and, once 0 is defined, we can express $y = 1$ as $(y > 0) \land \forall z \, (z < y) \implies z = 0$.

and the formula $\text{SUBS}(i, j, m, n)$, which is true if and only if $[i..i + m − 1] \subseteq [j..j + n − 1]$:

$$\text{SUBS}(i, j, m, n) := (j \le i) \wedge (i + m \le j + n).$$

Next, we have formulas to check if $n$ is odd or even:

$$\text{ODD}(n) := \exists i \; n = 2i + 1$$

$$\text{EVEN}(n) := \exists i \; n = 2i.$$

Strictly speaking, of course, we cannot write $2i$ in Presburger arithmetic, but we understand that this is a shorthand for $i + i$.

Although Presburger arithmetic does not explicitly include subtraction, we can test if $z = x − y$ by rewriting the expression as $x = y + z$. Of course, since the theory only deals with natural numbers, this is only meaningful if $x \ge y$.

We would also like to implement functions such as $n \bmod m$. This is most easily accomplished by rephrasing the function to be a relation or family of relations. For example, the relation $\text{MOD}_m(a, n)$ is true iff $n \equiv a \pmod{m}$. For any given constant $m$ then we can write

$$\text{MOD}_m(a, n) := \exists q \; n = m \cdot q + a.$$

The reason why we cannot define this as a relation $\text{MOD}(a, m, n)$ with three parameters is that multiplication by arbitrary integer variables is not valid in our logical theory, so we cannot express $q \cdot m$. In $\text{Th}(\mathbb{N}, +)$ we can, however, multiply by any *fixed natural number constant*, like 2 or 3. Thus we can instantiate this for a specific $m$; for example,

$$\text{MOD}_3(a, n) := \exists q \; n = 3q + a,$$

where again $3q$ is understood to be an abbreviation for $q + q + q$.

**Example 6.2.1**  Using Presburger arithmetic, we can express the so-called "Chicken McNuggets" theorem [378, Lesson 5.8, Problem 1] to the effect that 43 is the largest integer that cannot be represented as a non-negative integer linear combination of 6, 9, and 20, as follows:

$$(\forall n > 43 \; \exists x, y, z \ge 0 \; n = 6x + 9y + 20z)$$

$$\wedge \; \neg(\exists x, y, z \ge 0 \; 43 = 6x + 9y + 20z).$$

Again, "$6x$" is shorthand for the expression "$x + x + x + x + x + x$", and similarly for $9y$ and $20z$.

*Exercise* 33  Show that, for natural number constants $c$, there is a Presburger arithmetic formula of length $O(\log c)$ specifying that $x = cy$.

## 6.3 Decidability of Presburger arithmetic

Thanks to the work of Presburger [300, 301] we have the following result:

**Theorem 6.3.1** *There exists an algorithm that, given a well-formed first-order formula over* $\langle \mathbb{N}, + \rangle$*, with no free variables, will eventually halt and unerringly decide if it is true or false.*

This stands in stark contrast to some more powerful logical theories, where no such algorithm exists.

There is a relatively simple proof of Theorem 6.3.1, based on finite automata, and due to Büchi [61, 62], Elgot [134], and Hodgson [198]. More recently it has appeared (without attribution) in the textbook of Sipser [363, §6.2]. It proves even more:

**Theorem 6.3.2** *There is an algorithm that, given a well-formed first-order formula* $\varphi$ *over the structure* $\langle \mathbb{N}, + \rangle$*, with no free variables, decides whether* $\varphi$ *is true or not.*

*Furthermore, if* $\varphi$ *has* $t$ *free variables, the algorithm constructs a DFA recognizing the set of representations of* $t$*-tuples of natural numbers that make P true.*

*Proof* The idea of the proof is to represent integers in an integer base $k \geq 2$ using the alphabet $\Sigma_k = \{0, 1, \dots, k-1\}$. We can then represent $n$-tuples of integers as words over the alphabet $\Sigma_k^n$, padding with leading zeros, if necessary. Thus, for example, the pair $(21, 7)$ can be represented in base 2 by the word

$$[1,0]\,[0,0]\,[1,1]\,[0,1]\,[1,1].$$

At each step we are working with some subformula $\eta$ with $t$ free variables, and the corresponding DFA $M$ recognizing the set of representations of elements of $\mathbb{N}^t$ for which $\eta$ evaluates to true.

Each permitted operation in the theory corresponds to some transformation of $M$. For example, logical "and" ($\wedge$) corresponds to intersection of languages, logical "or" ($\vee$) corresponds to the union of languages, and logical "not" ($\neg$) corresponds to the complement of languages. These can be carried out using the constructions in Section 4.4.

The addition relation $x + y = z$ can be checked by a simple 2-state automaton depicted in Figure 6.1, where transitions not depicted lead to a nonaccepting "dead state". Also, in our automaton representation, we can easily check relations such as $x = y$ and $x < y$.

The quantifiers are handled as follows: if a formula is of the form

$$\exists x_1, x_2, \dots, x_n \; p(x_1, \dots, x_n),$$

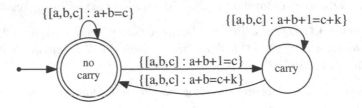

Figure 6.1 Checking addition in base $k$.

then we use nondeterminism to "guess" the $x_i$ and check them; this amounts to doing a projection on the transitions of the automaton, decreasing the number of variables. A projection is nothing more than applying a coding to the labels of the transitions. For example, suppose the formula is $\exists x\ p(x, y, z)$. Then transitions in the automaton for $p$ are on triples like $[a, b, c]$. To get an automaton for $\exists x\ p(x, y, z)$, we replace each transition $[a, b, c]$ with $[b, c]$. Of course, this transformation may result in an NFA, which then has to be determinized. Furthermore, projection may result in not all representations of a given number being accepted. In this case, some minor modification dealing with leading zeros may be needed (see Exercise 23).

If the formula is of the form $\forall x\ p(x)$, we use de Morgan's rule $\forall x\ p(x) \equiv \neg\exists x\ \neg p(x)$. In both cases, we then use the subset construction to convert the resulting NFA to a DFA.

Finally, if there are no free variables remaining, the resulting automaton is a single state on 0 inputs that either accepts everything ("true") or rejects everything ("false"). If there are free variables remaining, the resulting automaton accepts the representations of the values of the free variables that make the formula true.                                                                            □

This proof provides a decision procedure for Presburger arithmetic that runs in time at most

$$2^{2^{\cdot^{\cdot^{\cdot^{2^{q(n)}}}}}},$$

where the number of 2s in the exponents corresponds to the number of quantifier alternations, $q$ is a polynomial, and $n$ is the size of the quantifier-free portion of the formula. The tower of exponentiation of 2s comes from each time an NFA has to be converted to a DFA. This upper bound on the running time is truly astronomical! However, in practice, the decision procedure often runs much more quickly than this bound would suggest.

For Presburger arithmetic, this upper bound on the running time can be improved. Fischer and Rabin proved that Presburger arithmetic requires, in general, double exponential nondeterministic time [151] in the worst case. A matching upper bound on the nondeterministic complexity follows from the work of Ferrante and Rackoff [143, 144]. There is a triple exponential deterministic time upper bound [128]. For more information, see [183].

## 6.4 Extending Presburger arithmetic

Unfortunately, Presburger arithmetic is not so powerful. It is not strong enough to state very much that mathematicians or theoretical computer scientists actually want to prove, although it is used a bit in systems verification [340].

Luckily, a more powerful theory is still decidable. If we add the function $V_k : \mathbb{N} \to \mathbb{N}$ to our logical theory, where $V_k(x) = k^n$, and $k^n$ is the largest power of $k$ dividing $x$, the resulting logical theory is still decidable by a similar automaton-based technique [56]. This logical theory $\text{Th}(\mathbb{N}, +, V_k)$, which one might call *Büchi arithmetic,* is powerful enough to express finite automata and $k$-automatic sequences, as we will see in Section 6.6.

More generally, we introduce the concept of *regular numeration system S.* This is a way of associating strings of symbols over a finite alphabet $\Sigma$ with natural numbers $n$ such that

(a) Every natural number has a unique canonical $S$-representation as a word $w \in \Sigma^*$, and the only other valid $S$-representations are of the form $0^*w$.

(b) The set of all valid representations for $\mathbb{N}$ forms a regular language $L$.

(c) There is a DFA $M$ recognizing the relation $x + y = z$. This means that $M$ recognizes the language over $\Sigma^3$ where each element represents the $S$-representation of a triple $(x, y, z) \in \mathbb{N}^3$ such that $x + y = z$.

Examples of regular numeration systems include

(a) Base-$k$ representation for integers $k \geq 2$.

(b) Fibonacci representation.

(c) Tribonacci representation.

(d) Ostrowski $\alpha$-representation (and the special case of Pell representation).

We use $[w]_S$ to mean the integer represented by the word $w$ in the numeration system $S$, and $(n)_S$ to mean the canonical $S$-representation of $n$, lacking leading zeros. If the context is clear, we can omit the subscript.

Now we can give the formal definition of automatic sequence: a sequence $\mathbf{x} = (x_n)_{n\geq 0}$ over a finite alphabet is *automatic* if there exists a regular numeration system $S$ and a DFAO $M = (Q, \Sigma, \Delta, \delta, q_0, \tau)$ such that $x_n = \tau(\delta(q_0, 0^i(n)_S))$ for all $i \geq 0$, where $(n)_S$ is the canonical $S$-representation of $n$.

We now have enough background to prove the following theorem, which is the fundamental result on which the book depends.

**Theorem 6.4.1** *There is an algorithm that, given a formula $\varphi$ with no free variables, phrased in first-order logic, using only the universal and existential quantifiers, addition and subtraction of variables and constants, logical operations, comparisons, and indexing into a given automatic sequence $\mathbf{x}$, will decide the truth of that formula.*

*Furthermore, if $\varphi$ has $t \geq 1$ free variables, the algorithm produces a DFA $M$ that recognizes the language of all $S$-representations of $t$-tuples of natural numbers that make $\varphi$ evaluate to true.*

We call such a formula an *automatic formula*.

*Proof*   The idea of the proof is exactly the same as that we sketched for Presburger arithmetic. The only difference is that we start with a DFAO for $\mathbf{x}$. If we need to index by something like $\mathbf{x}[i + j]$, we just compute $\mathbf{x}[n]$ via the DFAO, in parallel with a DFA that checks the addition relation $n = i + j$. All the other steps are exactly as in the proof of Theorem 6.3.2.    □

To obtain a bound on the running time of this procedure, let us assume that the formula is written in prenex normal form, where all the quantifiers are on the left, and a quantifier-free formula $\varphi$ involving $t$ variables is on the right.

The formula $\varphi$ involves operations like "and" ($\wedge$), "or" ($\vee$), and so forth, and additions and subtractions of natural numbers. All of these can be implemented using the product constructions given in Section 4.4, and the adder given in Figure 6.1. So the total time needed to build an automaton for $\varphi$ is polynomial in the size of the original DFAO for $\mathbf{x}$.

Each quantifier alternation involves a conversion from NFA to DFA, which could blow up the size of the automaton by $n \to 2^n$. Thus we have

**Theorem 6.4.2** *Evaluating the formula $\xi$ on an automatic sequence $\mathbf{x}$ can be done in time at most*

$$2^{2^{\cdot^{\cdot^{\cdot^{2^{P(N)}}}}}},$$

where the number of 2s in the exponent is equal to the number of quantifier alternations, p is a polynomial depending on $\xi$, and N is the number of states in the DFAO for x.

Again, this upper bound on the running time is truly terrifying! However, this is just the worst-case time. It turns out that in practice, significantly better running times are often achieved. Why this is so is not well understood.

For more about the time complexity of Walnut's algorithm, see [223]. It is known that if one has only existential quantifiers, then evaluating the truth of a formula over $\langle \mathbb{N}, +, V_k \rangle$ is an NP-complete problem [182, 184, 185]. More generally, $\text{Th}(\mathbb{N}, +, V_k)$ is TOWER-complete, which means there is a nonelementary lower bound on its complexity. See [339, §3.1].

*Exercise* 34   Show that there is a first-order formula over $\langle \mathbb{N}, +, V_k \rangle$ of length $O(\log n)$, using only existential quantifiers, with one free variable $x$, for which the smallest $x$ making the formula true is $2^{n^{\Omega(1)}}$.

## 6.5 Useful formulas

Let us look at some of the kinds of formulas we can define in the extended theory. We will use these formulas throughout. Let x be an automatic sequence. Consider the formula

$$\text{FACTOREQ}(i, j, n) := \forall t \ (t < n) \implies \mathbf{x}[i + t] = \mathbf{x}[j + t].$$

It checks whether $\mathbf{x}[i..i + n - 1]$ and $\mathbf{x}[j..j + n - 1]$ are equal by comparing them at corresponding positions, $\mathbf{x}[i + t]$ and $\mathbf{x}[j + t]$, for $t = 0, \ldots, n - 1$.

Sometimes it is useful to specify the starting and ending position of one factor, instead of the length. The formula

$$\text{MATCH}(i, j, s) := \forall t \ (t \geq i \land t \leq j) \implies \mathbf{x}[t] = \mathbf{x}[(s + t) - i]$$

is true if $\mathbf{x}[i..j] = \mathbf{x}[s..s + j - i]$, and false otherwise.

From FACTOREQ, we derive other useful formulas. For instance, the formula

$$\text{OCCURS}(i, j, m, n) := (m \leq n) \land (\exists s \ (s + m \leq n) \land \text{FACTOREQ}(i, j + s, m))$$

tests whether $\mathbf{x}[i..i + m - 1]$ is a factor of $\mathbf{x}[j..j + n - 1]$.

Similarly, we can test whether $\mathbf{x}[i..i + n - 1]$ is a palindrome:

$$\text{PAL}(i, n) := \forall t \ (t < n) \implies \mathbf{x}[i + t] = \mathbf{x}[(i + n) - (t + 1)].$$

Some useful predicates are base-dependent. For example, if we are working with base-$k$ representations, then the predicate "$n$ is a power of $k$" is expressible in the theory, via the formula $n = V_k(n)$. For example, $\text{POWER}_2(n)$ asserts that $n$ is a power of 2. For more about $V_k$, see Section 10.2.

## 6.6 More about logic

Now we turn to a proof sketch that $\text{Th}(\mathbb{N}, +, V_k)$ defines exactly the $k$-automatic sequences. For the complete proof, the reader is referred to [56].

To make life easier, we'll work with automatic *subsets* of $\mathbb{N}$, instead of automatic *sequences*. Recall that a subset $S \subseteq \mathbb{N}$ is $k$-automatic if its associated characteristic sequence $(\chi_S(n))_{n \geq 0}$ defined by

$$\chi_S(n) = \begin{cases} 1, & \text{if } n \in S; \\ 0, & \text{otherwise}; \end{cases}$$

is $k$-automatic. Similarly, together with any automatic sequence taking values in an $\ell$-letter alphabet, we can write it as the term-by-term sum of the characteristic sequences for $\ell$ different automatic sets, one for each letter. Such a sequence is still automatic, as it can be generated by a product construction combining each of the automata for the different characteristic sequences; see Section 4.8.

**Theorem 6.6.1** *A set $S$ of integers is definable in $\text{Th}(\mathbb{N}, +, V_k)$ if and only if its characteristic sequence is $k$-automatic.*

*Proof* First we show how to construct a finite automaton $M_\varphi$ corresponding to any first-order formula $\varphi$ of $\langle \mathbb{N}, +, V_k \rangle$.

The idea again is that $M_\varphi$ will accept the base-$k$ representations of all $n$-tuples $(x_1, x_2, \ldots, x_n)$ of natural numbers making $\varphi(x_1, x_2, \ldots, x_n)$ true. We will use the *least-significant-digit first* representation for numbers, as it simplifies things a bit.

We observe that $\text{Th}(\mathbb{N}, R_+, R_{V_k})$ is equivalent to $\text{Th}(\mathbb{N}, +, V_k)$, where $R_+(x, y, z)$ is the relation $\{(x, y, z) : x + y = z\}$ and $R_{V_k}(x, y)$ is the relation $\{(x, y) : V_k(x) = y\}$.

We already saw automata for addition, so it suffices to give an automaton for $V_k(x) = y$.

*Exercise 35* Create an automaton accepting the base-$k$ representation of pairs $(x, y)$ such that $V_k(x) = y$.

For the other direction, we need to show how to encode a binary automatic sequence $(s(n))_{n \geq 0}$ in $\langle \mathbb{N}, +, V_k \rangle$. Since the domain of $\text{Th}(\mathbb{N}, +, V_k)$ is $\mathbb{N}$, and since automata process words, it may be hard at first glance to see how we could do this. So instead we actually encode the set of integers $\{n : s(n) = 1\}$ and we use the equivalent theory $\text{Th}(\mathbb{N}, R_+, R_{V_k})$.

The basic idea, given an integer $x$ for which $s(x) = 1$, is to assert the existence of another integer $y$ whose base-$k$ representation encodes, in lsd-first format, the sequence of states that the lsd-first input $(x)_k^R$ encounters as it is processed by the automaton.

One technical problem that we have to deal with is that multiple inputs are then encoded by the same integer. This is the "leading zeros" problem in disguise (in this case, you might call it the "trailing zeros" problem). For example, in lsd-first base-2 representation, both the words $101$ and $1010$ represent the integer 5. This is not a grave issue, however, since for an lsd-first DFAO we can always ensure that the output associated with the input word $x$ is the same as for $x0^i$, for all $i$.

*Exercise 36*   Justify this claim.

We now continue with the proof, under a simplifying assumption: we assume that the DFAO being encoded has at most $k$ states, numbered $0, 1, \ldots, k-1$, where the $k$ is the same $k$ as in $V_k$. If this is not the case, the proof becomes a bit more cumbersome, as we explain at the end.

We need some new relations

$$e_{j,k}(x, y)$$

for $0 \le j < k$. The meaning of this relation is that $y$ is some power of $k$, say $y = k^e$, and the coefficient of $k^e$ in the base-$k$ representation of $x$ is equal to $j$. We also need $\lambda_k(x)$, which is the greatest power of $k$ occurring with a nonzero coefficient in the base-$k$ representation of $x$. By definition we set $\lambda_k(0) = 1$. Finally, we also need $P_k(x)$, which is true if $x$ is a power of $k$ and false otherwise.

Now we show how to express the predicates $e_{j,k}(x, y)$ and $\lambda_k(x)$ and $P_k(x)$ in $\text{Th}(\mathbb{N}, +, V_k)$. The relation $P_k(x)$ is the easiest. Here $P_k(x)$ is the same as the assertion $V_k(x) = x$.

The formula $\lambda_k(x) = y$ is the next easiest. The basic idea is to observe that if we trap $x$ between two powers of $k$, say $k^e \le x < k^{e+1}$, then $\lambda_k(x) = k^e$. This works for every positive $x$; we need to handle $x = 0$ separately. So $\lambda_k(x) = y$ is the same as

$$(P_k(y) \wedge (y \le x) \wedge x < ky) \vee ((x = 0) \wedge (y = 1)).$$

Here $k$ is a constant, so multiplication by $k$ is expressible.

Finally, we can express $e_{j,k}(x, y)$ as follows: we group the powers of $k$ appearing in $x$ as follows: those appearing in $y$, those of exponent less than the one occurring in $y$, and those of exponent greater. So $e_{j,k}(x, y)$ is equivalent to

$$P_k(y) \wedge (\exists \ell \, \exists g \, (x = \ell + jy + g) \wedge (\ell < y) \wedge ((y < V_k(g)) \vee (g = 0))).$$

Here again $j$ is a constant.

Now that we have these relations, we can encode the computation of an automaton with a large formula (similar to the way we encode a polynomial-time bounded Turing machine with a SAT formula, if you are familiar with that):

If $x = \sum_{0 \le i \le l} a_i k^i$, the input is $a_0 a_1 \cdots a_l$ and the series of states encountered is $p_0, p_1, \ldots, p_{l+1}$. Our formula should say that

    (i) $p_0 = 0$.
    (ii) $\delta(p_i, a_i) = p_{i+1}$ for $0 \le i \le l$.
    (iii) $p_{l+1} \in F$.

We can encode these as follows:

    (i) $e_{0,k}(y, 1)$.
    (ii) $\forall t \, P_k(t) \wedge (t < z) \wedge \bigwedge_{\delta(q,b)=q'} \left( e_{q,k}(y, t) \wedge e_{b,k}(x, t) \implies e_{q',k}(y, kt) \right)$;
    (iii) $\bigvee_{q \in F} e_{q,k}(y, z)$.

Finally, the desired formula is

$$\exists y \, \exists z \, P_k(z) \wedge (z > y) \wedge (z > x) \wedge \text{(i)} \wedge \text{(ii)} \wedge \text{(iii)}.$$

Here the role of $z$ is to be a power of $k$, say $k^f$, so that $z$ is bigger than both $x$ and $y$. Thus it suffices to check the computation for powers of $k$ up to $z$.

This concludes the proof if the number of states in the DFAO is bounded above by $k$. What if the DFAO has more states than that? The trick here is to encode the states of the DFAO by *more than one variable*, each one representing a base-$k$ integer in lsd format. The transition function is then modified to handle states represented by $t$-tuples, where $k^t$ is an upper bound on the number of states. For full details, see [56]. $\qquad \square$

**Corollary 6.6.2** *The theory* $\mathrm{Th}(\mathbb{N}, +, V_k)$ *is decidable.*

*Proof* We can decide if a formula over $\langle \mathbb{N}, +, V_k \rangle$ is true, just as with Presburger arithmetic, by creating the automaton associated with the formula and checking if it accepts. $\qquad \square$

*Exercise 37* Let $h$ be a $k$-uniform morphism (not necessarily prolongable) and define $\mathbf{x} = y \, h(y) \, h^2(y) \cdots$ for some nonempty finite word $y$. Show that $\mathbf{x}$ is $k$-automatic and describe how to obtain an automaton for it. Hint: use a first-order formula.

The analogues of Theorem 6.6.1 and Corollary 6.6.2 for regular numeration systems also hold. Here the function $V_k$ has to be replaced by the map that sends $[wa0^i]$ for $a \neq 0$ to $[10^i]$.

## 6.7 Other kinds of automatic sequences

The same sorts of results we provided for base-$k$ representation hold for some other numeration systems, such as Fibonacci representation, Tribonacci representation, and the Ostrowski numeration system. The main requirements are that the set of canonical representations for $\mathbb{N}$ should form a regular language, and addition must be computable by a finite automaton.

For Fibonacci representation the set of canonical representations $C_F$ is represented by the regular expression $\epsilon \cup 1 (0 \cup 01)^*$. The adder is significantly more complicated than the one for base-$k$ addition, and can be deduced by at least two different methods.

The first is to obtain it directly. If a word $w \in \Sigma_2^3$ takes us from the initial state to a state $t$, and $w = x \times y \times z$, then we identify $t$ with the integer sequence $([x0^n]_F + [y0^n]_F - [z0^n]_F)_{n \geq 0}$. We then need to verify the identities implied by the transitions. This can be done more generally for any linear recurrence whose defining polynomial corresponds to a Pisot number; see [157, 158, 55].

The second method starts by obtaining an incrementer automaton; that is, an automaton $\text{INC}(x, y)$ that computes the relation $y = x+1$ for $x$ and $y$ in Fibonacci representation. Using the following easily-proven identities,

(a) $[x00 (10)^i]_F + 1 = [x010 2^i]_F$; and
(b) $[x0 (01)^i]_F + 1 = [x010 2^{i-1}]_F$,

we can obtain the incrementer depicted in Figure 6.2. Next, we "guess" the automaton, using the procedure given in Section 5.6. Once we have a guessed automaton for addition, represented (say) by $\text{ADD}(x, y, z)$, we can verify it in terms of $\text{INC}(x, y)$ as follows:

- Verify that $\forall x, y, z\ \text{ADD}(x, y, z) \iff \text{ADD}(y, x, z)$.
- Verify that $\forall x, z\ \text{ADD}(x, 0, z) \iff x = z$.
- Verify that $\forall x, y, r, s, t\ (\text{INC}(y, s) \wedge \text{INC}(r, t) \wedge \text{ADD}(x, y, r)) \implies \text{ADD}(x, s, t)$.

An induction on $y$ now completes the proof that the adder works as claimed. For more details, see [279].

Exactly the same sort of approach works for Tribonacci representation. Here the set of canonical representations is $\epsilon \cup (1 \cup 11) (0 \cup 01 \cup 011)^*$.

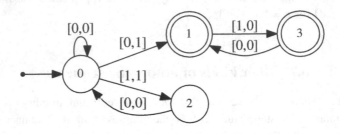

Figure 6.2 Incrementer for Fibonacci representation.

A more complicated approach is needed for the Ostrowski numeration system. See, for example, [27, 28].

## 6.8 Consequences

As a consequence of Theorem 6.6.1 and Corollary 6.6.2, we get the following two important corollaries.

**Corollary 6.8.1** *Let $P$ be any property of the factors of an automatic sequence $\mathbf{x}$ that is expressible as a first-order formula in $\langle \mathbb{N}, +, n \rightarrow \mathbf{x}[n] \rangle$. Then*

*(a) the set $\{n : \exists i$ such that $P$ holds for $\mathbf{x}[i..i + n - 1]\}$ is an automatic set;*

*(b) the set $\{(i, n) : P$ holds for $\mathbf{x}[i..i + n - 1]\}$ is an automatic set.*

**Corollary 6.8.2** *Let $P$ be a property of the factors of a $k$-automatic sequence $\mathbf{x}$ that is expressible as a first-order formula $\varphi$ in $\langle \mathbb{N}, +, n \rightarrow \mathbf{x}[n] \rangle$. Then there is a function $B(t)$, computable from $\varphi$, such that if $P$ holds for $\mathbf{x}[i..i + n - 1]$ and the DFAO for $\mathbf{x}$ has $t$ states, then $i, n \leq B(t)$.*

*Proof* Create the automaton $M'$ asserting that $P$ holds for $(i, n)$. It consists of a number of basic automaton operations (for which bounds on state complexity are known) applied to a $t$-state DFAO $M$ for $\mathbf{x}$. Hence we can find a function $C(t)$ bounding the number of states in $M'$. If $M'$ accepts any word at all, it must accept a word of length $< C(t)$. Hence $i, n \leq B(t) = k^{C(t)}$. □

## 6.9  Limitations

Not all morphic sequences have associated decidable logical theories. Consider the morphism $0 \to 0122$, $1 \to 122$, $2 \to 2$. The fixed point of this morphism is

$$\mathbf{s} = 01221222212222221222222221 \cdots .$$

It encodes, in the positions of the 1s, the characteristic sequence of the squares. So formulas over the first-order structure $\langle \mathbb{N}, +, n \to \mathbf{s}[n]\rangle$ are powerful enough to express the assertion that "$n$ is a square". With that, one can express multiplication, and so the theory is undecidable [89].

*Open Question* 6.9.1    Is the first-order theory $\mathrm{Th}(\mathbb{N}, +, p(n))$ decidable, where $p$ is a predicate for the prime numbers (true if $n$ is prime, false otherwise)? See [30].

*Open Question* 6.9.2    Is the first-order theory $\mathrm{Th}(\mathbb{N}, +, \varphi(n))$ decidable, where $\varphi$ is Euler's phi-function?

   Essential reading for these two problems is [48].

# 7

# Using Walnut

Walnut is free software originally designed and written in Java by Hamoon Mousavi [278], and recently modified by Aseem Raj Baranwal, Laindon C. Burnett, Kai Hsiang Yang, and Anatoly Zavyalov. This book is based on the most recent version of Walnut, called Walnut 3.7, which is available for free download at

https://cs.uwaterloo.ca/~shallit/walnut.html .

Walnut is constantly being improved, and new features are added all the time. Check at the URL above for the latest version.

Walnut essentially implements the decision procedure of Theorem 6.4.1. The default internal representation for natural numbers is base-2 representation, most significant digit first, but Walnut can also work with $k$-automatic sequences for arbitrary integers $k \geq 2$, with Fibonacci- and Tribonacci- and Pell-automatic sequences, and with Ostrowski-automatic sequences based on arbitrary quadratic irrationals. It is possible to work with representations of integers starting with either the most significant digit (the default) or the least-significant digit. For a detailed user's manual on how to use Walnut, see [278]. Walnut currently consists of about 10,000 lines of Java code, not including the dk package from BRICS.

A user interface is provided to enter queries in a language very similar to the language of first-order logic. The intermediate and final results of a query are all represented by automata. At every intermediate step, we perform determinization of the automaton, if necessary, and then minimization of the resulting DFA.

Each automaton accepts tuples of integers in a specified numeration system. In principle, Walnut can be used with any numeration system for which an automaton for addition is provided. These numeration system-specific automata can be declared in text files following a simple syntax. For the automaton resulting from a query, it is always guaranteed that if a tuple $t$ of integers is

accepted, all tuples obtained from *t* by addition or truncation of leading zeros
are also accepted. In Fibonacci representation, Tribonacci representation, and
so forth, only valid representations are accepted. For example, in Fibonacci
representation, the automata constructed by Walnut do not accept words with
two consecutive 1s.

All automata produced by Walnut are minimal and deterministic. However,
they may be incomplete, that is, they may omit a useless state and its associated
transitions. If an intermediate step results in the construction of an NFA, it is
converted to a DFA using the subset construction, and then minimized using
Valmari's algorithm, mentioned in Section 4.5.

Precursors of Walnut were written independently by Daniel Goč and Dane
Henshall.

## 7.1 Syntax of Walnut

Here is the basic syntax: words made up of capital letters (other than those
starting with A and E) refer to sequences (defined in terms of a DFAO) stored in
the directory Word Automata Library. For example, T is the Thue-Morse
sequence **t** and F refers to the Fibonacci word **f**.

You index a sequence by natural numbers using square brackets: T[n] refers
to the *n*th symbol of **t**. It is possible for DFAOs to have multiple arguments. In
this case you use multiple brackets: SCA[i][j] evaluates the two-dimensional
sequence **sca**[*i, j*]. In a Walnut command, natural numbers are always written
in base 10, even though they might be represented in other ways internally.

A complete list of those DFAOs provided with Walnut is given in Section 7.3. You can also add your own user-defined DFAO to this library by
creating a text file in the right format, with the name of the DFAO being the
name of the file.

E is Walnut's abbreviation for ∃ and A is the abbreviation for ∀. The symbol
=> is logical implication, & is logical AND, | is logical OR, and <=> is logical
IFF. Both the E and A can be followed by a single variable name, or a list of
variables.

Natural numbers can be used to index automatic sequences, and further can
be part of algebraic expressions. So, for example, one can write T[x+y] or
x+y=2*z. The allowed operations are addition, subtraction, multiplication by
a natural number constant, and integer division by a nonzero constant (x/c
represents $\lfloor x/c \rfloor$). When you write an algebraic expression, each variable must
occur at most once. So, for example, instead of x+y+x write 2*x+y in Walnut.
Remember that the domain of variables in Walnut is ℕ, so that negative num-

bers cannot be used. However, subtraction can be used meaningfully with the ordinary minus symbol, *provided the value of no subexpression is ever negative*. Some care must be taken in this regard, as the following exercise shows.

*Exercise* 38 Compare the two automata that `Walnut` produces here:

```
def aut1 "(x+y)-z=0":
def aut2 "x+(y-z)=0":
eval test1 "$aut1(1,1,2)":
eval test2 "$aut2(1,1,2)":
```

Why are the results different?

Sequences take their values in $\mathbb{Z}$, the integers. While arithmetic cannot be done on sequence values directly, they can be compared for equality (e.g., `T[n]=RS[n+1]`) or inequality (e.g., `T[n]<=RS[n+1]`). Constant values of sequences can be specified by preceding the constant with the @ sign, so that, for example, `T[n]=@0` specifies those $n$ for which $\mathbf{t}[n] = 0$, where $\mathbf{t}$ is the Thue-Morse sequence.

The phrase `?msd_3` preceding a formula specifies it should be evaluated in most-significant-digit-first format, in base 3. Here 3 can be replaced by any integer $\geq 2$. One can also use `lsd` in place of `msd`, which stands for least-significant-digit-first format. (The default is `msd_2`.) Similarly, `?msd_fib` evaluates the formula in Fibonacci representation, `?msd_trib` evaluates the formula in Tribonacci representation, and `?msd_pell` evaluates the formula in Pell representation. Unpredictable results, or errors, may occur if one attempts to mix multiple representations in the same expression.

A command of the form

```
ost name [0 1 2] [3 4]:
```

defines an Ostrowski numeration system. This particular example defines an Ostrowski numeration system based on the continued fraction

$$[0, 1, 2, 3, 4, 3, 4, 3, 4, \ldots]$$

and stores it under the name 'name'. Once defined, to use it, preface a query with `?msd_name` or `?lsd_name`.

Formulas can be defined and used in later work with the `def` command. For example, the formula

$$\text{FactorEq}(i, j, n) := \forall t < n \; \mathbf{x}[i + t] = \mathbf{x}[j + t]$$

can be defined in `Walnut` for the Fibonacci word $\mathbf{f}$ as follows:

```
def ffactoreq "?msd_fib At t<n => F[i+t]=F[j+t]":
```

This creates a predicate `$ffactoreq`, that takes three arguments: $i, j, n$ (in that order) that is true iff $\mathbf{f}[i..i + n - 1] = \mathbf{f}[j..j + n - 1]$, that is, if the length-$n$ factor beginning at position $i$ in the Fibonacci word is the same as the length-$n$ factor beginning at position $j$. The predicate is represented by a DFA that takes the Fibonacci representation of $(i, j, n)$ as input and accepts those inputs for which FACTOREQ$(i, j, n)$ evaluates to TRUE. When the predicate is used later in Walnut, it must be preceded by a dollar-sign. A crucial thing to remember is that *the order of arguments when a predicate is invoked is alphabetical order of the free variables that appear in it when it is defined.*

If you do not intend to save the result for later use, you can use `eval` in place of `def`. This is particularly useful if your expression has no free variables, because then `eval` will print the result TRUE or FALSE.

Although the formulas

    At Au $pred(t,u),   Au At $pred(t,u),   At,u $pred(t,u)

are logically equivalent, these three expressions are evaluated slightly differently by the algorithm used in Walnut. Recall that the universal quantifier is implemented by doing a complement, then a projection, an NFA-to-DFA conversion, and then another complement. The expression At Au $pred(t,u) forces Walnut to do these steps first for the variable $u$ and then for the variable $t$, while Au At $pred(t,u) causes this to be done in the opposite variable order. On the other hand, the formula At,u $pred(t,u) forces these steps where the projection acts on the variables $t$ and $u$ at the same time. This means the three variations can have wildly different requirements in terms of time and space. For example,

```
def ftmeqfact1 "?msd_fib At Au (t>=i & t<i+n & i+u=t+j)
   => FTM[t]=FTM[u]":
```

took about 36 seconds of CPU time on one Unix system, while

```
def ftmeqfact2 "?msd_fib At,u (t>=i & t<i+n & i+u=t+j)
   => FTM[t]=FTM[u]":
```

only took about 1.5 seconds on the same system.

Walnut can also compute linear representations for formulas with at least two free variables. This is also done with the `def` command, but the syntax is somewhat different. If you write

```
def name n "$func(i,n)":
```

for example, Walnut produces and stores in the filename name.mpl a Maple file that defines the linear representation $(v, \gamma, w)$ for the function $f(n)$ counting the number of $i$ for which $func(i,n)$ is true. If there are infinitely many such $i$, the result cannot be relied upon.

The command `inf` takes the name of an automaton as an argument, and returns TRUE if the automaton accepts infinitely many natural numbers, and FALSE otherwise.

## 7.2 Regular expressions

Formulas dealing with the representation of integers, expressed in terms of a regular expression, can be defined in Walnut using the `reg` command. The syntax is

```
reg name msd_k regex:
```

where `name` should be replaced by the predicate name, `k` should be replaced by the base of representation (or `fib` or `trib`) and `regex` is the regular expression. For regular expressions, the symbol | means union and * means Kleene closure.

For example, if we are working in base 2, then the command

```
reg power2 msd_2 "0*10*":
```

defines a predicate `$power2` that evaluates to TRUE if its argument is a power of 2, and FALSE otherwise. If you wish to use bases larger than 10, then digits larger than 9 must be enclosed in square brackets. For example, to define numbers in base 20 that look like a digit 19 followed by any number of 13s, write

```
reg tmp20 msd_20 "[19][13]*":
```

Regular expressions can work with tuples, by enclosing the tuple in square brackets and using commas as separators. For example, let us create an automaton `adjfib` with two free variables $x$ and $y$ that evaluates to TRUE if and only if $(x, y)$ represents two consecutive Fibonacci numbers, that is, $x = F_n$ and $y = F_{n+1}$ for some $n \geq 2$.

```
reg adjfib msd_fib msd_fib "[0,0]*[1,0][0,1][0,0]*":
```

The empty word is denoted by () in a regular expression.

If your regular expression is intended to represent a natural number, be sure that all representations having an arbitrary number of leading zeros (in msd-format) or trailing zeros (in lsd-format) are specified. Otherwise anomalous results may occur. This can be achieved by prefixing your regular expression with $0^*$ in the msd-case, and analogously for the lsd-case.

## 7.3 DFAOs included with Walnut

Some automatic sequences are built-in to Walnut, including all the sequences discussed in Section 2.4. They are stored in the directory Word Automata Library.

- T, the Thue-Morse sequence.
- TTM, the twisted Thue-Morse sequence.
- VTM, the ternary Thue-Morse sequence.
- P2, the characteristic sequence of the powers of 2.
- SB, the second-bit sequence.
- CA, the Cantor sequence.
- RS, the Rudin-Shapiro sequence.
- BS, the Baum-Sweet sequence.
- P, the regular paperfolding sequence (and its variant ZP).
- TH, the Tower of Hanoi solution sequence.
- PD, the period-doubling sequence.
- MW, the Mephisto Waltz sequence.
- SC, Stewart's choral sequence.
- LE, Leech's sequence.
- DEJ, Dejean's word.
- F, the Fibonacci word.
- RF, the Rote-Fibonacci word.
- FTM, the Fibonacci-Thue-Morse word.
- TR, the Tribonacci word.
- HC, the moves of the Hilbert curve.
- SCA, the Sierpiński carpet array.

Let us look at how two of these sequences are represented as files that Walnut uses. First, here is how T is stored in the file T.txt:

```
msd_2
0 0
0 -> 0
1 -> 1
1 1
0 -> 1
1 -> 0
```

The first line specifies the number system that the automaton is defined over. Lines with two numbers and no arrow give a state number (a natural number) first and an output (an integer) second. In this example, there are two states: a state numbered 0 with an output of 0 and a state numbered 1 with an output of

1. Finally, transitions for a state appear beneath that state and are of the form a -> b, where a is an input and b is a state.

State numbers should begin with state 0 and consist of consecutive numbers 0, 1, 2, .... For example, you should not have states numbered 0, 1, 3 and fail to include a state numbered 2.

To see how automata with two or more inputs are defined, consider the file SCA.txt, the DFAO for the Sierpiński carpet array. Compare this with Figure 5.12.

```
msd_3 msd_3

0 1
0 0 -> 0
0 1 -> 0
0 2 -> 0
1 0 -> 0
1 1 -> 1
1 2 -> 0
2 0 -> 0
2 1 -> 0
2 2 -> 0

1 0
0 0 -> 1
0 1 -> 1
0 2 -> 1
1 0 -> 1
1 1 -> 1
1 2 -> 1
2 0 -> 1
2 1 -> 1
2 2 -> 1
```

Here there are two inputs at once, so each transition looks like a b -> c, where a b represents a pair of input symbols read at once, and c is the next state to go to.

## 7.4 Creating DFAOs and morphisms

Walnut has several commands that allow the user to directly create DFAOs and uniform morphisms.

Let's start with the morphism command, which allows you to create a *k*-uniform morphism. For example,

```
morphism h "0->01 1->12 2->20":
```

defines a morphism called *h* that maps $0 \rightarrow 01$, $1 \rightarrow 12$, and $2 \rightarrow 20$.

If you have defined a uniform morphism, you can "promote" it to a DFAO generating the fixed point starting with 0 of the morphism using the command `promote`. For example,

```
promote T3 h:
```

defines a DFAO generating $h^{\omega}(0)$.

You can also apply a uniform morphism to a DFAO, getting a new DFAO as a result. If the morphism is *h* and the DFAO generates an infinite word **x** then the resulting DFAO generates $h(\mathbf{x})$. To do this, use the `image` command:

```
image F2 h F:
```

The resulting DFAO is defined over the same numeration system as the original DFAO.

By combining these three commands, you can define an arbitrary *k*-uniform DFAO. For example, let's define a *k*-uniform DFAO for the Rudin-Shapiro sequence:

```
morphism rud "0->01 1->02 2->31 3->32":
promote RS1 rud:
morphism codi "0->0 1->0 2->1 3->1":
image RS2 codi RS1:
eval test "An RS[n]=RS2[n]":
```

The resulting file, stored in `RS2.txt`, generates the Rudin-Shapiro sequence, as confirmed by the result `TRUE` at the end.

Another command allows the user to combine different DFAs into a single DFAO. The syntax is, for example,

```
combine Z dfa1 dfa2 dfa3:
```

The result is a DFAO `z` that outputs *x* on input *n* if the highest numbered DFA that accepts *n* is *x*, and outputs 0 if none of them do. This command can be used to turn one DFA into a DFAO computing the characteristic sequence simply by saying

```
combine <DFAO name> <DFA name>
```

Here the numeration system of the result is the numeration system of the first DFA provided, and all of them must be compatible.

A further refinement is that you can explicitly provide the outputs for each DFA. To do this, say, for example

```
combine Z dfa1=3 dfa2=5
```

which gives an output of 5 for those inputs accepted by `dfa2`, 3 for those inputs accepted by `dfa1`, and 0 for all other inputs.

## 7.5 **Invoking** Walnut

After you download Walnut for the first time, you will probably have to compile it. On a Linux system, go the Walnut directory and type

```
./build.sh
```

into a terminal window at the prompt. Now it should be installed and ready to go.

To start Walnut under Linux, use a terminal window and the command-line interface. Go to the bin directory of Walnut and type:

```
java Main.Prover
```

You will then see a prompt that looks like

```
[Walnut]$
```

You can then enter Walnut commands sequentially, or paste them in.

Results are stored in the directory called Result. Word automata (DFAOs) are stored in the directory called Word Automata Library. Ordinary automata (DFAs) are stored in the directory called Automata Library.

To use Walnut with Eclipse, start Eclipse up. Use the default workspace. Open Project from the File choices, and choose Walnut. Go to src/Main in the menu choices, right-click on Prover.java and choose Run As Java Application. You should now get a window where you can enter Walnut commands. To see results, go to the Eclipse file menu, right-click on Result and choose Refresh and the results should be there.

When you are done using Walnut, enter an EOF character (for example, CTRL-D under Linux) to stop the program. Or type exit; at the prompt.

## 7.6 **Output of a** Walnut **command**

Walnut has three modes of output. In terse mode, only a minimum of information is returned. To use the terse mode, an input query should end in a semicolon (;). In this case, if there are free variables, nothing is printed, while if there are no free variables, we get the answer TRUE or FALSE.

In the ordinary output mode, a query ends with a colon (:). In this case, Walnut provides some information about the progress of the computation. For example, let's redo the query from the Introduction about the presence of an overlap in **t**, but this time with a colon at the end:

```
eval thuetest "Ei,n n>=1 & Aj j<=n => T[i+j] = T[i+j+n]":
```

We get the following output:

```
n>=1:2 states - 0ms
 j<=n:2 states - 1ms
  T[(i+j)]=T[((i+j)+n)]:12 states - 4ms
   (j<=n=>T[(i+j)]=T[((i+j)+n)]):25 states - 1ms
    (A j (j<=n=>T[(i+j)]=T[((i+j)+n)])):1 states - 9ms
     (n>=1&(A j (j<=n=>T[(i+j)]=T[((i+j)+n)]))):1 states - 0ms
      (E i , n (n>=1&(A j (j<=n=>T[(i+j)]=T[((i+j)+n)])))):1 states - 0ms
Total computation time: 16ms.
```

---

FALSE

As you can see, `Walnut` reports on the status of your query by giving you information about subexpressions of your logical formula: namely, the sizes of the automata it produces and the time to produce each one.

Finally, in verbose mode, even more information about intermediate automata is printed. In this mode, a query should end with two colons (::).

In all three modes, one can find the answer in `thuetest.txt`. If you use a single colon, more information can be found in `thuetest_log.txt`. If you use a double colon, more information is in `thuetest_detailed_log.txt`. Furthermore, if an automaton is produced, a graphical depiction in `GraphViz` format[1] is stored as (in this case) `thuetest.gv`. On a Linux system, this can be converted to a pdf file with a command like

```
dot -Tpdf thuetest.gv > thuetest.pdf
```

All of these files go to the `Result` directory.

## 7.7 Defining your own DFAs and DFAOs

The `Word Automata Library` of `Walnut` is the place to define your own DFAOs. Give your DFAO a name of capital letters (but not starting with `A` or `E`, which are reserved symbols for the universal and existential quantifier) such as `GHI` and then store it in the file `GHI.txt`. It can then be invoked inside `Walnut`. The first line should say what the numeration system of the automaton is. For example, a first line of `msd_3` states that inputs are over the alphabet $\Sigma_3$ and are read msd-first. Use `msd_fib` for the Fibonacci numeration system and `msd_trib` for the Tribonacci numeration system. If you do not wish to specify a numeration system, but merely the size of the alphabet, you can use notation like $\{0, 1\}$, for example, to indicate a binary alphabet.

The `Automata Library` directory is the place to define your own DFAs. Here each state should have an output of 1 (accepting) or 0 (nonaccepting).

One useful item in the `Automata Library` is the DFA represented by the

---

[1] See http://www.graphviz.org.

predicate $shift. This takes two binary arguments and accepts if the second is the left shift of the first (with a 0 in the last position). The Walnut code for this is as follows:

```
{0,1} {0,1}
0 1
0 0 -> 0
0 1 -> 1
1 0
1 0 -> 0
1 1 -> 1
```

Here we see yet another feature of Walnut, which is that it is possible to define automata in the Automata Library that specify an input alphabet, but are untied to any particular numeration system. If you define an input alphabet of {0,1} {0,1}, as in the example above, this means the automaton is expecting two binary words in parallel as inputs. Such an automaton is compatible with msd_2 msd_2 or lsd_2 lsd_2 or msd_fib msd_fib, for example.

Another useful item is the DFA represented by the predicate $diffbyone. This takes two binary arguments and accepts if the second differs from the first in exactly one position. The Walnut code for this is as follows:

```
{0,1} {0,1}

0 0
0 0 -> 0
1 0 -> 1
0 1 -> 1
1 1 -> 0

1 1
0 0 -> 1
1 1 -> 1
```

*Exercise* 39  Give Walnut regular expressions for the DFAs diffbyone and shift.

## 7.8 Combining two different numeration systems

It is possible to combine two different numeration systems in one Walnut expression, but it is not possible to perform arithmetic operations on integers specified in two different systems. To specify a numeration system, use an expression like ?msd_3. The scope of such an expression is described as follows: if it appears outside parentheses, it modifies everything that follows. If it appears inside parentheses, the scope is restricted to the area between the command and the closing parenthesis.

It is also not possible to mix `lsd` and `msd` representations in the same `Walnut` command.

For some examples of the utility of this capability, see Section 10.10.

## 7.9 The correctness issue

We have *not* rigorously proved the correctness of the `Walnut` implementation.

However, it has been tested in a large number of different ways (including some results verified with independently-written programs). `Walnut` was tested against hundreds of different test cases, varying in simplicity from the most basic test cases testing only one feature at a time, to more comprehensive ones with many alternating quantifiers. We also used known facts about automatic sequences and the Fibonacci word in the literature to test `Walnut`, and in all those cases we were able to get the same result as in the literature. In a few cases, we were even able to find small errors in the statements of those earlier results (for example, see Section 9.11.6).

In this, we are squarely in the tradition of many other results in combinatorics on words that have been verified with machine computations—despite a lack of formal verification of the code. For one thing, programs in combinatorics on words are frequently hundreds or thousands of lines long, and proving even short programs correct is a nontrivial task. For another, typically one proves programs correct with the aid of a prover, but then who has verified the prover?

In our opinion, the only reasonable prescription is to (a) provide enough details that a reader could duplicate the computations, should he or she wish; and (b) provide access to the code used. We hope we have done (a). As for (b), the software can be downloaded from

```
https://cs.uwaterloo.ca/~shallit/papers.html   .
```

We view our work as part of a modern trend in mathematics. For other work on using computerized formal methods to prove theorems see, for example, [186, 228].

Please report any errors you find while using `Walnut`, but make sure they are really errors! I have found that every time I thought there was an error in the implementation, it was actually a mistake in the formula I wrote.

## 7.10 Some basic formulas in `Walnut`

Let us translate the basic formulas from Section 6.5 into `Walnut`:

- $\text{IN}(i, r, s) := (i \geq r) \wedge (i \leq s)$

  ```
  def in "i>=r & i<=s":
  ```

- $\text{SUBS}(i, j, m, n) := (j \leq i) \wedge (i + m \leq j + n)$

  ```
  def subs "j<=i & i+m<=j+n":
  ```

- $\text{ODD}(n) := \exists i \; n = 2 * i + 1$

  ```
  def odd "Ei n=2*i+1":
  ```

- $\text{EVEN}(n) := \exists i \; n = 2 * i$

  ```
  def even "Ei n=2*i":
  ```

- $\text{FACTOREQ}(i, j, n) := \forall k \, (k < n) \implies (\mathbf{x}[i + k] = \mathbf{x}[j + k])$

  ```
  def factoreq "Ak k<n => X[i+k]=X[j+k]":
  ```

- $\text{PAL}(i, n) := \forall k \, (k < n) \implies (\mathbf{x}[i + k] = \mathbf{x}[i + n - 1 - k])$

  ```
  def pal "Ak k<n => X[i+k] = X[(i+n)-(k+1)]":
  ```

- $\text{OCCURS}(i, j, m, n) := (m \leq n) \wedge (\exists k \, (k + m \leq n) \wedge \text{FACTOREQ}(i, j + k, m))$

  ```
  def occurs "m<=n & Ek k+m<=n & $factoreq(i,j+k,m)":
  ```

- $\text{POWER}_2(n) := n \text{ is a power of 2}$

  ```
  reg power2 msd_2 "0*10*":
  ```

This last formula works only for base 2, of course.

Of course, you should replace X with the appropriate file name from the `Word Automata Library`, and you may need to add a "`?msd`" specification if your sequence is automatic for other than base 2.

*Exercise* 40　A paper once claimed that "Every length $k$ factor of Thue-Morse appears as a factor of every length $8k - 1$ factor of Thue-Morse". Show that this claim is false in general, and determine those $k$ for which it is true.

## 7.11 Proving summation identities with Walnut

In some cases, Walnut can be used to prove summation identities about linear recurrence sequences, such as the Fibonacci numbers. We illustrate this by proving the identity

$$F_2 + F_5 + \cdots + F_{3n-1} = \frac{F_{3n+1} - 1}{2}$$

for $n \geq 1$.

If $y = F_2 + F_5 + \cdots + F_{3n-1}$, then the Fibonacci representation of $y$ is of the form $1(001)^{n-1}$. We can match $y$ with a regular expression of the form $1(001)^*$. Next, we create a formula adjfib that asserts that $x$ and $z$ are adjacent Fibonacci numbers, and $y$ matches the regular expression above. We use the fact that

$$F_{3n-1} \leq F_2 + F_5 + \cdots + F_{3n-1} \leq F_{3n}.$$

Then all we have to verify is that $y = (x + z - 1)/2$. Here's how to do this in Walnut:

```
reg adjfib msd_fib msd_fib "[0,0]*[1,0][0,1][0,0]*":
# asserts that x = F_{n+1} and y = F_n for some n
reg f3n1 msd_fib "0*1(001)*":
# asserts that argument is of the form F_2 + ... + F_{3n-1}
eval fibidentitycheck "?msd_fib Ax,y,z ($adjfib(z,x) &
    $f3n1(y) & x<=y & y<=z) => (2*y+1=x+z)":
```

which returns TRUE.

*Exercise* 41    Prove the following identities with Walnut:

  (a) $F_2 + F_3 + \cdots + F_n = F_{n+2} - 2, \quad n \geq 2.$
  (b) $F_2 + F_4 + \cdots + F_{2n} = F_{2n+1} - 1, \quad n \geq 1.$
  (c) $F_1 + F_4 + \cdots + F_{2n-1} = F_{2n}, \quad n \geq 1.$
  (d) $P_1 + P_2 + \cdots + P_n = (P_n + P_{n+1} - 1)/2, \quad n \geq 1.$

## 7.12 Custom numeration systems

Walnut gives you the capability of defining your own numeration systems (like Fibonacci, Tribonacci, Pell, etc.). To do so you will have to provide two automata and store them in the Custom Bases directory: an automaton recognizing all valid representations in the numeration system, and an adder.

The file with the first automaton should be called msd_name.txt, where name is replaced by the name of the numeration system. The adder should be called msd_name_addition.txt, and check the relation $x + y = z$.

*Exercise* 42  Develop a numeration system based on the sequence $(X_n)_{n \geq 1}$, where $X_1 = 1$, $X_2 = 2$, $X_3 = 4$, $X_4 = 7$, and $X_n = X_{n-1} + X_{n-2} + X_{n-4}$ for $n \geq 5$, where representations are given by the greedy algorithm. Find the automaton for all valid representations, and the adder.

## 7.13 Tips for using Walnut

Here are some things to keep in mind when formulating formulas for Walnut to evaluate.

- Whenever possible, break your formulas up into smaller pieces. This makes it easier to test and debug them.

- One of the most common errors is forgetting that when you call a defined automaton, the order of variables in its parameter list is given by alphabetical order of the free variable names in its original definition.

- Another common error is forgetting to specify the numeration system when evaluating a formula. This can only be omitted in the case of msd-first in base 2.

- To debug formulas, evaluate them on lots of small values to see if they agree with what you expect. This can help identify errors.

- Similarly, if your formula has no free variables, and you are anticipating a result like TRUE or FALSE, test your formula by removing some of the quantifiers and testing the modified formula on many values of the variables. For example, a formula like $\forall n\ P(n)$ can be tested by removing the universal quantifier and then testing $P(n)$ on many different values of $n$.

- If your goal is to prove results about finite words, try to phrase the claims about factors or prefixes of an appropriate infinite word instead.

- Be very careful with subtraction! While the subtraction operator is legitimate in Walnut, don't forget that all intermediate results must be non-negative to be meaningful. Hence an expression like $i - j - \ell + k$ should be rewritten as $(i + k) - (j + \ell)$.

- Be careful with edge cases, such as the empty word. Sometimes claims need to be restricted to nonempty words. For example, a predicate that asserts the presence of a square in a sequence (see Section 8.5) needs to specify that the length of the square is nonzero.

## 7.14 What to do if a query runs out of space

In rare cases, `Walnut` may not be able to provide an answer to a query because it runs out of space. If this happens, you will get an error message generated by the operating system. On a `Linux` machine, for example, you will probably see an error message like

```
Exception in thread "main" java.lang.OutOfMemoryError:
```

This is particularly true if you use a large base of representation (greater than 20, for example), or a more exotic numeration system, such as Tribonacci or an Ostrowski system, or if you use a large number of quantifiers, or start with an automaton with a large number of states.

If this happens, there are various tactics you can try:

- Try increasing the amount of space allocated to `Java`. To increase the amount of space available (at least on a Linux system), you can invoke `Walnut` with more memory. For example, typing

```
java -Xmx60G Main.Prover
```

will start `Walnut` with 60 Gigs of RAM. This number can be increased up to the memory capacity of your machine. Some computations done with `Walnut` can easily use more than 100 Gigs of RAM. On a `linux` system, the command `top` is useful for tracking how much space is being used.

- Reformulate your query in a different way, to use fewer variables that occur in the indexing of automatic words, or fewer quantifiers. For example, we can rewrite

$$\text{FactorEq}(i, j, n) := \forall t < n \; \mathbf{x}[i + t] = \mathbf{x}[j + t]$$

as the logically equivalent

$$\forall y, z \; (y \geq i \wedge y < i + n \wedge j + y = i + z) \implies \mathbf{x}[y] = \mathbf{x}[z].$$

This latter formula has only two variables that index $\mathbf{x}$ instead of three, so if the automaton for $\mathbf{x}$ is complicated, it might be substantially more efficient to process. Also see the discussion of the "substitute variables" trick in Section 8.5.

- Reformulate your query to use fewer quantifier alternations. Each quantifier alternation can, in principle, result in an exponential blowup in the number of states.

- A $k$-automatic sequence is also $k'$-automatic for every $k'$ that is multiplicatively dependent on $k$. In some cases, an automaton in a different base may use substantially fewer states.

- In some cases, a sequence with an lsd-first DFAO may need fewer states than an msd-first DFAO (and vice versa). You can try reformulating your DFAO to read the input in the opposite order.
- If you use many defined predicates, try making them less general to fit your particular case. The more parameters a predicate has, the more likely it will have many states in its representation. For example, if your goal is to prove some property of prefixes of an infinite word, don't define the property for all factors.
- If your goal is to show that some formula $P$ is true for infinitely many $n$, you might be tempted to use the formulation $\forall m \; \exists n \; (n > m) \wedge P(n)$. For very large automata, it's possible (see Section 10.13.2 for an example) that this might run out of space in determinizing a large NFA. Instead, just find a reachable state $q$ lying in a cycle, and from which one can reach an accepting state. This is doable in linear time and space in the size of the automaton by breadth-first search, and is implemented in Walnut with the inf command.
- In some cases, it may be possible to use the guessing procedure sketched in Section 5.7 to guess the automaton corresponding to a given formula, and then verify that your guess is correct using Walnut. As an example, consider the FACTOREQ formula from Section 6.5 based on some automatic sequence **x**:

```
def factoreq "At (t<n) => X[i+t]=X[j+t]":
```

This tests the assertion that $\mathbf{x}[i..i + n - 1] = \mathbf{x}[j..j + n - 1]$.

For some sequences Walnut may be unable to compute the corresponding automaton in a reasonable length of time. Instead, first "guess" the automaton, say feq.txt, and store it in the Automata Library directory. Then evaluate the following two Walnut commands:

```
eval zeros "Ai,j $feq(i,j,0)":
eval induc "Ai,j,n ($feq(i,j,n) & X[i+n]=X[j+n]) =>
    $feq(i,j,n+1)":
```

The first command asserts that feq is correct for $n = 0$; the second asserts that if it is correct for $n$, then it is correct for $n + 1$. If both return TRUE, then you have proved the correctness of the guessed automaton, by induction.

# 8

# First-order formulas for fundamental sequence properties

In this chapter we will examine about 80 different fundamental properties of automatic sequences, and show how each one can be encoded by first-order logical formulas. We then use `Walnut` to re-derive new proofs of known results, or prove new results, concerning some famous automatic sequences. You can use these examples to learn what `Walnut` is capable of, but also as a "catalogue" of first-order statements of fundamental properties of sequences.

Most of these properties can be phrased as some sort of transformation on automatic sequences. For example, consider the existence of squares in an automatic sequence **s**: this can be viewed as a map from **s** to a binary sequence **u**, where $u[n] = 1$ iff there is a square of order $n$ appearing as a factor in **s**. Exhibiting a first-order formula, then, constitutes a proof that the transformed sequence is automatic if the original sequence is—in other words, a closure property of automatic sequences. Thus, the logical approach we present in this book is a useful way to prove closure properties; in some cases, it is the only known way.

Furthermore, all our constructions are effective, and hence we can find an upper bound on the number of states in the DFA produced. Since every DFA of $N$ states accepts a word of length $\leq N - 1$ if it accepts anything at all, this leads to theorems like "If some factor $\mathbf{x}[i..i + n - 1]$ of an automatic sequence has property $P$, then there exists an example where $i, n$ are bounded by $f(N)$, where $f$ is an explicitly-calculable function, and $N$ is the number of states in the DFAO computing $\mathbf{x}$". For an example, see Theorem 8.4.1 or [78, Theorem 46].

One thing to observe, as you read each of these examples, is how we translate mathematical shorthand that is often used into the first-order language that `Walnut` expects.

Two important patterns are as follows:

113

- an assertion like $\forall x < y\ P(x)$ must be written as $\forall x\ (x < y) \implies P(x)$.
- an assertion like $\exists x < y\ P(x)$ must be written as $\exists x\ (x < y) \land P(x)$.

There is no need to read all of the sections of this chapter; feel free to browse to see what kinds of properties interest you.

## 8.1  Symbol and word occurrences

### 8.1.1  Occurrence of particular words

Let's start with one of the simplest properties of a sequence **x**: whether it contains some specific word $w$ as a factor.

For example, Thue observed in 1912 [374] that the squarefree word **vtm** discussed in Section 2.4.3 contains neither 212 nor 010 as factors. We can prove this as follows:

```
eval vtm212 "Ei (VTM[i]=@2 & VTM[i+1]=@1 & VTM[i+2]=@2)":
eval vtm010 "Ei (VTM[i]=@0 & VTM[i+1]=@1 & VTM[i+2]=@0)":
```

both of which evaluate to FALSE.

Similarly, if we want to determine the starting position of all occurrences of a particular factor, we can do so. Let us find the starting positions of all occurrences of the factor 01 in **t**:

```
eval tm01 "T[i]=@0 & T[i+1]=@1":
```

We get the automaton in Figure 8.1.

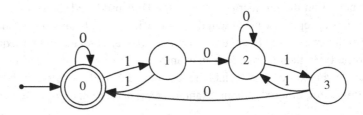

Figure 8.1 Starting positions of 01 in **t**.

This was previously observed in [54]. The first few starting positions of occurrences of 01 in **t** are therefore $0, 3, 6, 10, \ldots$.

### 8.1.2 Infinitely many occurrences of a symbol

We can test, given an automatic sequence **x** and a symbol $a$, whether $a$ occurs infinitely often in **x**.

To write this as a first-order formula, we just have to say that no matter how large $n$ is, there is some $i > n$ for which $\mathbf{x}[i] = a$:

$$\forall n \, \exists i \, (i > n) \wedge \mathbf{x}[i] = a.$$

Similarly, we can check whether every symbol that occurs, occurs infinitely often:

$$\forall n \, \exists i \, (i > n) \wedge \mathbf{x}[i] = \mathbf{x}[n].$$

The *literal* interpretation of this formula is that every symbol that occurs has a second occurrence later in the sequence, but this assertion is clearly equivalent to every symbol occurring infinitely often.

Let us check this latter formula on the Thue-Morse sequence:

```
eval thueinf "An Ei (i>n) & T[i]=T[n]":
```

which, naturally, returns TRUE.

### 8.1.3 Distance between symbol occurrences

Given an automatic sequence **x** and a symbol $a$, we can consider the distance between all occurrences of $a$ in **x**. For example, let's consider the distance between all occurrences of 1 in the Fibonacci word **f**:

```
def fibdist1 "?msd_fib Ei F[i]=@1 & F[i+d]=@1":
```

This gives a 5-state automaton recognizing the Fibonacci representation of the values of the free variable $d$, and is depicted in Figure 8.2. In Section 10.11 we will show how to characterize these distances $d$.

*Exercise* 43 Show that for all distances $d$, there are two occurrences of 0 in **f** at distance $d$.

### 8.1.4 Factors matching a regular expression

For some regular expressions $r$, we can find all factors of an automatic sequence that match $r$. For example, Currie, Harju, Ochem, and Rampersad [102]

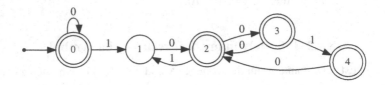

Figure 8.2 Distances between occurrences of 1 in **f**.

observed that for all $n \geq 2$, the word **vtm** contains a factor of the form $0w0$ with $|w| = n$, and the same is true for $2w2$. We can verify this as follows:

```
eval chor "An (n>=3) => ((Ei VTM[i]=@0 & VTM[i+n]=@0) &
   (Ej VTM[j]=@2 & VTM[j+n]=@2))":
```

which evaluates to TRUE.

Another interesting question is the following decision problem: given a regular expression $r$, does *every* element of the language specified by $r$ occur as a factor of a given automatic sequence **x**? This is decidable, as follows: If $L(r)$ contains $O(n)$ different words of length $n$—which is decidable, see [162]—then we know from the results in [370] that $L(r)$ must be a finite union of sets of the form $uv^*w$ for words $u, v, w$, and each of these patterns can be individually checked using the same approach we used for runs of a single symbol.

If, however, $L(r)$ does not contain $O(n)$ words of length $n$, then since the subword complexity of an automatic sequence is linear (as we will prove in Section 10.6.3), the answer is always "no" in this case.

### 8.1.5 Letters in arithmetic progression

An *arithmetic progression word* is a word of the form

$$\mathbf{x}[i] \, \mathbf{x}[i + j] \, \cdots \, \mathbf{x}[i + (k - 1)j]$$

for some $i \geq 0, j \geq 1, k \geq 2$. Such a word is said to be *monochromatic* if it consists of the $k$th power of a single letter.

Van der Waerden's celebrated theorem (see, e.g., [234]) states that no infinite word can avoid arbitrarily long finite monochromatic arithmetic progression words. But it's possible to avoid them for particular letters. Let us show, for example, that the Cantor word **ca** has no 3-term arithmetic progressions of 1s:

```
eval test3cantor "?msd_3 Ei,j (j>=1) & CA[i]=@1
   & CA[i+j]=@1 & CA[i+2*j]=@1":
```

This returns FALSE, so the Cantor word does not have any. (Of course it has arbitrarily long arithmetic progressions of 0s.)

We might also be interested in arithmetic progressions with specified difference. For example, sequence A339950 in the OEIS enumerates those $n$ for which there are length-2 monochromatic arithmetic progressions in the Fibonacci word **f** of difference $n$, but no length-3 monochromatic arithmetic progressions. We can construct a Walnut formula for this as follows:

```
def run3f "?msd_fib Ei (F[i]=F[i+n] & F[i]=F[i+2*n])":
def run2f "?msd_fib Ei F[i]=F[i+n]":
def a339950 "?msd_fib $run2f(n) & ~$run3f(n)":
```

Running this provides a 10-state Fibonacci DFA recognizing these $n$, depicted in Figure 8.3. For a follow-up discussion to this, see Section 10.11.

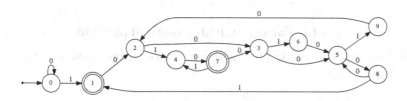

Figure 8.3 A Fibonacci DFA.

### 8.1.6 Testing Simon's congruence

Recall the definition of subsequence from Section 2.1. Given two words $y, z$ we say $y \sim_k z$ if the two sets of factors arising from length-$k$ subsequences of $y$ and $z$ are the same. For example, $0110011 \sim_3 1001100$.

For fixed $k$ we can write a first-order formula to check this condition (called Simon's congruence) for two factors of an automatic sequence **x**. For example, for $k = 3$ this can be done for the factors $\mathbf{t}[i..i + m - 1]$ and $\mathbf{t}[j..j + n - 1]$ of the Thue-Morse sequence, as follows:

```
def simon1 "A i1,i2,i3 (i<=i1 & i1<i2 & i2<i3 & i3<i+m) =>
   E j1,j2,j3 j<=j1 & j1<j2 & j2<j3 & j3<j+n & T[i1]=T[j1]
   & T[i2]=T[j2] & T[i3]=T[j3]":
def simon "$simon1(i,j,m,n) & $simon1(j,i,n,m)":
```

Notice that in the definition of `simon`, the first condition enforces one inclusion, and the second the other.

### 8.1.7 Incremented blocks

We can test for occurrences of patterns such as $xx'$, where $|x| = |x'| = n$ and $[x']_2 = [x]_2 + 1$. For example, $011100$ is an example of this kind of pattern, which we call an *incremented block* of order $n$. Let us find the positions and orders of such patterns in the Thue-Morse sequence. Study the example to see how it is done.

```
def incblock "Ej (i<=j & j<i+n & At (i<=t & t<j) =>
   T[t]=T[t+n]) & T[j]=@0 & T[j+n]=@1 & (Au (j<u & u<i+n)
   => (T[u]=@1 & T[u+n]=@0))":
# incblock(i,n) true if T[i..i+2n-1] is example of pattern
```

The resulting automaton shows that in the Thue-Morse sequence, there are such patterns for orders $n$ of the form $2^k$ or $3 \cdot 2^k$, for $k \geq 0$.

### 8.1.8 Factors matching unusual patterns

In many cases we can test for the occurrence of factors of unusual patterns, such as

$$1010^2 10^3 1 \cdots 10^s 1$$

for $s \geq 1$.

First let's write a predicate for $\mathbf{x}[j..k]$ belonging to $10^+1$:

$$\text{Test}101 := \mathbf{x}[j] = 1 \land \mathbf{x}[k] = 1 \land k \geq j+2 \land \forall t\, (t > j \land t < k) \implies \mathbf{x}[t] = 0.$$

Next let's write a predicate for $\mathbf{x}[m..n]$ being of the desired form. Basically it says that this factor begins correctly, ends correctly, and if we have a factor of the form $10^i 1$ not at the end, it is immediately followed by another factor of the form $10^{i+1}1$ that overlaps the first one in one symbol.

$$\mathbf{x}[m] = 1 \land \mathbf{x}[m+1] = 0 \land \mathbf{x}[m+2] = 1 \land \exists r\, \text{Test}101(r,n) \land \forall j,k$$

$$(j \geq m \land k \leq r \land j \leq k \land \text{Test}101(j,k)) \implies \text{Test}101(k,(2k+1) - j).$$

Let's try this in `Walnut`:

```
def test101 "T[j]=@1 & T[k]=@1 & k>=j+2 & At (t>j & t<k)
   => T[t]=@0":
def weirdfac "T[m]=@1 & T[m+1]=@0 & T[m+2]=@1
   & Er $test101(r,n) & A j,k (j>=m & k<=r & j<=k
   & $test101(j,k)) => $test101(k,(2*k+1)-j)":
def weirdfaclen "Em,n $weirdfac(m,n) & s+m=n+1":
```

The last automaton accepts only 3 and 6, so the only factors of the required form appearing in **t** are 101 and 101001.

We'll see another example of this idea in Section 9.11.4.

### 8.1.9 Runs of a single symbol

A *run* is a nonempty block consisting of repetitions of a single symbol $a$. Typically we are concerned with *maximal runs*; here "maximal" means it cannot be extended to the left or right. The first-order formula

$$\text{IsRun}(i, n) := (n \geq 1) \wedge (\forall t \, (t < n) \implies \mathbf{x}[i + t] = a) \wedge \mathbf{x}[i + n] \neq a$$
$$\wedge \, (i = 0 \vee \mathbf{x}[i - 1] \neq a)$$

asserts that $\mathbf{x}[i..i + n - 1]$ is a maximal run of $n$ $a$s. The formula

$$\exists i \, \text{IsRun}(i, n)$$

specifies those $n \geq 1$ for which there is a maximal run of $n$ $a$s in **x**. The formula

$$\forall m \, \exists i, n \, (n > m) \wedge \text{IsRun}(i, n)$$

asserts that there are arbitrarily long finite maximal runs of $a$s.

Let us determine whether there are arbitrarily large maximal runs of symbols in the Cantor sequence:

```
def carun0 "?msd_3 n>=1 & (At t<n => CA[i+t]=@0) &
  CA[i+n]!=@0 & (i=0|CA[i-1]!=@0)":
def carun1 "?msd_3 n>=1 & (At t<n => CA[i+t]=@1) &
  CA[i+n]!=@1 & (i=0|CA[i-1]!=@1)":
eval cantor0 "?msd_3 Am Ei,n (n>m) & $carun0(i,n)":
eval cantor1 "?msd_3 Am Ei,n (n>m) & $carun1(i,n)":
```

The first query returns TRUE, while the second returns FALSE. Hence there are arbitrarily long blocks of 0s, but not 1s, in this sequence.

Similarly, we can determine the longest runs occurring in a sequence. The formula

$$(\exists i \, \text{IsRun}(i, n)) \wedge (\forall j, m \, (m > n) \implies \neg \text{IsRun}(j, m))$$

asserts that $n$ is the length of the longest run of $a$s. Let us check this on the Rudin-Shapiro sequence:

```
def rsrun0 "n>=) & (At t<n => RS[i+t]=@0) & RS[i+n]!=@0
  & (i=0|RS[i-1]!=@0)":
def rsmaxrun0 "(Ei $rsrun0(i,n)) & (Aj,m m>n =>
  ~$rsrun0(j,m))":
```

The resulting automaton accepts only one number, which is 4. So the longest run of zeros in **rs** is of length 4.

## 8.1.10 Run positions and lengths

Given a sequence $\mathbf{s} = (s(n))_{n\geq 0}$, we can compute its run-length encoding, which is an expression of the form $\mathbf{s} = \prod_{i\geq 1} a_i^{e_i}$, where each $e_i \geq 1$ and $a_i \neq a_{i+1}$ for all $i \geq 1$. Then the set $\{0, e_1, e_1 + e_2, e_1 + e_2 + e_3, \ldots\}$ is the set of *beginning positions* of maximal runs, and the set $\{e_1, e_2, e_3, \ldots\}$ is the set of *run lengths* of $\mathbf{s}$. Thus we are, in effect, finding the consecutive maximal runs of all symbols appearing in $\mathbf{s}$.

Let us determine the set of maximal run lengths for the second-bit sequence:

```
eval sbrl "Ei n>=1 & (At t<n => SB[i+t]=SB[i]) &
   (SB[i+n]!=SB[i]) & (i=0 | SB[i-1]!=SB[i])":
```

Examining the resulting automaton shows that the only maximal runs in **sb** are of length 3 and length $2^i$ for $i \geq 0$.

Here is an example concerning Pell-automatic sequences. Recall the sequence **pad** defined in Section 5.11. We can make a DFAO PAD computing this sequence as follows:

```
reg validpell msd_pell "0*|0*(1|20)(0|1|20)*":
reg has0 msd_pell "(0|1|2)*(1|2)0(0|1|2)*":
reg has1 msd_pell "(0|1|2)*1(0|1|2)*":
reg has2 msd_pell "(0|1|2)*2(0|1|2)*":
def has012 "?msd_pell $validpell(n)&$has0(n)&$has1(n)&$has2(n)":
combine PAD has012:
```

We can determine the set of possible maximal run lengths in the sequence generated by this DFAO as follows:

```
eval padrunlengths "?msd_pell Ei n>=1 & (At t<n =>
   PAD[i+t]=PAD[i]) & (PAD[i+n]!=PAD[i]) & (i=0 |
   PAD[i-1]!=PAD[i])":
```

The resulting automaton is depicted in Figure 8.4, and demonstrates that the only maximal run lengths are (in Pell representation)

$$20 \cup 120 \cup 1(00)^* \cup 1(00)^*1 \cup 1^+.$$

With a bit of algebra, this corresponds to the set of run lengths

$$\{4\} \cup \{P_{2n+1} : n \geq 0\} \cup \{P_{2n} + 1 : n \geq 0\} \cup \left\{\frac{1}{2}(P_{n+1} - P_n - 1) : n \geq 3\right\}.$$

For a theorem about maximal run lengths in automatic sequences, see Corollary 10.8.7.

*Exercise* 44   Give first-order statements asserting that the maximal run lengths of a sequence **x** form an increasing (resp., strictly increasing) sequence.

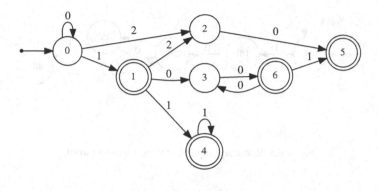

Figure 8.4 Maximal run lengths in the sequence PAD.

### 8.1.11 The boundary sequence

Let $\mathbf{s} = (s_n)_{n \geq 0}$ be a sequence over a finite alphabet $\Delta$. For each $n \geq 0$ consider the set $S_n = \{(s_i, s_{i+n}) : i \geq 0\}$. Chen and Wen [83] studied the *boundary sequence* of $\mathbf{s}$, which is the sequence $\mathbf{S} = (S_n)_{n \geq 0}$ over the alphabet $2^{\Delta \times \Delta}$.

It is easy to see that if $\mathbf{s}$ is automatic, then so is $\mathbf{S}$. Let us prove this by way of an example, namely, the Fibonacci word. For each pair

$$(a, b) \in \{(0, 0), (0, 1), (1, 0), (1, 1)\}$$

we can easily create a DFA recognizing the Fibonacci representation of the set $T_{a,b} = \{n : (a, b) \in S_n\}$.

```
def fib00 "?msd_fib Ei F[i]=@0 & F[i+n]=@0":
def fib01 "?msd_fib Ei F[i]=@0 & F[i+n]=@1":
def fib10 "?msd_fib Ei F[i]=@1 & F[i+n]=@0":
def fib11 "?msd_fib Ei F[i]=@1 & F[i+n]=@1":
```

Then we can combine each of the resulting automata into a single DFAO as in Section 4.8.

Letting

$$A = \{(0, 0), (1, 1)\},$$
$$B = \{(0, 0), (0, 1), (1, 0)\},$$
$$C = \{(0, 0), (0, 1), (1, 0), (1, 1)\},$$

we get the Fibonacci DFAO for the boundary sequence in Figure 8.5.

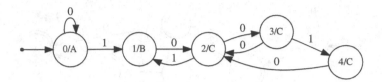

Figure 8.5  Boundary sequence for the Fibonacci word.

### 8.1.12 Novel factors

Call an occurrence $x[i..i + n - 1]$ of a factor *novel* if it is the first occurrence of that factor in $x$. We can write a formula that asserts that $x[i..i + n - 1]$ is novel:

$$\forall j\, (j < i) \implies \neg \text{FACTOREQ}(i, j, n).$$

This is one of the most fundamental examples in the book, because it shows how to consider the number of distinct *factors* having a given property, as opposed to *occurrences* of that factor.

Let us now find an automaton giving the positions and lengths of all novel factors of the Thue-Morse sequence $t$. Notice that we are using `tmfactoreq`, an implementation of FACTOREQ from Section 6.5; it asserts that $t[i..i + n - 1] = t[j..j + n - 1]$.

```
def tmfactoreq "At t<n => T[i+t]=T[j+t]":
def tmnovelf "Aj j<i => ~$tmfactoreq(i,j,n)":
```

This gives us the 8-state DFA depicted in Figure 8.6.

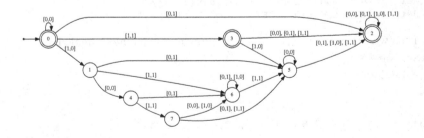

Figure 8.6  Automaton accepting $(i, n)$ where $t[i..i + n - 1]$ is a novel occurrence.

For example, the input `[1,1] [1,0] [0,1]` is accepted, indicating that the occurrence $t[6..10] = 01100$ is novel.

### 8.1.13 Weakly self-avoiding words

In [358] the authors studied infinite words $\mathbf{x}$ such that $\mathbf{x}[i..2i]$ is not a factor of $\mathbf{x}[j..2j]$ for $1 \le i < j < \infty$, and called them *weakly self-avoiding*. No such infinite words exist over a binary alphabet, but examples exist over a 3-letter alphabet, such as the word $\mathbf{w} = 220101101110 \cdots$ defined as follows:

$$\mathbf{w}[i] = \begin{cases} 2, & \text{if } i \le 2; \\ 0, & \text{if } i = 5 \cdot 2^n - 2 \text{ or } i = 7 \cdot 2^n - 2 \text{ for } n \ge 0; \quad (8.1) \\ 1, & \text{otherwise.} \end{cases}$$

It turns out that this $\mathbf{w}$ is 2-automatic. We can easily find a DFAO for it using the guessing procedure described in Section 5.6, and then verify it satisfies Eq. 8.1, as follows:

```
morphism g "0->01 1->23 2->45 3->46 4->54 5->66 6->66":
morphism h "0->2 1->2 2->2 3->0 4->1 5->0 6->1":
promote GG g:
image WSA h GG:
reg power2 msd_2 "0*10*":
eval wcheck "Ai WSA[i]=@0<=>(Ex $power2(x)&(i+2=5*x|i+2=7*x))":
```

Next, let us verify that $\mathbf{w}$ is weakly self-avoiding:

```
def wfactoreq "At (t<n) => WSA[i+t]=WSA[j+t]":
def woccurs "m<=n & Es (s+m<=n & $wfactoreq(i,j+s,m))":
eval wsatest "Ai,j (i>=1 & i<j) => ~$woccurs(i,j,i+1,j+1)":
```

and the result is TRUE.

## 8.2 Representation of integers

### 8.2.1 Matching a regular expression to the representation of $n$

Sometimes it is easy to write a regular expression that matches a given representation of an integer. For example, $0^*10^*(10^*10^*)^*$ is a regular expression for those binary words where the number of 1s is odd. Given the automaton for the Thue-Morse sequence (that is, `T` in `Walnut`), we can verify that this regular expression matches the base-2 representation of those integers $n$ for which $t[n] = 1$:

```
reg odd1 msd_2 "0*10*(10*10*)*":
eval tmchk "An $odd1(n) <=> T[n]=@1":
```

and it returns TRUE.

Similarly, for the paperfolding sequence, we have **zp**$[n] = 0$ for $n \geq 1$ if the base-2 expansion of $n$ has a suffix of the form $010^*$:

```
reg pfc msd_2 "0*10*|0*1(0|1)*010*":
eval pfchk "An n>=1 => ($pfc(n) <=> ZP[n]=@0)":
```

*Exercise* 45   Show that for Stewart's choral sequence **sc**, introduced in Section 2.4.13, we have **sc**$[n] = 1$ iff $(n)_3$ ends in a word of the form $21 \cdots 1$.

## 8.3  Properties of automatic sets

Recall that we say that a set $S \subseteq \mathbb{N}$ is automatic if its characteristic sequence $\mathbf{x} = (\chi_S(n))_{n \geq 0}$ is automatic.

### 8.3.1  Checking if an automatic set is finite or co-finite

An automatic set $S$ can be represented by a DFAO computing its characteristic sequence $(\chi_S(n))_{n \geq 0}$. A natural question to ask is then whether $S$ is finite or cofinite (that is, if its complement is finite). We can check this with the following first-order formulas:

$$\text{finite} := \exists n \, \forall m \, (m > n) \implies \chi_S(n) = 0,$$
$$\text{cofinite} := \exists n \, \forall m \, (m > n) \implies \chi_S(n) = 1.$$

Actually running this in Walnut may not be the most efficient strategy, because it involves a subset construction. For this reason, Walnut provides the inf command as discussed in Section 7.1.

### 8.3.2  Smallest and largest element of an automatic set

Given an automatic set $S$ with characteristic sequence $\mathbf{x}$, we can ask for the smallest and (provided $S$ is finite) largest element of $S$.

For the smallest element, we want a formula SMALLEST$(n)$ that is true if $n$ is the position of the first 1, and false otherwise:

$$\text{SMALLEST}(n) := (\mathbf{x}[n] = 1) \wedge \forall i \, (i < n) \implies (\mathbf{x}[i] \neq 1).$$

For the largest element, we want a formula LARGEST($n$) that is true if $n$ is the position of the last 1 in **x**, and false otherwise:

$$\text{LARGEST}(n) := (\mathbf{x}[n] = 1) \wedge \forall i \, (i > n) \implies (\mathbf{x}[n] \neq 1).$$

In both cases, the resulting automaton corresponding accepts at most one integer, which is the position of the first (resp., last) 1.

### 8.3.3 Greatest common divisor of automatic set

Suppose we are given a DFAO computing the characteristic sequence **x** of a $k$-automatic set $S$. We can compute gcd($S$) as follows: first, find the smallest nonzero element $t$ of $S$. This can be done by finding the DFA for

$$(t \geq 1) \wedge \mathbf{x}[t] = 1 \wedge \forall i \, (i \geq 1 \wedge i < t) \implies \mathbf{x}[i] = 0,$$

and then using breadth-first search to find the unique accepting path of the resulting DFA.

Next, compute all the divisors of $t$ and examine each one in descending order of size. For each divisor $d$ test whether every element of $S$ is a multiple of $d$, as follows:

$$\forall n \, \mathbf{x}[n] = 1 \implies \exists k \, n = dk.$$

Then gcd($S$) is the largest such $d$. See, for example, [35].

## 8.4 Periodicity, quasiperiodicity, and pseudoperiodicity

### 8.4.1 Ultimate periodicity

Recall that an infinite word **x** is *ultimately periodic* if there exist finite words $y, z$ with $z$ nonempty such that $\mathbf{x} = yz^\omega$. Ultimate periodicity is a classical property of sequences that has long been studied.

Using our approach, we can easily see that periodicity is decidable for automatic sequences [12]. It suffices to express ultimate periodicity as a first-order formula:

$$\exists p \geq 1, n \geq 0 \, \forall i \geq n \, \mathbf{x}[i] = \mathbf{x}[i + p].$$

*Exercise* 46   Check your understanding: why do we need to require that $p \geq 1$?

When we run this on the Thue-Morse sequence, we discover (as expected) that **t** is not ultimately periodic. The Walnut code is

```
eval tmup "Ep,n (p>=1) & (Ai (i>=n) => T[i]=T[i+p])":
```

and returns FALSE, as expected.

By considering the size of the automata generated by the decision procedure, we get bounds on the period and preperiod of ultimately periodic $k$-automatic sequences:

**Theorem 8.4.1**   *If a $k$-DFAO of $n$ states generates an ultimately periodic sequence* $\mathbf{x}$, *then the preperiod and period of* $\mathbf{x}$ *are both bounded above by* $k^{3 \cdot 2^{4n^2}}$.

*Proof*   We can make a DFA, using $n^2$ states, accepting those $(j, l)_k$ such that $\mathbf{x}[j] = \mathbf{x}[l]$. We can enforce the condition $(j \geq n) \wedge (l = k + p)$ using a total of $4n^2$ states. Checking $\forall j$ and $\forall l$ requires negating, some nondeterminism and another negation, giving $2^{4n^2}$. Finally, checking $p \geq 1$ takes 3 states, so a total $3 \cdot 2^{4n^2}$ states. Such an automaton, if it accepts anything at all, must accept $p$ and $n$ having at most $3 \cdot 2^{4n^2}$ symbols.                              □

*Remark* 8.4.2   Theorem 8.4.1 does not give the optimal upper bound, but that is not the point. The point is to illustrate that the logical approach to automatic sequences immediately provides analogous bounds for any of the first-order properties discussed in this chapter.

Honkala [200] was the first to prove that ultimate periodicity is decidable for automatic sequences. Later, Leroux [239], and, more recently, Marsault and Sakarovitch [258] gave efficient algorithms for the problem. For other related papers, see [244, 293, 192, 235, 33, 75]. In the greatest generality, it was solved by Mitrofanov [268, 269, 271] and Durand [131], independently.

Given that a sequence *is* ultimately periodic, we might want to compute the minimum possible period and preperiod. We do this by creating a first-order formula ULTPER$(i, p)$ that is true iff $\mathbf{x}$ is ultimately periodic with minimum period $p$ and minimum preperiod $i$.

For periods, we can do this as follows: first define a formula that asserts that $\mathbf{x}$ is ultimately periodic with preperiod $i$ and period $p$.

$$\text{HASPER}(i, p) := (p \geq 1) \wedge \forall j \, (j \geq i) \implies \mathbf{x}[j] = \mathbf{x}[j + p].$$

Then we define a formula that asserts that $i$ and $p$ are minimal:

$$\text{ULTPER}(i, p) := \text{HASPER}(i, p) \wedge (\forall \, q, k \, (q < p) \implies \neg \, \text{HASPER}(k, q))$$
$$\wedge \; (\forall \, q, k \, (k < i) \implies \neg \, \text{HASPER}(k, q)).$$

In `Walnut` this is

```
def hasper "p>=1 & Aj j>=i => X[j] = X[j+p]":
def ultper "$hasper(i,p) & (Aq,k (q<p) => ~$hasper(k,q))
   & (Aq,k k<i => ~$hasper(k,q))":
```

As an example, consider the DFAO in Figure 8.7 (where outputs are the state names). It generates the sequence 012(3456789)$^\omega$. Let us now execute

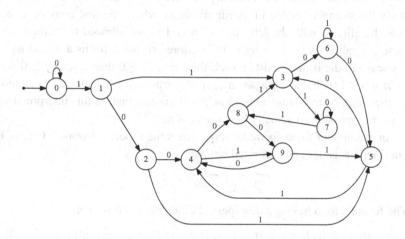

Figure 8.7 DFAO for 012(3456789)$^\omega$.

the following Walnut commands:

```
morphism g "0->01 1->23 2->45 3->67 4->89 5->34 6->56
   7->78 8->93 9->45":
promote UP g:
def hasper "(p>=1) & Aj (j>=i) => UP[j] = UP[j+p]":
def ultper "$hasper(i,p) & (Aq,k q<p => ~$hasper(k,q)) &
   (Aq,k k<i => ~$hasper(k,q))":
```

We find that the resulting automaton accepts only the pair (3,7), which means that the sequence has preperiod 3 and period 7.

*Exercise 47*  Justify the correctness of these formulas. How do we know that we can minimize $i$ and $p$ independently?

*Exercise 48*  Let $k \geq 3$. Show that the sequence of partial quotients in the continued fraction for the real number $\alpha_k = \sum_{n\geq 0} k^{-2^n}$ is 2-automatic and generated by a DFAO with 10 states. Use Walnut to prove that the resulting sequence is not ultimately periodic, and hence $\alpha_k$ is not rational or a quadratic irrational.

Do the same thing for $k = 2$. In this case, 14 states are needed. How about the numbers $k\alpha_k$? For more information, see [344, 299].

### 8.4.2 Quasiperiodicity

An infinite word **a** is said to be *quasiperiodic* if there is some finite nonempty word $x$ such that **a** can be completely "covered" with translates of $x$. Here we study the stronger version of quasiperiodicity where the first copy of $x$ used must be aligned with the left edge of **a** and is not allowed to "hang over"; these are called *aligned covers* in [87]. More precisely, for us $\mathbf{a} = a_0 a_1 a_2 \cdots$ is quasiperiodic if there exists $z$ such that for all $i \geq 0$ there exists $j \geq 0$ with $i - n < j \leq i$ such that $a_j a_{j+1} \cdots a_{j+n-1} = z$, where $n = |z|$. Such a $z$ is called a *quasiperiod*. Note that the condition $j \geq 0$ implies that, in this interpretation, any quasiperiod must actually be a *prefix* of **a**.

An example of a quasiperiodic sequence is the Fibonacci word **f**. One of its quasiperiods is 010, as illustrated below:

$$\overbrace{010}\ \overbrace{01\ 010}\ \underbrace{010}\ \cdots\ .$$

The formula for **a** having a quasiperiod of length $n > 0$ is then

$$(n > 0) \wedge \forall i\, \exists j\, (i < n + j) \wedge (j \leq i) \wedge (\forall \ell\, (\ell < n) \implies \mathbf{a}[\ell] = \mathbf{a}[\ell + j]).$$

The resulting automaton for Thue-Morse accepts nothing at all, so the Thue-Morse sequence is not quasiperiodic [257].

The quasiperiodicity of **f** was studied by Christou, Crochemore, and Iliopoulos [87], where we can (more or less) find the following theorem (also see [241]):

**Theorem 8.4.3** *A nonempty length-n prefix of* **f** *is a quasiperiod of* **f** *if and only if n is not of the form $F_k - 1$ for $k \geq 3$.*

In particular, the following prefix lengths are not quasiperiods: 0, 1, 2, 4, 7, 12, and so forth.

*Proof* Let us construct a formula for the assertion that the length-$n$ prefix of **f** is a quasiperiod:

$$\forall i \geq 0\ \exists j\ \text{with } i - n < j \leq i\ \text{FACTOREQ}(0, j, n).$$

In Walnut this is

```
def fibquasi "?msd_fib Ai (Ej i<j+n&j<=i&$ffactoreq(0,j,n))":
```

Inspection of the resulting automaton gives the result immediately, or we can use Walnut to verify it, as follows:

```
reg isfib msd_fib "0*10*":
eval fibquasicheck "?msd_fib An (~$fibquasi(n)) <=>
   (Es $isfib(s) & n=s-1)":
```

□

*Exercise* 49   Let **a** be the fixed point, starting with 0, of the morphism 0 → 01 and 1 → 011. Show that **a** is Fibonacci-automatic. What are its quasiperiods?

*Exercise* 50   How would you check in Walnut if a given *n* is an odd-indexed Fibonacci number? An even-indexed Fibonacci number?

*Exercise* 51   Give an example of a 2-automatic binary word that is quasiperiodic but not periodic.

*Exercise* 52   We proved that the Thue-Morse sequence is not quasiperiodic: it cannot be covered by translates of a single word. However, it is (what might be called) 2-quasiperiodic: it can be covered by translates of *exactly two* words. One family of such pairs is obvious: **t** can be covered by translates of $\mu^n(0)$ and $\mu^n(1)$ for all $n \geq 0$. Furthermore, prove that the only other pairs that work are $\mu^n(010)$ and $\mu^n(0110)$ for $n \geq 0$.

*Exercise* 53   Write a formula for the property of having a quasiperiod of length *n* for the weaker version of quasiperiodicity, where the quasiperiod need not be a prefix, but is allowed to "hang over" the left edge of the word.

For more on this topic, see [241, 242, 167, 165, 243].

## 8.4.3  Pseudoperiodicity

*Pseudoperiodicity* is a generalization of ordinary periodicity. We say a sequence **x** is *k*-pseudoperiodic if there exist positive integers $p_1, p_2, \ldots, p_k$ such that $\mathbf{x}[n] \in \{\mathbf{x}[n + p_1], \mathbf{x}[n + p_2], \ldots, \mathbf{x}[n + p_k]\}$ for all $n \geq 0$. It is easy to write a first-order logical formula for the property of being *k*-pseudoperiodic.

Let us show that the Thue-Morse sequence is 3-pseudoperiodic but not 2-pseudoperiodic:

```
eval ck2 "Ep,q 0<p & p<q & An (T[n]=T[n+p]|T[n]=T[n+q])":
eval ck3 "Ep,q,r 0<p & p<q & q<r &
   An (T[n]=T[n+p]|T[n]=T[n+q]|T[n]=T[n+r])":
```

The first assertion returns FALSE and the second TRUE.

## 8.5 Squares, cubes, and other powers

### 8.5.1 Squares

The following first-order formula asserts the presence of squares in a sequence:

$$\exists i, n \, (n \geq 1) \wedge \forall j \, (j < n) \implies \mathbf{x}[i + j] = \mathbf{x}[i + j + n].$$

Observe that we need to specify $n \geq 1$ here. The `Walnut` translation is

```
def hassquare "Ei,n n>=1 & Aj j<n => X[i+j]=X[i+j+n]":
```

By making the substitution $t = i + j$, we get an alternative formula for the existence of a square:

$$\exists i, n \, (n \geq 1) \wedge \forall t \, (t \geq i \wedge t < i + n) \implies \mathbf{x}[t] = \mathbf{x}[t + n].$$

Although logically equivalent to the previous formula, this one may run substantially faster on some sequences, because we are only indexing $\mathbf{x}$ by at most two variables. This is an example of the ploy known as the "substitute variables" trick.

Recall the sequence **vtm** discussed in Section 2.4.3. We can verify that **vtm** is squarefree using `Walnut`:

```
eval vtmsquare "Ei,n n>=1 & Aj j<n => VTM[i+j]=VTM[i+j+n]":
```

which evaluates to FALSE. Hence **vtm** is squarefree.

*Exercise* 54    Show how to verify with `Walnut` that $\mathbf{vtm}[n] = t_{n+1} - t_n + 1$, where $(t_n)_{n \geq 0}$ is the Thue-Morse sequence.

Now, let's turn to another example. Recall the Tower of Hanoi sequence **th** from Section 2.4.10. In a paper I co-wrote in 1994 [5], we proved that **th** is squarefree, but our proof took two pages and some case analysis. Instead, we can carry out the proof very easily in `Walnut`. The following formula asserts the existence of a square:

```
eval hanoisq "Ei,n n>=1 & Aj j<n => TH[i+j]=TH[i+j+n]":
```

and it evaluates to FALSE.

*Exercise* 55    Find a $k$-uniform morphism $h : \Sigma_3^* \to \Sigma_3^*$, prolongable on $a$, such that $h^\omega(a)$ is squarefree, and $k$ is as small as possible. Hint: use breadth-first search, as described in Section 2.6, to guess a candidate, and then verify it using `Walnut`.

## 8.5.2 Orders of squares

Next, we move on to a description of the *orders* of squares occurring in **f**. Recall that the order of a square $xx$ is defined to be $|x|$. An old result of Séébold [342] (also see [210, 156]) states

**Theorem 8.5.1** *All squares in* **f** *are of order* $F_n$ *for some* $n \geq 2$. *Furthermore, for all* $n \geq 2$, *there exists a square of order* $F_n$ *in* **f**.

*Proof* We create a formula for the orders of nonempty squares:

$$(n > 0) \wedge \exists i \, \forall t < n \, \mathbf{f}[i + t] = \mathbf{f}[i + n + t].$$

In Walnut this is

```
def fibsquarelen "?msd_fib n>0 & Ei At t<n => F[i+t]=F[i+n+t]":
```

Next, since the Fibonacci representation of $F_n$ is $10^{n-2}$, we can prove Séébold's result as follows:

```
reg isfib msd_fib "0*10*":
eval seebold "?msd_fib An $isfib(n) <=> $fibsquarelen(n)":
```

which evaluates to TRUE. □

We can easily get much more information about the square occurrences in **f**. The positions of all squares in **f** were computed by Iliopoulos, Moore, and Smyth [210, § 2], but the description is rather complicated and takes five pages to prove. Instead, let us define a formula asserting the existence of a square of order $n$ beginning at position $i$:

```
def fibsquarepos "?msd_fib n>0 & At t<n => F[i+t] = F[i+n+t]":
```

This produces the automaton in Figure 8.8. Note that it accepts the Fibonacci representation of $i$ and $n$ in parallel, with $(i)_F$ spelling out the first coordinates and $(n)_F$ spelling out the second.

Using the automaton for fibsquarepos, we can understand the positions at which squares begin in **f**. Not only is there a square starting at each position, even more is true: *arbitrarily* large squares begin at every position. We can assert this as follows:

```
eval fibals "?msd_fib Ai,m En n>m & At t<n => F[i+t]=F[i+n+t]":
```

It evaluates to TRUE.

*Exercise 56* In contrast, show that in the Thue-Morse sequence there are infinitely many positions where no square begins (sequence A345868 in the OEIS), and that no two squares begin at the same index.

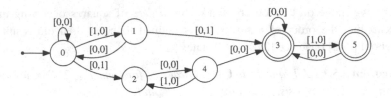

Figure 8.8  Automaton accepting positions and orders of all squares in **f**.

Next, let us try to determine the orders of squares in the Tribonacci word **tr**. One might be tempted to write

```
def tribsquarelen "?msd_trib n>0&Ei At t<n=>TR[i+t]=TR[i+n+t]":
```

but this required 1257 seconds of CPU time and 85 gigabytes of RAM.

Instead, as discussed above, substitute $j$ for $i + t$ and rewrite the formula as

```
def tribsquarelen "?msd_trib n>0 & Ei Aj (j>=i & j<i+n) =>
   TR[j]=TR[j+n]":
```

This terminated in one second and gives us the following result:

**Theorem 8.5.2**   *The orders of squares appearing in the Tribonacci word are $T_n$ for $n \geq 2$ and $T_n + T_{n-1}$ for $n \geq 3$.*

Similarly, arbitrarily large squares begin at every position of the Tribonacci word:

```
eval tribals "?msd_trib Ai,m En (n>=m) &
   Au,v (u>=i & u<i+n & v=u+n) => TR[u]=TR[v]":
```

It also evaluates to TRUE.

*Exercise 57*   Determine the orders of square prefixes of the Tribonacci word. Are any of the finite Tribonacci words squares?

### 8.5.3 Dean words

Consider the free group $G$ on two symbols $x, y$. Elements of $G$ can be considered as words over the alphabet $\{x, y, x^{-1}, y^{-1}\}$. A word is *reduced* if it contains none of the blocks $xx^{-1}, x^{-1}x, yy^{-1}, y^{-1}y$. Dean [113] constructed an infinite squarefree reduced word. Also see [190].

We can easily find an infinite squarefree reduced word using something we call *automatic breadth-first search*, a version of the idea we mentioned in Section 2.6.

We choose a regular numeration system, such as base $k$ for some $k \geq 2$, and a bound $B$ on the number of states in a DFAO. The idea is to use breadth-first search to examine the space of all words having the desired property, but stop expanding a node if the minimal DFAO generating the word has more than $B$ states. With luck, if we chose $k$ and $B$ appropriately, the search will converge on one or a small number of sequences generated by DFAO that are candidates for generating the word we want.

Let us encode a word using the correspondence

$$0 \leftrightarrow x, 1 \leftrightarrow y, 2 \leftrightarrow x^{-1}, 3 \leftrightarrow y^{-1}.$$

For $k = 2$ and a bound of 4 states, automatic breadth-first search quickly converges on the following candidate morphism:

$$0 \to 01, \ 1 \to 21, \ 2 \to 03, \ 3 \to 23.$$

Calling the corresponding DFAO DE, we can easily verify that the word it generates is squarefree and contains no occurrence of the factors 02, 20, 13, 31:

```
eval dean1 "Ei,n n>=1 & At t<n => DE[i+t]=DE[i+n+t]":
# check if there's a square

eval dean02 "Ei DE[i]=@0 & DE[i+1]=@2":
eval dean20 "Ei DE[i]=@2 & DE[i+1]=@0":
eval dean13 "Ei DE[i]=@1 & DE[i+1]=@3":
eval dean31 "Ei DE[i]=@3 & DE[i+1]=@1":
# check for existence of 02, 20, 13, 31
```

All of these return FALSE, so the word has the desired properties.

*Exercise 58*   Show that the odd-indexed subsequence of the word generated by DE is a recoding of the regular paperfolding word.

*Exercise 59*   Find a squarefree sequence $(g_n)_{n \geq 0}$ over the alphabet $\{-1, 0, 1\}$ with the property that $g_n = g_{2n+1} + g_{2n+2}$ for all $n \geq 0$. Hint: use automatic breadth-first search, restricting to 2-automatic sequences generated by a DFAO of at most 5 states, to identify a candidate. Then confirm with Walnut.

### 8.5.4 Pansiot encodings

Pansiot encodings are a general tool for studying repetition avoidance [292]. In the special case of squarefree words $\mathbf{x}$ over a three-letter alphabet, the encoding is as follows: 0 if $\mathbf{x}[n] = \mathbf{x}[n-2]$ and 1 otherwise. It is easy to see that given $\mathbf{x}[0..1]$ and its Pansiot encoding, one can reconstruct $\mathbf{x}$.

Let us compute the Pansiot encoding **y** of **vtm**:

```
eval pansiot "VTM[n]!=VTM[n+2]":
```

It gives the automaton in Figure 8.9 (where one interprets an accepting state as outputting 1 and a nonaccepting state as outputting 0): So, using the connection

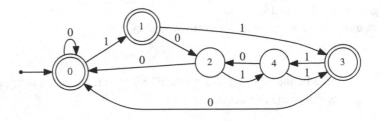

Figure 8.9  Automaton for Pansiot encoding of **vtm**.

between automata and morphisms mentioned in Section 5.4, we see that $\mathbf{y} = \xi(g^\omega(0))$, where

$$g(0) = 01 \qquad\qquad \xi(0) = 1$$
$$g(1) = 23 \qquad\qquad \xi(1) = 1$$
$$g(2) = 04 \qquad\qquad \xi(2) = 0$$
$$g(3) = 04 \qquad\qquad \xi(3) = 1$$
$$g(4) = 23 \qquad\qquad \xi(4) = 0.$$

## 8.5.5  Overlaps

We have already seen, in Section 1.3, a proof that the Thue-Morse sequence **t** is overlap-free.

Let's apply our technique to a related infinite word, the twisted Thue-Morse sequence introduced in Section 2.4.2. The following formula then asserts the existence of an overlap in **ttm**.

```
eval ttmolf "Ei, p (p>=1) & Aj (j<=p) => TTM[i+j]=TTM[i+j+p]":
```

When we run it, Walnut returns FALSE, so **ttm** is also overlap-free.

## 8.5.6 Underlaps

In analogy with overlaps, Rajasekaran et al. [307] defined an *underlap* to be a word of the form *axbxa*, where $a, b$ are distinct letters and $x$ is a possibly empty word. We call $|ax|$ the order of the underlap.

*Exercise* 60   Determine all the underlaps in the Thue-Morse sequence.

*Exercise* 61   Use breadth-first search, as discussed in Sections 2.6 and 8.5.3, to guess a ternary word that simultaneously avoids overlaps, overpals, underpals, and underlaps, and then prove your result with Walnut.

## 8.5.7 Cubes

There is a right way and a wrong way to check for the presence of cubes! First, the wrong way:

$$\text{IsCube}(i, n) := (\forall t \ (t < n) \implies x[i + t] = x[i + n + t])$$
$$\wedge \ (\forall t \ (t < n) \implies x[i + t] = x[i + 2n + t]).$$

This formula specifies that the word $y = x[i..i+n-1]$ matches $x[i+n..i+2n-1]$, and also that $y$ matches $x[i + 2n..i + 3n - 1]$. A better way is

$$\text{IsCube}(i, n) := \forall t \ (t < 2n) \implies x[i + t] = x[i + n + t].$$

This second formula only requires checking one condition instead of two. One could also write

$$\text{IsCube}(i, n) := \text{FactorEq}(i, i + n, 2n),$$

making use of a formula we already defined. And finally, the formula

$$\text{IsCube}(i, n) := \forall t \ (t \geq i \wedge t < i + 2n) \implies x[t] = x[t + n],$$

obtained by the "substitute variables" trick, may run significantly faster than all the others.

Let us try to find the orders of all cubes in the Fibonacci word:

**Theorem 8.5.3**   *The cubes in* **f** *are of order* $F_n$ *for* $n \geq 4$, *and a cube of each such order occurs.*

*Proof*   We use the formula

$$(n > 0) \wedge \exists i \ \text{FactorEq}(i, i + n, 2n).$$

In Walnut this is

```
eval fibcube "?msd_fib n>0 & Ei $ffactoreq(i,i+n,2*n)":
```

When we run `Walnut`, we obtain an automaton recognizing `(100)0*`, which corresponds to $F_n$ for $n \geq 4$.     □

Finally, one more example. Let us show that the Stewart choral sequence **sc** is cubefree. The following `Walnut` code asserts the existence of a cube:

```
eval sccube "?msd_3 Ei,n n>0& At (t<2*n)=>SC[i+t]=SC[i+n+t]":
```

and it evaluates to FALSE.

We might try to avoid arithmetic progression words of the form *abab*··· with $a \neq b$, which we call *alternating bichromatic words*. As stated, this is not so interesting, since every word of the form $a^n$ avoids these. So we might try to avoid both alternating bichromatic words in arithmetic progression *and* (say) ordinary cubes. An easy backtracking computation (as in Section 2.6) shows that the longest binary word avoiding both cubes and *abab* in arithmetic progression is of length 8 (e.g., `00100100`). We just saw that **sc** is cubefree. In addition, we can show the following:

**Theorem 8.5.4**  *Stewart's choral sequence contains no occurrence of the word ababa, $a \neq b$, in any arithmetic progression.*

*Proof*  Use the following `Walnut` command.

```
eval stewap "?msd_3 Ei,j,k,l,m k+i=2*j & j+l=2*k & m+k=2*l
    & SC[i]=SC[k] & SC[j]=SC[l] & SC[k]=SC[m] & SC[i]!=SC[j]":
```

□

## 8.5.8 Fourth powers

An old result, due to Karhumäki [219, Thm. 2], states that there are no fourth powers in the Fibonacci word **f**. The following `Walnut` code asserts the existence of a fourth power,

```
eval karhu "?msd_fib Ei,n n>0 & At (t>=i & t<i+3*n)
    => F[t]=F[t+n]":
```

and it evaluates to FALSE.

Similarly, there are no fourth powers in the Tribonacci word. The formula

```
eval trib4p "?msd_trib Ei,n n>0 & At (t>=i & t<i+3*n)
    => TR[t]=TR[t+n]":
```

also evaluates to FALSE.

### 8.5.9 Near-squares

A *near-square* is a word of length $2n-1$ and period $n > 1$. Examples in English include the words `magma` and `ingoing`. It is easy to check the existence of near-squares in a word $\mathbf{x}$:

$$\exists i, n \, (n > 1) \wedge \forall t \, (t + 2 \leq n) \implies \mathbf{x}[i + t] = \mathbf{x}[i + t + n].$$

Backtracking (see Section 2.6) easily proves that there are no words avoiding near-squares over a 3-letter (or smaller) alphabet. The automatic breadth-first search strategy, as described in Section 8.5.3 quickly converges on the following candidate morphism $g$ over a 4-letter alphabet:

$$0 \rightarrow 0123$$
$$1 \rightarrow 1032$$
$$2 \rightarrow 0132$$
$$3 \rightarrow 1023.$$

*Exercise 62*    Convert this morphism $g$ into a DFAO, and then execute the appropriate formula to prove that the fixed point of $g$, starting with 0, avoids near-squares.

### 8.5.10 Approximate squares

We say that a word $w = xx'$ is a *c-approximate square* if $|x| = |x'|$ and $H(x, x') < \min(c + 1, |x|)$, where $H$ is the Hamming distance (number of positions where $x, x'$ differ). A 0-approximate square is just an ordinary square, the English word `instinct` is a 1-approximate square, and the English word `distinguishing` is a 2-approximate square.

*Exercise 63*    Show that for each fixed $c$, the property of having a factor that is a $c$-approximate square is first-order expressible.

As an example, let us show that the word $\tau(h^{\omega}(0))$ avoids 1-approximate squares, where

| | |
|---|---|
| $h(0) = 01$ | $\tau(0) = 0$ |
| $h(1) = 20$ | $\tau(1) = 1$ |
| $h(2) = 34$ | $\tau(2) = 2$ |
| $h(3) = 34$ | $\tau(3) = 3$ |
| $h(4) = 53$ | $\tau(4) = 4$ |
| $h(5) = 01$ | $\tau(5) = 2.$ |

We then execute the `Walnut` commands:

```
morphism h "0->01 1->20 2->34 3->34 4->53 5->01":
morphism tau "0->0 1->1 2->2 3->3 4->4 5->2":
promote HH h:
image SA tau HH:
def satest "(At SA[t] != SA[t+1]) & Ai,n n>=2 => (Ej,k j<k
   & k<n & SA[i+j]!=SA[i+n+j] & SA[i+k]!=SA[i+n+k])":
```

and the result is TRUE. For more about avoiding approximate squares, see [288].

## 8.5.11 Arbitrary rational powers

Recall that we can talk about avoidance of arbitrary rational powers. Here are first-order formulas for avoiding, respectively, $p/q$ and $(p/q)^+$ powers.

$$\neg(\exists i, n \, (n \geq 1) \, \wedge \, \forall j \, (j \geq i \, \wedge \, qj < qi + (p - q)n) \implies \mathbf{x}[j] = \mathbf{x}[j + n])$$
$$\neg(\exists i, n \, (n \geq 1) \, \wedge \, \forall j \, (j \geq i \, \wedge \, qj \leq qi + (p - q)n) \implies \mathbf{x}[j] = \mathbf{x}[j + n]).$$

Of course, these formulas, as written, are not expressible in the logical theory $\mathrm{Th}(\mathbb{N}, +, V_k)$, because they involve multiplication by $q$ and $p - q$. Nevertheless, for any *specific* positive integers $p > q$ they become expressible.

Using this idea, let's consider an old construction of Leech [236]. Using a case analysis, he showed that the Leech word **le** defined in Section 2.4.14 is squarefree. We can verify this with `Walnut`, but in fact we can do more:

**Theorem 8.5.5**  *The Leech sequence* $\mathbf{le} = l_0 l_1 l_2 \cdots = 0121021201210120 \cdots$ *is* $\frac{15}{8}^+$*-free, and this exponent is optimal. Furthermore, if $x$ is a $\frac{15}{8}$ power occurring in* **l**, *then* $|x| = 15 \cdot 13^i$ *for some* $i \geq 0$.

*Proof*  We used our method to verify that there are no powers $> \frac{15}{8}$.

```
eval leech "?msd_13 Ei,n n>=1 & Aj (j>=i & 8*j<=8*i+7*n)
    => LE[j]=LE[j+n]":
```

The exponent 15/8 is optimal because, for example, the factor **le**[25..39] = 120102101201021 is easily seen to be a $\frac{15}{8}$ power. We can also compute an automaton that recognizes the base-13 expansion of those pairs $(i, n)$ for which a $\frac{15}{8}$ power of order $n$ begins at position $i$.

```
eval leechp "?msd_13 n>=1 & Aj (j>=i & 8*j<8*i+7*n)
    => LE[j]=LE[j+n]":
```

The resulting automaton has 3 states. We omit the automaton because it is not particularly attractive, but the regular expression it recognizes is

$$(\Sigma_{13} \times \{0\})^* \{[1, 0], \ [9, 0]\}[12, 8][0, 0]^*.$$

Hence all $\frac{15}{8}$ powers in **le** are of order $8 \cdot 13^i$ (and length $15 \cdot 13^i$) for $i \geq 0$. ☐

We can carry out a similar computation for Dejean's word **dej**. We find that it is $(7/4)^+$-power-free, but has $7/4$ powers of order $4 \cdot 19^i$ for every $i \geq 0$:

```
eval dej74e "?msd_19 Ei,n n>=1 & Aj (j>=i & 4*j<=4*i+3*n)
   => DEJ[j]=DEJ[j+n]":
eval dej74 "?msd_19 Ei n>=1 & Aj (j>=i & 4*j<4*i+3*n)
   => DEJ[j]=DEJ[j+n]":
```

This last formula recognizes the language `40*`, and hence the result.

*Exercise 64*   In ⌊104, Prop. 13⌋, the authors constructed an infinite binary word that contains no $7/3$-powers, but infinitely many overlaps. Use `Walnut` to prove it has those properties.

*Exercise 65*   Use automatic breadth-first search, as discussed in Section 8.5.3, to find a 3-automatic word over the alphabet $\{0, 1, 2\}$ that avoids $(7/4 + \epsilon)$-powers.

*Exercise 66*   Use `Walnut` to prove the following two results of Defant [116]:

(a) If $yvy$ is a factor of the Thue-Morse word **t** and $|y| = m$ then $2^{\lceil \log_2(m/3) \rceil}$ divides $|yv|$.

(b) This is best possible, in the sense that for each $m$ there exist $v$ and a length-$m$ word $y$ for which no higher power of 2 divides $|yv|$.

### 8.5.12 Rational powers in variations on factors

We have seen that the Thue-Morse sequence **t** avoids overlaps (that is, it has 2-powers, but no higher). We can consider what kinds of powers arise from "flipping" a single bit of **t** (that is, changing a 0 to a 1 and a 1 to a 0).

A little experimentation suggests the following theorem:

**Theorem 8.5.6**   *Flipping a single bit of* **t** *can result in an $\alpha$-power (but no higher power) for $\alpha \in \{\frac{5}{2}, \frac{8}{3}, 3, \frac{10}{3}, \frac{11}{3}, 4\}$, and no other $\alpha$.*

*Proof*   First we can construct a formula for the infinite word $\mathbf{t}_i$ that coincides with **t**, except that the $i$th bit is flipped. First we construct a DFA, and then we convert it to a DFAO using the `combine` command.

```
def tmc "(i=n & T[n]=@0) | (i!=n & T[n]=@1)":
combine TMC tmc:
```

Then for each possible $\alpha$-power in the above list, we can construct a formula specifying those $i$ such that $\mathbf{t}_i$ has an occurrence of an $\alpha$-power, but no higher. Finally, we check that we have covered all possible $i$, so there are no other possibilities.

```
def tmc52 "(Ej,n n>=1 & At (2*t<3*n) =>
   TMC[i][j+t]=TMC[i][j+t+n]) & (~Ej,n n>=1 & At (2*t<=3*n)
   => TMC[i][j+t]=TMC[i][j+t+n])":

def tmc83 "(Ej,n n>=1 & At (3*t<5*n) =>
   TMC[i][j+t]=TMC[i][j+t+n]) & (~Ej,n n>=1 & At (3*t<=5*n)
   => TMC[i][j+t]=TMC[i][j+t+n])":

def tmc31 "(Ej,n n>=1 & At (t<2*n) =>
   TMC[i][j+t]=TMC[i][j+t+n]) & (~Ej,n n>=1 & At (t<=2*n)
   => TMC[i][j+t]=TMC[i][j+t+n])":

def tmc103 "(Ej,n n>=1 & At (3*t<7*n) =>
   TMC[i][j+t]=TMC[i][j+t+n]) & (~Ej,n n>=1 & At (3*t<=7*n)
   => TMC[i][j+t]=TMC[i][j+t+n])":

def tmc113 "(Ej,n n>=1 & At (3*t<8*n) =>
   TMC[i][j+t]=TMC[i][j+t+n]) & (~Ej,n n>=1 & At (3*t<=8*n)
   => TMC[i][j+t]=TMC[i][j+t+n])":

def tmc41 "(Ej,n n>=1 & At (t<3*n) =>
   TMC[i][j+t]=TMC[i][j+t+n]) & (~Ej,n n>=1 & At (t<=3*n)
   => TMC[i][j+t]=TMC[i][j+t+n])":

eval test "(Ei $tmc52(i)) & (Ei $tmc83(i)) & (Ei $tmc31(i))
   & (Ei $tmc103(i)) & (Ei $tmc113(i)) & (Ei $tmc41(i)) &
   Ai ($tmc52(i)|$tmc83(i)|$tmc31(i)|$tmc103(i)|$tmc113(i)|
   $tmc41(i)))":
```

The final line returns TRUE, so we have proven our theorem.    □

We can then use Walnut's combine command to combine all the automata computed above into one DFAO that computes the critical exponent of **t** with the bit in position *i* flipped. See Figure 8.10.

*Exercise* 67    Call a binary word *delicate* if it is overlap-free, but flipping any single bit results in an overlap. Show that for all $n \geq 7$ the Thue-Morse sequence **t** has a length-*n* factor that is delicate.

*Exercise* 68    Flipping bit *i* of the Thue-Morse sequence can result in a number of different occurrences of overlaps. How many, as a function of *i*?

*Exercise* 69    Show that if the first symbol of the word **vtm** is changed to a 0, the resulting word is still squarefree, but any other change of a single position results in a square, a cube, or a $\frac{5}{2}$ power.

## 8.5.13 Extremal overlap-free words

Sometimes if you want to prove a property of a sequence of words, you can do it with Walnut by embedding the sequence into an automatic sequence

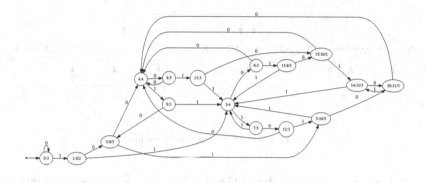

Figure 8.10 DFAO computing critical exponents for *i*th bit of **t** flipped.

somehow. Furthermore, although it is perhaps not immediately obvious, we can use Walnut to prove properties of words that are small variations of factors of an automatic sequence, such as those formed by inserting or deleting one symbol. We illustrate both of these ideas in this section.

A binary word $x$ is said to be *extremal overlap-free* if it is overlap-free, and for all factorizations $x = yz$, the two words $y0z$ and $y1z$ both contain overlaps.

Some experimentation suggests that all the words $\mu^k(0\mu(0011001)1)$ are extremal overlap-free, where $\mu$ is the Thue-Morse morphism defined in Chapter 1. We can verify this in a roundabout way, as follows: first we observe that $0\mu(0011001)1$ is a factor of $\mu^3(111)$. Hence $\mu^k(0\mu(0011001)1)$ is contained in $\mu^{k+3}(111)$. We can now define a 4-automatic sequence that has all the even powers $\mu^{2k}(111)$ appearing in it: namely, the image under the coding $0 \to 2$, $1 \to 1, 2 \to 0$ of the fixed point of the morphism

$$0 \to 0111, \quad 1 \to 1221, \quad 2 \to 2112.$$

We can build the corresponding DFAO x.txt as follows:

```
morphism ext "0->0111 1->1221 2->2112":
promote XT ext:
morphism codi "0->2 1->1 2->0":
image X codi XT:
```

Then we design a formula for the assertion that $\mathbf{X}[i..i + n - 1]$ is extremal overlap-free, as follows. The idea is to split the indices into five regions, as illustrated in Figure 8.11, and then verify that symbols occurring at the indices in the given regions match appropriately.

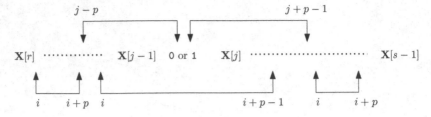

Figure 8.11 Extremal overlap-free word illustrated.

We can now verify that extremal($18 \cdot 4^i, 32 \cdot 4^i$) for $i \geq 0$ holds, which proves the claim.

```
def isover "?msd_4 Ep (p>=1) & 2*p+r+1=s & (Ai (r<=i & i+p<s)
   => X[i]=X[i+p])":
# X[r..s-1] is an overlap

def isover0 "?msd_4 Ep (p>=1) & (s=r+2*p) & (Ai (r<=i & i+p<j)
   => X[i]=X[i+p]) & (j>=r+p => X[j-p]=@0) & (Ai (r<=i & i<j
   & i+p>=j+1 & i+p<=s) => X[i]=X[(i+p)-1]) & (j+p<=s =>
   X[(j+p)-1]=@0) & (Ai (j<=i & i+p<s) => X[i]=X[i+p])":
#  X[r..j-1] 0 X[j..s-1] is an overlap

def isover1 "?msd_4 Ep (p>=1) & (s=r+2*p) & (Ai (r<=i & i+p<j)
   => X[i]=X[i+p]) & (j>=r+p => X[j-p]=@1) & (Ai (r<=i & i<j
   & i+p>=j+1 & i+p<=s) => X[i]=X[(i+p)-1]) & (j+p<=s =>
   X[(j+p)-1]=@1) & (Ai (j<=i & i+p<s) => X[i]=X[i+p])":
#  X[r..j-1] 1 X[j..s-1] is an overlap

def hasover "?msd_4 Er,s i<=r & r<=s & s<=i+n &
   $isover(r,s)":
# X[i..i+n-1] has an overlap X[r..s-1] in it somewhere

def extremal "?msd_4 (~$hasover(i,n)) & Aj (j>=i & j<=i+n)
   => ((Er,s r>=i & r<s & s<=i+n & $isover0(j,r,s)) &
   (Erp,sp rp>=i & rp<sp & sp<=i+n & $isover1(j,rp,sp)))":
# X[i..i+n-1] is extremal overlap-free
reg power4 msd_4 "10*":
eval test_extremal "?msd_4 Ai $power4(i)=>$extremal(18*i,32*i)":
```

For more on this topic, see [273, 274].

## 8.5.14 Primitive words

Recall that a word is *primitive* if it is nonempty and a non-power.[1]

---

[1] Some material in this section is reprinted from [173] by permission from Springer Nature.

Although at first glance it might look like this property is not first-order expressible, since the possible exponent of the power is arbitrary, a reformulation makes it clear that it is in fact expressible:

**Theorem 8.5.7** *A word w is primitive iff no nontrivial rotation of w equals* w.

Here a rotation of $w = w[0..n-1]$ is a word of the form $w[j..n-1]w[0..j-1]$ for some $j$, $0 \le j < n$. It is nontrivial if $j \ne 0$.

*Exercise* 70    Use Theorem 2.1.1 to prove Theorem 8.5.7.

We can therefore make a formula to check primitivity of $x[i..i+n-1]$ by comparing it to all of its nontrivial rotations:

$$\text{PRIM}(i, n) := \neg(\exists j\, (j > 0) \wedge (j < n)$$
$$\wedge\; \text{FACTOREQ}(i, i+j, n-j) \wedge \text{FACTOREQ}(i, (i+n)-j, j)).$$

For the Thue-Morse sequence, we can prove that every nonempty prefix is primitive.

```
def tmfactoreq "At t<n => T[i+t]=T[j+t]":
def tmprim "~(Ej j>0 & j<n & $tmfactoreq(i,i+j,n-j) &
    $tmfactoreq(i,(i+n)-j,j))":
def tmprimlength "n>0 & $tmprim(0,n)":
eval tmprimcheck "An n>=1 => $tmprimlength(n)":
```

This last command returns TRUE.

## 8.5.15 Unbounded exponents

Recall that if $|w| = n$ and per $w = p$ then we say that $\exp(w) = n/p$. Given a $k$-automatic sequence $x$, we would like to decide if $x$ contains factors of arbitrarily large exponent, that is, whether $\sup\{\exp(w) : w$ is a factor of $x\} = \infty$.

This question is a bit more subtle than it first appears. The easy case is where some nonempty factor $y = x[i..i+p-1]$ itself appears with unbounded exponent; that is, $y^s$ is a factor of $x$ for all $s$. We can write a first-order formula specifying such $y$ as follows:

$$(p \ge 1) \wedge \forall r\, \exists j, m\, (m > r) \wedge \text{FACTOREQ}(i, j, p) \wedge \text{FACTOREQ}(j, j+p, m).$$

So we can determine if $y$ exists, whether infinitely many $y$ exist, and what they are. We can also insist, for example, that $y$ be primitive and that $x[i..i+p-1]$ be the first occurrence of $y$ in $x$.

But—at least in principle—it could be that no individual $y$ occurs with unbounded exponent in $\mathbf{x}$, but rather for each $s$ there is a *different* $y$ such that $y^s$ appears in $\mathbf{x}$. We now show that this cannot happen for automatic sequences.

**Theorem 8.5.8**  *For each automatic sequence $\mathbf{x}$ there is a computable bound $B$ such that if $y^B$ occurs as a factor of $\mathbf{x}$ then $y$ occurs with unbounded exponent in $\mathbf{x}$.*

*Proof*  Let $M$ be a $k$-DFAO generating the sequence $\mathbf{x}$. As we will see in Section 10.5, for automatic sequences there is a computable constant $C$ such that if $y$ appears as a factor of $\mathbf{x}$, it must appear starting at a position that is $\leq C|y|$.

Now consider the following first-order formula $\varphi$:

$$\exists j \; \textsc{EarliestFac}(i, j, p) \wedge \textsc{Period}(j, p, n),$$

where

$$\textsc{Period}(j, p, n) = (p \geq 1) \wedge (p < n) \wedge \forall t \, (t + p < n) \implies \mathbf{x}[j+t] = \mathbf{x}[j+t+p]$$

and

$$\textsc{EarliestFac}(i, j, n) = \textsc{FactorEq}(i, j, n) \wedge \forall t \, \textsc{FactorEq}(t, j, n) \implies t \geq i.$$

The formula $\varphi$ asserts that there exists some $j$ such that

  (i)  $\mathbf{x}[i..i + p - 1] = \mathbf{x}[j..j + p - 1]$.
  (ii)  $i$ is the smallest index for which (i) holds.
  (iii)  there is some $p$, $1 \leq p \leq n$, for which $\mathbf{x}[j..j + n - 1]$ has period $p$.

Notice that this is asserting that $\mathbf{x}[j..j + n - 1]$ has exponent at least $n/p$.

From $M$ we can computably determine a DFA $M'$ accepting those triples $(i, p, n)_k$ in parallel satisfying $\varphi$. Suppose $M'$ has $r$ states. We now claim that $M'$ accepts $(i, p, n)_k$ with $n/p > k^r C$ iff $\mathbf{x}$ contains arbitrarily large powers of $\mathbf{x}[i..i + n - 1]$.

One direction is trivial. For the other direction, consider the base-$k$ representation of the triple $(i, p, n)$. From the discussion above we know that $i \leq Cp$. Since $n > k^r C p$ we have $n > k^r i$, and hence the base-$k$ representation of $(i, p, n)$ starts with at least $r$ 0s in the components corresponding to $i$ and $p$ and a nonzero digit in the $n$ component. We may now apply the pumping lemma to $z = (i, p, n)_k$ to get longer and longer words with the same value of $i$ and $p$, but arbitrarily large $n$. From the definition of $M'$ this means that there is an infinite sequence of increasing $n$ for which there exists a $j$ with $\mathbf{x}[j..j + n - 1]$ of exponent at least $n/p$. We may now take $B = k^r C$ to prove the result.  $\square$

So this rules out the second possibility mentioned above: once a factor $y$ occurs with sufficiently large exponent $B = k^r C$ in $\mathbf{x}$, it must occur with arbitrarily large exponent.

**Corollary 8.5.9** *We can decide if a k-automatic sequence has factors with arbitrarily large exponent.*

This last result is from [78].

Furthermore, if we want to check what these factors are, we can impose the additional requirements that $\mathbf{x}[i..i+n-1]$ be a novel occurrence, and primitive. Let us do this for the word **sb**, as follows:

```
def sbfactoreq "At t<n => SB[i+t]=SB[j+t]":
def sbprim "~(Ej j>0 & j<n & $sbfactoreq(i,i+j,n-j) &
   $sbfactoreq(i,(i+n)-j,j))":
def sbnovelf "Aj j<i => ~$sbfactoreq(i,j,n)":
def sbarbexp "Am m>n => Ej $sbfactoreq(i,j,n) &
   $sbfactoreq(j,j+n,m)":
def sbfirstarbexp "n>=1 & $sbnovelf(i,n) & $sbprim(i,n)
   & $sbarbexp(i,n)":
```

When we run this, we find that exactly two pairs $(i, n)$ are accepted: $(3, 1)$ and $(0, 1)$. This means that the only primitive words for which arbitrarily large powers appear in **sb** are **sb**[3] = 1 and **sb**[0] = 0.

### 8.5.16 Antisquares

An *antisquare* is a finite binary word of the form $x\,\overline{x}$; its order is defined to be $|x|$. We can check to see if $\mathbf{x}[i..i + 2n - 1]$ is an antisquare as follows:

$$\text{IsAnti}(i, n) := \forall j \, (j < n) \implies \mathbf{x}[i + j] \neq \mathbf{x}[i + j + n].$$

Let us instantiate this formula for the Fibonacci word $\mathbf{f}$:

```
def isantif "?msd_fib Aj j<n => F[i+j]!=F[i+j+n]":
def antisf "?msd_fib Ei $isantif(i,n)":
```

By inspecting the resulting automaton, we see that the only antisquares in $\mathbf{f}$ are of orders $0, 1, 2, 4$. This is a result of Apostolico and Brimkov [19].

### 8.5.17 Generalized powers

We call a word $w$ a *generalized rth power* if there exists a nonempty word $x$ such that $w = x_1 x_2 \cdots x_r$, with $x_i \in \{x, x^R\}$. For example, deeded is a generalized cube.

The period-doubling sequence is an example of a binary word that avoids generalized fourth powers. We can check this as follows:

```
def pdfactoreq "At t<n => PD[i+t]=PD[j+t]":
def pdrevcheck "At t<n => PD[i+t]=PD[(j+n)-(t+1)]":
eval checkpd4 "Ei,n n>=1 & ($pdfactoreq(i,i+n,n) |
   $pdrevcheck(i,i+n,n)) & ($pdfactoreq(i,i+2*n,n) |
   $pdrevcheck(i,i+2*n,n)) & ($pdfactoreq(i,i+3*n,n) |
   $pdrevcheck(i,i+3*n,n))":
```

which evaluates to FALSE, so **pd** contains no generalized fourth powers.

*Exercise* 71   Show that the fixed point of the morphism $0 \to 01$, $1 \to 12$, $2 \to 20$ is overlap-free and contains no generalized cubes.

### 8.5.18 Patterns with reversal

We can use Walnut as a "telescope" to explore complicated patterns that might be out of reach of existing methods.

For example, in [126], we looked for aperiodic binary infinite words that avoid the pattern $xxx^R$. Using the procedure outlined in Section 2.6, we found the following candidate: the Rote-Fibonacci word **rf** $= 0010011\cdots$, defined in Section 2.4.17.

**Theorem 8.5.10**   *The Rote-Fibonacci word* **rf** *avoids the pattern* $xxx^R$.

*Proof*   We run Walnut on the following formulas, which test for the existence of $xxx^R$:

```
def rffactoreq "?msd_fib At t<n => RF[i+t]=RF[j+t]":
def rfrevcheck "?msd_fib As,t (s>=i & t>=j &
   s+t+1=i+j+n) => RF[s]=RF[t]":
eval rfprop "?msd_fib Ei,n n>=1 & $rffactoreq(i,i+n,n)
   & $rfrevcheck(i,i+2*n,n)":
```

We get the result FALSE.                                                        □

*Exercise* 72   Use Walnut to prove these properties of the Rote-Fibonacci word:

(a) For $n \geq 0$ we have $\mathbf{f}[n+1] = \begin{cases} 1, & \text{if } \mathbf{rf}[n+1] = \mathbf{rf}[n]; \\ 0, & \text{otherwise.} \end{cases}$

(b) All squares in the Rote-Fibonacci word are of order $F_{3n+1}$ for $n \geq 0$, and each such order occurs.

(c) All cubes in the Rote-Fibonacci word are of order $F_{3n+1}$ for $n \geq 1$, and each such order occurs.

(d) There are palindromes of all lengths $\geq 0$ in the Rote-Fibonacci word.

(e) There are antipalindromes of all orders $\geq 0$ in the Rote-Fibonacci word.

(f) All antisquares in the Rote-Fibonacci word are of order $F_{3n+2}$ and $F_{3n+3}$ for $n \geq 0$, and all such orders occur.

(g) The Rote-Fibonacci word is mirror invariant.

(h) The critical exponent of the Rote-Fibonacci word is $(5 + \sqrt{5})/2$.

(i) The Rote-Fibonacci word also avoids the pattern $x\, x^R\, x^R$.

## 8.5.19 Avoiding other patterns

Mercaş, Ochem, Samsonov, and Shur [262] gave examples of binary cube-free words avoiding various kinds of patterns. With Walnut we can provide simple computational proofs of their results.

Let's start with the Stewart choral word **sc**, introduced in Section 2.4.13. We already saw, in Section 8.5.7, that it avoids cubes. Let us show it also avoids the pattern $xxyyxx$. Here $x$ must be nonempty, but $y$ is allowed to be empty.

The idea is to let $|x| = m$ and $|y| = n$. Then we can test the existence of the pattern with the following Walnut code. Carefully examine the ideas to see how to handle similar patterns.

```
# SC avoids the pattern xxyyxx, m = |x|, n = |y|
def factoreq "?msd_3 At (t<n) => SC[i+t]=SC[j+t]":
eval xxyyxx "?msd_3 Ei,m,n (m>=1) & $factoreq(i,i+m,m) &
    $factoreq(i+2*m,i+2*m+n,n) & $factoreq(i,i+2*m+2*n,2*n)":
```

For a generalization of this result, see [149].

Here are Walnut proofs for the other patterns in the paper [262]: $xxyxyy$, $xxyyxyx$, and $xyxxyxy$. For each one we construct a different binary automatic sequence and test it.

```
#Avoid the pattern xxyxyy
morphism h1 "0->0110010 1->1001101":
promote H1 h1:
def factoreq "?msd_7 At (t<n) => H1[i+t]=H1[j+t]":
eval testh1 "?msd_7 Ei,m,n (m>=1) & $factoreq(i,i+m,m) &
    $factoreq(i,i+2*m+n,m) & $factoreq(i+2*m,i+3*m+n,n) &
    $factoreq(i+3*m+n,i+3*m+2*n,n)":
eval cubetesth1 "?msd_7 Ei,n (n>=1) & $factoreq(i,i+n,2*n)":

#Avoid the pattern xxyyxyx
morphism h2 "0->01001 1->10110":
promote H2 h2:
def factoreq "?msd_5 At (t<n) => H2[i+t]=H2[j+t]":
eval testh2 "?msd_5 Ei,m,n (m>=1) & $factoreq(i,i+m,m) &
    $factoreq(i,i+2*m+2*n,m) & $factoreq(i,i+3*m+3*n,m) &
    $factoreq(i+2*m,i+2*m+n,n) & $factoreq(i+2*m,i+3*m+3*n,n)":
eval cubetesth2 "?msd_5 Ei,n (n>=1) & $factoreq(i,i+n,2*n)":
```

```
#Avoid the pattern xyxxyxy
morphism h3 "0->010011 1->011001":
promote H3 h3:
def factoreq "?msd_6 At (t<n) => H3[i+t]=H3[j+t]":
eval testh3 "?msd_6 Ei,m,n (m>=1) & $factoreq(i,i+m+n,m) &
    $factoreq(i,i+2*m+n,m) & $factoreq(i,i+3*m+2*n,m) &
    $factoreq(i+m,i+3*m+n,n) & $factoreq(i+m,i+4*m+2*n,n)":
eval cubetesth3 "?msd_6 Ei,n (n>=1) & $factoreq(i,i+n,2*n)":
```

## 8.5.20 Least periods

Given a factor $x[i..i + n - 1]$ of an automatic sequence, we may determine its least period as follows:

$$\textsc{Peri}(i, n, p) := (p > 0) \wedge (p \leq n)$$
$$\wedge \; \forall j \, (j \geq i \wedge j + p < i + n) \implies x[j] = x[j + p]$$
$$\textsc{Lper}(i, n, p) := \textsc{Peri}(i, n, p) \wedge \forall q \, (q < p) \implies \neg \textsc{Peri}(i, n, q).$$

Here $\textsc{Peri}(i, n, p)$ asserts that $x[i..i + n - 1]$ has period $p$ and $\textsc{Lper}(i, n, p)$ asserts that $x[i..i + n - 1]$ has least period $p$.[2]

Currie and Saari [105] proved that for the Thue-Morse sequence **t** and every period $p$ there is a factor with least period $p$. We can check this as follows:

```
def tmperi "p>0 & p<=n & Aj (j>=i & j+p<i+n) => T[j]=T[j+p]":
def tmlper "$tmperi(i,n,p)&(Aq (q>=1&q<p)=>~$tmperi(i,n,q))":
eval tmleastpcheck "Ap p>=1 => Ei,n n>=1 & $tmlper(i,n,p)":
```

This evaluates to TRUE.

It is sometimes the case that the set of least periods, considered over all nonempty factors, is a relatively sparse set. For example, for the Fibonacci word **f**, the only possible periods are of length $F_n$ for $n \geq 2$, a fact first observed by Saari [328, 105]. We can prove it in Walnut as follows:

```
def fibperi "?msd_fib p>0 & p<=n & Aj (j>=i & j+p<i+n)
    => F[j]=F[j+p]":
def fiblper "?msd_fib $fibperi(i,n,p) & (Aq (q>=1 & q<p)
    => ~$fibperi(i,n,q))":
def fibleastp "?msd_fib Ei,n n>=1 & $fiblper(i,n,p)":
```

The automaton produced by the last command recognizes the language $10^*$, which represents $F_n$ for $n \geq 2$ in Fibonacci representation.

The analogous characterization for the Tribonacci word is far more complex. We use the Walnut code

---

[2] Some material in this section is reprinted from [168] by permission from Springer Nature.

```
def tribperi "?msd_trib p>0 & p<=n & Aj (j>=i & j+p<i+n) =>
   TR[j]=TR[j+p]":
def triblper "?msd_trib $tribperi(i,n,p) & (Aq (q>=1 & q<p) =>
   ~$tribperi(i,n,q))":
def tribleastp "?msd_trib Ei,n n>=1 & $triblper(i,n,p)":
```

and get the automaton of 24 states depicted in Figure 8.12.

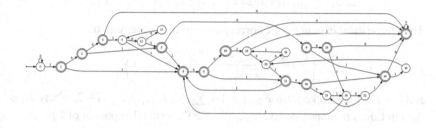

Figure 8.12 Least periods of the Tribonacci word.

## 8.5.21 Critical exponents

Recall that the critical exponent of an infinite word **x** is $\sup\{\exp(w) : w \in \text{Fac}(\mathbf{x})\}$. We saw in Section 8.5.11 how to test whether a given automatic sequence contains a power with a specific rational exponent $p/q$. With that idea, we can usually compute the critical exponent of an automatic sequence, if it is rational and we already have a good guess as to what it is.

In fact, for $k$-automatic sequences, it is known that the critical exponent is computable [335]. However, this algorithm is not currently implemented in Walnut.

For words that are Fibonacci- and Tribonacci-automatic, however, the critical exponent may not be rational. For these words we need a different approach.

In the previous section we saw how to compute the least periods of an infinite word using the formulas PERI and LPER. For each least period $p$, we can find the length $\ell(p)$ of the longest word having this as least period. The formula LONGEST$(n, p)$ asserts that $n$ is the length of the longest factor having $p$ as its least period.

$$\text{LONGEST}(n, p) := (\exists i \ \text{LPER}(i, n, p)) \wedge (\forall r, i \ \text{LPER}(i, r, p) \implies r \leq n).$$

Then the critical exponent of **x** is $\sup_{p \in P} \ell(p)/p$.

Here is the Walnut code for the specific case of the Fibonacci word:

```
def fibperi "?msd_fib p>0 & p<=n & Aj j+p<n => F[i+j]=F[i+j+p]":
def fiblper "?msd_fib $fibperi(i,n,p) & Aq q<p =>
  ~$fibperi(i,n,q)":
def fiblongest "?msd_fib (Ei $fiblper(i,n,p)) &
  (Ar,i $fiblper(i,r,p) => r<=n)":
```

Running this gives us the following language for LONGEST($n, p$):

$$([1,0] \cup [0,0][0,1]([1,0][0,0])^*[0,0])[1,0].$$

Thus the critical exponent of **f** corresponds to the supremum of

$$\left\{ \frac{F_{2n+4} + 1 + \sum_{2 \le i \le n} F_{2i+1}}{F_{2n+2}} : n \ge 1 \right\}.$$

But it is readily checked that $F_{2n+4} + 1 + \sum_{2 \le i \le n} F_{2i+1} = L_{2n+3} - 2$, where $L_n$ is the $n$th Lucas number (see Exercise 15). So the critical exponent of **f** is

$$\sup\{(L_{2n+3} - 2)/F_{2n+2} : n \ge 1\} = (5 + \sqrt{5})/2,$$

a result originally due to Mignosi and Pirillo [263].

There are many interesting variations on the critical exponent that can be studied using the same kinds of ideas. For example, ice(**x**), the "initial critical exponent", is equal to sup{exp($w$) : $w$ is a prefix of **x**}. Let us compute this for **t**. To do so, we compute for each $p$ the length of the longest prefix having $p$ as its least period.

```
def pptm "p>0 & p<=n & Aj j+p<n => T[j]=T[j+p]":
def lpertm "$pptm(n,p) & Aq q<p => ~$pptm(n,q)":
def longestm "$lpertm(n,p) & (Ar $lpertm(r,p) => r<=n)":
```

Inspection of the result shows there are four possible accepting paths:

- [1,0][0,1][1,1][0,0]$^*$, corresponding to the exponent 5/3.
- [1,1] and [1,1][0,0], corresponding to the exponent 1.
- [1,1][1,0][0,1][0,0]$^*$, corresponding to the exponent 6/5.

So ice(**t**) = 5/3.

*Exercise 73*   The "lazy" or "three-in-a-row" Tower of Hanoi sequence is defined as the fixed point of the morphism $0 \to 010$, $1 \to 321$, $2 \to 012$, $3 \to 323$. See [13].

Determine the critical exponent of this sequence.

*Exercise 74*   Consider the morphism defined by $0 \to 012$, $1 \to 103$, $2 \to 123$, $3 \to 032$, and the two words that are fixed points starting with 0 and 1. Compute their critical exponent.

### 8.5.22 Circular factors

Recall that $\exp(w) = |w| / \operatorname{per}(w)$, where $\operatorname{per}(w)$ is the length of the shortest period of $w$.

The *circular critical exponent* of a finite or infinite word $x$ is defined to be

$$\operatorname{cce}(x) := \sup\{\exp(w) : w \in \operatorname{Fac}(\operatorname{Conj}(x))\}.$$

The term "circular" here refers to regarding $x$ as a "circular word" where the last symbol wraps around to the first.

In this section we prove the following result of Aberkane and Currie:

**Theorem 8.5.11** *For all $n \geq 1$ there is a length-$n$ factor $x$ of the Thue-Morse sequence $\mathbf{t}$ satisfying $\operatorname{cce}(x) \leq 5/2$.*

*Proof* We start by developing a useful first-order logical formula with free variables $i, m, n, p, s$. We want it to assert that

in the circular word given by the length-$n$ word starting

at position $s$ in the Thue-Morse sequence, there is a factor     (8.2)

$w$ of length $m$ and (not necessarily least) period $p \geq 1$ starting at position $i$.

In order to do this, we will conceptually repeat the word $x = \mathbf{t}[s..s + n - 1]$ twice, as depicted in Figure 8.13, where the black vertical line separates the two copies. The factor $w$ is indicated in grey; it may or may not straddle the boundary between the two copies. Here indices should be interpreted as

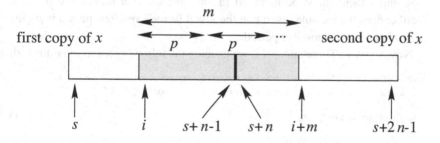

Figure 8.13 Factor of a circular word of length $n$. Reprinted from [359] by permission from EDP Sciences.

"wrapping around"; the index $s + n + j$ is the same as $s + j$ for $0 \leq j < n$. Then the assertion that $w$ has period $p$ potentially corresponds to three different ranges of $j$:

- Both $j$ and $j + p$ lie in the first copy of $x$, so we compare $\mathbf{t}[j]$ to $\mathbf{t}[j + p]$ for all $j$ in this range: $i \leq j < \min(s + n - p, i + m - p)$.

- $j$ lies in the first copy of $x$, but $j + p$ lies in the second copy, so we compare $t[j]$ to $t[j + p - n]$ for all $j$ in this range: $\max(i, s + n - p) \le j < \min(s + n, i + m - p)$.
- Both $j$ and $j + p$ lie in the second copy of $x$, so we compare $t[j - n]$ to $t[j + p - n]$ for all $j$ in this range: $\max(i, s + n) \le j < i + m - p$.

Putting this all together, we get the following logical formula that asserts the truth of statement (8.2):

$$\mathrm{crep}(i, m, n, p, s) :=$$
$$(\forall j((j \ge i) \wedge (j < s + n - p) \wedge (j < i + m - p)) \implies t[j] = t[j + p])$$
$$\wedge \; (\forall j((j \ge i) \wedge (j < s + n) \wedge (j \ge s + n - p) \wedge (j < i + m - p))$$
$$\implies t[j] = t[j + p - n]) \wedge (\forall j((j \ge i) \wedge (j \ge s + n)$$
$$\wedge \; (j < i + m - p)) \implies t[j - n] = t[j + p - n]).$$

The translation into `Walnut` is as follows:

```
def crep "(Aj (j>=i & j+p<s+n & j+p<i+m) => T[j]=T[j+p]) &
   (Aj (j>=i & j<s+n & j+p>=s+n & j+p<i+m) =>
   T[j]=T[(j+p)-n]) & (Aj (j>=i & j>=s+n & j+p<i+m)
   => T[j-n]=T[(j+p)-n])":
```

The resulting automaton implementing $\mathrm{crep}(i, m, n, p, s)$ has 1423 states. Note that our formula does not impose conditions such as $p \ge 1$ or $p \le n$ or $m \le n$, which are required for crep to make sense. These conditions (or stronger ones that imply them) must be included in any formula that makes use of crep. Neither does the formula assert that the given factor's *smallest* period is $p$; just that $p$ is one of the possible periods.

Now, to prove Theorem 8.5.11, we execute the following `Walnut` command:

```
eval aberkane "An n>=1 => Es Am,p,i (p>=1 & m>=1 & m<=n &
   i>=s & i<s+n & $crep(i,m,n,p,s)) => 2*m <= 5*p":
```

which evaluates to TRUE.                                                    □

This proof is from [359].

### 8.5.23 Disposable positions

As we saw in Section 8.5.13, it's possible to prove properties of variations on factors of automatic sequences.

Milosevic and Rampersad [267] introduced the notion of disposable position in an infinite squarefree word. The position $k$ is *disposable* if removing the symbol at that position preserves squarefreeness of the word.

We can test this for the word **vtm** by separately considering the positions lying in $\mathbf{x}[i..i + n - 1]$ and in $\mathbf{x}[i + n..i + 2n - 1]$. Let us carry this out for the word **vtm**:

```
def vfactoreq "At t<n => VTM[i+t]=VTM[j+t]":
def dispos "~Ei,n n>=1 & ((i<=k & k<=i+n &
   $vfactoreq(i,i+n+1,k-i) & $vfactoreq(k+1,n+k+1,(n+i)-k))
   | (i+n<=k & k<=i+2*n & $vfactoreq(i,i+n,k-(i+n)) &
   $vfactoreq(k-n,k+1,(i+2*n)-k)))":
```

The resulting automaton encodes the positions of **vtm** that are disposable, and is depicted in Figure 8.14.

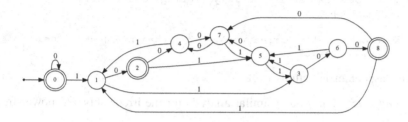

Figure 8.14 Disposable positions in **vtm**.

### 8.5.24 Irreducibly overlap-free words

Harju [189] introduced the notion of irreducibly squarefree word; this is a finite word of length $\geq 3$ that is squarefree, but deleting any symbol (except the first and last) causes a square to appear. Analogously we could consider the notion of *irreducibly overlap-free* word. For example, 101101 is irreducibly overlap-free, as deleting any of the interior letters causes an occurrence of either 111 or 10101.

We can now prove a theorem of Przybocki [304]:

**Theorem 8.5.12** *The Thue-Morse word contains irreducibly overlap-free factors of length precisely* $\{6, 8, 9, 10\} \cup \{n : n \geq 12\}$.

*Proof* We use the following Walnut commands:

```
def delsp "(i+t<j => T[i+t]=@1) & (i+t>=j => T[i+t+1]=@1)":
# delsp(i,j,t) = true if tth symbol of T[i..infinity] after
# deleting T[j] is equal to 1
```

```
def deloverlap "Ac c<=s => ($delsp(i,j,r+c) <=>
  $delsp(i,j,r+c+s))":
# deloverlap(i,j,r,s) = true if there is an overlap
# beginning at position r and of order s in
# T[i..infinity] after deleting T[j]

def delover "Er,s (s>=1) & (r+2*s+2<=n) & $deloverlap(i,j,r,s)":
# delover(i,j,n) = true if there's a nonempty overlap in
# T[i..i+n-1]$ after deleting T[j]

def irredover "Aj (i<j & j+1<i+n) => $delover(i,j,n)":
# true if T[i..i+n-1] is irreducibly overlap-free

def irredoverlength "(n>=3) & Ei $irredover(i,n)":
# Thue-Morse has an irreducibly overlap-free factor
# of length n

eval checkover "An $irredoverlength(n) <=> n=6 | n=8 | n=9
  | n=10 | n>=12":
```

The last command returns TRUE.                                    □

*Exercise 75*    Carry out a similar analysis for the irreducibly 7/3-power-free words.

## 8.5.25 Antipowers

Fici, Restivo, Silva, and Zamboni [148] introduced the notion of *r-antipower:* *r* consecutive blocks of the same length, no two of which are the same. For example, orange is a 3-antipower, but banana is not.

Fici, Postic, and Silva proved [146] proved that the Cantor word **ca** avoids 11-antipowers. We can improve this result optimally to:

**Theorem 8.5.13**    *The Cantor word* **ca** *contains no* 10-*antipowers, but does contain a* 9-*antipower.*

*Proof*    It is easy to verify that

$$\mathbf{ca}[157..246] = (0000010100)\ (0101000000)\ (0001010001)$$
$$(0100000000)\ (0000000000)\ (0000000001)\ (0100010100)$$
$$(0000000101)\ (0001010000)$$

is a 9-antipower. To show that **ca** has no 10-antipowers, it suffices to show that every block of size $10n$ can be split into 10 consecutive blocks of size $n$, with at least two being identical. In general, proving this requires comparison of $10 \cdot 9/2 = 45$ different pairs of blocks. However, for the particular case of the Cantor word **ca**, we can get by with comparison of only 14 blocks, as follows:

```
def cfaceq "?msd_3 At t<n => CA[i+t]=CA[j+t]":
eval cno10 "?msd_3 Ai,n n>=1 => (
    $cfaceq(i+0*n,i+1*n,n) | $cfaceq(i+0*n,i+5*n,n) |
    $cfaceq(i+2*n,i+3*n,n) | $cfaceq(i+2*n,i+8*n,n) |
    $cfaceq(i+3*n,i+4*n,n) | $cfaceq(i+3*n,i+7*n,n) |
    $cfaceq(i+3*n,i+9*n,n) | $cfaceq(i+4*n,i+5*n,n) |
    $cfaceq(i+4*n,i+9*n,n) | $cfaceq(i+5*n,i+6*n,n) |
    $cfaceq(i+5*n,i+8*n,n) | $cfaceq(i+6*n,i+7*n,n) |
    $cfaceq(i+7*n,i+8*n,n) | $cfaceq(i+8*n,i+9*n,n))":
```

which evaluates to TRUE.                                               □

For more information, see [315].

*Exercise* 76   Define the characteristic sequence of the powers of 4 in Walnut, and show that it has 3-antipowers but no 4-antipowers.

## 8.5.26  Thue's irreducible words

Thue [374] called a word **x** *irreducible* if every pair of consecutive occurrences of the same length-$n$ factor, say $x[i..i + n - 1]$ and $x[j..j + n - 1]$, with $i < j$, has at least two symbols separating the two occurrences, that is, satisfies the inequality $j \geq i + n + 2$. It is easy to see that there are no infinite irreducible squarefree words over a three-letter alphabet. Thue constructed a family of such words over a 4-letter alphabet.

We can easily find such a word using automatic breadth-first search and Walnut. Breadth-first search using a criterion of being 2-automatic with at most 8 states quickly converges on six candidate words, one of which is

$$0120321031230210312032130123021031203\cdots,$$

which a DFAO guesser says can be generated with 8 states. It has the morphic representation $\tau(g^{\omega}(0))$, where $g$ maps

| | | | |
|---|---|---|---|
| $0 \to 01$; | $1 \to 23$; | $2 \to 45$; | $3 \to 63$; |
| $4 \to 41$; | $5 \to 27$; | $6 \to 05$; | $7 \to 67$ |

and $\tau(01234567) = 01203213$. We can verify its correctness with Walnut as follows:

```
morphism g "0->01 1->23 2->45 3->63 4->41 5->27 6->05 7->67":
promote GG g:
morphism tau "0->0 1->1 2->2 3->0 4->3 5->2 6->1 7->3":
image TI tau GG:
def tifaceq "At t<n => TI[i+t]=TI[j+t]":
eval titest "An,i,j (n>=1 & i<j & $tifaceq(i,j,n)) => j>=i+n+2":
```

Here titest returns TRUE, so indeed this infinite word has the desired property of Thue irreducibility. For more about this word, see Section 10.8.17.

## 8.6 Conjugates, palindromes, and borders

### 8.6.1 Conjugates

Recall that finite words $y, z$ are conjugates if one is a rotation of the other. We can construct a first-order logical formula asserting that $x[j..j + n - 1]$ is a conjugate of $x[i..i + n - 1]$ as follows:

$$\exists t \, (t \le n) \wedge \text{FACTOREQ}(j, i + t, n - t) \wedge \text{FACTOREQ}(i, (j + n) - t, t).$$

(There is a small amount of subtlety here: we write $t \le n$ and not $t < n$ because we want the formula to work correctly when $n = 0$.) We say a factor $y$ of $x$ is *cyclically isolated* if no conjugate of $y$, 0 except $y$ itself, belongs to $x$.

We can find those $n$ for which there is a cyclically isolated factor of length $n$ of the Thue-Morse sequence $t$, as follows:

```
def tmconj "Et t<=n & $tmfactoreq(j,i+t,n-t) &
    $tmfactoreq(i,(j+n)-t,t)":
def tmcu "Aj $tmconj(i,j,n) => $tmfactoreq(i,j,n)":
def tmculen "Ei $tmcu(i,n)":
```

The resulting DFA accepts all $n$ except $0, 3, 4, 5, 9$, so there are cyclically isolated factors of $t$ for all lengths $\ge 10$.

Now let's consider another property of words. Say that an infinite word $x$ has property $P_i$ if, for all factors $w$ of length $\ge i$, some conjugate of $w$ does not appear in $x$. Bell and Madill [38] constructed an infinite word over a 12-letter alphabet satisfying $P_2$. Gamard, Ochem, Richomme, and Séébold [160] constructed

  (a) a 2-automatic binary sequence with property $P_5$.
  (b) a 2-automatic sequence over $\{0, 1, 2, 3\}$ with property $P_3$.
  (c) a 2-automatic sequence over $\{0, 1, 2, 3, 4, 5\}$ with property $P_2$.

Finally, Badkobeh and Ochem [25] constructed a sequence over $\{0, 1, 2, 3, 4\}$ with property $P_2$.

We can verify properties (a)–(c) above with Walnut. To do so, we need to construct DFAOs for the corresponding sequences, which is not difficult based on the definitions in [160].

```
morphism gam "0->01 1->21 2->03 3->23":
promote B4 gam:
```

```
morphism g2 "0->0000101001110110100 1->0011100010100111101
   2->0000111100010110100 3->0011110110100111101":
morphism g3 "0->0010 1->1122 2->0200 3->1212":
morphism g6 "0->01230 1->24134 2->52340 3->24513":
image G2B4 g2 B4:
image G3B4 g3 B4:
image G6B4 g6 B4:

def gamard6factoreq "Au,v (i+v=j+u & u>=i & u<i+n) =>
   G6B4[u]=G6B4[v]":
def gamard6shift "$gamard6factoreq(j,i+t,n-t) &
   $gamard6factoreq(i,(j+n)-t,t)":
def gamard6conj "Et t<=n & $gamard6shift(i,j,n,t)":
def gamard6allconj "At t<=n => Ej $gamard6shift(i,j,n,t)":
eval gamard6check "An n>=2 => ~(Ei $gamard6allconj(i,n))":

def gamard3factoreq "Au,v (i+v=j+u & u>=i & u<i+n) =>
   G3B4[u]=G3B4[v]":
def gamard3shift "$gamard3factoreq(j,i+t,n-t) &
   $gamard3factoreq(i,(j+n)-t,t)":
def gamard3conj "Et t<=n & $gamard3shift(i,j,n,t)":
def gamard3allconj "At t<=n => Ej $gamard3shift(i,j,n,t)":
eval gamard3check "An n>=3 => ~(Ei $gamard3allconj(i,n))":

def gamard2factoreq "Au,v (i+v=j+u & u>=i & u<i+n) =>
   G2B4[u]=G2B4[v]":
def gamard2shift "$gamard2factoreq(j,i+t,n-t) &
   $gamard2factoreq(i,(j+n)-t,t)":
def gamard2conj "Et t<=n & $gamard2shift(i,j,n,t)":
def gamard2allconj "At t<=n => Ej $gamard2shift(i,j,n,t)":
eval gamard2check "An n>=5 => ~(Ei $gamard2allconj(i,n))":
```

The last check took 300 Gigs of storage and 9329 seconds of CPU time. This was one of the biggest computations I ever did with `Walnut`.

### 8.6.2 Mesosomes

A *mesosome* is a word of the form $xx'$ with $x'$ a conjugate of $x$ and $x \neq x'$; the English word `mesosome` is itself an example. See [100].

We can determine for which $n$ there is a mesosome factor $t[i..i + 2n - 1]$ of the Thue-Morse word, as follows:

```
def tmconj "Et t<=n & $tmfactoreq(j,i+t,n-t) &
   $tmfactoreq(i,(j+n)-t,t)":
def tmmeso "$tmconj(i,i+n,n) & ~$tmfactoreq(i,i+n,n)":
def tmmesolength "Ei $tmmeso(i,n)":
```

The result is a 12-state automaton, accepting and rejecting infinitely many $n$.

### 8.6.3 Palindromes

Palindromes in words have a very long history of being studied; for example, see [6, 150, 78].

It is easy to write a first-order logic formula for a sequence to have a palindromic factor of length $n$:

$$\exists i \, \forall t \, (t < n) \implies \mathbf{x}[i + t] = \mathbf{x}[(i + n) - (t + 1)]. \tag{8.3}$$

We can translate this directly to Walnut, and evaluate it on the Thue-Morse sequence:

```
def thuepal "Ei At t<n => T[i+t] = T[(i+n)-(t+1)]":
```

The resulting automaton is depicted in Figure 8.15. By inspection of this au-

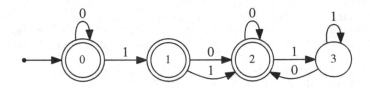

Figure 8.15 Palindromes in Thue-Morse.

tomaton, we easily see that the set of lengths of palindromic factors is $\{1, 3\} \cup \{2n : n \geq 0\}$.

*Exercise* 77    Verify this last claim with Walnut.

The formula we gave in (8.3) is quite natural, but because it requires indexing by three different variables, it can be very slow to evaluate in some cases.

We can find an equivalent faster formula by observing that when we check to see if $\mathbf{x}[i..i+n-1]$ is a palindrome, the indices we compare—$i$ against $i+n-1$, $i + 1$ against $i + n - 2$, and so forth—always sum to $2i + n - 1$. This gives the following alternative formula:

$$\text{PAL}(i, n) := \exists i \, \forall s, t \, (s \geq i \, \wedge \, t \geq i \, \wedge \, s + t + 1 = 2i + n) \implies \mathbf{x}[s] = \mathbf{x}[t],$$

which will run much more quickly on many examples, particularly if the automaton for $\mathbf{x}$ is large.

As an example, let us prove the following result of Chuan [88]:

**Theorem 8.6.1** *There exist palindromes of every length $\geq 0$ in the Fibonacci word* **f**.

*Proof* We use the `Walnut` formula

```
eval fibpal "?msd_fib An Ei As,t (s>=i & t>=i &
   s+t+1=2*i+n) => F[s]=F[t]":
```

which evaluates to TRUE.  □

We could also characterize the positions and lengths of all nonempty palindromes, using the formula

```
eval pal "?msd_fib n>=1 & As,t (s>=i & t>=i & s+t+1=2*i+n)
   => F[s]=F[t]":
```

The resulting 20-state automaton is not particularly enlightening, and so is omitted here.

Next, we turn to a result of Droubay [123]:

**Theorem 8.6.2** *The Fibonacci word* **f** *contains exactly one palindromic factor of length n if n is even, and exactly two palindromes of length n if n is odd.*

*Proof* First, we construct a formula for the lengths $n$ for which there is exactly one palindromic factor of length $n$:

$$\exists i \, (\text{PAL}(i, n) \wedge \forall j \, \text{PAL}(j, n) \implies \text{FACTOREQ}(i, j, n)).$$

This asserts that the word $\mathbf{x}[i..i + n - 1]$ is a palindrome, and all words of the same length that are palindromes must equal this word.

Next, we construct a formula for the length $n$ for which there are exactly two palindromic factors of length $n$:

$$\exists i, j \, (\text{PAL}(i, n) \wedge \text{PAL}(j, n) \wedge \neg\text{FACTOREQ}(i, j, n)$$

$$\wedge \, \forall k \, \text{PAL}(k, n) \implies (\text{FACTOREQ}(i, k, n) \vee \text{FACTOREQ}(j, k, n))).$$

This formula asserts first, that there are two distinct palindromes of length $n$ and second, that every length-$n$ palindrome must be one of these two.

Now that we have these formulas, we can check that the first specifies all even numbers and the second specifies all odd numbers. Here is the `Walnut` code:

```
def fpal "?msd_fib As,t (s>=i&t>=i&s+t+1=2*i+n) => F[s]=F[t]":
def feven "?msd_fib Em n=2*m":
def fodd "?msd_fib Em n=2*m+1":
def ffactoreq "?msd_fib At t<n => F[i+t]=F[j+t]":
def onepal "?msd_fib Ei ($fpal(i,n) & Aj $fpal(j,n) =>
```

```
    $ffactoreq(i,j,n))":
def twopal "?msd_fib Ei,j ($fpal(i,n) & $fpal(j,n) &
    (~$ffactoreq(i,j,n)) & Ak ($fpal(k,n)=>($ffactoreq(i,k,n)|
    $ffactoreq(j,k,n))))":
eval checkonepal "?msd_fib An $onepal(n) <=> $feven(n)":
eval checktwopal "?msd_fib An $twopal(n) <=> $fodd(n)":
```

When we evaluate this, we obtain the result TRUE for the last two formulas. This proves the result of Droubay. □

The prefixes of **f** are factors of particular interest. Let us determine which prefixes of **f** are palindromes:

**Theorem 8.6.3** *The prefix* **f**$[0..n-1]$ *of length n is a palindrome if and only if* $n = F_i - 2$ *for some* $i \geq 3$.

*Proof* First, we construct a Walnut formula isfib which checks if $s$ is a Fibonacci number. Then we verify that every length of a palindrome is a Fibonacci number minus 2.

```
reg isfib msd_fib "0*10*":
eval fpalp "?msd_fib An $fpal(0,n)<=>(Es ($isfib(s) & s=n+2))":
```

□

*Exercise 78* Prove an analogous theorem for the prefixes of the Tribonacci word that are palindromes: a length-$n$ prefix of **tr** is a palindrome iff there exists $s$ such that $n = (T_{s+2} + T_s - 3)/2$.

*Exercise 79* Show that the word **vtm** contains no even-length palindromes, but contains palindromes of every odd length.

*Exercise 80* Find an infinite binary word that is not ultimately periodic, such that it has no word $w$, $|w| \geq 8$, with a conjugate that is a palindrome.

### 8.6.4 Maximal palindromes

There are two distinct notions of maximal palindromes in words. One involves *maximal occurrences*: an occurrence $\mathbf{x}[i..i+n-1]$ is maximal if it is a palindrome, but $\mathbf{x}[i-1..i+n]$ is not [206]. The other involves *maximal palindromes*: a word $y = \mathbf{x}[i..i+n-1]$ is maximal if it is a palindrome, but for all $a$, the word $aya$ does not occur in $\mathbf{x}$.

A formula for checking if $\mathbf{x}[i..i+n-1]$ is a maximal occurrence is therefore

$$\text{Pal}(i, n) \wedge \neg\text{Pal}(i-1, n+2).$$

A formula for checking if $x[i..i + n - 1]$ is a maximal palindrome is

$$\text{PAL}(i, n) \land \lnot(\exists j \, \text{FACTOREQ}(i, j, n) \land x[j - 1] = x[j + n]).$$

In Walnut we can check these for the Thue-Morse sequence as follows:

```
def tmpal "At t<n => T[i+t] = T[(i+n)-(t+1)]":
def tmfactoreq "At t<n => T[i+t]=T[j+t]":
def mpotm "Ei $tmpal(i,n) & ~$tmpal(i-1,n+2)":
def mptm "Ei $tmpal(i,n) & ~(Ej $tmfactoreq(i,j,n) &
   T[j-1]=T[j+n])":
```

For the Thue-Morse sequence we find that there are maximal occurrences of palindromes of length 0 and $4^n$ and $3 \cdot 4^n$ for $n \geq 0$, while there are maximal palindromes of length $3 \cdot 4^n$ for $n \geq 0$ only.

In contrast, for the Rudin-Shapiro sequence there are only finitely many of these. The following Walnut code shows that there are maximal palindromic occurrences of lengths $0, 1, 2, 3, 5, 6, 7, 10, 14$ only, and there are maximal palindromes of lengths $5, 10, 14$ only.

```
def rspal "At t<n => RS[i+t] = RS[(i+n)-(t+1)]":
def rsfaceq "At t<n => RS[i+t]=RS[j+t]":
def mpors "Ei $rspal(i,n) & ~$rspal(i-1,n+2)":
def mprs "Ei $rspal(i,n) & ~(Ej $rsfaceq(i,j,n) &
   RS[j-1]=RS[j+n])":
```

See [336] for more examples.

### 8.6.5 Factorization into palindromes

For each $k$, we can make a first-order formula that says that the length-$n$ prefix $x[0..n - 1]$ can be factorized as the concatenation of $k$ nonempty palindromes. For example, for $x = t$ and $k = 3$, we have

```
def ispal "Au,v (u>=j & u<k & u+v+1=j+k) => T[u]=T[v]":
def threepal "Ej,k j>0 & j<k & k<n & $ispal(0,j) &
   $ispal(j,k) & $ispal(k,n)":
```

This gives a 22-state DFA recognizing the set of valid $n$ for $t$.

*Exercise 81*    What modifications would be needed to allow the palindromes to be empty?

*Exercise 82*    Determine the factors of the Thue-Morse sequence that are the products of two (possibly empty) palindromes. (Compare [52].)

### 8.6.6 Mirror invariance

The property of mirror invariance of a sequence $\mathbf{x}$ states that if $w$ is a factor of $\mathbf{x}$, then so is $w^R$. This is also called *reversal closed*. A useful formula is

$$\text{RevChk}(i, j, n) := \forall s, t\, (s \geq i \wedge t \geq j \wedge s + t + 1 = i + j + n) \implies \mathbf{x}[s] = \mathbf{x}[t],$$

which is true iff $\mathbf{x}[i..i + n - 1] = \mathbf{x}[j..j + n - 1]^R$.

Let us now check that the Thue-Morse sequence is mirror invariant:

```
def revchktm "As,t (s>=i & t>=j & s+t+1=i+j+n) => T[s]=T[t]":
eval tmmi "Ai,n Ej $revchktm(i,j,n)":
```

This returns TRUE.

*Exercise* 83    Which of the sequences that we have studied so far are mirror invariant?

### 8.6.7 Near-palindromes

Define a word $x$ to be a *near-palindrome* if $x$ differs from $x^R$ in exactly two positions; these words are of interest in genomics. Let us determine for which lengths $n$ the Fibonacci word $\mathbf{f}$ has a near-palindrome of length $n$:

```
def fibnearpal "?msd_fib Ek 2*k+1<n & F[i+k]!=F[(i+n)-(k+1)] &
    At (2*t+1<n & t!=k) => F[i+t]=F[(i+n)-(t+1)]":
def fibnearpallen "?msd_fib Ei $fibnearpal(i,n)":
```

The resulting Fibonacci automaton has 13 states; it is depicted in Figure 8.16.

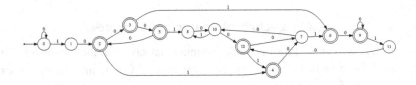

Figure 8.16 Fibonacci automaton for lengths of near-palindromes in the Fibonacci word.

### 8.6.8 Reversal-free sequences

A sequence $\mathbf{x}$ is *k-reversal-free* if whenever $w$ is a factor of $\mathbf{x}$, and $|w| \geq k$, the word $w^R$ is not a factor of $\mathbf{x}$. Clearly no 1-reversal-free sequences exist. Over a ternary alphabet, the only 2-reversal-free sequences are periodic. If we want an aperiodic 3-reversal-free sequence, we can get one by applying the morphism $0 \rightarrow 0012$, $1 \rightarrow 0112$ to the Thue-Morse sequence [152, 153]. Then we can check to see that the resulting sequence is aperiodic and 3-reversal-free as follows:

```
morphism revmor "0->0012 1->0112":
image FS revmor T:
def fsrevchk "As,t (s>=i & t>=j & s+t+1=i+j+n) => FS[s]=FS[t]":
eval fsrevfree "Ai,j,n (n>=3) => ~$fsrevchk(i,j,n)":
eval fsaper "~Ep,n (p>=1) & (Ai (i>=n) => FS[i]=FS[i+p])":
```

which returns TRUE.

### 8.6.9 Antipalindromes

An *antipalindrome* is a binary word $x$ satisfying $x = \overline{x^R}$. Let us construct a first-order formula for $\mathbf{x}[i..i + n - 1]$ being an antipalindrome:

$$\text{ANTIPAL}(i, n) := \exists i\, \forall s, t\, (s \geq i \wedge t \geq i \wedge s + t + 1 = 2i + n) \implies \mathbf{x}[s] \neq \mathbf{x}[t].$$

Using this formula, we can prove

**Theorem 8.6.4** *The only nonempty antipalindromes in the Fibonacci word* **f** *are* 01, 10, (01)$^2$, *and* (10)$^2$.

*Proof* Let us construct a formula specifying that $\mathbf{f}[i..i + n - 1]$ is an anti-palindrome, and further that it is a first occurrence of such a factor:

```
def antipalf "?msd_fib As,t (s>=i & t>=i & s+t+1=2*i+n)
    => F[s]!=F[t]":
def ffactoreq "?msd_fib At t<n => F[i+t]=F[j+t]":
def foapf "?msd_fib $antipalf(i,n)&Aj j<i=>~$ffactoreq(i,j,n)":
```

When we run this through our program, the pairs $(i, n)$ satisfying this formula are accepted by the automaton in Figure 8.17.

It follows that the only $(i, n)$ pairs accepted are

$$(0, 0), (0, 2), (1, 2), (3, 4), (4, 4),$$

corresponding to the words $\epsilon$, 01, 10, (01)$^2$, and (10)$^2$. $\square$

### 8.6.10 Overpals

In analogy with overlaps, Rajasekaran et al. [307] defined an *overpal* to be a word of the form $axax^Ra$, where $a$ is a single letter and $x$ a possibly empty word.

We can prove that the Thue-Morse sequence contains no overpals as follows. Here $n$ represents $|ax|$; this is called the order of the overpal.

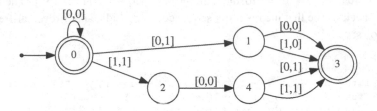

Figure 8.17 Automaton accepting positions and orders of first occurrences of nonempty antipalindromes in **f**.

```
eval tmhasoverpal "Ei,n n>=1 & (T[i]=T[i+n]) & (T[i]=T[i+2*n])
    & At (t>=1 & t<n) => T[i+t]=T[(i+2*n)-t]":
```

*Exercise* 84    Determine the orders of overpals in the Fibonacci word **f**.

### 8.6.11 Underpals

Rajasekaran et al. [307] defined an *underpal* to be a word of the form $axbx^{R}a$, where $a, b$ are distinct letters and $x$ is a possibly empty word. The order of an underpal is $|ax|$.

*Exercise* 85    Determine the orders of all underpals in the Fibonacci word.

### 8.6.12 Borders

Recall that a *border* of a word $x$ is a nonempty proper prefix of $x$ that is also a suffix.[3] Let us start by constructing a formula asserting that a factor $\mathbf{x}[i..i+n-1]$ is bordered. Examine the diagram in Figure 8.18. As we can see from the figure, the factor $\mathbf{x}[i..i + n - 1]$ is bordered, with border length $j$, if $\mathbf{x}[i + t] = \mathbf{x}[i + n + t - j]$ for $0 \leq t < j$. So the formula

$$\exists j\, (1 \leq j < n) \wedge \text{FactorEq}(i, (i + n) - j, j)$$

is true iff $\mathbf{x}[i..i + n - 1]$ is bordered.

Although the decision procedure we discussed in this book is mostly geared to proving results about infinite words, in some cases it can prove results about finite words instead, provided those finite words appear as factors of an appropriate infinite word. Let's see an example.

---

[3] Some material in this section is reprinted from [168] by permission from Springer Nature.

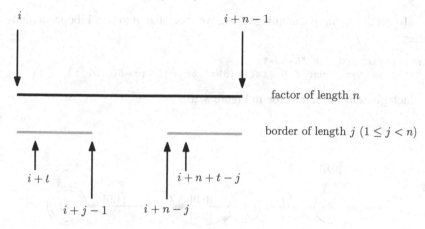

Figure 8.18 A bordered factor in a word.

Recall the finite Fibonacci words from Section 2.4.16: these are defined by $X_1 = 1$, $X_2 = 0$, and $X_n = X_{n-1}X_{n-2}$ for $n \geq 3$. Cummings, Moore, and Karhumäki [98] proved that the borders of the finite Fibonacci word $X_n$ are precisely the words $X_{n-2k}$ for $0 < 2k < n - 1$. We can reprove this (and more!) by computing the borders of the prefixes of **f**, and observing that $X_n = \mathbf{f}[0..F_n - 1]$.

```
def ffactoreq "?msd_fib At t<n => F[i+t]=F[j+t]":
def fibbord "?msd_fib j>=1 & j<n & $ffactoreq(i,(i+n)-j,j)":
def bordfibpref "?msd_fib $fibbord(0,m,n)":
```

Here `fibbord` asserts that $\mathbf{f}[i..i + n - 1]$ has a border of length $j$. The resulting automaton, depicted in Figure 8.19, encodes not just borders of the Fibonacci words, but borders of *all* prefixes of **f**.

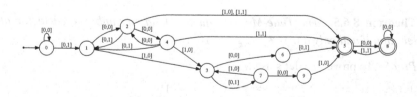

Figure 8.19 Borders of prefixes of **f**.

To get the result of Cummings et al., we specialize $n$ to be a Fibonacci number:

```
reg isfib msd_fib "0*10*":
def cummings "?msd_fib $isfib(n) & $bordfibpref(m,n)":
```

which gives us the automaton in Figure 8.20.

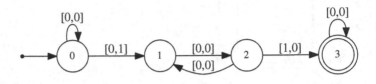

Figure 8.20  Automaton for Cummings' theorem.

Examining the automaton gives the proof.

### 8.6.13 Unbordered factors

Next we look at unbordered factors. Currie and Saari [105] studied the unbordered factors of the Thue-Morse sequence, and proved that if $n \not\equiv 1 \pmod 6$, then the Thue-Morse sequence has an unbordered factor of length $n$.

However, these are not the only lengths with an unbordered factor; for example,

$$0011010010110100110010110100101$$

is an unbordered factor of length 31. Currie and Saari left it open to decide for which lengths congruent to 1 (mod 6) this property holds. This was solved in [168], as follows:

**Theorem 8.6.5**  *The Thue-Morse sequence* **t** *has an unbordered factor of length $n$ if and only if $(n)_2 \notin 1\,(01^*0)^*10^*1$.*

*Proof*  To prove this, let's use Walnut.

```
def tmfactoreq "At t<n => T[i+t]=T[j+t]":
def tmbord "j>=1 & j<n & $tmfactoreq(i,(i+n)-j,m)":
def tmunblength "Ei Am ~$tmbord(i,m,n)":
reg nobord msd_2 "0*1(01*0)*10*1":
eval tmchk "An $tmunblength(n) <=> ~$nobord(n)":
```

and `Walnut` returns TRUE.                                                    □

Now let's look at the unbordered factors of the Fibonacci word. We reprove the following result of Harju and Kärki [191, Lemma 3].

**Theorem 8.6.6** *The only unbordered nonempty factors of* **f** *are of length* $F_n$ *for* $n \geq 2$, *and there are two distinct ones for each such length. For* $n \geq 3$ *these two unbordered factors have the property that one is a reverse of the other.*

*Proof* We can check this with the following formulas, and observing the automata in the last three.

```
def ffactoreq "?msd_fib At t<n => F[i+t]=F[j+t]":
def fibrevchk "?msd_fib As,t (s>=i & t>=j & s+t+1=i+j+n)
   => F[s]=F[t]":
def fibbord "?msd_fib m>=1 & m<n & At t<m =>
   $ffactoreq(i,(i+n)-m,m)":
def funbord "?msd_fib Am ~$fibbord(i,m,n)":
def funbordlength "?msd_fib Ei $funbord(i,n)":
def funbordtwo "?msd_fib Ei,j ($funbord(i,n) &
   $funbord(j,n) & ~$ffactoreq(i,j,n))":
def funbordrev "?msd_fib $funbordlength(n) & Ai,j ($funbord(i,n)
   & $funbord(j,n)) => ($ffactoreq(i,j,n) | $fibrevchk(i,j,n))":
```

                                                                              □

## 8.6.14 Frames

Harju and Kärki [191] defined a *frame* to be a word of the form $xx$, where $x$ is unbordered. Let us compute the frames in the Thue-Morse sequence.

```
def tmfactoreq "At t<n => T[i+t]=T[j+t]":
def tmbord "m>=1 & m<n & At t<m => $tmfactoreq(i,(i+n)-m,m)":
def tmsquare "$tmfactoreq(i,i+n,n)":
def tmunb "Am ~$tmbord(i,m,n)":
def tmframe "n>=1 & $tmunb(i,n) & $tmsquare(i,n)":
```

The resulting automaton encodes the starting positions and orders $|x|$ of all frames $xx$ in **t**.

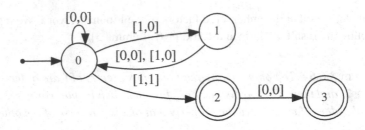

So the only frames in **t** are $0^2$, $1^2$, $(01)^2$, and $(10)^2$.

### 8.6.15 Approximate borders

There has been some interest in what might be called *k-approximate borders*: a prefix and suffix of the same length that agree on all but *k* positions. For example, the English word added has a 2-approximate border of length 3. See, for example, [224].

Let us determine the factors with 2-approximate borders in the Thue-Morse word. In particular, there is a factor with a 2-approximate border for every length $\geq 3$.

```
def factordist2 "Ek,l k<l&l<n&T[i+k]!=T[j+k]&T[i+l]!=T[j+l]
    & At (t<n & t!=k & t!=l) => T[i+t]=T[j+t]":
def border2m "$factordist2(i,(i+n)-k,k)":
eval b2test "An (n>=3) <=> Ei,k k>0 & k<n & $border2m(i,k,n)":
```

## 8.7 Recurrence, uniform recurrence, linear recurrence

### 8.7.1 Recurrence

Recall that a sequence is recurrent if every factor that occurs, occurs infinitely often. Let us write a first-order formula for the property that **x** is recurrent:

$$\forall i, n \ \exists j \ (j > i) \land \text{FACTOREQ}(i, j, n) .$$

With this formula we can check, for example, that **t** is recurrent, but **sb** is not.

## 8.7.2 Uniform recurrence

Recall that a sequence **x** is uniformly recurrent if it is recurrent, and for every factor $w$ there exists a constant $c$ such that every occurrence of $w$ in **x** is followed by another occurrence at distance at most $c$. We can write a first-order formula for this property, as follows:

$$\forall n \; \exists c \; \forall i \; \exists j \; (i < j \leq i + c) \land \text{FACTOREQ}(i, j, n).$$

We have therefore proved a theorem of [284]:

**Theorem 8.7.1** *It is decidable, given an automatic sequence **x**, whether **x** is uniformly recurrent.*

Also see [130].

Here is the Walnut formula for the Thue-Morse sequence.

```
eval tmur "An Ec Ai Ej j<=i+c & j>i & $tmfactoreq(i,j,n)":
```

Of course, it evaluates to TRUE.

*Exercise 86* Show that the Cantor sequence is recurrent but not uniformly recurrent.

*Exercise 87* Define $G_0 = 001101000110$ and $G_{n+1} = G_n 01 G_n^R$ for $n \geq 0$. Let $\mathbf{G} = \lim_{n \to \infty} G_n$. Find a 2-DFAO generating **G**. Next, use Walnut to verify that **G** is uniformly recurrent, closed under reversal of factors, aperiodic, and contains exactly 13 distinct palindromes (including the empty word).

## 8.7.3 Linear recurrence

Recall that a sequence **x** is linearly recurrent if it is uniformly recurrent, and the constant $c$ mentioned in the previous section is at most linear in $n$.

A direct translation of this property into first-order logic is

$$\exists c \; \forall n \geq 1 \; \forall i \; \exists j \; (i < j \land j < cn \land \text{FACTOREQ}(i, j, n)),$$

but this is not a legitimate statement in $\text{Th}(\mathbb{N}, +, n \to \mathbf{x}[n])$, because of the multiplication $cn$.

In Theorem 10.8.4 we will see that if an automatic sequence is uniformly recurrent, then it is in fact linearly recurrent.

In the meantime, if we have good reason to guess a specific value of $c$, we can then test linear recurrence for the constant $c$. For example, let's show that for the Thue-Morse sequence **t** every factor of length $n \geq 3$ is followed by another occurrence of the same factor at distance at most $9n - 18$:

```
def tmlinrec "Ai,n n>=3 => Ej (j>=1 & j+18<=9*n &
   $tmfactoreq(i,i+j,n))":
```

Walnut proves that the claim is TRUE. This is optimal because $9n - 18$ works for infinitely many $n$, $9n - 19$ fails for infinitely many $n$, and 9 cannot be replaced by any smaller number.

### 8.7.4 Grouped factors

Recall that $\rho_\mathbf{x}(n)$ is the subword complexity function for $\mathbf{x}$. Cassaigne [72] introduced the notion of *grouped factors*. A sequence $\mathbf{x} = (a_i)_{i \geq 0}$ has grouped factors of length $n$ if there exists some position $m = m(n)$ such that $\mathbf{x}[m..m + \rho_\mathbf{x}(n) + n - 2]$ contains all the $\rho_\mathbf{x}(n)$ length-$n$ factors of $\mathbf{x}$, each factor occurring exactly once.

One consequence of his results is that the Fibonacci word $\mathbf{f}$ has grouped factors for all $n \geq 1$. This is essentially the optimal condensation of factors (see Section 10.8.7). We can prove this as follows:

```
def ffactoreq "?msd_fib At (t<n => F[i+t] = F[j+t])":
def fibgf "?msd_fib Ai Ej (j>=s & j<s+t & $ffactoreq(i,j,n)
   & (Ak (k>=s & k<s+t &  j!=k) => (~$ffactoreq(i,k,n))))":
eval fibhasgf "?msd_fib An Es,t $fibgf(n,s,t)":
```

The first part of the formula `fibgf` specifies that every length-$n$ factor appears at least once somewhere in the $t$ consecutive factors beginning at position $s$, and the second part specifies that it appears exactly once.

*Exercise* 88   For which $n$ does the Thue-Morse sequence have grouped factors of length $n$?

## 8.8  Types of words

### 8.8.1 Return words

Let $\mathbf{x}$ be a recurrent infinite word (so that every factor that occurs, occurs infinitely often). Then $\mathbf{x}[i..j - 1]$ is called a *return word* for a length-$n$ word $w$ if $\mathbf{x}[i..i + n - 1]$ and $\mathbf{x}[j..j + n - 1]$ are two consecutive occurrences of $w$ in $\mathbf{x}$. See [129].

The formula asserting that $\mathbf{x}[i..j - 1]$ is a return word is then

$$\exists n \text{ FACTOREQ}(i, j, n) \land \forall m \ (i < m < j) \implies \neg \text{FACTOREQ}(i, m, n).$$

For the Thue-Morse sequence we have

```
def returntm "En $tmfactoreq(i,j,n) & Am (i<m & m<j)
   => ~$tmfactoreq(i,m,n)":
```

which creates a DFA accepting those $(i, j)$ such that $\mathbf{x}[i..j-1]$ is a return word. For bounds on return word length (in terms of $n$), see Section 10.8.4.

### 8.8.2 Lyndon words and factorizations

A word $w$ is called *Lyndon* if it is primitive and also lexicographically less than any of its proper nonempty suffixes.[4] We can implement this for the Thue-Morse sequence, as follows:

```
def tmfactoreq "At t<n => T[i+t]=T[j+t]":
def tmprim "~(Ej j>0 & j<n & $tmfactoreq(i,i+j,n-j) &
   $tmfactoreq(i,(i+n)-j,j))":
def tmpref "m<n & $tmfactoreq(i,j,m)":
def tmlesst "$tmpref(i,j,m,n) | (Et t<m & t<n &
   (Al (l<t) => T[i+l]=T[j+l]) & T[i+t]=@0 & T[j+t]=@1)":
def tmlyndon "$tmprim(i,n) & Aj (i<j & j<i+n) =>
   $tmlesst(i,j,n,(n+i)-j)":
def tmlynlen "Ei $tmlyndon(i,n)":
```

and prove [173]:

**Theorem 8.8.1** *There is a Lyndon factor of length $n$ in the Thue-Morse sequence* $\mathbf{t}$ *iff* $n = 2^k$ *or* $3 \cdot 2^k$ *or* $5 \cdot 2^k$, *for* $k \geq 0$.

Recall the Lyndon factorization from Section 2.1. Ido and Melançon [260, 207] gave an explicit description of the Lyndon factorization of the Thue-Morse sequence $\mathbf{t}$ and the period-doubling sequence $\mathbf{pd}$ (among other things). For the Thue-Morse sequence, this factorization is given by

$$\mathbf{t} = w_1 w_2 w_3 w_4 \cdots = (011)(01)(0011)(00101101) \cdots,$$

where each term in the factorization, after the first, is double the length of the previous. Séébold [343] and Černý [73] generalized these results to other related automatic sequences.

We can prove that the Lyndon factorization of a $k$-automatic sequence is itself $k$-automatic. Of course, we need to explain how the factorization is encoded. The easiest and most natural way to do this is to use an infinite word over $\{0, 1\}$, where the 1s indicate the positions where a new term in the factorization begins. Thus the $i$th 1, for $i \geq 0$, appears at index $|w_1 w_2 \cdots w_i|$. For example, for the Thue-Morse sequence, this encoding is given by

$$100101000100000001 \cdots.$$

---

[4] Some material in this section is reprinted from [173] by permission from Springer Nature.

If the factorization is infinite, then there are infinitely many 1s in its encoding; otherwise there are finitely many 1s.

In order to prove the theorem, we need a number of results. An occurrence $[i..j]$ is said to be Lyndon if the word $\mathbf{x}[i..j]$ at that position is Lyndon. We say an occurrence $O_1 = [i..j]$ is *inside* an occurrence $O_2 = [i'..j']$ if $i' \le i$ and $j' \ge j$. If, in addition, either $i' < i$ or $j < j'$ (or both), then we say $O_1$ is *strictly inside* $O_2$. These definitions are easily extended to the case where $j$ or $j'$ are equal to $\infty$, and they correspond to the formulas $I$ (inside) and $SI$ (strictly inside) given below:

$$I(i, j, i', j') \quad \text{is} \qquad i' \le i \text{ and } j' \ge j$$

$$SI(i, j, i', j') \quad \text{is} \qquad I(i, j, i', j') \text{ and } ((i' < i) \text{ or } (j' > j)).$$

An infinite Lyndon factorization

$$\mathbf{x} = w_1 w_2 w_3 \cdots$$

then corresponds to an infinite sequence of occurrences

$$[i_1..j_1], [i_2..j_2], \cdots$$

where $w_n = \mathbf{x}[i_n..j_n]$ and $i_{n+1} = j_n + 1$ for $n \ge 1$, while a finite Lyndon factorization

$$\mathbf{x} = w_1 w_2 \cdots w_r \mathbf{w}$$

corresponds to a finite sequence of occurrences

$$[i_1..j_1], [i_2..j_2], \ldots, [i_r..j_r], [i_{r+1}..\infty]$$

where $w_n = \mathbf{x}[i_n..j_n]$ and $i_{n+1} = j_n + 1$ for $1 \le n \le r$.

Then in [173] the authors prove the following two results:

**Theorem 8.8.2**  *Let $\mathbf{x}$ be an infinite word. Every Lyndon occurrence in $\mathbf{x}$ appears inside a term of the Lyndon factorization of $\mathbf{x}$.*

**Corollary 8.8.3**  *The occurrence $[i..j]$ corresponds to a term in the Lyndon factorization of $\mathbf{x}$ if and only if both of the following hold:*

*(a) $[i..j]$ is Lyndon.*

*(b) $[i..j]$ does not occur strictly inside any other Lyndon occurrence.*

This means that the Lyndon factorization of an automatic sequence is automatic. Let us carry out the factorization for the Thue-Morse sequence:

```
def isin "ip<=i & jp>=j":
def strictlyin "$isin(i,ip,j,jp) & (ip<i | jp>j)":
def tmfactoreq "At t<n => T[i+t]=T[j+t]":
def tmprim "~(Ej j>0 & j<n & $tmfactoreq(i,i+j,n-j) &
    $tmfactoreq(i,(i+n)-j,j))":
def tmpref "m<n & $tmfactoreq(i,j,m)":
def tmlesst "$tmpref(i,j,m,n) | (Et t<m & t<n & (Al l<t
    => T[i+1]=T[j+1]) & T[i+t]=@0 & T[j+t]=@1)":
def tmlyndon "$tmprim(i,n) & Aj (i<j & j<i+n) =>
    $tmlesst(i,j,n,(n+i)-j)":
def islynd "$tmlyndon(i,(j+1)-i)":
def lyndonf "$islynd(i,j) & A ip,jp $strictlyin(i,ip,j,jp)
    => ~$islynd(ip,jp)":
```

The resulting automaton, depicted in Figure 8.21, proves that the Lyndon factorization of **t** is $[0..2], [3..4], [5..8], [9..16], \dots, [2^i + 1 .. 2^{i+1}], \dots$.

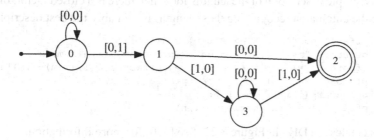

Figure 8.21 Lyndon factorization automaton.

*Exercise* 89  Suppose **w** is $k$-automatic. Show that the following decision problems are decidable:

(a) Given $t$ words of the same length $r$, is **w** factorizable as a product of these words?
(b) Given a length $r$ and a bound on the number of words $t$, is $w$ factorizable using at most $t$ different factors of length $r$?
(c) Given a length $r$, is $w$ factorizable using a set of factors of the same length $r$ such that each factor is a permutation of the others?

*Open Question* 8.8.4  How can the above problem be solved if you do not know $r$?

### 8.8.3 Closed words

Recall that a word is closed if it is of length ≤ 1, or has a border that occurs exactly twice. A closed word is also called a *complete first return*. We can create a formula CLOSED($i, n$) that asserts that $\mathbf{x}[i..i + n - 1]$ is closed as follows:

$$(n \le 1) \lor (\exists j \; j < n \land \text{BORDER}(i, j, n) \land neg\text{OCCURS}(i, i + 1, j, n - 2)).$$

Let's apply this to the Thue-Morse sequence. We can prove that there is a closed factor of **t** of every length:

```
def tmfactoreq "At t<n => T[i+t]=T[j+t]":
def tmoccurs "m<=n & Ek k+m<=n & $tmfactoreq(i,j+k,m)":
def tmbord "m>=1 & m<n & At t<m => $tmfactoreq(i,(i+n)-m,m)":
def tmclo "n<=1 | (Ej j<n & $tmbord(i,j,n) &
    ~$tmoccurs(i,i+1,j,n-2))":
eval tmclosall "An n>=1 => Ei $tmclo(i,n)":
```

For other sequences, such as the regular paperfolding sequence, there is no really simple description of the lengths for which there is a closed factor. In this case the automaton recognizing these lengths is probably the best description.

```
def pffactoreq "At t<n => P[i+t]=P[j+t]":
def pfoccurs "m<=n & Ek k+m<=n & $pffactoreq(i,j+k,m)":
def pfbord "m>=1 & m<n & At t<m => $pffactoreq(i,(i+n)-m,m)":
def pfclosed "n<=1 | (Ej j<n & $pfbord(i,j,n) &
    ~$pfoccurs(i,i+1,j,n-2))":
def pfclosedlen "Ei $pfclosed(i,n)":
```

This creates the DFA in Figure 8.22. See [336] for more information.

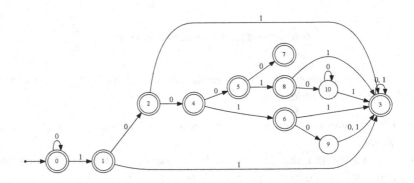

Figure 8.22 Automaton for lengths of closed factors of the paperfolding sequence.

### 8.8.4 Rich words

As we have seen in Section 2.1, a finite word $x$ is rich if and only if it has $|x| + 1$ distinct palindromic factors. As stated, it does not seem easy to phrase this in first-order logic, since there is no obvious way to count.

Luckily, there is an alternative characterization of rich words, which can be found in [124, Prop. 3]: a finite word is rich if every prefix $p$ of $w$ has a palindromic suffix $s$ that occurs only once in $p$. This property can be stated as follows:

$$\text{Rich}(i, n) := \forall m \; \text{In}(m, 1, n) \implies$$

$$(\exists j \; \text{Subs}(j, i, 1, m) \wedge \text{Pal}(j, i + m - j) \wedge \neg \text{Occurs}(j, i, i + m - j, m - 1)).$$

Finally, we can express the property that **x** has a rich factor of length $n$ as follows:

$$\exists i \; \text{Rich}(i, n).$$

With this we can prove, for example, that every factor of the period-doubling word is rich:

```
def in "i>=r & i<=s":
def subs "j<=i & i+m<=j+n":
def pdpal "Ak k<n => PD[i+k] = PD[i+n-1-k]":
def pdfactoreq "Ak k<n => PD[i+k]=PD[j+k]":
def pdoccurs "m<=n & (Ek k+m<=n & $pdfactoreq(i,j+k,m))":
def pdrich "Am $in(m,1,n) => Ej $subs(j,i,1,m) &
    $pdpal(j,(i+m)-j) & ~$pdoccurs(j,i,(i+m)-j,m-1)":
eval testpdrich "Ai,n $pdrich(i,n)":
```

For more about rich words in automatic sequences, see [336].

### 8.8.5 Privileged words

The recursive definition for privileged words given above in Section 2.1 is not obviously expressible in first-order logic. Luckily, there is an alternative characterization from [336] that is expressible.

Let us say a word $w$ has property $P$ if for all $n$, $1 \leq n \leq |w|$, there exists a word $x$ such that $1 \leq |x| \leq n$, and $x$ occurs exactly once in the first $n$ symbols of $w$, as a prefix, and $x$ also occurs exactly once in the last $n$ symbols of $w$, as a suffix. Then we have [336]:

**Theorem 8.8.5** *A nonempty word $w$ is privileged if and only if it has property $P$.*

To implement this in first-order logic, let us write a formula that is true if and only if the prefix $\mathbf{x}[i..i + m - 1]$ occurs exactly once in $\mathbf{x}[i..i + n - 1]$:

$$\text{UniPref}(i, m, n) := \forall j \, \text{In}(j, 1, n - m - 1) \implies \neg\text{FactorEq}(i, i + j, m).$$

There is a similar expression for whether the suffix $\mathbf{x}[i + n - m..i + n - 1]$ occurs exactly once in $\mathbf{x}[i..i + n - 1]$:

$$\text{UniSuff}(i, m, n) := \forall j \, \text{In}(j, 1, n - m - 1) \implies \neg\text{FactorEq}(i + n - m, i + n - m - j, m).$$

Finally, our characterization of privileged words is

$$\text{Priv}(i, n) := (n \le 1) \lor (\forall m \, \text{In}(m, 1, n) \implies (\exists p \, \text{In}(p, 1, m)$$
$$\land \, \text{Border}(i, p, n) \land \text{UniPref}(i, p, m) \land \text{UniSuff}(i + n - m, p, m))).$$

In Walnut this is

```
def in "i>=r & i<=s":
def pdfactoreq "Ak k<n => PD[i+k] = PD[j+k]":
def unipref "Aj (j>0 & j+m<n) => ~$pdfactoreq(i,i+j,m)":
def unisuff "Aj (j>0 & j+m<n) =>
   ~$pdfactoreq((i+n)-m,(i+n)-(m+j),m)":
def pdbord "$in(m,1,n) & $pdfactoreq(i,(i+n)-m,m)":
def pdpriv "n>=1&Am $in(m,1,n) => Ep p<=m&p>=1&$unipref(i,p,m)
   & $unisuff((i+n)-m,p,m) & $pdbord(i,p,n)":
eval pdprivlen "Ei $pdpriv(i,n)":
```

The resulting automaton is depicted in Figure 8.23.

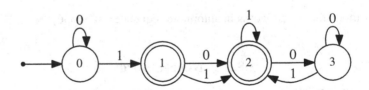

Figure 8.23 Lengths of privileged factors in **pd**.

Inspection of this automaton then proves the following:

**Theorem 8.8.6** *The lengths of nonempty privileged factors in the period-doubling word are given by the set $\{2\} \cup \{2n + 1 : n \ge 0\}$.*

Now let's turn to another example. Peltomäki [296] conjectured that there are arbitrarily long, but not infinite, runs of $n$ for which there are no length-$n$ privileged factors in the Thue-Morse sequence. We can prove this conjecture, as follows:

```
def in "i>=r & i<=s":
def tmfactoreq "Ak k<n => T[i+k] = T[j+k]":
def tmunipref "Aj (j>0 & j+m<n) => ~$tmfactoreq(i,i+j,m)":
def tmunisuff "Aj (j>0 & j+m<n) =>
    ~$tmfactoreq((i+n)-m,(i+n)-(m+j),m)":
def tmbord "$in(m,1,n) & $tmfactoreq(i,(i+n)-m,m)":
def tmpriv "n>=1 & Am $in(m,1,n) => Ep p<=m & p>=1 &
    $tmunipref(i,p,m)&$tmunisuff((i+n)-m,p,m)&$tmbord(i,p,n)":
def tmprivlen "Ei $tmpriv(i,n)":
eval tmunprivlrun "An Ei At t<n => ~$tmprivlen(i+t)":
eval tmprivlinf "Am En (n>m) & $tmprivlen(n)":
```

Here

- `tmpriv(i,n)` asserts that $\mathbf{t}[i..i + n - 1]$ is a privileged factor.
- `tmprivlen(n)` asserts the existence of a privileged factor of length $n$ in $\mathbf{t}$.
- `tmunprivlrun` asserts there are arbitrarily long runs where `tmprivlen(n)` evaluates to FALSE. It evaluates to TRUE.
- `tmprivlinf` asserts there are infinitely many $n$ for which `tmprivlen(n)` evaluates to TRUE; it also evaluates to TRUE.

### 8.8.6 Special factors

Recall that a factor $w$ of a word $\mathbf{x}$ is said to be *right-special* if there exist two different letters $a$ and $b$ such that both $wa$ and $wb$ are factors of $\mathbf{x}$. For a binary word $\mathbf{x}$ we can test whether $\mathbf{x}[i..i + n - 1]$ is right-special, as follows:

$$\text{IsRs}(i, n) := \exists j \ \textsc{FactorEq}(i, j, n) \land \mathbf{x}[i + n] \neq \mathbf{x}[j + n].$$

For the Fibonacci word there is exactly one right-special factor of each length, which we can test as follows:

```
def isrs "?msd_fib Ej $ffactoreq(i,j,n) & F[i+n] != F[j+n]":
eval unirs "?msd_fib (An Ei $isrs(i,n)) & ~(En,i,j
    $isrs(i,n) & $isrs(j,n) & ~$ffactoreq(i,j,n))":
```

It returns TRUE.

It would be nice to actually get our hands on this unique special factor. For this, we have the following result of Berstel [43].

**Theorem 8.8.7** *The right-special factor of length n of* $\mathbf{f}$ *is equal to* $\mathbf{f}[0..n-1]^R$.

*Proof*  To prove this, execute the `Walnut` command

```
def berstel "?msd_fib Aj,n,i (j<n & $isrs(i,n)) =>
  F[i+j]=F[n-(j+1)]":
```

which returns TRUE.                                                    □

We now turn to bispecial factors of binary words **x**. These are words $w$ such that $w0, w1, 0w, 1w$ are all factors of **x**. We can easily make a formula similar to IsRs above to test bispeciality. Let us use this to prove the following result of de Luca and Mione [249]:

**Theorem 8.8.8**  *There are exactly two bispecial factors of Thue-Morse of length $2^k$ and $3 \cdot 2^k$ for $k \geq 0$, and for all other lengths, there are none.*

*Proof*  Use the following `Walnut` commands:

```
def isbi "Ej,m $tmfactoreq(i,j,n)&T[i+n]!=T[j+n]
  & $tmfactoreq(i,m,n) & T[i-1]!=T[m-1]":
def hasbi "Ei $isbi(i,n)":
def hastwobi "Ei,j $isbi(i,n)&$isbi(j,n)&~$tmfactoreq(i,j,n)":
eval hasthreebi "Ei,j,k,n $isbi(i,n)&$isbi(j,n)&$isbi(k,n)&
  ~$tmfactoreq(i,j,n)&~$tmfactoreq(i,k,n)&~$tmfactoreq(j,k,n)":
```

□

*Exercise* 90    An *Arnoux-Rauzy* word [21] over an alphabet $\Sigma$ can be characterized as an infinite word that is closed under reversal, and having exactly one right-special factor of each length, where each such factor has exactly $|\Sigma|$ extensions of one letter (see [251]). Show that the Tribonacci word is Arnoux-Rauzy.

*Exercise* 91    The *maximum-order complexity* of a binary sequence **s** is a function $M : \mathbb{N} \to \mathbb{N}$ mapping $n$ to the smallest positive integer $m$ for which there is a $GF(2)$-function $f$ such that $\mathbf{s}[i+m] = f(\mathbf{s}[i], \ldots, \mathbf{s}[i+m-1])$ for $0 \leq i < n-m$. First, show that $M(n)$ is equal to $1+$ the length of the longest special factor in a length-$n$ prefix of **s**.

Second, compute $M$ for the Thue-Morse sequence, the Rudin-Shapiro sequence, and the Fibonacci-Thue-Morse sequence from Section 2.4.18. Compare your results with those of Sun and Winterhof [369] and Shallit [357].

### 8.8.7  Minimal forbidden words

A word $w$ is *minimal forbidden* for an infinite word **x** if $w$ is not a factor of **x**, but every proper factor of $w$ is. Alternatively, writing $w = atb$ for letters $a, b$, we want $atb \notin \text{Fac}(\mathbf{x})$, but $at, tb \in \text{Fac}(\mathbf{x})$. We would like to compute the minimal forbidden words for a binary word **x**. For example, 000 is a minimal forbidden word for **t**.

Here we are faced with a bit of a problem, since it is not possible to provide indices $i, n$ such that $\mathbf{x}[i..i + n - 1]$ is not a factor of **x**! So we would need to encode our answer somehow.

Provided that **x** is a binary word, a reasonable encoding is the following: we accept the pair $(i, n)$ if $y = \mathbf{x}[i..i + n - 1]\overline{\mathbf{x}[i + n]}$ is a minimal forbidden word. In the terminology we used above, $a = \mathbf{x}[i]$, $t = \mathbf{x}[i + 1..i + n - 1]$, and $b = \overline{\mathbf{x}[i + n]}$.

It then suffices to check that

(i) $y$ does not appear in **x**.

(ii) $\mathbf{x}[i + 1..i + n - 1]\overline{\mathbf{x}[i + n]}$ does.

We can do this with the following formula:

$$\text{IsMF}(i, n) := (\neg\exists j \; \text{FACTOREQ}(i, j, n) \;\wedge\; \mathbf{x}[i + n] \neq \mathbf{x}[j + n])$$
$$\wedge \; (\exists j' \; \text{FACTOREQ}(i + 1, j', n - 1) \;\wedge\; \mathbf{x}[i + n] \neq \mathbf{x}[j' + n - 1]).$$

From this we can recover the following result of Shur [361]:

**Theorem 8.8.9** *The minimal forbidden factors of* **t** *are of length* 3 *and* $3 \cdot 2^n + 2$ *for* $n \geq 0$.

*Proof* We use the following Walnut code:

```
def ismf "(~Ej $tmfactoreq(i,j,n) & T[i+n]!=T[j+n]) &
   (Ejp $tmfactoreq(i+1,jp,n-1) & T[i+n]!=T[(jp+n)-1])":
def lengthmf "Ei $ismf(i,n-1)":
def firstmf "$ismf(i,n) & Aj (j<i & $ismf(j,n)) =>
   ~$tmfactoreq(i,j,n)":
reg power2 msd_2 "0*10*":
eval shurtest "An $lengthmf(n) <=> ((n=3) |
   Ei $power2(i) & n=3*i+2)":
```

Here `lengthmf` accepts those $n$ such that there is a forbidden factor of **t** of length $n$, and `firstmf` accepts those pairs $(i, n)$ such that $i$ is the smallest index for which $\mathbf{x}[i..i + n - 1]\overline{\mathbf{x}[i + n]}$ is forbidden. Then `shurtest` asserts that the claim of Shur holds, and it returns TRUE. $\square$

For more information about minimal forbidden words, see, for example, [97, 266].

*Exercise 92* Show how to obtain a complete description of all of the minimal forbidden factors in terms of $\mu$, the Thue-Morse morphism.

### 8.8.8 Trapezoidal words

Trapezoidal words, introduced in Section 2.1, have many different character-izations. The characterization that proves useful to us is the following [58, Prop. 2.8]: a word $w$ is trapezoidal if and only if $|w| = R_w + K_w$. Here $R_w$ is the minimal length $\ell$ for which $w$ contains no right-special factor of length $\ell$, and $K_w$ is the minimal length $\ell$ for which there is a length-$\ell$ suffix of $w$ that appears nowhere else in $w$.

This can be translated into a first-order formula as follows: $\textsc{RtSp}(j, n, p)$ is true if and only if $\mathbf{x}[j..j + n - 1]$ has a right special factor of length $p$, and false otherwise:

$$\textsc{RtSp}(j, n, p) := \exists r\, \exists s\, (\textsc{Subs}(r, j, p + 1, n) \wedge \textsc{Subs}(s, j, p + 1, n)$$
$$\wedge\ \textsc{FactorEq}(r, s, p) \wedge \mathbf{x}[s + p] \neq \mathbf{x}[r + p]).$$

Next, we create a formula $\textsc{MinRt}(j, n, p)$ that is true if and only if $p$ is the smallest integer such that $\mathbf{x}[j..j + n - 1]$ has no right-special factor of length $p$:

$$\textsc{MinRt}(j, n, p) := ((\neg\textsc{RtSp}(j, n, p)) \wedge (\forall c\, (\neg\textsc{RtSp}(j, n, c)))) \implies c \geq p.$$

Next, $\textsc{UnrepSuf}(j, n, q)$ is true if and only if the suffix of length $q$ of $\mathbf{x}[j..j + n - 1]$ is unrepeated in $\mathbf{x}[j..j + n - 1]$:

$$\textsc{UnrepSuf}(j, n, q) := \neg\textsc{Occurs}(j + n - q, j, q, n - 1).$$

Next, $\textsc{MinUnrepSuf}(j, n, p)$ is true if and only if $p$ is the length of the shortest unrepeated suffix of $\mathbf{x}[j..j + n - 1]$:

$$\textsc{MinUnrepSuf}(j, n, p) := \textsc{UnrepSuf}(j, n, q) \wedge (\forall c\, \textsc{UnrepSuf}(j, n, c) \implies c \geq q).$$

The formula $\textsc{Trap}(j, n)$ is true if and only if $\mathbf{x}[j..j + n - 1]$ is trapezoidal:

$$\textsc{Trap}(j, n) := \exists p\, \exists q\, (n = p + q) \wedge \textsc{MinUnrepSuf}(j, n, p) \wedge \textsc{MinRt}(j, n, q).$$

Finally, we can determine those $n$ for which $\mathbf{x}$ has a trapezoidal factor of length $n$ as follows:

$$\exists j\, \textsc{Trap}(j, n).$$

*Exercise* 93  Show that the period-doubling sequence has only finitely many distinct trapezoidal factors. How many are there?

See [336] for more examples.

### 8.8.9 Balanced words

Our definition of balanced word given in Section 2.1 does not obviously lend itself to a definition in first-order arithmetic, since it involves counting. However, for binary words there is an alternative characterization (due to Coven and Hedlund [95]) that we can use: a binary word $w$ is unbalanced if and only if there exists a word $v$ such that both $0v0$ and $1v1$ are factors of $w$.

Thus we can write define $\textsc{Unbal}(i, n)$, a formula that is true if and only if $x[i..i + n - 1]$ is unbalanced, as follows:

$$\exists m\, (m \geq 2) \wedge (\exists j, k\, (\textsc{Subs}(j, i, m, n) \wedge \textsc{Subs}(k, i, m, n)$$
$$\wedge\, \textsc{FactorEq}(j + 1, k + 1, m - 2) \wedge x[j] = x[(j + m) - 1]$$
$$\wedge\, x[k] = x[(k + m) - 1] \wedge x[j] \neq x[k])).$$

With this we can easily prove

**Theorem 8.8.10** *Every factor of the Fibonacci word is balanced.*

*Proof* We use the Walnut commands implementing the idea above

```
def fibsubs "?msd_fib j<=i & i+m<=j+n":
def ffactoreq "?msd_fib At t<n => F[i+t]=F[j+t]":
def fibunbal "?msd_fib Em m>=2 & (Ej,k $fibsubs(j,i,m,n) &
    $fibsubs(k,i,m,n) & $ffactoreq(j+1,k+1,m-2) &
    F[j]=F[(j+m)-1] & F[k]=F[(k+m)-1] & F[j]!=F[k])":
eval fibbal "?msd_fib Ai,n ~$fibunbal(i,n)":
```

and `fibbal` returns `TRUE`. □

Of course this is already known in much greater generality: every factor of every Sturmian word is balanced [277].

*Exercise 94* Show that the Thue-Morse sequence **t**, the Rudin-Shapiro sequence **r**, the regular paperfolding sequence **p**, and the period-doubling word **pd** have only finitely many balanced factors, but have unbalanced factors of all sufficiently large lengths.

See [336] for more examples.

### 8.8.10 Christoffel words

A binary word $w$ is called a *Christoffel word* if it is balanced and of the form $0v1$ for some palindrome $v$. See, for example, [46]. We can easily write a predicate asserting that a factor of the Fibonacci word is Christoffel, as follows:

```
def fibispal "?msd_fib As,t (s>=i&t>=i&s+t+1=2*i+n)=>F[s]=F[t]":
def christof "?msd_fib (~$fibunbal(i,n)) & F[i]=@0 &
    F[i+n-1]=@1 & $fibispal(i+1,n-2)":
```

*Exercise* 95   Show that there is a Christoffel factor of length $n$ in the Fibonacci word if and only if $n = F_k$ for $k \geq 3$, and there is only one such factor for each such length.

## 8.9  Comparing two or more sequences

### 8.9.1  One sequence as a shift of another

Given two automatic sequences $\mathbf{x}$ and $\mathbf{y}$ defined over the same numeration system, we can decide if $\mathbf{y}$ is a shift of $\mathbf{x}$ by some amount with the formula

$$(\exists t \; \forall n \; \mathbf{y}[n + t] = \mathbf{x}[n]) \; \vee \; (\exists t \; \forall n \; \mathbf{y}[n] = \mathbf{x}[n + t]).$$

Since the shift could be left or right, we need to check both possibilities.

### 8.9.2  Perfect shuffle and unshuffle

Let's recall the Mephisto Waltz word $\mathbf{m}$ from Section 1. If we split $\mathbf{m}$ into even- and odd-indexed subsequences, we get $\mathbf{m} = \mathbf{y} \text{Ш} \mathbf{z}$ for some infinite words $\mathbf{y} = 01010001110101001101 \cdots$ and $\mathbf{z} = 00110101011000101000 \cdots$. This operation is called *unshuffle*.

**Theorem 8.9.1**   *Let $h$ be the morphism defined as follows:*

$$0 \rightarrow 012 \qquad\qquad 1 \rightarrow 302$$
$$2 \rightarrow 031 \qquad\qquad 3 \rightarrow 321,$$

*and let $\tau_1, \tau_2$ be the codings defined by*

$$\tau_1(0) = 0 \qquad\qquad \tau_2(0) = 0$$
$$\tau_1(1) = 1 \qquad\qquad \tau_2(1) = 0$$
$$\tau_1(2) = 0 \qquad\qquad \tau_2(2) = 1$$
$$\tau_1(3) = 1 \qquad\qquad \tau_2(3) = 1.$$

*Then $\mathbf{y} = \tau_1(h^\omega(0))$ and $\mathbf{z} = \tau_2(h^\omega(0))$.*

*Proof*   This can be verified with Walnut as follows:

```
morphism h "0->012 1->302 2->031 3->321":
morphism tau1 "0->0 1->1 2->0 3->1":
morphism tau2 "0->0 1->0 2->1 3->1":
promote HH h:
image MA tau1 HH:
image MB tau2 HH:
```

```
eval meph1 "?msd_3 Ai MW[2*i]=MA[i]":
eval meph2 "?msd_3 Ai MW[2*i+1]=MB[i]":
```

□

Now we can answer an old question of Prodinger and Urbanek [302], following the strategy in [313]:

**Theorem 8.9.2** *Both* **y** *and* **z** *have squares of bounded order, but their perfect shuffle* **m** *has squares of unbounded order.*

*Proof* For the first assertion, we can write Walnut formulas for the orders of squares appearing in **y** and **z**, and check that the orders are bounded:

```
def mephasq "?msd_3 Ei Aj j<n => MA[i+j]=MA[i+j+n]":
def mephbsq "?msd_3 Ei Aj j<n => MB[i+j]=MB[i+j+n]":
eval mephabcheck "?msd_3 Ec An ($mephasq(n) => n<c) &
   ($mephbsq(n) => n<c)":
```

For the second assertion, we can write

```
def mwsq "?msd_3 Ei Aj j<n => MW[i+j]=MW[i+j+n]":
eval mwsqcheck "?msd_3 Ac En n>c & $mephsq(n)":
```

to check that **mw** has squares of arbitrarily large order. Everything returns TRUE. □

### 8.9.3 Common factors

Given two automatic sequences *defined over the same numeration system*, we can find the factors they have in common. For example, let's find the lengths of factors in common between the Thue-Morse sequence **t** and the Rudin-Shapiro sequence.

```
def common "Ei,j At t<n => T[i+t]=RS[j+t]":
```

The resulting automaton accepts the base-2 representation of the integers 0 through 8. So no factor of length 9 or larger occurs in both sequences.

*Exercise* 96    Show how to obtain the list of factors themselves.

Notice that our method cannot deal with the factors in common between the Thue-Morse sequence (say) and the Fibonacci word, because these are defined over different numeration systems. However, since sufficiently long factors of the Fibonacci word have a density of 0s close to $(\sqrt{5}-1)/2$, while sufficiently long factors of Thue-Morse have a density of 0s close to $1/2$, we know that there can only be finitely many different factors in common between these two sequences. Now it is easy to simply enumerate them until we find a length having no factors in common.

We now turn to questions of factors shared by two automatic sequences. For $k$-automatic sequences, Fagnot [142] showed that it is decidable whether two automatic sequences **x** and **y** have exactly the same set of factors. This is also decidable by our methods, as follows: the factors of **x** are a subset of those of **y** if and only if for all $i \geq 0$, $n \geq 1$ there exists $j \geq 0$ such that $\mathbf{x}[i..i + n - 1] = \mathbf{y}[j..j + n - 1]$. As an example, let's show that the factors of **t** and **ttm** coincide, by running the `Walnut` commands

```
def tmsubttm "Ej At t<n => T[i]=TTM[j]":
def ttmsubtm "Ej At t<n => TTM[i]=T[j]":
eval equal "Ai,n $tmsubttm(i,n) & $ttmsubtm(i,n)":
```

and `Walnut` returns `TRUE`.

### 8.9.4 Proximal sequences

Bucci, De Luca, and Zamboni [60] introduced the notion of proximality. Two sequences **x** and **y** are said to be *proximal* if they agree on arbitrarily long consecutive blocks of indices.

The following problem is decidable: given two $k$-automatic sequences **x** and **y**, are they proximal? It is easy to see that **x** and **y** are proximal if and only if for all integers $n \geq 0$ there exists an integer $i \geq 0$ such that $\mathbf{x}[i..i + n - 1] = \mathbf{y}[i..i + n - 1]$. Our method now applies.

Let us apply this idea to show that **t**, the Thue-Morse sequence, and **ttm**, the word introduced in Section 2.4.2, are proximal:

```
eval checkproxttm "An Ei Aj j<n => T[i+j]=TTM[i+j]":
```

It evaluates to `TRUE`, so these sequences are indeed proximal.

## 8.10  Two-dimensional arrays

Just as there is a theory of automatic sequences, there is also a theory of automatic two-dimensional arrays. See, for example, [329, 330, 332] and [16, Chap. 14]. We can think of these as maps from $\mathbb{N} \times \mathbb{N} \to \Delta$, for a finite alphabet.

## 8.10.1 Picture frames

A *picture frame* is a finite rectangular array of points in the plane lattice, with at least two rows and columns, such that the first row equals the last row, and the first column equals the last column. In other words, **y** has a picture frame iff there exist indices $m < n$ and $p < q$ such that the $\mathbf{y}[m..n, p] = \mathbf{y}[m..n, q]$ and $\mathbf{y}[m, p..q] = \mathbf{y}[n, p..q]$. Figure 8.24 indicates a picture frame in an array of letters. Now the following natural question occurs: is there a 2-coloring of

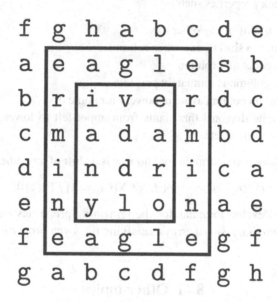

Figure 8.24 A picture frame.

the quarter-plane containing no picture frames at all? We might call such a coloring *frameless*.

**Theorem 8.10.1** *Define the two-dimensional array* $\mathbf{y}[i, j] = t_{i+j}$*, where* $\mathbf{t} = t_0 t_1 t_2 \cdots$ *is the Thue-Morse sequence. Then* **y** *is frameless.*

*Proof* We use the following `Walnut` code to check for the existence of a frame:

```
def yy "T[i+j]=@1":
eval framecheck "Em,n,p,q m<n & p<q &
    (Ai (m<=i & i<=n) => ($yy(i,p) <=> $yy(i,q))) &
    (Aj (p<=j & j<=q) => ($yy(m,j) <=> $yy(n,j)))":
```

which returns FALSE.     □

For more information, see [218].

*Exercise* 97    Show how to construct a frameless two-coloring of $\mathbb{Z} \times \mathbb{Z}$.

### 8.10.2  Properties of two-dimensional arrays

Suppose we are given an automatic two-dimensional array **X**. We can use Walnut to check properties such as:

- no row is a shift of any other row.
- no column is a shift of any other column.
- no row is equal to a column.
- no row or column is ultimately periodic.
- every row and column avoid $\alpha$-powers for some $\alpha$.
- every infinite diagonal that slants from upper left to lower right avoids $\alpha$-powers for some $\alpha$, etc.

For example, here is the formula for "no row is a shift of any other row":

$$\forall i, j \, (i \neq j) \implies (\neg(\exists c \, \forall \ell \, \mathbf{X}[i, l] = \mathbf{X}[j, l + c])).$$

*Exercise* 98    Develop formulas for the remaining properties and find some examples of two-dimensional arrays satisfying the given properties.

## 8.11  Other topics

### 8.11.1  Orbit closure

Recall that the *orbit closure* of a sequence **x** is the set of all sequences having arbitrarily long finite prefixes appearing as factors of **x**. The lexicographically least and greatest sequences of the orbit closure are of particular interest.

Let us see how to calculate the lexicographically least sequence in the orbit closure of a binary sequence. We need a series of formulas:

- L$\tau(i, j, n)$ asserts that $\mathbf{x}[i..i+n-1]$ is lexicographically less than $\mathbf{x}[j..j+n-1]$.
- FACTOREQ$(i, j, n)$ asserts that the factors $\mathbf{x}[i..i + n - 1]$ and $\mathbf{x}[j..j + n - 1]$ are equal.
- L$\tau$E$(i, j, n)$ asserts that $\mathbf{x}[i..i + n - 1]$ is lexicographically less than or equal to $\mathbf{x}[j..j + n - 1]$.
- LLEAST$(n)$ is true if the lexicographically least sequence in the orbit closure of **x** has a 1 in position $n$.

These formulas are as follows:

$$\textsc{FactorEq}(i, j, n) := \forall t \ (t < n) \implies \mathbf{x}[i + t] = \mathbf{x}[j + t]$$

$$\textsc{Lt}(i, j, n) := \exists t \ (t < n) \wedge \textsc{FactorEq}(i, j, t) \wedge \mathbf{x}[i + t] < \mathbf{x}[j + t]$$

$$\textsc{Lte}(i, j, n) := \textsc{Lt}(i, j, n) \vee \textsc{FactorEq}(i, j, n)$$

$$\textsc{Lleast}(n) := \exists i \ (\mathbf{x}[i + n] = 1) \wedge (\forall j \ \textsc{Lte}(i, j, n + 1)).$$

This allows us to prove the following theorem:

**Theorem 8.11.1** *The lexicographically least sequence in the orbit closure of the Thue-Morse sequence* $\mathbf{t} = t_0 t_1 t_2 \cdots$ *is* $\overline{t_1} \ \overline{t_2} \ \overline{t_3} \ \dots$.

*Proof* We implement the formulas above for $\mathbf{t}$. In the last step, we check to see that the automaton produced generates the word $\overline{t_1} \ \overline{t_2} \ \overline{t_3} \ \dots$.

```
def tmfactoreq "At t<n => T[i+t]=T[j+t]":
def tmlt "Et t<n & $tmfactoreq(i,j,t) & T[i+t]<T[j+t]":
def tmleq "$tmlt(i,j,n) | $tmfactoreq(i,j,n)":
def lleast "Ei T[i+n]=@1 & Aj $tmleq(i,j,n+1)":
def checklltm "An $lleast(n) <=> T[n+1]=@0":
```

□

Similarly, we can prove the following result of Currie [101]:

**Theorem 8.11.2** *The lexicographically least sequence in the orbit closure of the Rudin-Shapiro sequence* $\mathbf{rs}$ *is* $0\mathbf{rs}$.

*Proof* We implement the formulas above for $\mathbf{rs}$. In the last step, we check to see that the automaton produced generates the word $0\mathbf{rs}$.

```
def rfactoreq "At t<n => RS[i+t]=RS[j+t]":
def ltr "Et t<n & $rfactoreq(i,j,t) & RS[i+t]<RS[j+t]":
def leqr "$ltr(i,j,n) | $rfactoreq(i,j,n)":
def lleastr "Ei RS[i+n]=@1 & Aj $leqr(i,j,n+1)":
def checkllrs "(~$lleastr(0)) & An (n>=1) =>
   ($lleastr(n) <=> RS[n-1]=@1)":
```

□

## 8.11.2 Automatic real numbers

Let $b$ be an integer $\geq 2$. Given a real number $x$, we can consider its base-$b$ representation

$$x = a_0 + \sum_{i \geq 1} a_i b^{-i},$$

where $a_0 \in \mathbb{Z}$ and $a_i \in \Sigma_b = \{0, 1, \ldots, b - 1\}$ for $i \geq 1$. For example, $-\pi$ is associated with the sequence $(-4, 8, 5, 8, 4, 0, 7, \ldots)$.

Notice that some numbers have two distinct representations as sequences. For example, in base $k$ the number $0$ has two representations: $(0, 0, 0, \ldots)$ and $(-1, b - 1, b - 1, b - 1, \ldots)$.

We say that such a real number $x$ is $(k, b)$-automatic if its base-$b$ representation $(a_i)_{i \geq 0}$ is $k$-automatic. The set of all such real numbers is $L(k, b)$. The sets $L(k, b)$ have some interesting properties that are discussed in [16, Chap. 10].

In this section, we show how to prove a basic result about the automatic reals using our method. This greatly simplifies the proof given in [237] and [16, Chap. 10].

**Lemma 8.11.3**   *If $x, y \in L(k, b)$, then $x + y \in L(k, b)$.*

*Proof*   The whole difficulty of the proof is that when we add $x$ to $y$, the carries that influence a given position could, potentially, come from arbitrarily far to the right of that position.

Let $b \geq 2$ and define

$$x = a_0 + \sum_{i \geq 1} a_i b^{-i}$$

$$y = b_0 + \sum_{i \geq 1} b_i b^{-i}$$

$$x + y = c_0 + \sum_{i \geq 1} c_i b^{-i},$$

where $c_i = a_i + b_i$ for $i \geq 0$. Using the cross-product construction, we see that $\mathbf{c} = (c_i)_{i \geq 0}$ is a $k$-automatic sequence, but may not be a "legitimate" base-$b$ expansion, because some of the $c_i$ for $i \geq 1$ could exceed $b - 1$. Thus, we have to "normalize" the representation of $x + y$ and show that this process still results in a $k$-automatic sequence. Normalization involves correctly processing the carries.

Just like when we add $1$ to $999 \cdots 9$ in base $10$, when we add two numbers in base $b$ and get a carry at position $i$, it can influence arbitrarily many digits to the left, but only if there is a long block of consecutive digits equal to $b - 1$. For $i \geq 0$ define

$$d_i := \begin{cases} 1, & \text{if } \exists j > i \text{ such that } c_j \geq b \text{ and } c_{i+1}, \ldots, c_{j-1} = b - 1; \\ 0, & \text{otherwise,} \end{cases}$$

and $e_i = (c_i + d_i) \bmod b$. Then the reader can check again that $x + y = \sum_{i \geq 0} e_i b^{-i}$ and $0 \leq e_i < b$ for $i \geq 1$. So it just remains to prove that the sequence $\mathbf{e} = (e_i)_{i \geq 0}$ is $k$-automatic.

The definition of $d_i$ is clearly specified by a first-order formula and hence $(d_i)_{i \geq 0}$ is $k$-automatic. Hence $(e_i)_{i \geq 0}$ is $k$-automatic, and the result is proved. ☐

**Example 8.11.4** Consider the automatic real number $x$ whose base-2 representation $\mathbf{a} = (a_i)_{i \geq 0}$ is given by $a_i = 1$ if $(i)_2$ starts with 10, and 0 otherwise, and the automatic real number $y$ whose base-2 representation $\mathbf{b} = (b_i)_{i \geq 0}$ is given by $b_i = 1$ if $(i)_2$ starts with 101, and 0 otherwise. Here are the first few terms of the sequences in the proof:

| $i$ | 0 | 1 | 2 | 3 | 4 | 5 | 6 | 7 | 8 | 9 | 10 | 11 | 12 | 13 | 14 |
|-----|---|---|---|---|---|---|---|---|---|---|----|----|----|----|----|
| $a_i$ | 0 | 0 | 1 | 0 | 1 | 1 | 0 | 0 | 1 | 1 | 1 | 1 | 0 | 0 | 0 |
| $b_i$ | 0 | 0 | 0 | 0 | 0 | 1 | 0 | 0 | 0 | 0 | 1 | 1 | 0 | 0 | 0 |
| $c_i$ | 0 | 0 | 1 | 0 | 1 | 2 | 0 | 0 | 1 | 1 | 2 | 2 | 0 | 0 | 0 |
| $d_i$ | 0 | 0 | 0 | 1 | 1 | 0 | 0 | 1 | 1 | 1 | 1 | 0 | 0 | 0 | 0 |
| $e_i$ | 0 | 0 | 1 | 1 | 0 | 0 | 0 | 1 | 0 | 0 | 1 | 0 | 0 | 0 | 0 |

The corresponding automata are depicted in Figures 8.25–8.27.

*Exercise* 99 The $k$-automatic sequences form a vector space over $\mathbb{Q}$, under the operation of term-by-term addition of sequences, and multiplication of every term of a sequence by a rational number.

Show that the following problem is decidable: given DFAOs $M_1, M_2, \ldots, M_t$ computing $k$-automatic sequences, decide whether the corresponding sequences are $\mathbb{Q}$-linearly independent.

### 8.11.3 Continued fractions

In [344] we find the following result: let $\alpha_n = \sum_{0 \leq i \leq n} 3^{-2^i}$. Then for $n \geq 2$, the continued fraction for $\alpha_n$ is given by

$$[a_0, a_1, \ldots, a_{r-1}, a_r + 1, a_r - 1, a_{r-1}, a_{r-2}, \ldots, a_1], \tag{8.4}$$

where $\alpha_{n-1} = [a_0, a_1, \ldots, a_r]$.

Let $[b_0, b_1, b_2, \ldots]$ be the continued fraction for $\alpha = \lim_{n \to \infty} \alpha_n$. It is not hard to see that the continued fractions for $\alpha_n$ and $\alpha$ agree on the first $2^n$ terms. Let $\mathbf{b} = b_0 b_1 b_2 \cdots$. Let us show that $\mathbf{b}$ is a 2-automatic sequence. To do so, we compute the first 10,000 terms by the recursion, and then use the guessing procedure of Section 5.6. This gives us the DFAO depicted in Figure 8.28. We can now use Walnut to prove that our guessed automaton is correct, by verifying that the continued fraction obeys the rule (8.4). Storing the DFAO as B.txt in the Word Automata Library, it suffices to check that $\mathbf{b}[2..2^n - 1] = \mathbf{b}[2^n + 2..2^{n+1} - 1]^R$, $\mathbf{b}[2^n] = 3$, and $\mathbf{b}[2^n + 1] = 1$ for $n \geq 2$.

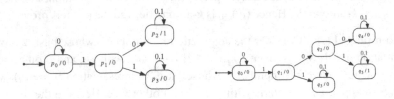

Figure 8.25  Automata for the sequences **a** and **b**.

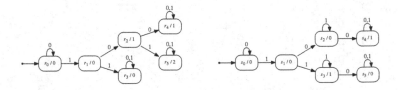

Figure 8.26  Automata for the sequences **c** and **d**.

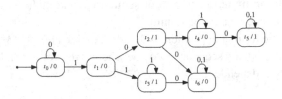

Figure 8.27  Automaton for the sequence **e**.

```
reg power2 msd_2 "0*10*":
eval bcheck1 "Ax,i ($power2(x) & x>=4 & i>=2 & i<x) =>
   B[i]=B[2*x+1-i]":
eval bcheck2 "Ax ($power2(x) & x>=4) => (B[x]=@3 & B[x+1]=@1)":
```

### 8.11.4  String attractors

A *string attractor* for a finite word $w$ is a set $P$ of positions of $w$ such that every nonempty factor $f$ of $w$ has an occurrence in $w$ that touches at least one of the positions of $P$. For example, $P = \{2, 4\}$ is a string attractor for the word 01001. See, for example, [222, 227, 232, 255, 256].

We can determine the length-$n$ prefixes of Thue-Morse that have a string attractor of cardinality 2 as follows:

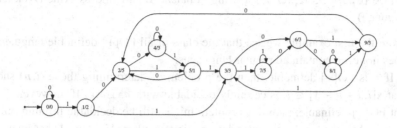

Figure 8.28 Automaton for a continued fraction.

```
def tmfe "A u,v (u>=i & u<=j & v+j=u+k) => T[u]=T[v]":
def stringatt2 "Ei1,i2 (i1<n) & (i2<n) & Ak,l (k<=l & l<n)
  => (Er,s r<=s & s<n & (s+k=r+l) & $tmfe(k,l,s) &
  ((r<=i1 & i1<=s) | (r<=i2 & i2<=s)))":
```

and this returns the set $\{1, 2, 3, 4, 5, 6\}$. For example, see [337].

## 8.12 What properties of factors can `Walnut` check?

All the examples in the previous section suggest a natural question: what are the kinds of properties of factors of automatic sequences that `Walnut` can check?

Many of these properties can be expressed as follows: given a language $L$, write a first-order statement asserting that the pair $(i, n)$ is such that $\mathbf{x}[i..i + n - 1] \in L$. What is the class of languages $L$ for which this be done?

As we have seen, this class of languages contains (for example):

- $\{x \in \Sigma^* : x = x^R\}$ (palindromes)
- $\{xx : x \in \Sigma^+\}$ (squares)
- $\{x : \nexists y \in \Sigma^+, n \geq 2 \text{ such that } x = y^n\}$ (primitive words)

and many other examples.

It turns out that the class has a name, the FO[+]-*definable languages*, and has been studied by several authors—see [341, 326] and especially [84]. Despite this, we still do not have a full understanding of what this language class is. We do know, however, that the following languages are *not* FO[+]-definable.

- $\{x \in \{0, 1\}^* : |x|_1 \equiv 0 \pmod 2\}$ (parity—words with an even number of 1s)
- $\{xx' : x, x' \in \Sigma^+ \text{ and } x' \text{ is a permutation of } x\}$ (abelian squares)

- $\{x \in \{0, 1\}^* : x$ represents a string of balanced parentheses $\}$ (the Dyck language)

From the first example we see that the class of all FO[+]-definable languages does not even contain all regular languages.

If $L$ is FO[+]-definable, then the problem of determining those $(i, n)$ such that $\mathbf{x}[i..i + n - 1] \in L$ is certainly decidable with Walnut. If, however, $L$ is not FO[+]-definable, then this problem might still be decidable through other means. As an example, consider determining whether $\mathbf{x}[i..i + n - 1]$ has an even number of 1s. This can be done indirectly, as follows: first, we can create a simple 2-state finite-state transducer $T$ that maps a word to the running sum of the number of 1s in the word, taken modulo 2. Define $\mathbf{y} = T(\mathbf{x})$. By a theorem of Cobham [91, Thm. 4], we know that from the DFAO for $\mathbf{x}$, we can computably determine a DFAO for $\mathbf{y}$. Then $\mathbf{x}[i..i + n - 1]$ has an even number of 1s if and only if $\mathbf{y}[i + n - 1] \equiv \mathbf{y}[i - 1] \pmod 2$. Currently, this sort of DFAO transformation is not built-in to Walnut, although it may be available in some future version.

More generally, using results in [334] we can prove the following result.

**Theorem 8.12.1**    *Given a DFA $M$ and a $k$-automatic sequence $\mathbf{x}$, we can compute a DFA of two arguments $i$ and $n$ such that $(i, n)_k$ is accepted if and only if $\mathbf{x}[i..i + n - 1]$ is accepted by $M$. Hence it is decidable if (a) any factor or (b) all factors of $\mathbf{x}$ belong to $L(M)$.*

# 9

# Regular sequences and enumeration problems

Although the automatic sequences form a large and interesting class, one draw-back is that they need to take their values in a finite set. But many interesting sequences, such as $(s_2(n))_{n \geq 0}$ (counting the sum of the bits in the base-2 representation of $n$), take their values in $\mathbb{N}$ (or $\mathbb{Z}$, or any semiring). We would like to find a generalization that allows this.

In this chapter we discuss this generalization of the automatic sequences, called the regular sequences. We show how these sequences can be represented, and how they relate to enumerating various aspects of automatic sequences. When the base of representation is base $k$, these sequences are called $k$-regular, but they can be generalized for any regular numeration system. For example, we can speak of Fibonacci-regular or Tribonacci-regular sequences. However, in what follows, most of our discussion is about $k$-regular sequences.

The two principal papers about $k$-regular sequences are [14] and [17]. Connections with rational series can be found in [47]. Number-theoretic aspects of $k$-regular sequences can be found in [94].

## 9.1 Two characterizations of $k$-regular sequences

The first way to characterize the $k$-regular sequences is to generalize the $k$-kernel. Instead of demanding that the $k$-kernel be finite, as is the case with $k$-automatic sequences, we require that there exists a finite set $S$ of sequences such that each sequence in the $k$-kernel belongs to $\langle S \rangle$, the set of all linear combinations of the sequences in $S$.

The second characterization uses the notation of recognizable formal series that we introduced in Section 4.10. Recall that $C_k = \{\epsilon\} \cup (\Sigma_k - \{0\})\Sigma_k^*$, the set of all canonical base-$k$ representations. A sequence of natural numbers $\mathbf{a} =$

$(a(n))_{n \geq 0}$ is $k$-regular if the function $f : \Sigma_k^* \to \mathbb{N}$ defined by

$$f(x) = \begin{cases} 0, & \text{if } x \notin C_k; \\ a(n), & \text{if } x \in C_k \text{ and } [x]_k = n \end{cases}$$

is recognizable. In other words, there exist vectors $v, w$ and a matrix-valued morphism $\gamma$ such that $a(n) = v\gamma((n)_k)w$ for all $n \geq 0$. As we have seen, the triple $(v, \gamma, w)$ is called a *linear representation* for **a**. Linear representations are, in general, not unique. The *rank* of a linear representation $(v, \gamma, w)$ is $n$ if $v$ and $w$ are $n$-element vectors.

Alternatively, we could do this for the reverse representations $(n)_k^R$ by transposing all the matrices and interchanging the roles of $v$ and $w$. This corresponds to an lsd-first reading of the base-$k$ representation of $n$.

**Example 9.1.1**   Let us work this all out for $s_2(n)$, the sum of the bits in the base-2 representation of $n$. Clearly

$$s_2(2n) = s_2(n)$$
$$s_2(2n + 1) = s_2(n) + 1,$$

and therefore $s_2(2^e \cdot n + i) = s_2(n) + s_2(i)$ for $e \geq 0, 0 \leq i < 2^e$. Thus every element of the 2-kernel of $(s_2(n))_{n \geq 0}$ can be written as a $\mathbb{Z}$-linear combination of the two sequences $(s_2(n))_{n \geq 0}$ and the constant sequence 1.

We can also find a representation for $s_2(n)$ in terms of "smaller" sequences in the 2-kernel only:

$$s_2(2n) = s_2(n)$$
$$s_2(4n + 1) = s_2(2n + 1) \tag{9.1}$$
$$s_2(4n + 3) = -s_2(n) + 2s_2(2n + 1).$$

To know if such a system is "complete"—that is, if the relations allow computing the sequence for all $n$, given a finite number of initial values—we draw a $k$-ary tree with the nodes labeled with elements of the $k$-kernel. We consider a node to be a leaf if there is an expression for the corresponding sequence in the $k$-kernel in terms of "smaller sequences"—that is, sequences higher up in the tree. If all paths from the root end at a leaf, and the tree is finite, then the system of relations is complete. The tree corresponding to the system (9.1) above is depicted in Figure 9.1.

To find a linear representation for $(s_2(n))_{n \geq 0}$, we write down the basis elements $(s_2(n))$ and the constant sequence 1 and consider the effect of *right* multiplication by matrices $\gamma(0)$ and $\gamma(1)$. We want these matrices to act as

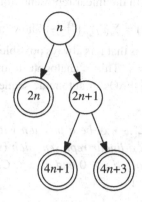

Figure 9.1 The 2-ary tree corresponding to the system (9.1).

follows:

$$[s_2(n) \quad 1] \cdot \gamma(0) = [s_2(2n) \quad 1]$$
$$[s_2(n) \quad 1] \cdot \gamma(1) = [s_2(2n + 1) \quad 1]$$

and so we can choose

$$v = \begin{bmatrix} 0 & 1 \end{bmatrix}; \quad \gamma(0) = \begin{bmatrix} 1 & 0 \\ 0 & 1 \end{bmatrix}; \quad \gamma(1) = \begin{bmatrix} 1 & 0 \\ 1 & 1 \end{bmatrix}; \quad w = \begin{bmatrix} 1 \\ 0 \end{bmatrix}.$$

The choice for $v$ corresponds to setting $n = 0$, and the choice for $w$ corresponds to picking out the particular sequence we are interested in.

Alternatively, we can find a representation from the sequences of the $k$-kernel. Here the basis elements are

$$(s_2(n))_{n \geq 0} \text{ and } (s_2(2n + 1))_{n \geq 0}.$$

We want

$$[s_2(n) \quad s_2(2n + 1)] \cdot \gamma(0) = [s_2(2n) \quad s_2(4n + 2)]$$
$$[s_2(n) \quad s_2(2n + 1)] \cdot \gamma(1) = [s_2(2n + 1) \quad s_2(4n + 3)].$$

We can choose

$$v = \begin{bmatrix} 0 & 1 \end{bmatrix}; \quad \gamma(0) = \begin{bmatrix} 1 & 0 \\ 0 & 1 \end{bmatrix}; \quad \gamma(1) = \begin{bmatrix} 0 & -1 \\ 1 & 2 \end{bmatrix}; \quad w = \begin{bmatrix} 1 \\ 0 \end{bmatrix}.$$

This example shows that even if a sequence takes only non-negative values, the entries of the matrices in the linear representation could be negative.

*Exercise* 100   Define $f(n) = \sum_{1 \le k \le n} \binom{n}{k} \frac{k}{n+k}$. Show that $v_2(f(n)) = -s_2(n)$.

One fine technical point is that it is always possible to choose the matrix $\gamma(0)$ in such a way that $v\gamma(0) = v$. This is analogous to the condition $\delta(q_0, 0) = q_0$ that we often require for DFAOs in automatic sequences. More precisely, we have

**Lemma 9.1.2**   *Let* $f : \Sigma_k^* \to \mathbb{N}$ *be a function with a linear representation* $(v, \gamma, w)$. *Then there exists a linear representation* $(v', \gamma', w')$ *for a function* $g$ *satisfying* $g(0^i x) = f(x)$ *for all* $i \ge 0$ *and all* $x \in C_k$. *Furthermore,* $v'$ *can be chosen such that* $v'\gamma'(0) = v'$.

For the proof, see [78].

*Exercise* 101   Let

$$v = \begin{bmatrix} 0 & 1 \end{bmatrix}; \qquad \gamma(0) = \begin{bmatrix} 2 & 0 \\ 0 & 1 \end{bmatrix}; \qquad \gamma(1) = \begin{bmatrix} 2 & 0 \\ 1 & 1 \end{bmatrix}; \qquad w = \begin{bmatrix} 1 \\ 0 \end{bmatrix}.$$

Prove that this is a linear representation for the function $f(n) = n$.

## 9.2 Examples of $k$-regular sequences

**Example 9.2.1**   Let $f_k(n)$ denote the number of "runs" of consecutive identical symbols in the base-$k$ expansion of $n$. Note that $f_k(0) = 0$. Then $(f_k(n))_{n \ge 0}$ is $k$-regular. For example, for $k = 2$ we get the following relations for $f = f_2$:

$$f(4n) = f(2n)$$
$$f(4n + 1) = f(2n) + 1$$
$$f(4n + 2) = f(2n + 1) + 1$$
$$f(4n + 3) = f(2n + 1).$$

This shows that the 2-kernel of $f$ is a linear combination of $(f(2n))_{n \ge 0}$, $(f(2n + 1))_{n \ge 0}$, and the constant sequence 1.

*Exercise* 102   Show that $|f(n + 1) - f(n)| \le 1$ for all $n$.

**Example 9.2.2**   Consider the sequence $s(n)$, defined by the relations $s(0) = 0$, $s(2n) = -s(n)$, and $s(2n + 1) = s(n) + 1$ for $n \ge 0$. This sequence was invented by the Danish composer Per Nørgård, who used it in some of his musical compositions [22]. From this we can find the following linear representation for

$s(n)$:

$$v = \begin{bmatrix} 0 & 1 \end{bmatrix}; \quad \gamma(0) = \begin{bmatrix} -1 & 0 \\ 0 & 1 \end{bmatrix}; \quad \gamma(1) = \begin{bmatrix} 1 & 0 \\ 1 & 1 \end{bmatrix}; \quad w = \begin{bmatrix} 1 \\ 0 \end{bmatrix}.$$

**Example 9.2.3** Take the linear representation for the function $f(n) = n$ from Exercise 101:

$$v = \begin{bmatrix} 0 & 1 \end{bmatrix}; \quad \gamma(0) = \begin{bmatrix} 2 & 0 \\ 0 & 1 \end{bmatrix}; \quad \gamma(1) = \begin{bmatrix} 2 & 0 \\ 1 & 1 \end{bmatrix}; \quad w = \begin{bmatrix} 1 \\ 0 \end{bmatrix}.$$

Now reverse it by taking the transpose of each array, and exchanging the role of $v$ and $w$:

$$v = \begin{bmatrix} 1 & 0 \end{bmatrix}; \quad \gamma(0) = \begin{bmatrix} 2 & 0 \\ 0 & 1 \end{bmatrix}; \quad \gamma(1) = \begin{bmatrix} 2 & 1 \\ 0 & 1 \end{bmatrix}; \quad w = \begin{bmatrix} 0 \\ 1 \end{bmatrix}.$$

This linear representation now computes the map that reverses the base-2 representation of $n$ and evaluates it; that is, it computes the function $n \to [(n)_2^R]_2$.

The following theorem shows that every polynomial generates a $k$-regular sequence.

**Theorem 9.2.4** *Let $p(X)$ be a polynomial with integer coefficients. Then $(p(n))_{n \geq 0}$ is $k$-regular for all $k \geq 2$.*

*Proof* Let $p(X) = \sum_{0 \leq i \leq t} a_i X^i$. We have

$$p(k^e \cdot n + j) = \sum_{0 \leq i \leq t} a_i (k^e \cdot n + j)^i$$

$$\in \langle 1, n, n^2, \dots, n^t \rangle,$$

where we have used the binomial theorem. $\square$

**Theorem 9.2.5** *Let $0 \leq a < k$ be an integer. Then the sequence $(|(n)_k|_a)_{n \geq 0}$ is $k$-regular.*

*Proof* We have

$$|(kn + b)_k|_a = \begin{cases} |(n)_k|_a, & \text{if } a \neq b; \\ 1 + |(n)_k|_a, & \text{if } a = b \text{ and } n > 0; \\ 0, & \text{if } a = b = n = 0. \end{cases}$$

The case $a = b = n = 0$ needs to be treated specially because, for example, if $k = 2$ then $|(2n)_2|_0 = |(n)_2|_0 = 0$ for $n = 0$.

So every sequence in the $k$-kernel of $(|(n)_k|_a)_{n \geq 0}$ is a linear combination of the three sequences $((|(n)_k|_a)_{n\geq 0}$, the constant sequence 1, and the sequence $[n = 0]$ taking the value 1 at $n = 0$, and 0 otherwise.                    □

*Exercise* 103   Show that if $t(0) = 1$, $t(2n) = n + 1$, $t(2n + 1) = t(n) + 1$, then $(t(n))_{n\geq 0}$ is a 2-regular sequence. Find its linear representation.

## 9.3  Converting between the two representations of $k$-regular sequences

Given one of the two kinds of representation of $k$-regular sequence, we would like to (computably) convert it to the other.

We first describe an algorithm to deduce the system of relations for the $k$-kernel, given a linear representation $(v, \gamma, w)$ of $f$. We assume the linear representation satisfies $v\gamma(0) = v$. If this is not the case, we can ensure it using Lemma 9.1.2.

Each element of the $k$-kernel of $f$ is of the form $(f(k^{|z|}n + [z]_k))_{n\geq 0}$ for some word $z \in \Sigma_k^*$. Now $f(k^{|z|}n + [z]_k) = v\gamma(xz)w = v\gamma(x)\gamma(z)w$ for $x = (n)_k$. The idea is to assemble relations for $\gamma(z)w$ as a linear combination of $\gamma(z')w$ for $z'$ preceding $z$ in radix order. For example, if $k = 2$, if we find an identity like

$$\gamma(101)w = 2\gamma(11)w - 3\gamma(010)w,$$

then left multiplication by $v\gamma(x)$ gives

$$v\gamma(x)\gamma(101)w = 2v\gamma(x)\gamma(11)w - 3v\gamma(x)\gamma(010),$$

and hence $f(8n + 5) = 2f(4n + 3) - 3f(8n + 2)$.[1]

Finding the relations, therefore, amounts to exploring the $k$-ary tree of all possible $z \in \Sigma_k^*$ in a breadth-first manner, using a queue, until enough relations are found. Initially the queue holds the empty word $\epsilon$.

At every stage we pop the queue, obtaining a word $z$, and computing the vector $\gamma(z)w$. We attempt to express this as a linear combination of the vectors $\gamma(z')w$ for $z' <_r z$ that we have already computed. If we cannot find such an expression for $\gamma(z)w$, we push $az$ onto the queue for each $a$, $0 < a < k$.

On the other hand, if we succeed in writing $\gamma(z)w$ as a linear combination of the $\gamma(z')w$, then this gives a relation for $f(k^{|z|}n + [z]_k)$ in terms of "smaller" elements of the $k$-kernel.

---

[1] This is an example of why we need $v\gamma(0) = v$, because when $n = 0$ we need $v\gamma(010)$ to be the same as $v\gamma(10)$.

**Example 9.3.1** Let's consider an example. Suppose $k = 2$ and

$$v = [-1\,1\,0]; \qquad \gamma(0) = \begin{bmatrix} 1 & 1 & 0 \\ 0 & 2 & 0 \\ 3 & 1 & -1 \end{bmatrix}; \qquad \gamma(1) = \begin{bmatrix} -1 & 3 & 0 \\ 1 & -1 & 2 \\ 0 & -1 & 1 \end{bmatrix}; \qquad w = \begin{bmatrix} 0 \\ 0 \\ 1 \end{bmatrix}.$$

The reader can easily verify that $v\gamma(0) = v$. We pop $\epsilon$ and compute $\gamma(\epsilon)w = w = [0\,0\,1]^T$. Here the $T$ as an exponent denotes, as usual, the transpose of the vector.

Next, we push 0 and 1 onto the queue. Again matrix multiplication gives us

$$\gamma(0)w = [0\,0\,-1]^T$$
$$\gamma(1)w = [0\,2\,1]^T.$$

The first of these gives us the relation $\gamma(0)w = -\gamma(\epsilon)w$, and hence $f(2n) = -f(n)$. However, it is impossible to write $\gamma(1)w$ as a linear combination of $\gamma(\epsilon)w$, so we push 01 and 11 onto the queue.

We can now verify that

$$\gamma(01)w = [2\,4\,1]^T$$
$$\gamma(11)w = [6\,0\,-1]^T.$$

It is not possible to express $\gamma(01)w$ as a linear combination of $\gamma(\epsilon)w$ and $\gamma(1)w$, so we push 001 and 101 onto the queue. However, by solving a linear system, we see that $\gamma(11)w = 2\gamma(\epsilon)w - 6\gamma(1)w + 3\gamma(01)w$, so we get the relation $f(4n + 3) = 2f(n) - 6f(2n + 1) + 3f(4n + 1)$.

Next, we can verify that

$$\gamma(001)w = [6\,8\,9]^T$$
$$\gamma(101)w = [10\,0\,-3]^T.$$

Again, solving linear systems we get

$$\gamma(001)w = 8\gamma(\epsilon)w - 2\gamma(1)w + 3\gamma(01)w$$
$$\gamma(101)w = 2\gamma(\epsilon)w - 10\gamma(1)w + 5\gamma(01)w,$$

which give us $f(8n + 1) = 8f(n) - 2f(2n + 1) + 3f(4n + 1)$ and $f(8n + 5) = 2f(n) - 10f(2n + 1) + 5f(4n + 1)$, respectively. At this point there is nothing left in the queue, so we have found a complete set of relations, namely

$$f(2n) = -f(n)$$
$$f(4n + 3) = 2f(n) - 6f(2n + 1) + 3f(4n + 1)$$
$$f(8n + 1) = 8f(n) - 2f(2n + 1) + 3f(4n + 1)$$
$$f(8n + 5) = 2f(n) - 10f(2n + 1) + 5f(4n + 1).$$

This concludes this example.

It is also possible to find relations in "the other direction". This doesn't produce relations for the $k$-kernel, but rather for the "reverse $k$-kernel", where the first few bits of the number's representation are fixed. Sometimes these relations are more useful than the ones for the $k$-kernel. Practically the same algorithm can be used, except instead of finding relations for $\gamma(z)w$ we find them for $v\gamma(z)$.

Next, we describe how to find a linear representation for a $k$-regular sequence, given the $k$-kernel. Let the $k$-kernel of $f$ be generated by the sequences $f_1 = f, f_2, \ldots, f_t$. Define the vector

$$V(n) = \begin{bmatrix} f_1(n) & f_2(n) & \cdots & f_t(n) \end{bmatrix}.$$

Since every element of the $k$-kernel can be written as a linear combination of $f_1, \ldots, f_t$, we can define the matrix $\gamma(a)$ by $V(kn + a) = V(n)\gamma(a)$. Set $v = V(0)$ and

$$w = \begin{bmatrix} 1 \\ 0 \\ \vdots \\ 0 \end{bmatrix}.$$

Then $v\gamma(0) = v$, and an easy induction gives $v\gamma((n)_k)w$.

**Example 9.3.2**   Consider a sequence $f$ defined by the following relations:

$$f(0) = 0$$
$$f(1) = 1$$
$$f(2) = 3$$
$$f(4n) = 2f(2n)$$
$$f(4n + 1) = f(2n) + f(2n + 1)$$
$$f(4n + 3) = -2f(n) + f(2n + 1) + f(4n + 2)$$
$$f(8n + 2) = 2f(2n) + f(4n + 2)$$
$$f(8n + 6) = -4f(n) + 2f(2n + 1) + 2f(4n + 2).$$

The 2-kernel of $f$ is therefore generated by the subsequences

$$(f(n))_{n\geq 0}, \quad (f(2n))_{n\geq 0}, \quad (f(2n + 1))_{n\geq 0}, \quad (f(4n + 2))_{n\geq 0}.$$

To find a linear representation for $f$, write

$$V(n) = \begin{bmatrix} f(n) & f(2n) & f(2n + 1) & f(4n + 2) \end{bmatrix}.$$

Then the relations for $f$ give

$$V(2n) = \begin{bmatrix} f(2n) & f(4n) & f(4n+1) & f(8n+2) \end{bmatrix}$$

$$= V(n) \begin{bmatrix} 0 & 0 & 0 & 0 \\ 1 & 2 & 1 & 2 \\ 0 & 0 & 1 & 0 \\ 0 & 0 & 0 & 1 \end{bmatrix}$$

$$V(2n+1) = \begin{bmatrix} f(2n+1) & f(4n+2) & f(4n+3) & f(8n+6) \end{bmatrix}$$

$$= V(n) \begin{bmatrix} 0 & 0 & -2 & -4 \\ 0 & 0 & 0 & 0 \\ 1 & 0 & 1 & 2 \\ 0 & 1 & 1 & 2 \end{bmatrix},$$

which gives us the linear representation

$$v = \begin{bmatrix} 0 & 0 & 1 & 3 \end{bmatrix} \quad ; \quad \gamma(0) = \begin{bmatrix} 0 & 0 & 0 & 0 \\ 1 & 2 & 1 & 2 \\ 0 & 0 & 1 & 0 \\ 0 & 0 & 0 & 1 \end{bmatrix}; \quad \gamma(1) = \begin{bmatrix} 0 & 0 & -2 & -4 \\ 0 & 0 & 0 & 0 \\ 1 & 0 & 1 & 2 \\ 0 & 1 & 1 & 2 \end{bmatrix}; \quad w = \begin{bmatrix} 1 \\ 0 \\ 0 \\ 0 \end{bmatrix}.$$

By the way, this $f(n)$ is the Mallows sequence: the unique increasing sequence of natural numbers such that $f(f(n)) = 2n$ for $n \neq 1$; see [16, Example 4].

## 9.4 Basic properties of $k$-regular sequences

The class of $k$-regular sequences is closed under many useful operations.

**Theorem 9.4.1** *Let* $\mathbf{u} = (u(n))_{n\geq 0}$ *and* $\mathbf{v} = (v(n))_{n\geq 0}$ *be $k$-regular sequences. Then*

(a) $\mathbf{u} + \mathbf{v} = (u(n) + v(n))_{n\geq 0}$
(b) $\mathbf{uv} = (u(n)v(n))_{n\geq 0}$
(c) $c\mathbf{u} = (c \cdot u(n))_{n\geq 0}$

*are all $k$-regular sequences.*

*Proof* Let the $k$-kernel of $\mathbf{u}$ be contained in $\langle \mathbf{u}_1, \mathbf{u}_2, \ldots, \mathbf{u}_r \rangle$ and let the $k$-kernel of $\mathbf{v}$ be contained in $\langle \mathbf{v}_1, \mathbf{v}_2, \ldots, \mathbf{v}_{r'} \rangle$.

(a) The $k$-kernel of $\mathbf{u} + \mathbf{v}$ is evidently contained in $\langle \mathbf{u}_1, \ldots, \mathbf{u}_r, \mathbf{v}_1, \ldots, \mathbf{v}_{r'} \rangle$.

(b) The $k$-kernel of $\mathbf{uv}$ is evidently contained in $\langle A \rangle$, where $A = \{ \mathbf{u}_i \mathbf{v}_j : 1 \leq i \leq r, 1 \leq j \leq r' \}$.

(c) Similarly, the $k$-kernel of $c\mathbf{u}$ is contained in $\langle c\mathbf{u}_1, c\mathbf{u}_2, \ldots, c\mathbf{u}_r \rangle$.

$\square$

**Theorem 9.4.2** *Let $i < k$, and let $p(X_1, X_2, \ldots, X_i)$ be a multivariate polynomial in $i$ indeterminates with rational coefficients. Then*

$$(p(|(n)_k|_1, |(n)_k|_2, \ldots, |(n)_k|_i))_{n \geq 0}$$

*is a $k$-regular sequence.*

*Proof* From Theorem 9.2.5 we know each $(|(n)_k|_i)_{n \geq 0}$ is $k$-regular sequence. The theorem then follows from the closure properties of $k$-regular sequences in Theorem 9.4.1. □

We can now show that a fundamental decision problem about $k$-regular sequences over $\mathbb{Z}$ is, in general, undecidable. Recall Hilbert's tenth problem: it is the problem to decide, given a multivariate polynomial $p(X_1, X_2, \ldots, X_i)$ with integer coefficients, whether there exist natural numbers $c_1, c_2, \ldots, c_i$ such that $p(c_1, c_2, \ldots, c_i) = 0$. A classic result, due to Putnam-Robinson-Matiyasevich, is that this problem is recursively unsolvable (undecidable) [259].

**Theorem 9.4.3** *Given a $k$-regular sequence $(f(n))_{n \geq 0}$, it is undecidable (recursively unsolvable) to determine if there exists $n_0 \in \mathbb{N}$ such that $f(n_0) = 0$.*

*Proof* We reduce from Hilbert's tenth problem. Given the polynomial

$$p(X_1, X_2, \ldots, X_i),$$

transform it to the $k$-regular sequence $f$ defined by

$$f(n) := (p(|(n)_k|_1, |(n)_k|_2, \ldots, |(n)_k|_i))_{n \geq 0}$$

where $k = i + 1$. Then $f(n_0) = 0$ for some $n_0$ iff

$$p(|(n_0)_k|_1, |(n_0)_k|_2, \ldots, |(n_0)_k|_i) = 0$$

for some $n_0$ iff there exist

$$c_1 = |(n_0)_k|_1, c_2 = |(n_0)_k|_2, \ldots, c_i = |(n_0)_k|_i$$

such that $p(c_1, c_2, \ldots, c_i) = 0$. So an algorithm to detect the presence of 0s in a $k$-regular sequence would allow us to solve Hilbert's tenth problem. □

For more undecidable problems involving $k$-regular sequences, see [231, 201].

The next result concerns finite-state transducers (see Section 4.12).

**Lemma 9.4.4** *Let $T = (Q, \Sigma_k, \Sigma_k, \delta, q_0, \lambda)$ be a deterministic finite-state transducer. Let $(f(n))_{n \geq 0}$ be a $k$-regular sequence. Let the domain of $\delta$ and $\lambda$ be extended to $\Sigma_k^*$ in the obvious way. Define $g(n) = f(T((n)_k))$. Then $(g(n))_{n \geq 0}$ is also a $k$-regular sequence.*

*Proof* Let $(v, \gamma, w)$ be a rank-$s$ linear representation for $f$. We create a linear representation $(v', \gamma', w')$ for $g$.

The idea is that $\gamma'(a)$, $0 \le a < k$, is an $n \times n$ matrix, where $n = rs$. It is easiest to think of $\gamma'(a)$ as an $r \times r$ matrix, where each entry is itself an $s \times s$ matrix. In this interpretation, $(\gamma'(a))_{i,j} = \gamma(\lambda(q_i, a))$ if $\delta(q_i, a) = q_j$.

An easy induction now shows that if $\delta(q_i, x) = q_j$ and $\lambda(q_i, x) = y$, then $(\gamma'(x))_{i,j} = \gamma(y)$. If we now let $v'$ be the vector $[v \quad 0 \quad \cdots \quad 0]$ and $w'$ be the vector $[w \quad w \quad \cdots \quad w]^T$, then it follows that $v'\gamma'(x)w' = v\gamma(T(x))w$. This gives a linear representation for $(g(n))_{n \ge 0}$. $\qquad\square$

**Corollary 9.4.5** *If $(f(n))_{n \ge 0}$ is k-regular, then so are the sequences*

   *(a) $(f(\lfloor n/a \rfloor))_{n \ge 0}$ for $a \in \mathbb{N}$, $a \ge 1$.*
   *(b) $(f(an + b))_{n \ge 0}$ for $a, b \in \mathbb{N}$.*

*Proof* We prove only (a), leaving (b) to the reader.

First, construct a finite-state transducer $T$ that outputs the base-$k$ representation of $\lfloor n/a \rfloor$ on input $(n)_k$. The idea is just to use long division, keeping track of the carries (which can be at most $a$) in the state. The transducer $T$ is depicted in Figure 9.2. A slight complication is to avoid outputting leading zeros, but this is easily handled (see the example for $a = 3$, $k = 2$). Next, we use the

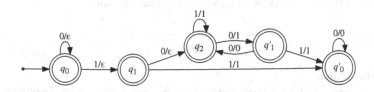

Figure 9.2 Transducer dividing by 3.

lemma above to see that $(f(T((n)_k)))_{n \ge 0}$ is $k$-regular. Thus we have shown that $(f(\lfloor n/a \rfloor))_{n \ge 0}$ is $k$-regular.

$\qquad\square$

The analogue of Theorem 5.8.1 is the following:

**Theorem 9.4.6** *A sequence is k-regular iff it is $k^f$-regular for some $f \ge 1$.*

*Proof* The same proof we used for Theorem 5.8.1 (essentially) works here, replacing "the kernel is finite" with "the kernel is a subset of a finitely generated module".                                                                    □

## 9.5 Non-closure of the class of regular sequences

The class of $k$-regular sequences is, unfortunately, *not* closed under some operations that, a priori, you might suspect it would be. For example, it is not closed under the operation of term-by-term division: $\mathbf{a}/\mathbf{b} = (a(n)/b(n))_{n\geq0}$. Take $\mathbf{a} = 1$, and $b(0) = 1$, $b(2n) = n + 1$, $b(2n + 1) = b(n) + 1$. Exercise 103 shows that $\mathbf{b}$ is 2-regular.

For $j \geq 1$ define $b_j(n) = b(2^j \cdot n + 2^{j-1} - 1)$; each $(b_j(n))_{n\geq0}$ is an element of the 2-kernel. Observe that $b_j(n) = n + j$ for $j \geq 1$. Suppose $1/\mathbf{b} = (1/b(n))_{n\geq0}$ were 2-regular. Then the module generated by

$$(1/b_1(n))_{n\geq0}, (1/b_2(n))_{n\geq0}, \ldots,$$

would have finite rank. Then for some $m \geq 1$, the rows of the $m \times m$ matrix $M = M_{i,j}$ defined by

$$M_{i,j} = \frac{1}{b_j(i-1)} = \frac{1}{i+j-1}$$

for $1 \leq i, j \leq m$ would be linearly independent and hence $\det M = 0$. But $M$ is an $m \times m$ Hilbert matrix, well known to have determinant

$$\frac{1}{\pm \prod_{1\leq k<m}(2k+1)\binom{2k}{k}^2} \neq 0,$$

a contradiction.

Similarly, the class of $k$-regular sequences is not closed under absolute value. Define $e_i(n)$ for $i \in \{0, 1\}$ to be the number of occurrences of the digit $i$ in the base-2 expansion of $n$. Define $f(n) = e_0(n) - e_1(n)$.

*Exercise* 104   Show that $f(n)$ is a 2-regular sequence.

Now $(f(2^j \cdot n))_{n\geq0}$ is a sequence in the 2-kernel of $(f(n))_{n\geq0}$, and we have

$$|f(2^j \cdot n)| = |e_0(n) - e_1(n) + j| \text{ for } n \geq 1, j \geq 0 .$$

Assume (to get a contradiction) that there is a finite linear combination, with not all $c_i = 0$, such that $\sum_{0\leq i\leq b} c_i f(2^i \cdot n) = 0$ for all $n$. Choose the least $i$ such that $c_i \neq 0$, and call it $a$. Then

$$f(2^a \cdot n) = \sum_{a+1\leq i\leq b} -(c_i/c_a)f(2^i n) \tag{9.2}$$

for all $n \geq 0$. Let $x_m$ be the least nonzero integer such that $e_0(x_m) - e_1(x_m) = 0$. It is easy to see that $x_m = 2^{-m} - 1$ for $m < 0$ and $x_m = 2^{m+1}$ for $m \geq 0$. Evaluate Eq. (9.2) at $n = x_m$ for $m \in \mathbb{Z}$. On the left-hand side of Eq. (9.2) we have

$$|f(2^a \cdot x_m)| = |e_0(x_m) - e_1(x_m) + a| = |m + a|.$$

On the right-hand side we have

$$\sum_{a+1 \leq i \leq b} -(c_i/c_a)|m + i|.$$

So

$$|m + a| = \sum_{a+1 \leq i \leq b} -(c_i/c_a)|m + i|$$

for all $m$. But for $m \geq -(a + 1)$ the right-hand side is of the form $Am + B$ for constants $A, B$, and hence is monotone. But the left-hand side is 1 for $m = -(a + 1)$, 0 for $m = -a$, and 1 for $m = 1 - a$, which is not monotone, a contradiction.

*Exercise 105*  Show that the class of $k$-regular sequences is not closed under the operations of elementwise max and min.

*Exercise 106*  Define $h(n)$ to be the length of the longest block of contiguous 1s in the binary expansion of $n$.

(a) Show that $h(2n) = h(n)$ and $h(2n + 1) = \max(h(n), v_2(n + 1) + 1)$ for $n \geq 0$.
(b) Show that $h$ is not 2-regular.

*Exercise 107*  Is the class of $k$-regular sequences closed under composition? That is, if $(f(n))_{n \geq 0}$ and $(g(n))_{n \geq 0}$ are both $k$-regular sequences taking values in $\mathbb{N}$, must $(f(g(n)))_{n \geq 0}$ be $k$-regular?

## 9.6 *k*-regular sequences and *k*-automatic sequences

**Theorem 9.6.1**  *A sequence* $\mathbf{a} = (a(n))_{n \geq 0}$ *taking finitely many values in* $\mathbb{Z}$ *is $k$-regular iff* $\mathbf{a}$ *is $k$-automatic.*

*Proof*  One direction is easy. If $\mathbf{a}$ is $k$-automatic then there is a DFAO $M = (Q, \Sigma, \Delta, \delta, q_0, \tau)$ generating it. We can then find a linear representation $(v, \gamma, w)$ for it by letting $v = [1\ 0\ 0 \cdots\ 0]$, $w$ be the column vector where the $i$th entry is $\tau(q_i)$, and $\gamma(a)$ be the matrix where the entry in row $i$ and column $j$ is 1 if $\delta(q_i, a) = q_j$ and 0 otherwise.

If **a** is $k$-regular, let its $k$-kernel be generated by some finite subset $\mathbf{a}_i :=$ $(a_i(n))_{n \geq 0}$ of the $k$-kernel, for $1 \leq i \leq r$, with $\mathbf{a} = \mathbf{a}_1$. Then

$$
V(n) = \begin{bmatrix} a_1(n) \\ a_2(n) \\ \vdots \\ a_r(n) \end{bmatrix},
$$

then $V(kn + a) = \gamma(a) \cdot V(n)$ for $0 \leq a < k$, and $n \geq 0$, and the appropriate matrix $\gamma(a)$. Note that when $n = 0$ and $a = 0$, the relation implies that $V(0) = \gamma(0)V(0)$.

Since **a** takes only finitely many values, the same is true of $(V(n))_{n \geq 0}$. Call the set of these values $S$. For $x \in S$ define the $k$-uniform morphism

$$
\sigma(x) = (\gamma(0) \cdot x)(\gamma(1) \cdot x) \cdots (\gamma(k-1) \cdot x).
$$

Then the infinite word

$$
\alpha = V(0)V(1)V(2) \cdots
$$

is the fixed point of $\sigma$ and $(a(n))_{n \geq 0}$ is given by an image of $\alpha$ under the coding that maps each vector to its first component.          □

**Example 9.6.2**   Consider the 3-regular sequence $(a(n))_{n \geq 0}$ defined by

$$
\begin{aligned}
a(n) &= n \text{ for } n = 0, 1, 2 \\
a(3n) &= a(n) \\
a(9n + 1) &= a(3n + 1) \\
a(9n + 2) &= a(3n + 2) \\
a(9n + 4) &= a(3n + 2) \\
a(9n + 5) &= -a(n) \\
a(9n + 7) &= 0 \\
a(9n + 8) &= -a(n) + a(3n + 2).
\end{aligned}
$$

Then one can prove that $(a(n))_{n \geq 0}$ takes the values $\{-3, -2, -1, 0, 1, 2, 3\}$ only (and 3 occurs for the first time at $a(401)$).

It follows that $(a(n))_{n \geq 0}$ is 3-automatic. In fact, using the technique in Section 4.11, we can show that it is generated by a 3-DFAO with 56 states.

## 9.7 Growth rate of *k*-regular sequences

In this section we prove a theorem about the growth rate of $k$-regular sequences. We can use it to show, for example, that $(2^n)_{n \geq 0}$ is not $k$-regular for any $k$. For more about this topic, see [78, 74].

**Theorem 9.7.1** *Suppose* $\mathbf{f} = (f(n))_{n \geq 0}$ *is a $k$-regular sequence. Then there exists a real number* $\alpha > 0$ *such that* $f(n) = O(n^{\alpha})$.

*Proof* Since $\mathbf{f}$ is $k$-regular, there exists a linear representation $(v, \gamma, w)$ such that

$$f(n) = v\gamma((n)_k)w = v\gamma(a_1)\gamma(a_2)\cdots\gamma(a_r)w,$$

where $(n)_k = a_1 a_2 \cdots a_r$.

Let $\| \cdot \|$ denote the $L_\infty$ norm of a vector, extended to matrices in the usual way. Then

$$
\begin{aligned}
|f(n)| &\leq \|v\| \, \|\gamma(a_1)\| \, \|\gamma(a_2)\| \, \cdots \, \|\gamma(a_r)\| \, \|w\| \\
&\leq \|v\| \, m^r \, \|w\| \\
&\leq cm^{1+\log_k n} \\
&= (cm)m^{\log_k n} \\
&= (cm)n^{\log_k m} \\
&= Cn^{\alpha},
\end{aligned}
$$

where $m = \max_{0 \leq i < k} \|\gamma(i)\|$ and $C = cm$ and $\alpha = \log_k m$. $\qquad\square$

Another result, which we will not prove, is that if $(f(n))_{n \geq 0}$ is unbounded and $k$-regular, then there exists a constant $c > 0$ such that $|f(n)| > c \log n$ infinitely often. See [34].

## 9.8 Principles of enumeration

In this section we will establish a fundamental connection between automatic sequences and $k$-regular sequences that will allow us to enumerate many aspects of automatic sequences. Here by "enumerate" we mean "give a good formula for" the particular quantity $f(n)$.

But what do we mean by "formula"? The usual but distressingly vague answer is that a formula for $f(n)$ is an expression involving familiar mathematical operations such as addition, subtraction, multiplication, division, exponentiation, and perhaps additional functions such as factorial, binomial coefficient, trig and inverse trig functions, $n$th roots, logarithm, floor, ceiling, summation, product, special functions, and so forth.

A more modern and precise answer is that a good formula for $f(n)$ is an *algorithm* that runs in little-$o$ of the time required to actually list the objects being enumerated, that is, in time $o(f(n))$; see the excellent article of Herb Wilf [381].

In particular, in the discussion that follows we prove the following basic result. Here the logical structures are those considered in Chapter 6.

**Theorem 9.8.1** *Let* x *be an automatic sequence, and let* P *be a first-order definable property of the factors of* x *such that, for each n,* P *holds for finitely many factors* x[i..i + n − 1]. *Then the function*

$$f(n) = |\{i \ : \ P \text{ holds for } \mathbf{x}[i..i + n - 1]\}|$$

*is a regular sequence.*

We will see that our method produces a linear representation for $f(n)$, and hence $f$ is computable by multiplying at most $(\log_k n)+1$ matrices together, and then pre- and post-multiplying by two vectors. Hence if $f$ enumerates objects connected with an automatic sequence x that are first-order definable, we get an algorithm that can compute $f(n)$ in $O(\log n)$ operations on integers about the size of $n$. We can consider this as a new tool to include in our "combinatorial toolkit" of computable techniques, along with more traditional enumeration decision methods (e.g., those of Wilf, Gosper, Zeilberger, etc.).

From the linear representation for $f$, we can computably determine a set of defining relations for the $k$-kernel. Sometimes these defining relations allow us to prove more detailed results about the behavior of $f$.

Let $P$ be a first-order property of a factor $\mathbf{x}[i..i + n - 1]$ of a $k$-automatic sequence. There are three fundamental enumeration problems we can handle. Each of the following sequences is $k$-regular, and we can "automatically" compute them by finding their linear representation:

- the total number of occurrences of factors of x having property $P$ that occur in a prefix of length $n$ of x.
- the number of distinct length-$n$ factors of x having property $P$.
- the total number of distinct factors of x having property $P$ that occur in a prefix of length $n$ of x.

However, the method can do even more than this:

- We can get an exact formula for $f(n)$ in terms of exponentials and polynomials for those $n$ for which $(n)_k$ is simply expressible (for example, of the form $uv^iw$ for some words $u, v, w$). This is true, for example, for $n$ of the form $k^r$ or $k^r \pm 1$. If $f(n)$ is an increasing function, this also gives us the asymptotic behavior of $f$. In some cases we can compute $\lim_{n\to\infty} f(n)/n$ or $\limsup_{n\to\infty} f(n)/n$, which are two common quantities of interest.

• We can get an exact formula for the *average behavior* of $f(n)$ in intervals like $0 \le n < k^r$ and $k^r \le n < k^{r+1}$.

• In some cases we can deduce an explicit formula for $f(n)$ in terms of familiar functions, or verify a previously-guessed formula.

• If $f(n)$ is bounded above by a constant, we can verify this, and "automatically" construct a DFAO computing $f$.

The cornerstone of our enumeration method is based on Corollary 4.9.2. Recall that it gives for $w \in \Delta^*$, $x \in \Sigma^*$, a linear representation for the number of accepting paths labeled with the word $w \times x$ in a DFA with input alphabet $\Delta \times \Sigma$.

Our enumeration method works (more or less) as follows: use `Walnut` to create a DFA, with inputs in base $k$, for a formula $P$ of two or more variables, $i_1, i_2, \ldots, i_t$ and $n$. Then the number $f(n)$ of $t$-tuples $(i_1, \ldots, i_t)$ for which $P(i_1, \ldots, i_t, n)$ is true is then given by $v\gamma((n)_k)w$, where $v, \gamma, w$ are as in the statement of Corollary 4.9.2. This gives a good formula for $f(n)$. We say "more or less" because there is a small bit of subtlety about leading zeros, which we will discuss in a minute.

Let's look at an example. Let us choose $\Sigma = \{0, 1\}$ and $\Delta = \Sigma \times \Sigma$. The automaton in Figure 9.3, created with `Walnut` using the command

```
def pairs "i<j & j<=n":
```

accepts those triples $(i, j, n)$ with $i < j$ and $j \le n$. (We have modified the output `Walnut` produces to make it more readable. Here the $*$ symbol in a transition means "either 0 or 1".) The number of such triples for a particular value of $n$ is easily seen to be $n(n-1)/2$. From this the corresponding linear representation is

$$v = [1\,0\,0\,0] \qquad \gamma(0) = \begin{bmatrix} 1&0&0&0\\0&2&0&1\\0&0&2&0\\0&0&0&4 \end{bmatrix} \qquad \gamma(1) = \begin{bmatrix} 1&1&1&0\\0&2&0&1\\0&0&2&2\\0&0&0&4 \end{bmatrix} \qquad w = \begin{bmatrix} 0\\0\\1\\1 \end{bmatrix}$$

which gives a good formula for the function $f(n) = n(n-1)/2$ for $n \ge 0$. It can be computed with `Walnut` with the command

```
eval pairmat n "i<j & j<=n":
```

which produces a file `pairmat.mpl` in the `Result` directory that defines the arrays $v, \gamma(0), \gamma(1), w$ in a format that `Maple` can understand.

In general we can use this idea to compute the number of $t$-tuples $(i_1, \ldots, i_t)$

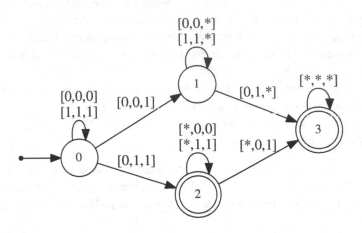

Figure 9.3  Automaton for $i < j$ and $j \le n$.

such that $P(i_1, i_2, \ldots, i_t, n)$ evaluates to TRUE. However, there are two small wrinkles to consider:

The first is that there may be infinitely many $t$-tuples corresponding to a given $n$. This would be true, for example, if $P(i, n)$ is defined to be "$i \ge n$". In this case the quantity $f(n)$ is, depending on your point of view, either infinite or not well defined, and so we cannot expect any sensible answer from our matrix approach.[2] More precisely, the linear representation will give larger and larger values when we evaluate it on the inputs $(n)_k$, $0(n)_k$, $00(n)_k$, etc., violating our convention that leading zeros should make no difference in our computations with automata. Caution: formulas involving the empty word often may result in infinitely many $i$ for $n = 0$.

The second wrinkle is that some of the $t$-tuples we wish to count might have a base-$k$ representation that is *longer* than that of $n$. In this case, computing $v\gamma((n)_k)w$ is *not* sufficient; it will miss some tuples where an $i_j > n$ and not count them. So we might have to compute $v\gamma(0^i(n)_k)w$ for an appropriate value of $i$ instead. However, provided $f(n)$ is not infinite, a pumping lemma argument easily shows that $i$ can be no larger than the number of states in our original DFA. So to correctly handle the case of large $i$, we just replace $v$ in our linear

---

[2]  There is a way around this, which is to use the semiring $\mathbb{N} \cup \{\infty\}$ in place of $\mathbb{N}$; see [78].

representation with $v' = v\gamma(0)^i$ where $i$ is the number of states in the DFA. This works provided that our DFA has the property that $\delta(q_0, [0, 0, \ldots 0]) = q_0$, which we can easily ensure and is a guaranteed feature of the automata that Walnut produces. Alternatively, we can simply multiply $v$ by $\gamma(0)$ on the right until the result stabilizes, and call the result $v'$. This replacement is done automatically in Walnut 3.

Let us now see how to produce first-order formulas for each of the three fundamental enumeration problems listed above.

The first problem is to find the total number of occurrences of factors of $\mathbf{x}$ having property $P$ that occur in a prefix of length $n$ of $\mathbf{x}$. An occurrence is of the form $\mathbf{x}[i..i+m-1]$. To say that this occurs in the length-$n$ prefix of $\mathbf{x}$ means that $i + m - 1 \leq n - 1$, which is equivalent to the inequality $i + m \leq n$. This gives us the following formula:

$$(i + m \leq n) \wedge P(i, n).$$

The number of triples $(i, m, n)$ for which this formula evaluates to TRUE then gives us the desired number of factors in a length-$n$ prefix.

The second of the three basic enumeration problems on automatic sequences is to find the number of distinct length-$n$ factors having property $P$. At first glance one might think the appropriate formula is just $P(i, n)$. However, a little reflection shows this will not work: typically there will be infinitely many such $i$ because the associated formula counts *occurrences* of factors with the property, and not the factors themselves. As we saw in Section 8.1.12, the way to resolve this is to count *novel occurrences* only: these are indices $i$ such that $\mathbf{x}[i..i+n-1]$ is a factor that never occurred previously in the sequence. We can therefore use the formula

$$P(i, n) \wedge \forall j\, (j < i) \implies \neg\text{FactorEq}(i, j, n)$$

and enumerate the pairs $(i, n)$ for which this is true.

The third problem is to count the total number of distinct factors having property $P$ that occur in a prefix of length $n$. Here we combine the two previous ideas, obtaining the formula

$$(i + m \leq n) \wedge P(i, m) \wedge \forall j\, (j < i) \implies \neg\text{FactorEq}(i, j, n).$$

With these three formulas as templates, we can find good formulas for a large number of different properties of automatic sequences and recover many results from the literature.

Next, let us see how to find exact formulas for $f(n)$ for $n$ of a special form. To do so we need to detour a bit into the theory of linear recurrences with constant coefficients.

If $(a(n))_{n\geq 0}$ is a sequence of complex numbers satisfying the relation

$$a(n) = \sum_{1 \leq i \leq t} c_i a(n - i),$$

for $n \geq i$ and constants $c_1, c_2, \ldots, c_t$, we say that $a(n)$ satisfies a linear recurrence of order $t$. For example, the Fibonacci numbers satisfy the linear recurrence $F_n = F_{n-1} + F_{n-2}$ for $n \geq 2$. Note that this usage of the term "linear recurrence" unfortunately conflicts with the same term as the property defined in Section 2.2.

The *annihilating polynomial* for $(a(n))_{n\geq 0}$ is defined to be

$$p(x) = X^t - c_1 X^{t-1} - \cdots - c_{t-1} X - c_t.$$

The fundamental theorem of linear recurrences (see, e.g., [141, §1.1]) is the following:

**Theorem 9.8.2** *Suppose a linear recurrence sequence $(a(n))_{n\geq 0}$ has annihilating polynomial $p$, which factors as $X^r \prod_{1 \leq i \leq j}(X - \alpha_i)^{e_i}$ for some distinct complex numbers $\alpha_1, \alpha_2, \ldots, \alpha_j$ and positive integers $e_1, e_2, \ldots, e_j$. Then*

$$a(n) = \sum_{1 \leq i \leq j} p_i(n)\alpha_i^n,$$

*for $n \geq r$, where each $p_i$ is a polynomial of degree at most $e_i - 1$.*

An expression of the form $\sum_{1 \leq i \leq j} p_i(n)\alpha_i^n$ is called an *exponential polynomial*.

The values of $\alpha_i$ are the zeros of the annihilating polynomial $p$ and can be determined by factoring the polynomial $p$ over $\mathbb{C}$ with a computer algebra system, such as `Maple`. The values of the coefficients of the polynomials $p_i$ can then be computed by solving a suitable system of linear equations.

**Example 9.8.3** Suppose $g(0) = 0$, $g(1) = 1$, and $g(n) = g(n-1) + g(n-2) + n$. Then

$$g(n) = g(n - 1) + g(n - 2) + n$$
$$g(n - 1) = g(n - 2) + g(n - 3) + n - 1$$
$$g(n - 2) = g(n - 3) + g(n - 4) + n - 2,$$

so adding together the first line, $-2$ times the second line, and the third line gives us (after simplification)

$$g(n) = 3g(n - 1) - 2g(n - 2) - g(n - 3) + g(n - 4).$$

Hence an annihilating polynomial for $g$ is $X^4 - 3X^3 + 2X^2 + X - 1$, which factors into $(X - 1)^2(X^2 - X - 1)$. Let $\alpha > \beta$ be the two zeros of $X^2 - X - 1$. Then the fundamental theorem gives us that $g(n) = c_1\alpha^n + c_2\beta^n + c_3n + c_4$ for some constants $c_1, c_2, c_3, c_4$. Letting $n = 0, 1, 2, 3$ and solving the resulting linear system gives us $c_1 = (5 + \sqrt{5})/2$, $c_2 = -(3 + \sqrt{5})/2$, $c_3 = \sqrt{5}$, $c_4 = -1$.

While this is indeed an exact formula for $g(n)$, we can obtain a better formula as follows: observe that any linear combination of $\alpha^n$ and $\beta^n$ can be rephrased as a linear combination of the Fibonacci numbers $F_{n+1}$ and $F_n$. Hence we can write $g(n) = d_1F_{n+1} + d_2F_n + d_3n + d_4$ for some constants $d_1, d_2, d_3, d_4$. Again letting $n = 0, 1, 2, 3$ and solving the resulting linear system gives us $d_1 = 1$, $d_2 = 1$, and $d_3 = -1$, and so we have proved $g(n) = 3F_{n+1} + 2F_n - n - 3 = F_{n+4} - n - 3$, which is perhaps a more satisfying formula.

Now we connect the powers of matrices with linear recurrences.

**Theorem 9.8.4** *Let $M$ be an $n \times n$ matrix with minimal polynomial $p(X)$ of degree $d$. Let $0 \leq i, j < n$ and define $A(n) = (M^n)_{i,j}$. Then $(A(n))_{n \geq 0}$ satisfies a linear recurrence with annihilating polynomial $p$.*

*Proof* A matrix $M$ satisfies its own minimal polynomial $p$; that is, $p(M) = 0$. In other words, if $p(X) = X^t - c_1X^{t-1} - \cdots - c_{t-1}X - c_t$, then

$$M^t = c_1M^{t-1} + \cdots + c_{t-1}M + c_t.$$

Multiplying both sides by $M^n$ we get

$$M^{n+t} = c_1M^{n+t-1} + \cdots + c_{t-1}M^{n+1} + c_tM^n.$$

But if this relation holds for the matrix $M$, it also holds for the entry in the $i$th row and $j$th column. Hence

$$A(n + t) = c_1A(n + t - 1) + \cdots + c_{t-1}A(n + 1) + c_tA(n),$$

for all $n \geq 0$. □

**Corollary 9.8.5** *Let $v$ be a row vector of dimension $t$, let $M$ be a $t \times t$ matrix, and $w$ be a column vector of dimension $t$. Let $p(x)$ be the minimal polynomial of $M$. Then the sequence $(vM^nw)_{n \geq 0}$ satisfies a linear recurrence with annihilating polynomial $p$.*

*Proof* If $p$ annihilates two or more linear recurrences simultaneously, then it also annihilates any linear combination of them. □

## 9.9 Asymptotic behavior of $k$-regular sequences

By combining Theorem 9.8.2 and Corollary 9.8.5, we get an algorithm for determining an exact formula for $f(k^n)$, if $f$ is expressible as the number of tuples $(i_1, \ldots, i_t, n)$ making some automatic formula $P(i_1, \ldots, i_t, n)$ evaluate to TRUE:

1 Use Walnut to find a linear representation $(v, \gamma, w)$ for $f(n)$.

2 Find the minimal polynomial $p(X)$ of $\gamma(0)$. This can be done with a computer algebra system, such as Maple.

3 Factor the minimal polynomial $p(X)$, writing $p(X) = X^r \prod_{1 \leq i \leq j} (X - \alpha_i)^{e_i}$. Again, this can be done with any computer algebra system.

4 Suppose the corresponding exponential polynomial

$$\sum_{1 \leq i \leq j} p_i(n) \alpha_i^n$$

has $t$ degrees of freedom; that is, $t = \sum_i \deg p_i$. Evaluate $f(k^n)$ for $n = r, r+1, \ldots, r+t-1$ both via the linear representation and the exponential polynomial.

5 Solve the resulting linear system to find the coefficients of the polynomials $p_i(n)$.

More generally, we can find an exact formula for $f(m)$ for any $m$ such that $(m)_k$ is of the form $uv^n w$ for some words $u, v, w$. In this case, instead of working with the minimal polynomial for $\gamma(0)$, we work with the minimal polynomial for $\gamma(v)$. The roots of the resulting polynomial then need to be raised to the $1/|v|$ power.

Sometimes we are not so concerned with an exact formula for $f(k^n)$, but rather its asymptotic behavior. This corresponds to understanding the behavior of the dominant terms of an exponential polynomial. If the annihilating polynomial has a single dominant zero $\alpha$ (i.e., one that dominates the others in terms of absolute value), then the asymptotic behavior of $f(k^n)$ is (up to less quickly growing terms) $p(n)\alpha^n$. If, for example, $f(m)$ is monotonically increasing, then we now understand its asymptotic growth rate.

The reason why an exact formula for $f(m)$ in terms of an exponential polynomial is easy to obtain for $m = k^n$ is that it depends, essentially, on the powers of a *single* matrix—namely, $\gamma(0)$—and powers of a single matrix are completely understood. In general, $m$ will usually have a representation in terms of two or more distinct digits, which corresponds to the product of two or more different matrices. That kind of product is *much* harder to understand! Even in the asymptotic case, we need to understand something called the "joint spectral radius" [93], which can be very hard to compute.

For many of the enumeration problems we want to solve, the function $f(n)$ we are concerned with is $O(n)$. In this case it is often of interest to compute $\sup_{n \geq 1} f(n)/n$, $\liminf_{n \to \infty} f(n)/n$, $\inf_{n \geq 1} f(n)/n$, and $\limsup_{n \to \infty} f(n)/n$. While evaluating these limits is undecidable in general, sometimes the following strategy will give us some bounds. First, using the linear representation we can graph $f(n)/n$ for the first thousand or million values. This will often suggest the $n$ for which extremal values of $f(n)/n$ occur locally, and these values of $n$ often will have simple base-$k$ representations, of the form $xy^*z$ for some words $x, y, z$.[3] One can then use the method above to compute the exact behavior of $f$ at these special values of $n$, which will produce lower bounds on the sup and lim sup, and upper bounds on the inf and lim inf. Upper bounds on $f(n)$ can also be obtained by using matrix norms on the elements of a linear representation, such as the $L_\infty$ norm, but these are usually weak. Even a simple finite decision problem involving $k$-regular sequences is NP-complete [92].

In some cases $f(n)$ is bounded above by a constant. This can be determined through the algorithms of Mandel and Simon [254] or Jacob [211, 212, 213]. However, to the best of my knowledge, publicly-available implementations of these are not available. Therefore, instead, we can use the "semigroup trick" as discussed in Section 4.11. If $f(n)$ is indeed bounded by a constant, the semigroup trick will prove this fact. Further, it can actually produce a DFAO computing $f$. If we start with a minimized linear representation, and $f(n)$ is bounded above by a constant, then the semigroup trick is guaranteed to halt and produce a finite automaton computing $f(n)$. This follows from [47, Cor. II.2.3].

Most of what we have said above for $k$-automatic sequences also works for Fibonacci- and Tribonacci-automatic sequences, with minor modifications. The main modification is that powers of $k$ are replaced by the Fibonacci numbers and Tribonacci numbers, respectively.

We say a sequence $(s_n)$ is "Fibonacci-regular" if there is a linear representation for it in Fibonacci representation. That is, there are vectors $v, w$ and a matrix-valued morphism $\gamma$ such that if $z$ is the Fibonacci representation of $n$, then $s_n = v\gamma(z)w^T$.

**Exercise 108** Consider the linear representation $(v, \gamma, w)$ defined as follows:

$$v = [1\,0\,0\,0\,0\,0] \quad \gamma(0) = \begin{bmatrix} 1 & 0 & 0 & 0 & 0 & 0 \\ 0 & 0 & 0 & 1 & 1 & 0 \\ 1 & 0 & 0 & 0 & 0 & 0 \\ 0 & 0 & 0 & 1 & 1 & 0 \\ 0 & 0 & 0 & 1 & 0 & 0 \\ 0 & 0 & 0 & 1 & 0 & 0 \end{bmatrix} \quad \gamma(1) = \begin{bmatrix} 0 & 1 & 1 & 0 & 0 & 0 \\ 0 & 0 & 0 & 0 & 0 & 0 \\ 0 & 0 & 0 & 0 & 0 & 0 \\ 0 & 1 & 0 & 0 & 0 & 1 \\ 0 & 1 & 0 & 0 & 0 & 0 \\ 0 & 0 & 0 & 0 & 0 & 0 \end{bmatrix} \quad w = \begin{bmatrix} 0 \\ 1 \\ 0 \\ 1 \\ 1 \\ 1 \end{bmatrix}.$$

Prove that $v\gamma((n)_F)w = n$ for all $n \geq 0$. Hint: prove by induction that if $r = |x|$,

---

[3] But not always! This was the so-called *Lagarias-Wang finiteness conjecture*, which has been disproven [49].

then

$$\gamma(xa0) = \begin{bmatrix} 1 & 0 & 0 & [xa]_F & [x]_F + a & 0 \\ 0 & 0 & 0 & 0 & 0 & 0 \\ 0 & 0 & 0 & 0 & 0 & 0 \\ 0 & 0 & 0 & F_{r+1} & F_r & 0 \\ 0 & 0 & 0 & F_r & F_{r-1} & 0 \\ 0 & 0 & 0 & 0 & 0 & 0 \end{bmatrix}$$

for $a \in \{0, 1\}$ and

$$\gamma(x01) = \begin{bmatrix} 0 & [x0]_F & 1 & 0 & 0 & [x]_F \\ 0 & 0 & 0 & 0 & 0 & 0 \\ 0 & 0 & 0 & 0 & 0 & 0 \\ 0 & F_{r+1} & 0 & 0 & 0 & F_r \\ 0 & F_r & 0 & 0 & 0 & F_{r-1} \\ 0 & 0 & 0 & 0 & 0 & 0 \end{bmatrix}.$$

*Exercise* 109    Define $f(n)$ to be the number of partitions of $n$ as a sum of distinct Fibonacci numbers $\geq 1$, where order does not matter. For example, $f(11) = 3$ because $11 = 8 + 3 = 8 + 2 + 1 = 5 + 3 + 2 + 1$. Show that $f(n)$ is Fibonacci-regular. Further, show that for each $k \geq 1$, the set $\{n : f(n) = k\}$ is Fibonacci-automatic. For more information about $f(n)$, see [85].

*Exercise* 110    Consider the White-Robbins-Ardila power series

$$F(x) = \prod_{n \geq 2} (1 - x^{F_n}) = (1 - x)(1 - x^2)(1 - x^3) \cdots = \sum_{i \geq 0} e_i x^i,$$

where $F_n$ is the $n$th Fibonacci number, with $F_0 = 0$, and $F_1 = 1$ [379, 321, 20, 352]. Show that the sequence $(e_i)_{i \geq 0}$ is Fibonacci-regular. Then use the "semigroup trick" to show that $e_i \in \{-1, 0, 1\}$ for all $i$.

## 9.10 Average values of regular sequences

If $f$ is $k$-regular, we can also get an exact, closed-form expression for sums like $\sum_{0 \leq n < k^r} f(n)$ and $\sum_{k^r \leq n < k^{r+1}} f(n)$, and hence for the average values of $f$ over intervals like $[0, k^r)$ and $[k^r, k^{r+1})$.

Suppose $f$ has linear representation $(v, \gamma, w)$. Then

$$\sum_{0 \leq n < k^r} f(n) = \sum_{x \in \Sigma_k^r} v\gamma(x)w = v \left( \sum_{x \in \Sigma_k^r} \gamma(x) \right) w = v \left( \sum_{a \in \Sigma_k} \gamma(a) \right)^r w,$$

and so the sum $S(r) := \sum_{0 \leq n < k^r} f(n)$ can be written as an exponential polynomial in terms of the zeros of the minimal polynomial of the matrix $M :=$

$\sum_{a\in\Sigma_k}\gamma(a)$. Once we have that, the average value of $f(n)$ in the interval $0 \le n < k^r$ is $k^{-r}S(r)$. To compute $\sum_{k^r\le n<k^{r+1}} f(n)$, it suffices to compute $S(r+1)-S(r)$.

For the average-case behavior of regular sequences in other numeration systems, we can use the same sort of idea, provided that the linear representation $v\gamma(x)w$ evaluates to 0 on all words $x$ that correspond to "illegal" representations. For example, for Fibonacci-regular sequences, we can require that $v\gamma(x)w$ be 0 on all words $x$ having two consecutive 1s. If this requirement is not fulfilled, we have to work a bit harder: let $Y_r$ be the set of all binary words of length $r$ that do not contain the factor 11. Then it is easy to see that $Y_r = 0Y_{r-1} \cup 10Y_{r-2}$. Let $f$ be Fibonacci-regular with linear representation $(v, \gamma, w)$ and suppose we want to compute $\sum_{0\le n<F_r} f(n)$ for $r \ge 2$. Then

$$\sum_{0\le n<F_r} f(n) = \sum_{0\le n<F_r} v\gamma((n)_F)w = \sum_{x\in Y_{r-2}} v\gamma(x)w = v\left(\sum_{x\in Y_{r-2}} \gamma(x)\right)w,$$

so it suffices to show how to compute $S_r := \sum_{x\in Y_r} \gamma(x)$. Here we have used the fact that $\gamma(x) = \gamma(0^ix)$ for all $i \ge 0$.

We have

$$S_r = \sum_{x\in Y_r} \gamma(x)$$

$$= \sum_{x\in 0Y_{r-1}\cup 10Y_{r-2}} \gamma(x)$$

$$= \left(\sum_{x\in 0Y_{r-1}} \gamma(x)\right) + \left(\sum_{x\in 10Y_{r-2}} \gamma(x)\right)$$

$$= \gamma(0)\left(\sum_{x\in Y_{r-1}} \gamma(x)\right) + \gamma(10)\left(\sum_{x\in Y_{r-2}} \gamma(x)\right)$$

$$= \gamma(0)S_{r-1} + \gamma(10)S_{r-2}.$$

Now suppose $S_r$ is the matrix with entries $[s^r_{i,j}]_{0\le i,j<t}$ for some $t$. Define

$$C^r_j = \begin{bmatrix} s^r_{0,j} \\ s^r_{1,j} \\ \vdots \\ s^r_{t-1,j} \end{bmatrix},$$

the $j$th column of $S_r$. Let

$$M = \begin{bmatrix} \gamma(0) & \gamma(10) \\ I_t & 0_t \end{bmatrix},$$

where $I_t$ is the $t \times t$ identity matrix and $\mathbf{0}_t$ is the $t \times t$ matrix of all 0s. Then

$$\begin{bmatrix} C_j^r \\ C_j^{r-1} \end{bmatrix} = M \cdot \begin{bmatrix} C_j^{r-1} \\ C_j^{r-2} \end{bmatrix}. \tag{9.3}$$

Hence each column of $S_r$, and hence each entry of $S_r$, satisfies a linear recurrence whose annihilating polynomial is the minimal polynomial of $M$. Thus we can obtain an annihilating polynomial $p(X)$ for $\sum_{0 \le n < F_r} f(n)$ and we can use our previous techniques to determine an exact formula (an exponential polynomial) for this sum.

A similar technique works for Tribonacci-regular sequences.

## 9.11 Enumeration examples

In this section we show how to enumerate more than a dozen different properties of automatic sequences using the methods of the previous section. (About a dozen more, using a different method, are discussed in the next chapter.)

We start with subword complexity.

### 9.11.1 Subword complexity

Subword complexity counts the number of distinct length-$n$ factors in an infinite word. To use our approach, we have to count novel occurrences: factors that never occurred previously. Let us carry this out for the Thue-Morse sequence **t**:

```
eval tmsubc n "Aj j<i => ~$tmfactoreq(i,j,n)":
```

The formula asserts that the factor $\mathbf{x}[i..i + n - 1]$ never occurred earlier in **t**. Walnut produces a file `tmsubc.mpl` with the corresponding linear representation, and it is stored in the `Result` directory. We now need to modify the vector $v$ as discussed in Section 9.8, and this gives the following linear representation for $\rho_t(n)$:

$$v = [1\,1\,0\,0\,1\,0\,0\,0] \quad \gamma(0) = \begin{bmatrix} 1&1&0&0&0&0&0&0 \\ 0&0&0&0&1&0&0&0 \\ 0&0&2&0&0&0&0&0 \\ 0&0&1&0&0&1&0&0 \\ 0&0&0&0&0&0&0&0 \\ 0&0&1&0&0&1&0&0 \\ 0&0&0&0&0&0&1&0 \\ 0&0&0&0&0&0&2&0 \end{bmatrix} \quad \gamma(1) = \begin{bmatrix} 0&0&1&1&0&0&0&0 \\ 0&0&0&0&0&1&1&0 \\ 0&0&2&0&0&0&0&0 \\ 0&0&2&0&0&0&0&0 \\ 0&0&0&0&0&0&1&1 \\ 0&0&2&0&0&0&0&0 \\ 0&0&0&0&0&1&1&0 \\ 0&0&0&0&0&2&0&0 \end{bmatrix} \quad w = \begin{bmatrix} 1 \\ 0 \\ 1 \\ 1 \\ 0 \\ 0 \\ 0 \\ 0 \end{bmatrix}.$$

If we graph $f(n) := \rho_t(n)/n$ for some small values of $n$ (using the linear representation, of course, and not computing directly from examining factors of **t**!) we obtain the picture in Figure 9.4, which suggests that $f$ has a local minimum

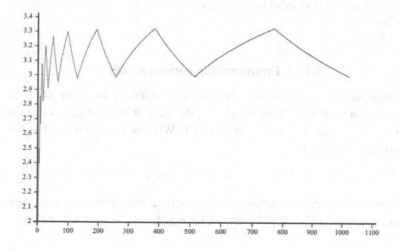

Figure 9.4 Graph of $f(n)$.

at $n = 2^r + 1$ and a local maximum at $n = 3 \cdot 2^r + 1$. Now the minimal polynomial for $\gamma(0)$ is $X^2(X - 1)(X - 2)$, so this means that $\rho_t(2^r + 1) = c_1 2^r + c_2$ for $r \geq 2$. By solving the associated linear system, we get $c_1 = 3$ and $c_2 = 0$. Therefore $\rho_t(2^r + 1) = 3 \cdot 2^r$, an identity that actually holds for $r \geq 1$. Similarly we find $\rho_t(3 \cdot 2^r + 1) = 10 \cdot 2^r$, which holds for $r \geq 0$. Thus we have shown $\limsup_{n \to \infty} \rho_t(n)/n \geq 10/3$ and $\liminf_{n \to \infty} \rho_t(n)/n \leq 3$.

In fact, close examination of the values of $\rho_t(n)$ suggests the following conjecture for $n \geq 3$:

$$\rho_t(n) = \begin{cases} 3 \cdot 2^r + 4(i - 1), & \text{if } n = 2^r + i, \, 1 \leq i \leq 2^{r-1}; \\ 5 \cdot 2^r + 2(i - 1), & \text{if } n = 3 \cdot 2^{r-1} + i, \, 1 \leq i \leq 2^{r-1}. \end{cases} \tag{9.4}$$

We will see a different approach to subword complexity in Section 10.8.14, which will allow us to *prove* the formula in (9.4).

Let us now compute the average value of $\rho_t(n)$ in the range $2^r \leq n < 2^{r+1}$. To do so, we start by computing the minimal polynomial of $\gamma(0) + \gamma(1)$: it is $X^3(X-1)(X-2)(X-4)$. So we know that $g(r) := \sum_{0 \leq n < 2^r} \rho_t(n) = c_1 \cdot 4^r + c_2 \cdot 2^r + c_3$ for some constants $c_1, c_2, c_3$ and $r \geq 3$. Solving the linear system, we get $c_1 = 19/12$, $c_2 = -9/2$, and $c_3 = 17/3$. So this gives $g(r) = \frac{19}{12} \cdot 4^r - \frac{9}{2} 2^r + 17/3$, which actually holds for $r \geq 1$. Hence

$$g(r + 1) - g(r) = \frac{57}{12} \cdot 4^r - \frac{9}{2} 2^r.$$

So the average value of $\rho_t(n)$ in the range $2^r \leq n < 2^{r+1}$ is $\frac{57}{12} \cdot 2^r - \frac{9}{2}$, which holds for $r \geq 1$.

## 9.11.2 Enumerating subsequences

Instead of factors we can count (scattered) subsequences, which do not have to be contiguous. For example, let $f(n)$ be the number of subsequences of the form $0 \cdots 1 \cdots 0$ in the length-$n$ prefix of **t**. What is $f(n)$? We can use the following Walnut code:

```
def tmsubseq n "i<j & j<k & k<n & T[i]=@0 & T[j]=@1 & T[k]=@0":
```

This gives a linear representation for the function, from which we can prove formulas such as $f(2^n) = 8^n/48 - 2^n/12$ for $n \geq 3$.

## 9.11.3 Enumerating palindromes

Damanik [108] studied $P_{pd}(n)$, the number of length-$n$ palindromes in the period-doubling sequence, and proved the following result:

**Theorem 9.11.1**   *We have* $P_{pd}(n) \in \{0, 1, 2, 3, 4\}$. *Furthermore,* $P_{pd}(n) = 0$ *for* $n \geq 4$ *even,* $P_{pd}(n) = P_{pd}(2n - 1) = P_{pd}(2n + 1)$ *for* $n \geq 5$ *odd.*

We can rederive Damanik's results as follows. We have already seen, in Section 8.6.3, that we can create a two-variable formula $\text{Pal}(i, n)$ asserting that the length-$n$ factor beginning at position $i$ of a word **x** is a palindrome:

$$\text{Pal}(i, n) := \forall j\, (j < n) \implies \mathbf{x}[i + j] = \mathbf{x}[(i + n) - (j + 1)].$$

The next step is to modify this so that we only count *novel palindromes*: that is, palindromes that have never occurred before, earlier in the sequence. As we have seen above, we can do this as follows:

$$\text{NovelPal}(i, n) := \text{Pal}(i, n) \wedge \forall j\, (j < n) \implies \neg\text{FactorEq}(i, j, n).$$

Now $P_\mathbf{x}(n)$, the number of distinct length-$n$ palindromes occurring in **x**, is just

$$|\{i \,:\, \text{Novel}(i, n) \text{ is true}\}|.$$

We can therefore obtain a linear representation for $P_\mathbf{x}(n)$ using the method discussed in the previous section.

Let us now show how to do this with Walnut for the period-doubling sequence:

```
def pdpal "Aj j<n => PD[i+j]=PD[(i+n)-(j+1)]":
def pdfactoreq "Ak k<n => PD[i+k]=PD[j+k]":
def pdnovelpal "$pdpal(i,n) & Aj j<i => ~$pdfactoreq(i,j,n)":
eval pdnp n "$pdnovelpal(i,n)":
```

This produces the following `Maple` representation for $v, \gamma(0), \gamma(1), w$ and stores it in the file `pdnp.mpl`.

$$v = [1\,1\,0\,0\,0\,0] \quad \gamma(0) = \begin{bmatrix} 1&1&0&0&0&0 \\ 0&0&0&0&0&0 \\ 0&0&0&0&1&0 \\ 0&0&0&0&0&1 \\ 0&0&0&0&1&0 \\ 0&0&0&0&2&0 \end{bmatrix} \quad \gamma(1) = \begin{bmatrix} 0&0&1&1&0&0 \\ 0&0&0&0&1&0 \\ 0&0&1&0&0&0 \\ 0&0&1&0&0&0 \\ 0&0&1&0&0&0 \\ 0&0&2&0&0&0 \end{bmatrix} \quad w = \begin{bmatrix} 1 \\ 0 \\ 1 \\ 1 \\ 0 \\ 1 \end{bmatrix},$$

a linear representation for $P_{pd}(n)$.

A little experimentation suggests that $P_{pd}(n)$ is bounded above by a constant. So we can now use the "semigroup trick" to compute $P_{pd}(n)$ to verify this. A simple program, modeled after that given in Section 4.11 produces a DFAO of 7 states, as shown in Figure 9.5. Here the name of the state is a vector of the

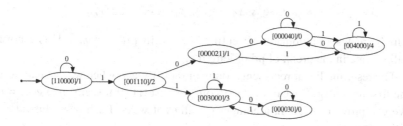

Figure 9.5 Automaton for palindrome complexity of the period-doubling sequence.

form $v\gamma(x)$ for some $x$. If the state's name is $s$, then the output is $s \cdot w$.

Inspection of this automaton now proves the first part of Damanik's theorem. For the second part, we take the automaton in Figure 9.5 and turn it into a `Walnut` word automaton called `PDP.txt`. Finally, we write `Walnut` formulas for the remaining claims in Damanik's theorem:

```
morphism g "0->01 1->23 2->46 3->53 4->46 5->53 6->46":
morphism h "0->1 1->2 2->1 3->3 4->0 5->0 6->4":
promote G g:
image PDP h G:

def even "Em n=2*m":
def odd "Em n=2*m+1":
eval dam1 "An (n>=4 & $even(n)) => PDP[n]=@0":
eval dam2 "An (n>=5 & $odd(n)) => (PDP[n]=PDP[2*n-1] &
```

```
PDP[n]=PDP[2*n+1])":
```

and the last two formulas return TRUE. This completes the proof of Damanik's theorem.

Next, let us count the total number of nonempty palindrome occurrences in **pd**[0..$n$ − 1]. Call this $f(n)$. We use the Walnut command

```
def pdpalpref n "m>0 & i+m<=n & $pdpal(i,m)":
```

This gives us a linear representation of rank 13. Using the technique described above in Section 9.9, we find

$$f(2^n) = \frac{5}{6}n2^n - \frac{8}{9}2^n + \frac{n}{2} + \frac{7}{4} + \frac{5}{36}(-1)^n,$$

which proves, since $f$ is increasing, that $f(n) = \Theta(n \log n)$.

Finally, let's turn to the problem of determining $g(n)$, the number of *distinct* nonempty palindromes in a prefix of length $n$ of **pd**. We can do this as follows:

```
def pdpalprefdis n "m>0 & i+m<=n & $pdnovelpal(i,n)":
```

which creates an automaton accepting $(i, m, n)$ iff **pd**[$i..i + m − 1$] is a novel palindrome in the prefix of **pd** of length $n$.

The resulting linear representation is of rank 13, and when we evaluate it on the first few integers we discover (to our surprise!) that it seems like $g(n) = n$. We can prove this fact in a number of different ways. Each way illustrates a different approach.

First, we could minimize the resulting linear representation using the algorithm mentioned at the end of Section 9.1. When we do so, we get the following linear representation:

$$u = \begin{bmatrix} 1 & 0 \end{bmatrix} \quad \gamma(0) = \begin{bmatrix} 1 & 0 \\ -1 & 2 \end{bmatrix} \quad \gamma(1) = \begin{bmatrix} 0 & 1 \\ -2 & 3 \end{bmatrix} \quad v = \begin{bmatrix} 0 \\ 1 \end{bmatrix}.$$

After calculating $\gamma(x)$ for some short binary words $x$ we are led to the following conjecture:

$$\gamma(x) = \begin{bmatrix} 1 - [x]_2 & [x]_2 \\ 1 - 2^{|x|+1} - [x]_2 & 2^{|x|+1} + [x]_2 \end{bmatrix},$$

which is easily proved by induction. Now the claim $v\gamma((n)_2)w = n$ easily follows.

Second, we could take the rank-13 representation (or the minimized representation of the previous paragraph) and combine it with a known representation for the function $n$ (such as that in Exercise 101), obtaining a linear representation for their difference. When we minimize the resulting linear representation the result is of rank 0, so the two representations give the same function (as in Theorem 4.10.2).

Third, we could observe that $g(n) = n$ iff $g(0) = 0$ and $g(n) - g(n-1) = 1$ for all $n \geq 1$. We can obtain $g(n) - g(n-1)$ by modifying the definition of pdpalprefdis to count only the novel palindromes that end at position $n-1$:

```
def pdpalconj n "m>0 & i+m=n & $pdnovelpal(i,n)":
```

The resulting linear representation $(v, \gamma, w)$ has the following easily-verified property:

$$\gamma(1x) = \begin{bmatrix} 0 & 0 & 1 & 0 & 0 & 1 \\ 0 & 0 & 0 & 0 & 0 & 0 \\ 0 & 0 & 1 & 0 & 0 & 1 \\ 0 & 0 & 0 & 0 & 0 & 0 \\ 0 & 0 & 1 & 0 & 0 & 1 \\ 0 & 0 & 0 & 0 & 0 & 0 \end{bmatrix}$$

for all $|x| \geq 2$. This proves that the function evaluates to 1 for all $n \geq 1$.

Finally, we could simply make the assertion that exactly one novel palindrome ends at every position of **pd**, and verify it:

```
def pdpalrich "(An Ei,m (i+m=n) & $pdnovelpal(i,m)) &
    An ~Ei,j,m,mp (i+m=n) & (j+mp=n) & $pdnovelpal(i,m) &
    $pdnovelpal(j,mp) & (i!=j)":
```

which returns TRUE. The first clause says there is a novel palindrome ending at position $n - 1$ and the second says there is only one.

*Exercise* 111    Carry out the same sort of analysis for the Thue-Morse sequence.

### 9.11.4 Counting finitely many factors

Suppose there are only finitely many distinct factors with a given property $P$. We can use our enumeration method to count them. There are two steps. The first step is to find the length $\ell$ of the longest factor with the given property $P$. Once we have this, we use our enumeration method to count the number of factors of length $\leq \ell$ with property $P$.

Let's illustrate this idea by counting the number of rich factors of the Rudin-Shapiro sequence.

```
def rsfaceq "At t<n => RS[i+t]=RS[j+t]":
def rsoccurs "n<=s & Ek k+n<=s & $rsfaceq(i,j+k,n)":
def rspal "At t<n => RS[i+t] = RS[(i+n)-(t+1)]":
def rsrich "Am $in(m,1,n) => (Ej $subs(j,i,1,m) &
    $rspal(j,(i+m)-j) & ~$rsoccurs(j,i,(i+m)-j,m-1))":
def rsrichlongest "Ei $rsrich(i,n)&Am m>n => ~Ej $rsrich(j,m)":
```

The last `Walnut` command produces an automaton that accepts only the number 30, so the longest rich factor is of length 30.

Next we compute the number of rich factors of length $\leq n$, using the "novel occurrences" idea mentioned earlier. The first step is to produce the linear representation:

```
eval rsrichm n "m<=n & $rsrich(i,m) & Aj j<i =>
  ~$rsfaceq(i,j,m)":
```

This gives us a linear representation $(v, \gamma, w)$ of rank 159. We then evaluate the linear representation at $n = 30$, and obtain the number 975. Thus we have proved

**Theorem 9.11.2** *The Rudin-Shapiro sequence has 975 rich factors (including the empty word).*

## 9.11.5 Enumerating factors in families

We might want to enumerate factors that match certain regular expressions, such as

$$0 \cup 1 \cup 0 (0 \cup 1)^* 0 \cup 1 (0 \cup 1)^* 1,$$

specifying that the first and last symbol are the same. Let's do this for the Thue-Morse sequence. As usual, we need to ensure we count only novel occurrences of each factor.

```
eval tmfl n "T[i]=T[i+n-1] & Aj j<i => ~$tmfactoreq(i,j,n)":
```

This gives us a linear representation $(v, \gamma, w)$ of rank 17 for $f(n)$, the number of length-$n$ factors of **t** with first and last symbol the same. The minimal polynomial of $\gamma(0)$ is $X^2(X-1)(X-2)(X+1)$, so we know $f(2^r) = c_1 2^r + c_2 + c_3(-1)^r$ for $r \geq 2$. When we solve for $c_1, c_2, c_3$ we find $c_1 = 5/3$, $c_2 = -1$, $c_3 = 1/3$. Hence $f(2^r) = \frac{5}{3} 2^n + \frac{1}{3}(-1)^n - 1$, which holds for $r \geq 1$.

## 9.11.6 Enumerating squares

Let us count the number $s(n)$ of order-$n$ squares in the Fibonacci word **f**. (Recall that the order of a square $xx$ is $|x|$.)

```
def ffactoreq "?msd_fib At t<n => F[i+t]=F[j+t]":
def fnovelsq "?msd_fib $ffactoreq(i,i+n,n) & Aj j<i =>
   ~$ffactoreq(i,j,2*n)":
eval fibsqm n "?msd_fib $fnovelsq(i,n)":
```

This gives us a linear representation $(v, \gamma, w)$ of rank 9. We already know from Theorem 8.5.1 that $s(n) > 0$ iff $n$ is a Fibonacci number. We can now compute $s(F_n)$ using the method in Section 9.9. The minimal polynomial of $\gamma(0)$ is $x(x-1)(x+1)(x^2-x-1)$, which implies that $s(n) = c_1 + c_2(-1)^n + c_3 F_n + c_4 F_{n+1}$ for some constants $c_1, c_2, c_3, c_4$. Solving the corresponding linear system, we see that $s(F_n) = F_n$. We have therefore proved the following result:

**Theorem 9.11.3**  *The Fibonacci word* **f** *has exactly* $F_n$ *distinct squares of order* $|F_n|$.

One feature of the logic-based approach is that it applies not only to properties of the infinite Fibonacci word **f**, but also to the finite Fibonacci words $X_n$. Recall from Section 2.4.16 that these words are defined as follows:

$$X_n = \begin{cases} \epsilon, & \text{if } n = 0; \\ 1, & \text{if } n = 1; \\ 0, & \text{if } n = 2; \\ X_{n-1}X_{n-2}, & \text{if } n > 2. \end{cases}$$

Note that $|X_n| = F_n$ for $n \geq 1$. Since the word $X_n$ (for $n \neq 1$) is the prefix of length $F_n$ of **f**, our method can prove claims about the words $X_n$ by rephrasing those claims in terms of prefixes of **f**. In so doing our method gives a bonus—it proves characterizations for *all* such prefixes of **f**, not just those of a particular length.

To illustrate the idea, we now turn to a result of Fraenkel and Simpson [156]. They computed the exact number of squares (blocks of the form $xx$ for $x$ a nonempty word) appearing in the words $X_n$; this was previously estimated by Crochemore [96].

There are two variations of the problem: we can either count the number of distinct squares in $X_n$, or we can count what Fraenkel and Simpson called the number of "repeated squares" in $X_n$ (i.e., the total number of *occurrences* of squares in $X_n$).

We can construct the linear representations as follows. For the number of squares in **f**$[0..n-1]$, we write

```
eval fibds n "?msd_fib j>=1 & i+2*j<=n & $ffactoreq(i,i+j,j) &
   Am m<i => ~$ffactoreq(m,i,2*j)":
```

For the total number of occurrences of squares in **f**$[0..n-1]$, we write

```
eval fibdos n "?msd_fib j>=1 & i+2*j<=n & $ffactoreq(i,i+j,j)":
```

Let us focus on $b(n)$, the total number of square occurrences in **f**$[0..n-1]$. Let $B(n)$ denote the number of square occurrences in the finite Fibonacci word $X_n$,

so that $B(n) = b(F_n)$. This corresponds to considering the Fibonacci representation of the form $10^{n-2}$; that is, $B(n) = b([10^{n-2}]_F)$. The corresponding matrix
$\gamma(0)$ has minimal polynomial

$$X^4(X-1)^2(X+1)^2(X^2-X-1)^2.$$

It now follows from the theory of linear recurrences that there are constants
$c_1, c_2, \ldots, c_8$ such that

$$B(n+1) = (c_1 n + c_2)\alpha^n + (c_3 n + c_4)\beta^n + c_5 n + c_6 + (c_7 n + c_8)(-1)^n$$

for $n \geq 3$, where $\alpha = (1 + \sqrt{5})/2, \beta = (1 - \sqrt{5})/2$ are the roots of $X^2 - X - 1$.
(The reason why we're computing $B(n+1)$ is to be compatible with Fraenkel
and Simpson.) We can find these constants by computing $B(4), B(5), \ldots, B(11)$
(using the linear representation) and then solving for the values of the constants
$c_1, \ldots, c_8$.

When we do so, we find

$$c_1 = \frac{2}{5} \qquad c_2 = -\frac{2}{25}\sqrt{5} - 2 \qquad c_3 = \frac{2}{5} \qquad c_4 = \frac{2}{25}\sqrt{5} - 2$$
$$c_5 = 1 \qquad c_6 = 1 \qquad \qquad c_7 = 0 \qquad c_8 = 0.$$

A little simplification, using the fact that $F_n = (\alpha^n - \beta^n)/(\alpha - \beta)$, leads to

**Theorem 9.11.4** *Let $B(n)$ denote the number of square occurrences in $X_n$.*
*Then*

$$B(n+1) = \frac{4}{5}nF_{n+1} - \frac{2}{5}(n+6)F_n - 4F_{n-1} + n + 1$$

*for $n \geq 3$.*

This statement corrects a small error in Theorem 2 in [156] (the coefficient
of $F_{n-1}$ was wrong; note that their $F$ and their Fibonacci words are indexed
differently from ours), which was first pointed out to us by Kalle Saari.

### 9.11.7 Enumerating cubes

In a similar way, we can count the cube occurrences in $X_n$. These are blocks
of the form $xxx$, where $x$ is a nonempty word. Using analysis exactly like the
square case, we easily obtain the following new result:

**Theorem 9.11.5** *Let $C(n)$ denote the number of cube occurrences in the Fibonacci word $X_n$. Then for $n \geq 3$ we have*

$$C(n) = (d_1 n + d_2)\alpha^n + (d_3 n + d_4)\beta^n + d_5 n + d_6$$

*where*

$$d_1 = \frac{3 - \sqrt{5}}{10} \qquad d_2 = \frac{17}{50}\sqrt{5} - \frac{3}{2} \qquad d_3 = \frac{3 + \sqrt{5}}{10}$$

$$d_4 = -\frac{17}{50}\sqrt{5} - \frac{3}{2} \qquad d_5 = 1 \qquad d_6 = -1.$$

### 9.11.8 Enumerating powers in arbitrary factors

We can also enumerate squares (and other kinds of powers) in arbitrary factors, not just prefixes. For example, in [204], the authors count the number of distinct $r$-powers occurring in a factor $f[i..i + n - 1]$ of the Fibonacci word $\mathbf{f}$, for $r \in \{2, 2 + \epsilon, 3\}$. We can easily do this with our method. For example, let's compute the number of distinct squares in $\mathbf{f}[i..i + n - 1]$:

```
def fibsquareinterval i n "?msd_fib m>=1 & $ffactoreq(j,j+m,m) &
   i<=j & j+2*m<=i+n & Ak (i<=k & k<j & k+2*m<=i+n) =>
   ~$ffactoreq(j,k,2*m)":
```

Here we make the assertion that $\mathbf{f}[j..j + 2m - 1]$ is a square, lies inside $[i..i + n - 1]$, and is not equal to any square $\mathbf{f}[k..k + 2m - 1]$ previously occurring in that interval. This gives us a linear representation for this quantity, of rank 162. Notice that here we are summing over all $j$ and $m$ that correspond to a particular $i$ and $n$, so there are actually four different matrices corresponding to the possible digit combinations of $i$ and $n$.

### 9.11.9 Enumerating unbordered factors

Let $U_x(n)$ denote the number of unbordered factors of length $n$ in $\mathbf{x}$. Let us compute $U(n) = U_t(n)$ for the Thue-Morse word $\mathbf{t}$. In Sections 8.6.12 and 8.6.13 we already constructed formulas for the property of being bordered or unbordered. If we write

```
def tmfactoreq "At t<n => T[i+t]=T[j+t]":
def tmbord "m>=1 & m<n & $tmfactoreq(i,(i+n)-m,m)":
def tmunb "Am ~$tmbord(i,m,n)":
eval tmunbm n "$tmunb(i,n) & Aj j<i => ~$tmfactoreq(i,j,n)":
```

then after adjusting the vector (as discussed in Section 9.8), we get the linear representation $(v, \gamma, w)$ for $U(n)$.

From this linear representation it is possible to deduce the following identities for $U(n)$:

$$U(4n) = 2U(2n), \qquad (n \geq 2) \tag{9.5}$$

$$U(4n + 1) = U(2n + 1), \qquad (n \geq 0) \tag{9.6}$$

$$U(8n + 2) = U(2n + 1) + U(4n + 3), \qquad (n \geq 1) \tag{9.7}$$

$$U(8n + 3) = -U(2n + 1) + U(4n + 2) \qquad (n \geq 2) \tag{9.8}$$

$$U(8n + 6) = -U(2n + 1) + U(4n + 2) + U(4n + 3) \qquad (n \geq 2) \tag{9.9}$$

$$U(8n + 7) = 2U(2n + 1) + U(4n + 3) \qquad (n \geq 3). \tag{9.10}$$

Eq. (9.6) is the easiest to verify. By explicit calculation we get $(\gamma(01) - \gamma(1))w = [0^{22}]^T$, so multiplication on the left by $v\gamma(z)$ gives $v\gamma(z01)w - v\gamma(z1)w = 0$, and so $U(4n + 1) - U(2n + 1) = 0$ for all $n \geq 0$.

For the other identities we need to understand something about the pattern of 0s in $v\gamma(z)$. It is easy to verify by multiplying that for $a \in \{0, 1\}$ we have $v\gamma(1a) = [0^6 *^{16}]^T$, where the $*$ denotes an entry that may be nonzero. However, the first six columns of both $\gamma(0)$ and $\gamma(1)$ have no nonzero entries below row 6, and so

$$v\gamma(1az) = [0^6 *^{16}]^T \tag{9.11}$$

for all $z \in \{0, 1\}^*$.

It is now easy to check by multiplying that

$$(\gamma(00) - 2\gamma(0))w = [-1\ 0\ -2\ 0^{19}]^T$$
$$(\gamma(010) - \gamma(1) - \gamma(11))w = [-2\ -2\ 0^{20}]^T$$
$$(\gamma(011) + \gamma(1) - \gamma(10))w = [4\ 0\ 1\ 0\ 0\ 1\ 0^{16}]^T$$
$$(\gamma(110) + \gamma(1) - \gamma(10) - \gamma(11))w = [1\ -1\ 1\ 0\ 2\ 1\ 0^{16}]^T,$$

which, together with (9.11) suffices to prove the identities (9.5)–(9.9) for $n \geq 2$. Eq. (9.10) is the hardest to verify. By two multiplications we get

$$(\gamma(b111) - 2\gamma(b1) - \gamma(b11))w = [*\ 0\ *\ 0\ 0\ *\ 0^{16}]^T$$

for $b \in \{0, 1\}$. Hence, together with Eq. (9.11), this suffices to prove (9.10) for $n \geq 4$.

The few remaining $n$ in the statement of the theorem not covered by the analysis above can now be verified by direct calculation. Once we have these identities, we can prove

**Theorem 9.11.6** *We have* $U(n) \leq n$ *for* $n \geq 4$. *Furthermore,* $U(n) = n$ *infinitely often. Thus,* $\limsup_{n \geq 1} U(n)/n = 1$.

*Proof* We now verify, by induction on $n$, that $U(n) \le n$ for $n \ge 4$. The base case is $n = 4$, and $U(4) = 2$. Now assume $n \ge 5$. Otherwise,

- If $n \equiv 0 \pmod 4$, say $n = 4m$ and $m \ge 2$. Then $U(4m) = 2U(2m) \le 2 \cdot 2m \le 4m$ by (9.5) and induction.

- If $n \equiv 1 \pmod 4$, say $n = 4m + 1$ for $m \ge 1$, then $U(4m + 1) = U(2m + 1)$ by (9.6). But $U(2m + 1) \le 2m + 1$ by induction for $m \ge 2$. The case $m = 1$ corresponds to $U(5) = 4 \le 5$.

- If $n \equiv 2 \pmod 8$, say $n = 8m + 2$, then for $m \ge 2$ we have $U(8m + 2) = U(2m + 1) + U(4m + 3) \le 6m + 4$ by induction, which is less than $8m + 2$. If $m = 1$, then $U(10) = 4 < 10$.

- If $n \equiv 3 \pmod 8$, say $n = 8m + 3$ for $m \ge 1$, then $U(8m + 3) = -U(2m + 1) + U(4m + 2) \le U(4m + 2) \le 4m + 2$ by induction.

- If $n \equiv 6 \pmod 8$, say $n = 8m + 6$, then $U(8m + 6) = -U(2m + 1) + U(4m + 2) + U(4m + 3) \le U(4m + 2) + U(4m + 3) \le 8m + 5$ by induction, provided $m \ge 2$. For $m = 0$ we have $U(6) = 6$ and for $m = 1$ we have $U(14) = 4$.

- If $n \equiv 7 \pmod 8$, say $n = 8m + 7$, then $U(8m + 7) = 2U(2m + 1) + U(4m + 3) \le 2(2m + 1) + 4m + 3 = 8m + 5$ for $m \ge 3$, by induction. The cases $m = 0, 1, 2$ can be verified by inspection.

This completes the proof that $U(n) \le n$.

It remains to see that $U(n) = n$ infinitely often. We do this by showing that $U(n) = n$ for $n$ of the form $3 \cdot 2^i$, $i \ge 1$. Let us prove this by induction on $i$. It is true for $i = 1$ since $U(6) = 6$. Otherwise $i \ge 2$, and using (9.5) we have $U(3 \cdot 2^{i+1}) = 2U(3 \cdot 2^i) = 2 \cdot 3 \cdot 2^i = 3 \cdot 2^{i+1}$ by induction. This also implies the claim $\limsup_{n \ge 1} U(n)/n = 1$. □

*Exercise* 112  Show that for the period-doubling sequence **pd** there are exactly 2 unbordered factors of every length $n \ge 1$. Hint: either compute the relations for $U_{\mathbf{pd}}(n)$ or use the "semigroup trick".

### 9.11.10 Enumerating distinct frames

Harju and Kärki [191] determined the number of frames (cf. Section 8.6.14) in the finite Fibonacci word $X_n$. We can do this more generally for the prefix of length $n$ of the Fibonacci word **f**:

```
def ffactoreq "?msd_fib At t<n => F[i+t]=F[j+t]":
def fibbord "?msd_fib m>=1 & m<n & $ffactoreq(i,(i+n)-m,m)":
def fibsquare "?msd_fib $ffactoreq(i,i+n,n)":
```

```
def fibunbord  "?msd_fib Am ~$fibbord(i,m,n)":
def fibframe   "?msd_fib n>=1&$fibunbord(i,n)&$fibsquare(i,n)":
def fibcountframe n "?msd_fib (i+2*r<=n) & $fibframe(i,r) &
   Aj (j+2*r<=n & $ffactoreq(i,j,2*r)) => (j>=i)":
```

This gives a linear representation $(v, \gamma, w)$ for the number of frames.

The minimal polynomial for the matrix $\gamma(0)$ is $X^6(X + 1)(X - 1)^2$, which shows that the number of distinct frames in a prefix of length $F_n$ is of the form $a(-1)^n + bn + c$ for $n \geq 8$. Solving for $a, b, c$, we find that the number of distinct frames in $X_n$, the finite Fibonacci word (or prefix of $\mathbf{f}$ of length $F_n$) is $2n - 10$ for $n \geq 8$.

### 9.11.11 Enumerating closed factors

Let $C_\mathbf{x}(n)$ denote the number of closed factors of length $n$ in $\mathbf{x}$. Let us determine $C(n) = C_\mathbf{t}(n)$, the number of such length-$n$ factors of $\mathbf{t}$. Here are the first few values of $C(n)$:

| $n$ | 0 | 1 | 2 | 3 | 4 | 5 | 6 | 7 | 8 | 9 | 10 | 11 | 12 | 13 |
|------|---|---|---|---|---|---|---|---|---|---|----|----|----|----|
| $C(n)$ | 1 | 2 | 2 | 2 | 4 | 4 | 6 | 4 | 8 | 8 | 10 | 8 | 12 | 8 |

```
def tmfactoreq "At t<n => T[i+t]=T[j+t]":
def tmoccurs "m<=n & Ek k+m<=n & $tmfactoreq(i,j+k,m)":
def tmbord "m>=1 & m<n & $tmfactoreq(i,(i+n)-m,m)":
def tmclo "(i=0 & n=0) | (i<=1 & n=1) | (Ej j<n &
   $tmbord(i,j,n) & ~$tmoccurs(i,i+1,j,n-2))":
eval tmclom n "$tmclo(i,n) & Aj j<i => ~$tmfactoreq(i,j,n)":
```

This gives us a linear representation $(v, \gamma, w)$ for computing $C(n)$. If we now explicitly compute $C(n)$ for $1 \leq n \leq 1000$, and graph it, the graph suggests the conjecture that $C$ achieves its local maximum when $n = 11 \cdot 2^r + 1$. Now $(11 \cdot 2^r + 1)_2 = 1101 \, 0^{r-1}1$ for $r \geq 1$, so by using the ideas in Section 9.9, we see that $C(11 \cdot 2^r + 1)$ satisfies a linear recurrence whose annihilating polynomial is the minimal polynomial of $\gamma(0)$. We compute this minimal polynomial and find it is $X^3(X-1)(X-2)$. Thus $C(11 \cdot 2^r + 1) = c_1 \cdot 2^r + c_2$ for $r \geq 3$. Solving the linear system for $c_1, c_2$ gives us the identity $C(11 \cdot 2^r + 1) = 12 \cdot 2^r$, which actually holds for $r \geq 0$. Thus we have proved that $\limsup_{n \to \infty} C(n)/n \geq 12/11$.

### 9.11.12 Enumerating privileged words

Let us count the number $\mathrm{Pr}_\mathbf{t}(n)$ of length-$n$ privileged factors of the Thue-Morse sequence $\mathbf{t}$. Here are the first few values of this sequence

| $n$ | 0 | 1 | 2 | 3 | 4 | 5 | 6 | 7 | 8 | 9 | 10 | 11 | 12 | 13 | 14 |
|---|---|---|---|---|---|---|---|---|---|---|---|---|---|---|---|
| $a(n)$ | 1 | 2 | 2 | 2 | 2 | 0 | 4 | 0 | 8 | 0 | 8 | 0 | 4 | 0 | 0 |

We use the following `Walnut` code:

```
def in "i>=r & i<=s":
def tmfactoreq "Ak k<n => T[i+k] = T[j+k]":
def tmunipref "Aj (j>0 & j+m<n) => ~$tmfactoreq(i,i+j,m)":
def tmunisuff "Aj (j>0 & j+m<n) =>
   ~$tmfactoreq((i+n)-m,(i+n)-(m+j),m)":
def tmbord "$in(m,1,n) & $tmfactoreq(i,(i+n)-m,m)":
def tmpriv "n<=1 | Am $in(m,1,n) => Ep p<=m & p>=1 &
   $tmunipref(i,p,m) & $tmunisuff((i+n)-m,p,m) &
   $tmbord(i,p,n)":
eval tmprivm n "$tmpriv(i,n) & Aj j<i =>
   ~$tmfactoreq(i,j,n)":
```

Computing $\mathrm{Pr}(n)$ for $1 \le n \le 1000$ suggests that the local maximum of $\mathrm{Pr}(n)$ occurs at $n = 2^{2r+1} + 2$. Let us evaluate $\mathrm{Pr}(n)$ at these values. Since $(2^{2r+1} + 2)_2 = 1\,0^{2r-1}\,10$, we need to determine the minimal polynomial of $\gamma(00)$. It is $X^3(X - 1)(X - 2)$. Therefore $\mathrm{Pr}(2^{2r+1} + 2) = c_1 2^r + c_2$ for $r \ge 3$. Solving the linear system gives $c_1 = 4$, $c_2 = -2$. Hence $\mathrm{Pr}(2^{2r+1} + 2) = 2^{r+2} - 2$ for $r \ge 3$. It now follows that $\limsup_{n\to\infty} \mathrm{Pr}(n)/\sqrt{n} \ge 2\sqrt{2}$.

We can also do the same thing for the number $\mathrm{Prp}(n)$ of length-$n$ privileged palindromes in the Thue-Morse sequence. Here are the first few values:

| $n$ | 0 | 1 | 2 | 3 | 4 | 5 | 6 | 7 | 8 | 9 | 10 | 11 | 12 | 13 | 14 |
|---|---|---|---|---|---|---|---|---|---|---|---|---|---|---|---|
| $b(n)$ | 1 | 2 | 2 | 2 | 2 | 0 | 4 | 0 | 4 | 0 | 4 | 0 | 4 | 0 | 0 |

```
def tmpal "At t<n => T[i+t] = T[(i+n)-(t+1)]":
def tmprivpal "$tmpriv(i,n) & $tmpal(i,n)":
eval tmprivpalm n "$tmprivpal(i,n) & Aj j<i =>
   ~$tmfactoreq(i,j,n)":
```

We can now use the "semigroup trick" to prove that $\mathrm{Prp}(n)$ is bounded above by 4, and construct a DFAO calculating it.

## 9.11.13 Counting irreducibly overlap-free factors

We continue our analysis started in Section 8.5.24. There we defined the notion of irreducibly overlap-free factor. We can count the number of length-$n$ irreducibly overlap-free factors of the Thue-Morse word **t** as follows:

```
def factoreq "At (t<n) => T[i+t]=T[j+t]":
def irredovernovel n "(n>=3) & $irredover(i,n) &
   Aj $factoreq(i,j,n) => j>=i":
```

This gives us a linear representation of rank 252 for the number of such factors.

With this representation, and the methods of this chapter, we can easily prove results like:

**Theorem 9.11.7**   *Let $f(n)$ denote the number of irreducibly overlap-free factors of length n of* t. *Then*

*(a) $f(2^n + 2^{n-1} + 6) = 35 \cdot 2^{n-4} - 4$ for $n \geq 7$.*
*(b) $f(2^n + 1) = 2^{n-1}$ for $n \geq 3$.*

*Hence* $\limsup_{n \to \infty} f(n)/n \geq 35/24$ *and* $\liminf_{n \to \infty} f(n)/n \leq 1/2$.

*Open Question* 9.11.8    Can you prove equality in the last statement of Theorem 9.11.7?

### 9.11.14  Counting recurrent factors

Recall that a factor $y$ of an infinite sequence **x** is said to be *recurrent* if it occurs infinitely often in **x**. We can count the number of length-$n$ recurrent factors using our technique.

Let us carry this out for the second-bit sequence **sb**:

```
def sbfactoreq "At t<n => SB[i+t]=SB[j+t]":
def sbrecur "Am Ej j>m & $sbfactoreq(i,j,n)":
eval sbrecurm n "$sbrecur(i,n) & Aj j<i => ~$sbfactoreq(i,j,n)":
```

This gives us a linear representation of order 25.

*Exercise* 113    Use the linear representation to show that **sb** has exactly $2n$ recurrent factors of length $n$ for $n \geq 1$.

### 9.11.15  Cyclic complexity

The cyclic complexity function $C_\mathbf{x}(n)$ counts the number of length-$n$ factors, where factors that are conjugates of each other are treated as the same. Let us enumerate this for $\mathbf{x} = \mathbf{t}$, the Thue-Morse sequence. We use the following Walnut code:

```
def tmconj "Et t<=n & $tmfactoreq(j,i+t,n-t) &
    $tmfactoreq(i,(j+n)-t,t)":
eval tmcc n "Aj j<i => ~$tmconj(i,j,n)":
```

This gives a linear representation $(v, \gamma, w)$ of rank 50 for $C_\mathbf{t}(n)$. We can compute the exact value of $C(n) = C_\mathbf{t}(n)$ for $n$ a power of 2 as before, by determining the minimal polynomial of $\gamma(0)$. It is $X^3(X - 1)(X - 2)(X + 1)$, so $C(2^r) = c_1 \cdot 2^r + c_2 + c_3(-1)^r$ for $r \geq 3$. By solving the appropriate linear system, we find $c_1 = 2$, $c_2 = -4$, $c_3 = 0$, so $C(2^r) = 2^{r+1} - 4$ for $r \geq 3$. (Actually, it also holds for $r \geq 2$.) Similarly, one can prove $C(2^r + 2) = \frac{4}{3} \cdot (2^r - (-1)^r)$ for $r \geq 3$. See [229].

**Open Question 9.11.9** Prove that $(4/3)n - 4 \leq C(n) \leq 2n$ for $n \geq 1$.

We can do the same thing for the Fibonacci word:

```
def ffactoreq "?msd_fib At t<n => F[i+t]=F[j+t]":
def fconj "?msd_fib Et t<=n & $ffactoreq(j,i+t,n-t) &
   $ffactoreq(i,(j+n)-t,t)":
eval fcc n "?msd_fib Aj j<i => ~$fconj(i,j,n)":
```

and show that $C_f(F_n) = 2$ for $n \geq 1$, while $C_f(F_{2n} + 1) = 2F_{2n-2}$ for $n \geq 4$.

## 9.11.16 Permutational complexity

Given an aperiodic infinite word $\mathbf{x}$, write $i <_p j$ if $\mathbf{x}[i..\infty)$ precedes $\mathbf{x}[j..\infty)$ in the lexicographic order. This defines a total order on $\mathbb{N}$. Hence an interval $[i..i + n - 1]$ corresponds to a certain permutation of $\{1, 2, \ldots, n\}$. For example, let $\mathbf{x} = \mathbf{t}$, the Thue-Morse sequence. Then you can easily verify that $[1..5]$ corresponds to the permutation

$$\begin{pmatrix} 1 & 2 & 3 & 4 & 5 \\ 5 & 4 & 2 & 3 & 1 \end{pmatrix}$$

because $5 <_p 4 <_p 2 <_p 3 <_p 1$.

Now we can count the number of distinct permutations corresponding to intervals of length $n$. This is called the permutation complexity, $W_{\mathbf{x}}(n)$. Widmer [380] found the following expression for $W_{\mathbf{t}}(n)$:

$$W_{\mathbf{t}}(n) = 2^{a+2} + 2b - 4$$

if $n \geq 6$ and $n = 2^a + b$ for $0 < b \leq 2^a$.

We can show that if $\mathbf{x}$ is $k$-automatic then $W_{\mathbf{x}}$ is $k$-regular, by constructing a formula to count it [78, Thm. 41]. For Thue-Morse this is

```
def lessthan "Et T[i+t]=@0&T[j+t]=@1&Ak k<t => T[i+k]=T[j+k]":
def sameperm "Al,m (1<n & m<n) => ($lessthan(i+1,i+m) <=>
   $lessthan(j+1,j+m))":
eval widmer n "At t<s => ~$sameperm(s,t,n)":
```

The first formula defines an order on suffixes of $\mathbf{t}$. The second formula asserts that the permutation induced by $[i..i + n - 1]$ is the same as that induced by $[j..j + n - 1]$. Finally, the last formula counts the number of distinct permutations: it asserts that all length-$n$ blocks at a position $< s$ represent a different permutation than that at position $s$. This gives a linear representation for $W_{\mathbf{t}}$ of rank 11. With this linear representation, we can reprove the result of Widmer. To do so, we need to find the "reverse" relations. We do so using the analogue of the algorithm described in Section 5.7. This produces the following relations, where we have written $W$ for $W_t$.

$$W([110x]_2) = -\frac{1}{4}W([11x]_2) + \frac{5}{4}W([101x]_2)$$

$$W([111x]_2) = -\frac{1}{2}W([11x]_2) + \frac{3}{2}W([101x]_2)$$

$$W([1000x]_2) = -2W([10x]_2) + 3W([100x]_2)$$

$$W([1001x]_2) = -2W([11x]_2) + 3W([101x]_2)$$

$$W([1010x]_2) = -\frac{9}{4}W([11x]_2) + \frac{13}{4}W([101x]_2)$$

$$W([1011x]_2) = -\frac{5}{2}W([11x]_2) + \frac{7}{2}W([101x]_2).$$

Once we have these, the result of Widmer easily follows by a long but not difficult induction on $n$.

**Exercise 114**   Carry out the same calculation for the "doubled" Thue-Morse sequence, obtained from **t** by applying the morphism $0 \to 00, 1 \to 11$.

### 9.11.17 Lie complexity

In [39] the authors defined the following notion: let $L_\mathbf{x}(n)$ be the number of length-$n$ factors $w$ of $\mathbf{x}$ such that every conjugate of $w$ is also a factor of $\mathbf{x}$. Here two factors that are cyclic shifts of each other are regarded as the same.

By constructing a first-order formula we can easily show that if $\mathbf{x}$ is an automatic sequence then $L_\mathbf{x}(n)$ is a regular sequence. Let us compute it for the Fibonacci word **f**:

```
def fibfactoreq "?msd_fib Au,v (i+v=j+u & u>=i & u<i+n)
    => F[u]=F[v]":
def fibshift "?msd_fib $fibfactoreq(j,i+t,n-t) &
    $fibfactoreq(i,(j+n)-t,t)":
# asserts that F[j..j+n-1] is a conjugate of F[i..i+n-1]
# but shifted by t

def fibconj "?msd_fib Et (t<=n) & $fibshift(i,j,n,t)":
# asserts that F[j..j+n-1] is a conjugate of F[i..i+n-1]

def fibpref "?msd_fib (m<=n) & $fibfactoreq(i,j,m)":
def fiblt "?msd_fib Et (t<n) & $fibfactoreq(i,j,t) &
    F[i+t]<F[j+t]":
def fibleq "?msd_fib $fiblt(i,j,n) | $fibfactoreq(i,j,n)":
def fiballconj "?msd_fib At (t<=n) => Ej $fibshift(i,j,n,t)":
```

```
# all conjugates of F[i..i+n-1] appear in F

def fiblexleast "?msd_fib Aj $fibconj(i,j,n) => $fibleq(i,j,n)":
# F[i..i+n-1] is lex least among all its conjugates in F

def fiblie "?msd_fib $fiballconj(i,n) & $fiblexleast(i,n) &
  (Aj $fibfactoreq(i,j,n) => (j>=i))":
# F[i..i+n-1] has all conjugates appearing and is lex least
# among all its conjugates in F, and is first to appear

def matfiblie n "?msd_fib $fiblie(i,n)":
```

The resulting linear representation is of rank 9. By using the semigroup trick, we can easily prove

**Theorem 9.11.10** *We have*

$$
L_f(n) = \begin{cases} 2, & \text{if } n = 1, 2; \\ 1, & \text{if } n = 0 \text{ or } n = F_k \text{ for } k \geq 4 \text{ or } n = F_k + F_{k-3} \text{ for } k \geq 4; \\ 0, & \text{otherwise.} \end{cases}
$$

*Exercise* 115   Find an automatic sequence with critical exponent strictly less than 2, with the property that its Lie complexity is nonzero infinitely often.

## 9.11.18 Counting white squares in the Sierpiński carpet array

As we have seen in Figure 2.5, we can think of the Sierpiński carpet array as consisting of white squares on a black background. A white square is an $n \times n$ subarray consisting entirely of white cells (i.e., 0s), having a border consisting entirely of black cells (i.e., 1s) all around it. This gives the following Walnut code for counting $f(n)$, the number of white squares occurring in the first $n$ rows and columns:

```
def is0square "?msd_3 (Ar,s (r>=i & r<i+n & s>=j & s<j+n) =>
  SCA[r][s]=@0) & (At (t+1>=j & t<=j+n) => (SCA[i-1][t]=@1 &
  SCA[i+n][t]=@1)) & (Au (u+1>=i & u<=i+n) => (SCA[u][j-1]=@1 &
  SCA[u][j+n]=@1))":
# is n x n subarray starting at position (i,j) a white square?

def zerosqcount n "?msd_3 m>=1 & i+m<=n & j+m<=n &
  $is0square(i,j,m)":
```

This gives a linear representation for $f$:

$$v = [1\,0\,0\,0\,0]; \qquad \gamma(0) = \begin{bmatrix} 1\,0\,0\,0\,0 \\ 0\,8\,0\,0\,1 \\ 0\,0\,3\,0\,0 \\ 0\,0\,0\,3\,0 \\ 0\,0\,0\,0\,1 \end{bmatrix}; \qquad \gamma(1) = \begin{bmatrix} 0\,1\,1\,1\,0 \\ 0\,8\,0\,0\,1 \\ 0\,3\,2\,0\,0 \\ 0\,3\,0\,2\,0 \\ 0\,0\,0\,0\,1 \end{bmatrix};$$

$$\gamma(2) = \begin{bmatrix} 1\,3\,2\,2\,1 \\ 0\,8\,0\,0\,1 \\ 0\,5\,3\,0\,1 \\ 0\,5\,0\,3\,1 \\ 0\,0\,0\,0\,1 \end{bmatrix}; \qquad w = \begin{bmatrix} 0 \\ 0 \\ 0 \\ 0 \\ 1 \end{bmatrix}.$$

We can now use this representation to prove, for example, that there are $(8^n - 1)/7$ white squares appearing in the first $3^n$ rows and columns.

## 9.12  How to guess the relations for a $k$-regular sequence

It is often possible, given the first hundred or thousand terms of a $k$-regular sequence, to guess the relations of the $k$-kernel that define it, using a heuristic procedure.

To do so, we use a procedure similar to that for $k$-automatic sequences, as discussed in Section 5.6. We maintain a queue of sequences to examine, starting with the sequence $(f(n))_{n\geq 0}$ itself. At each stage we try to write the current sequence as a $\mathbb{Q}$-linear combination of previous sequences, based on the terms we know so far. If this fails, we decimate by replacing $n$ with $kn+a$, $0 \leq a < k$, and appending these new sequences to the queue of sequences to examine. If it succeeds, we output the relation.

Let us try this procedure with the sequence defined by $f(n) = [(n)_2^R]_2$, in other words, the sequence that results by taking the base-2 representation of $n$, reversing the order of the digits, and evaluating the result as a base-2 number. See Example 9.2.3.

We quickly find the guess $f(2n) = f(n)$, but $f(2n + 1)$ cannot be written as a linear combination of $f(n)$. Next we find $f(4n + 3) = -2f(n) + 3f(2n + 1)$, but $f(4n + 1)$ cannot be written as a linear combination of $f(n)$ and $f(2n + 1)$. Finally, we find that $f(8n + 1) = -2f(2n + 1) + 3f(4n + 1)$ and $f(8n + 5) = -4f(n) + 5f(2n + 1)$. This gives a complete set of relations for $f$, from which we can determine a linear representation, as in Section 9.3.

Once guessed, we can often easily verify these identities by induction.

*Exercise* 116   Prove the guessed relations for $f$ defined above.

# 10

## Synchronized sequences

In this chapter, we discuss a class of sequences that is "halfway between" the automatic sequences and the regular sequences.[1]

This is the class of *synchronized sequences*. These sequences can be used to enumerate many properties of automatic sequences in a different and often more convenient way than we saw in the previous chapter for regular sequences. In particular, synchronization makes it possible to directly check guessed formulas for sequences.

## 10.1 Automata computing relations

An automaton $M$ that takes inputs from an alphabet $\Delta \times \Sigma$ can be viewed as computing a relation $R$ on equal-length words, one from $\Delta^*$ and one from $\Sigma^*$, where $(x, y) \in R$ iff $M$ accepts $x \times y$.

If $\Sigma = \Sigma_k$ and $\Delta = \Sigma_\ell$ for two integers $k, \ell \geq 2$, then we can also view $M$ as computing a relation on $\mathbb{N}$. Here $(m, n) \in R$ if $(m, n)_{k,\ell}$ is accepted by $M$. If this is the case, we call the relation $(k, \ell)$-automatic. If $k = \ell$, we just call it $k$-automatic.

**Example 10.1.1** Consider the relation $R$ on pairs $(n, s)$, which is true if $s = a \cdot k^i$ for some $i \geq 0$, $a \neq 0$, and the base-$k$ representation of $n$ has the nonzero digit $a$ in the digit position representing $k^i$; that is, if $n = \sum_{0 \leq j < t} e_j k^j$, and $e_i = a > 0$.

For $k = 3$, the relation is computed by the automaton in Figure 10.1.

If we want to check whether the relation $R$ is actually a total function on $\mathbb{N}$

---

[1] Much of the material in this chapter is reprinted from [355] by permission from Springer Nature.

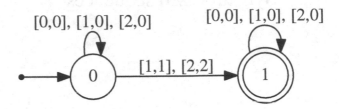

Figure 10.1 Synchronized automaton computing digit in specified position.

(that is, whether the pairs accepted are of the form $(m, f(m))$), we can do that with a first-order formula:

$$(\forall m \; \exists n \; R(m, n)) \wedge (\forall m, n, n' \; (R(m, n) \wedge R(m, n')) \implies n = n').$$

Here the first clause states that $f(m)$ has at least one value for each $m$, and the second clause says that $f(m)$ has at most one value for each $m$.

If this criterion is satisfied, we say the automaton computes the function $f$ in a synchronized fashion.

*Exercise* 117    Suppose we are given an automaton $M$ computing a function $f(n)$. How can we tell whether $f$ is one-one?

## 10.2 $k$-synchronized sequences

Carpi and Maggi [70] introduced the class of $k$-synchronized sequences. Recall that $(m, n)_k$ denotes the base-$k$ representation of the pair $(m, n) \in \mathbb{N} \times \mathbb{N}$, over the alphabet $(\Sigma_k \times \Sigma_k)^*$.

A *$k$-synchronized sequence* or *$k$-synchronized function* $(f(n))_{n \geq 0}$ is one for which the language $[0, 0]^* \{(n, f(n))_k \; : \; n \geq 0\}$ is regular, that is, recognized by a DFA $M$. Such a DFA is itself called synchronized. In what follows, when we talk about the language recognized by a synchronized automaton, we will often use the convention mentioned in Section 5.3 and talk about the corresponding subset $S = \{(n, f(n)) \; : \; n \geq 0\}$ of $\mathbb{N}^2$, instead of the set of all of its representations $[0, 0]^*(S)_k$.

**Example 10.2.1** As a simple example of a $k$-synchronized sequence, consider $f(n) = n + 1$. This is recognized by the DFA in Figure 10.2 for the case $k = 2$.

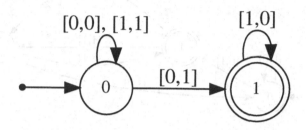

Figure 10.2 Synchronized DFA for $k = 2$ and $f(n) = n + 1$.

**Example 10.2.2** Here is another example. Let $\mathbf{t} = t_0 t_1 t_2 \cdots$ be the Thue-Morse sequence. The *odious numbers*

$$1, 2, 4, 7, 8, 11, \ldots,$$

are those for which $t_n = 1$; they form sequence A000069 in the OEIS. If we let $o_n$ be the $n$th odious number, with $o_0 = 1$, then it is easy to see that $o_n = 2n + 1 - t_n$. The sequence $(o_n)_{n \geq 0}$ is thus 2-synchronized. It can be computed in Walnut as follows:

```
def odious "(T[n]=@0 => s=2*n+1) & (T[n]=@1 => s=2*n)":
```

which gives us the synchronized automaton computing $o_n$ in Figure 10.3.

Similarly, the evil numbers are those for which $t_n = 0$; they are defined by $e_n = 2n + t_n$ and form sequence A001969 in the OEIS. This terminology comes from [41, p. 431].

Let's look at three other examples. The first is the function $n \to k^{\lfloor \log_k n \rfloor}$, defined for $n \geq 1$. For example, for $k = 3$, the DFA in Figure 10.4 demonstrates the synchronization. The second is the function $V_k(n) = k^{v_k(n)}$ defined above in Section 6.4, again for $n \geq 1$. For example, for $k = 3$, we can use the DFA in Figure 10.5 at left. The third is the function $V'_k(n)$, which is defined to be $e_i k^i$,

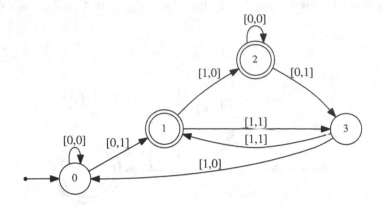

Figure 10.3 Synchronized automaton for $o_n$.

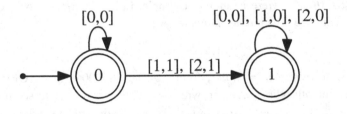

Figure 10.4 Synchronized DFA for $n \to 3^{\lfloor \log_3 n \rfloor}$.

where $(n)_k = e_t e_{t-1} \cdots e_1 e_0$ and $i$ is the smallest index such that $e_i \neq 0$. For $k = 3$ the automaton in Figure 10.5 at right suffices.

*Exercise* 118    Define the three synchronized DFAs above via `Walnut`'s regular expression capabilities.

As we will see in this chapter, many other, less trivial aspects of $k$-automatic

Figure 10.5 Synchronized DFAs for $V_3(n)$ and $V'_3(n)$.

sequences are also synchronized. The main tool for proving this is the following consequence of Theorem 6.3.2:

**Theorem 10.2.3** *Let* $\varphi(n, s)$ *be a first-order logical formula involving indexing into an automatic sequence* **x**, *logical operations, comparisons, and addition of natural numbers, with two free variables* $n$ *and* $s$, *and asserting that* $s = f(n)$ *for some function* $f$. *Then the DFA recognizing the language* $\{(n, f(n))_k : n \geq 0\}$ *is synchronized.*

Obviously this concept can be further generalized to functions that map to pairs or tuples, such as $n \to (x_n, y_n)$. The following exercise illustrates this.

*Exercise* 119 Show that the Nim-sum $x \oplus y$ of natural numbers, defined by the exclusive-or of their base-2 representations, is a synchronized 2-dimensional sequence. See [16, Example 24].

## 10.3 Closure properties of synchronized sequences

Before we start discussing the properties of synchronized sequences, let us generalize the concept a bit. Let $k, \ell \geq 2$ be two natural numbers. We say a sequence $(a(n))_{n \geq 0}$ is $(k, \ell)$-*synchronized* if there exists a DFA recognizing, in parallel, the base-$k$ representation of $n$ and the base-$\ell$ representation of $a(n)$. We write $(n)_{k,\ell}$ for this representation, consisting of a word over the alphabet $\Sigma_k \times \Sigma_\ell$.

**Theorem 10.3.1** *Suppose* $(a(n))_{n \geq 0}$ *and* $(b(n))_{n \geq 0}$ *are* $(k, \ell)$-*synchronized sequences. Then so are the sequences*

*(a)* $(a(n) + b(n))_{n \geq 0}$.
*(b)* $(a(n) \dot{-} b(n))_{n \geq 0}$, *where* $x \dot{-} y$ *is the "monus" function, defined by* $\max(0, x - y)$.
*(c)* $(|a(n) - b(n)|)_{n \geq 0}$.
*(d)* $(\lfloor \alpha a(n) \rfloor)_{n \geq 0}$, *where* $\alpha$ *is a non-negative rational number.*

*(e)* $(\max(a(n), b(n)))_{n \geq 0}$.

*(f)* $(\min(a(n), b(n)))_{n \geq 0}$.

*(g)* *running maximum, defined by* $c(n) = \max_{0 \leq i \leq n} a(n)$.

*(h)* *running minimum, defined by* $d(n) = \min_{0 \leq i \leq n} a(n)$.

*Proof* Let $A$ be a $(k, \ell)$-synchronized DFA computing $a(n)$ and $B$ be a $(k, \ell)$-synchronized DFA computing $b(n)$. Here we treat $A$ as a boolean function that returns TRUE if $A$ accepts $(n)_k$ and $(x)_\ell$ in parallel and similarly for $B$. To prove these results, it suffices (by Theorem 10.2.3) to provide first-order formulas asserting $s = f(n)$ for each transformation $f(n)$. We do this as follows:

(a) $\forall x, y \, (A(n, x) \wedge B(n, y)) \implies s = x + y$.

(b) $\forall x, y \, (A(n, x) \wedge B(n, y)) \implies ((x \geq y \implies x = s + y) \wedge (x < y \implies s = 0))$.

(c) $\forall x, y \, (A(n, x) \wedge B(n, y)) \implies ((x \geq y \implies x = s + y) \wedge (x < y \implies y = s + x))$.

(d) Write $\alpha = p/q$. Then the formula is $\forall x \, A(n, x) \implies (qs \geq px \wedge qs < px + q)$. As stated, this is not a first-order formula, but it becomes one if $q$ and $p$ are replaced by their particular values. Here we understand $2x$ to mean "$x + x$", $3x$ to mean "$x + x + x$", etc.

(e) $\forall x, y \, (A(n, x) \wedge B(n, y)) \implies ((x \geq y \implies s = x) \wedge (x < y \implies s = y))$.

(f) $\forall x, y \, (A(n, x) \wedge B(n, y)) \implies ((x \geq y \implies s = y) \wedge (x < y \implies s = x))$.

(g) $(\exists i \, (i \leq n) \wedge A(i, s)) \wedge (\forall j, t \, (j \leq n \wedge A(j, t)) \implies s \geq t)$.

(h) $(\exists i \, (i \leq n) \wedge A(i, s)) \wedge (\forall j, t \, (j \leq n \wedge A(j, t)) \implies s \leq t)$.

□

*Remark* 10.3.2 Not all of these properties hold for $k$-regular sequences. For example, the $k$-regular sequences are not closed under absolute value, min, or max, as we saw in Section 9.5.

Assume that $(a(n))_{n \geq 0}$ is unbounded. The first discrete inverse is defined by $g(n) = \min\{i : a(i) \geq n\}$. If further we have $\lim_{n \to \infty} a(n) = \infty$, the second discrete inverse is defined to be $h(n) = \max\{i : a(i) \leq n\}$.

**Theorem 10.3.3** *Suppose* $(a(n))_{n \geq 0}$ *is $k$-synchronized. Then so are the first and second discrete inverses.*

*Proof* Again, it suffices to provide the appropriate first-order formulas. Let $A$ be a $k$-synchronized DFA computing $a(n)$. For $g(n)$ the corresponding formula is

$$\exists i \, A(i, s) \wedge s \geq n \wedge (\forall j \, (A(j, t) \wedge t \geq n) \implies j \geq i),$$

and for $h(n)$ it is

$$\exists i\, A(i, s) \wedge s \leq n \wedge (\forall j\, (A(j, t) \wedge t \leq n) \implies j \leq i).$$

□

Our next theorem concerns composition of synchronized sequences.

**Theorem 10.3.4** *Suppose $(a(n))_{n \geq 0}$ is $(k, \ell)$-synchronized and $(b(n))_{n \geq 0}$ is $(\ell, m)$-synchronized. Then $(b(a(n)))_{n \geq 0}$ is $(k, m)$-synchronized.*

*Proof* Let $A$ be an automaton recognizing pairs $(n, a(n))$ represented in bases $k$ and $\ell$, respectively, and similarly $B$ for $(t, b(t))$ in bases $\ell$ and $m$. Consider the first-order formula $\exists t\, A(n, t) \wedge B(t, s)$; it is true iff $s = b(a(n))$. □

*Exercise* 120 Let $c \in \mathbb{N}, d \in \mathbb{Z}$. Show that the function $n \to \max(0, cn + d)$ is $(k, \ell)$-synchronized for all $k, \ell \geq 2$.

## 10.4 Automatic, synchronized, and regular sequences

**Theorem 10.4.1** *Let $(a(n))_{n \geq 0}$ be a $(k, \ell)$-synchronized sequence taking values in $\mathbb{N}$. Then $(a(n))_{n \geq 0}$ is $k$-automatic if and only if it is bounded.*

*Proof* Let $M = (Q, \Sigma_k \times \Sigma_\ell, \delta, q_0, F)$ be a $(k, \ell)$-synchronized DFA computing $a(n)$.

Suppose $a(n)$ is bounded. Then it takes on only finitely many values, say $b_1, b_2, \ldots, b_t$. For each $b_i$ form the DFA $M_i$ that arises from intersecting $M$ with a DFA that recognizes all words over $(\Sigma_k \times \Sigma_\ell)^*$ whose second component spells out $0^*(b_i)_\ell$. The result is a DFA $M_i$ recognizing the base-$k$ representations of those $n$ for which to $a(n) = b_i$. Now, using the familiar cross-product construction, we can simply combine all these different DFAs $M_i$ into one $k$-DFAO computing $(a(n))_{n \geq 0}$.

For the other direction, if $\mathbf{a} = (a(n))_{n \geq 0}$ is $k$-automatic, then its range has to be finite by definition, and hence bounded. □

**Theorem 10.4.2** *Suppose $\mathbf{a} = (a(n))_{n \geq 0}$ is a $(k, \ell)$-synchronized sequence taking values in $\mathbb{N}$, and let $S$ be the range of the sequence $\mathbf{a}$. Then the characteristic sequence $(\chi_S(i))_{i \geq 0}$, defined to be 1 if $i \in S$ and 0 otherwise, is $\ell$-automatic.*

*Proof* Let $A$ be a $(k, \ell)$-synchronized DFA computing $a(n)$. Consider the first-order formula

$$\exists n\, A(n, s);$$

then by Theorem 6.4.1, the set of values of $s$ making this formula evaluate to TRUE is $\ell$-automatic.                                                                    □

**Theorem 10.4.3**   *Let* $(a(n))_{n\geq 0}$ *be a* $(k, \ell)$-*synchronized sequence. Then it is* *k-regular.*

*Proof*   Suppose $A$ is a DFA recognizing the pairs $(n, a(n))$ with $n$ represented in base $k$ and $a(n)$ in base $\ell$. Consider the first-order formula

$$\exists s\ i < s \wedge A(n, s);$$

the set of pairs $(i, n)$ for which this formula evaluates to TRUE forms an $(\ell, k)$-automatic sequence and we can constructively find the appropriate DFA $B$. Furthermore, for a given $n$, the number of $i$ making this formula true is $a(n)$. Then, as in Section 4.10, we can compute a linear representation for $a(n)$ directly from $B$, and hence $(a(n))_{n\geq 0}$ is $k$-regular.                                    □

**Example 10.4.4**   Consider the DFA in Figure 10.6. This one-state DFA $A$,

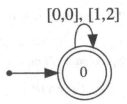

$$[0,0],\ [1,2]$$

Figure 10.6  (2, 3)-synchronized DFA for the Cantor sequence.

which is $(2, 3)$-synchronized, computes the $n$th term of the Cantor sequence $(c(n))_{n\geq 0} = (0, 2, 6, 8, 18, 20, 24, 26, \ldots)$ of numbers having no 1s in their base-3 representation; it is sequence A005823 in the *On-Line Encyclopedia of Integer Sequences* (OEIS) [365]. See Section 2.4.6.

However, using the formula $\exists s\ i < s \wedge A(n, s)$ given above, and computing the corresponding linear representation, gives

$$v = \begin{bmatrix} 1 & 0 \end{bmatrix}; \quad \zeta(0) = \begin{bmatrix} 1 & 0 \\ 0 & 3 \end{bmatrix}; \quad \zeta(1) = \begin{bmatrix} 1 & 2 \\ 0 & 3 \end{bmatrix}; \quad w = \begin{bmatrix} 0 \\ 1 \end{bmatrix},$$

so the sequence $(c(n))_{n\geq 0}$ itself is 2-regular.

On the other hand, the characteristic sequence of the range of $(c(n))_{n\geq 0}$ is **ca**, which is 3-automatic.

One great advantage to a synchronized representation for a function is that we can easily verify identities. For example, for the Cantor sequence, let's verify with Walnut that $s_{2n} = 3s_n$ and $s_{2n+1} = 3s_n + 2$ for all $n \geq 0$.

```
reg cs msd_2 msd_3 "([0,0]|[1,2])*":
eval test1 "An,r,s ($cs(n,?msd_3 r) & $cs(2*n,?msd_3 s))
   => ?msd_3 s=3*r":
eval test2 "An,r,s ($cs(n,?msd_3 r) & $cs(2*n+1,?msd_3 s))
   => ?msd_3 s=3*r+2":
```

Notice that since msd_2 is the default representation, we do not need to explain to Walnut that $n$ is represented in base 2, but we do need to declare the variables r and s as represented in base 3.

## 10.5 An example: the appearance function

In this section we look at an example of a useful synchronized function in detail: appearance [78].

The *appearance* function $A_\mathbf{x}(n)$ of a sequence $\mathbf{x}$ is the length of the shortest prefix of $\mathbf{x}$ that contains all length-$n$ factors of $\mathbf{x}$. We claim that $A_\mathbf{x}(n)$ is $k$-synchronized for $k$-automatic sequences $\mathbf{x}$. To see this, write a first-order formula $\mathrm{pr}(n, s)$ that states that the prefix of length $s$ contains all length-$n$ factors of $\mathbf{x}$:

$$\forall j \, \exists i \, (i + n \leq s) \, \wedge \, \forall t \, (t < n) \implies \mathbf{x}[j + t] = \mathbf{x}[i + t].$$

Next, write the first-order formula stating that $s$ is the smallest such:

$$\mathrm{app}(n, s) := \mathrm{pr}(n, s) \, \wedge \, \neg\,\mathrm{pr}(n, s - 1).$$

Thus $\mathrm{app}(n, s)$ evaluates to TRUE iff $s = A_\mathbf{x}(n)$.

It now follows from Theorem 6.4.1 that if $\mathbf{x}$ is a $k$-automatic sequence, then one can construct an automaton recognizing $\{(n, A_\mathbf{x}(n)) : n \geq 0\}$. This shows that $A_\mathbf{x}(n)$ is $k$-synchronized.

As an example, let us carry out this construction for the Thue-Morse sequence using Walnut. We obtain the automaton in Figure 10.7. The first few values of the appearance function in this case are given in Table 10.1.

| $n$ | 1 | 2 | 3 | 4 | 5 | 6 | 7 | 8 | 9 | 10 | 11 | 12 | 13 | 14 |
|------|---|---|---|----|----|----|----|----|----|----|----|----|----|----|
| $A(n)$ | 2 | 7 | 8 | 15 | 16 | 29 | 30 | 31 | 32 | 57 | 58 | 59 | 60 | 61 |

Table 10.1 $A(n)$ for $1 \leq n \leq 14$.

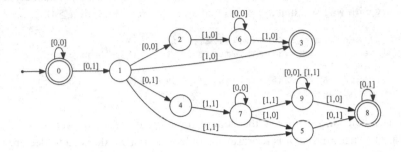

Figure 10.7 Synchronized 2-automaton computing $A_t(n)$.

Having such an automaton for $A_x(n)$ can make verification of identities involving $A_x(n)$ trivial. Often these identities can be conjectured on the basis of numerical examples, and then verified with `Walnut`. Inspection of Table 10.1 and a few more values suggests the following identities for $n \geq 1$ and $A = A_t$:

$$A(2n + 1) = A(2n) + 1$$
$$A(4n) = 2A(2n) + 1$$
$$A(8n + 2) = 2A(4n + 2) - 1$$
$$A(8n + 6) = 2A(4n + 2) + 3.$$

One way to verify these identities with `Walnut` is as follows. Study the example closely to see how the binary relation app can be massaged into identity verification:

```
def tmpr "Aj Ei i+n<=s & At t<n => T[i+t]=T[j+t]":
def tmap "$tmpr(n,s) & ~$tmpr(n,s-1)":
eval test1 "A n,s,t (n>=1 & $tmap(2*n,s) & $tmap(2*n+1,t))
    => (t=s+1)":
eval test2 "A n,s,t (n>=1 & $tmap(2*n,s) & $tmap(4*n,t))
    => (t=2*s+1)":
eval test3 "A n,s,t (n>=1 & $tmap(4*n+2,s) & $tmap(8*n+2,t))
    => (t+1=2*s)":
eval test4 "A n,s,t (n>=1 & $tmap(4*n+2,s) & $tmap(8*n+6,t))
    => (t=2*s+3)":
```

We can also verify an explicit formula for $A = A_t$, as follows.

$$A(n) = \begin{cases} 0, & \text{if } n = 0; \\ 2, & \text{if } n = 1; \\ 7, & \text{if } n = 2; \\ 7 \cdot 2^j + i - 1, & \text{if } n = 2^j + i \text{ for } j \geq 0 \text{ and } 2 \leq i \leq 2^j + 1. \end{cases} \tag{10.1}$$

To verify this, the basic idea is to replace $2^j$ by a variable $t$, which can be enforced to be a power of 2 using a regular expression in Walnut, as follows:

```
reg power2 msd_2 "0*10*":
eval idcheck "A n,t,i,s ($power2(t) & n=t+i & i>=2 & i<=t+1 &
   n>=3 & $app(n,s)) => (s+1=7*t+i)":
```

which evaluates to TRUE. This proves the claim (10.1) for $n \geq 3$.

## 10.6 Growth rate of synchronized sequences

A $k$-regular sequence $(f(n))_{n \geq 0}$ can grow as fast as any polynomial in $n$, but no faster. However, for synchronized sequences, their growth rate is much more constrained.

**Theorem 10.6.1** *Let* $k, \ell \geq 2$ *be integers, let* $(f(n))_{n \geq 0}$ *be a* $(k, \ell)$-*synchronized sequence, and define* $\beta = (\log \ell)/(\log k)$. *Then*

*(a)* $f(n) = O(n^\beta)$.
*(b) If* $f(n) = o(n^\beta)$, *then* $f(n) = O(1)$.
*(c) If there exists an increasing subsequence* $0 < n_1 < n_2 < \cdots$ *such that* $\lim_{i \to \infty} f(n_i)/n_i^\beta = 0$, *then there exists a constant* $C$ *such that* $f(n) = C$ *for infinitely many* $n$.

*Proof*

(a) Suppose $f \neq O(n^\beta)$. Then there exists an increasing subsequence $(n_i)_{i \geq 0}$ such that $f(n_i)/n_i^\beta \to \infty$. Suppose the DFA accepting $\{(n, f(n))_{k,\ell} : n \geq 0\}$ has $t$ states; then $t$ is the pumping lemma constant. Choose $i$ such that $n_i \geq k^t$ and $f(n_i)/n_i^\beta > \ell^{t+1}$, and in the pumping lemma let $z = (n_i, f(n_i))_{k,\ell}$. Then $|z| > t$, and furthermore we have

$$|f(n_i)_\ell| > \log_\ell f(n_i) > \log_\ell(n_i^\beta \ell^{t+1}) = (\log_\ell n_i^\beta) + t + 1 = (\beta \log_\ell n_i) + t + 1$$
$$= (\log_k n_i) + t + 1 \geq |(n_i)_k| + t.$$

Hence the first component of $z$ starts with at least $t$ 0s, while the second component starts with a nonzero digit. When we pump (that is, write $z = uvw$ with $|uv| \le t$ and $|v| \ge 1$ and consider $uv^2w$) we only add to the number of leading $0$s in the first component, but the second component's base-$\ell$ value increases in size (since it starts with a nonzero digit). This implies that $f$ is not a function, a contradiction.

(b) We prove the contrapositive. Since $L = \{(n, f(n))_{k,\ell} : n \ge 0\}$ is regular, so is the reversed language $L^R = \{(n, f(n))_{k,\ell}^R : n \ge 0\}$. Let $M$ be a DFA recognizing $L^R$, and let $t$ be the number of states of $M$ (which is the pumping lemma constant). Assume that $f \ne O(1)$. Then there must be an $n_0 > 0$ for which $f(n_0) > \ell^t$. Let $z = (n_0, f(n_0))_{k,\ell}^R$. Then $|z| > t$. Using the pumping lemma, write $z = uvw$ with $|uv| \le t$ and $|v| \ge 1$, and consider the sequence of words $z_i = uv^{i+1}w \in L^R$ for $i \ge 0$. Then $z_i = (a_i, b_i)_{k,\ell}^R$ for some integers $a_i, b_i$ and hence $f(a_i) = b_i$. Let $r, s$ be integers such that $k^r \le n_0 < k^{r+1}$ and $\ell^s \le f(n_0) < \ell^{s+1}$. Then $a_i < k^{r+1+i|v|}$ and $b_i > \ell^{s+i|v|}$. Thus $\log_\ell b_i - \log_k a_i > s - r - 1$, and so $f(a_i) = b_i > \ell^{s-r-1} a_i^\beta$. Thus $f(n) > cn^\beta$ for infinitely many $n$, with $c = \ell^{s-r-1}$, and hence $f(n) \ne o(n^\beta)$.

(c) Suppose the synchronized DFA for $f$ has $t$ states. From the fact that $\lim_{i \to \infty} f(n_i)/n_i^\beta = 0$, there must exist some $n_i > k^t$ for which $f(n_i)/n_i^\beta < \ell^{-(t+1)}$. Then

$$|f(n_i)_\ell| \le (\log_\ell f(n_i)) + 1 \le (\log_\ell n_i^\beta \ell^{-(t+1)}) + 1 = (\beta \log_\ell n_i) - t$$
$$= (\log_k n_i) - t \le |(n_i)_k| - t.$$

Let $z$ be the base-$k$ representation of the pair $(n_i, f(n_i))$. The second component of $z$ then starts with at least $t$ $0$s. Applying the pumping lemma to $z$ then implies there are infinitely many $n$ for which $f(n) = f(n_i)$. Take $C = f(n_i)$ to obtain the result.

□

**Corollary 10.6.2**  *Let $f(n)$ be a $(k, \ell)$-synchronized sequence that is increasing. Then either $f = O(1)$ or $f = \Theta(n^\beta)$, where $\beta = (\log \ell)/(\log k)$.*

As another corollary, we immediately get that the subword complexity of automatic sequences is small:

**Corollary 10.6.3**  *Let $\mathbf{x}$ be a $k$-automatic sequence, and let $\rho_\mathbf{x}(n)$ be the number of distinct factors of length $n$ appearing in $\mathbf{x}$. Then $\rho_\mathbf{x}(n) = O(n)$.*

*Proof*   Clearly the number of distinct factors of length $n$ is bounded above by the appearance function $t := A_\mathbf{x}(n)$ (because $\mathbf{x}[0..t - 1]$ contains all factors of length $n$). However, we proved in Section 10.5 that $A_\mathbf{x}(n)$ is $k$-synchronized, so by Theorem 10.6.1 (a) it is $O(n)$, and the same is true for $\rho_\mathbf{x}(n)$.   □

**Theorem 10.6.4** *If $f(n)$ is a synchronized sequence that is $O(1)$, then it is automatic.*

*Proof* If $f = O(1)$, then it takes only finitely many values. For each value $a$ it takes, we can form the finite automaton recognizing those $n$ for which $f(n) = a$, and then recombine them into a single automaton computing $f$, as in Section 4.8. □

We should stress that synchronized functions need not be smooth at all. For example, the 2-synchronized function $f(n) = (n \bmod 16) + n - 2^{\lfloor \log_2 n \rfloor}$ is very erratic, as Figure 10.8 illustrates.

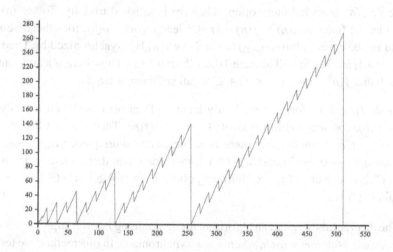

Figure 10.8 $f(n)$ for $1 \le n < 2^{10}$.

Here $f(n) = 0$ infinitely often, $f(n) = n/3$ infinitely often, and $f(n) \sim \sqrt{n}$ infinitely often, etc.

We now turn to another question. Suppose $f(n)$ is a $k$-synchronized function. By results of [336] the following quantities are all rational numbers, and computable:

- $\sup_{n \ge 1} f(n)/n$.
- $\limsup_{n \ge 1} f(n)/n$.
- $\inf_{n \ge 1} f(n)/n$.
- $\liminf_{n \ge 1} f(n)/n$.

Based on this, we can prove the following new result:

**Theorem 10.6.5** *Suppose $f(n)$ is $k$-synchronized. Then $\limsup_{n\geq 1} f(n)/n = r$ iff there exist constants $C, C' \geq 0$ such that both of the following hold:*

*(a) $f(n) \leq rn + C$ for all sufficiently large $n$.*

*(b) $f(n) \geq rn - C'$ for infinitely many $n$.*

*Proof* The reverse direction ($\Longleftarrow$) is clearly sufficient, so let us prove the forward direction.

By the remarks above $r$ is rational. There are two cases to consider.

*Case 1:* $f(n) \geq rn$ infinitely often. Then (b) is satisfied trivially. To see (a), consider the function $g(n) = f(n) \dot{-} \lfloor rn \rfloor$. Clearly $g(n) = o(n)$, for otherwise $r$ could not be equal to $\limsup_{n\geq 1} f(n)/n$. Now $g(n)$ is $k$-synchronized by Theorem 10.3.1, and hence by Theorem 10.6.1 (b) it is $O(1)$. Thus there is a constant $C$ such that $f(n) \leq \lfloor rn \rfloor + C \leq rn + C$ for all sufficiently large $n$.

*Case 2:* $f(n) \leq rn$ for all sufficiently large $n$. Then (a) is satisfied trivially. To see (b), consider the function $h(n) = \lceil rn \rceil \dot{-} f(n)$. Then the fact that $r = \limsup_{n\geq 1} f(n)/n$ implies that there is an increasing subsequence $(n_i)_{i\geq 1}$ such that $h(n_i)/n_i \to 0$. By Theorem 10.6.1 (c) we know that there must be a constant $C' \geq 0$ such that $h(n) = C'$ infinitely often. Then $f(n) \geq \lceil rn \rceil - C' \geq rn - C'$ infinitely often. □

The theorem above gives an algorithm for determining $r = \limsup_{n\geq 1} f(n)/n$ by *continued fraction search*, when $f$ is $k$-synchronized. In this method we test the first-order formula

$$\exists m, c \; \forall n \; (n \geq m \wedge F(n, s)) \implies qs \leq pn + cq$$

for rational numbers $r = p/q$ to determine the smallest $r$ for which it holds, where $F$ is a $k$-DFAO computing $f(n)$. (Binary search does not suffice to determine $r$ since $q$ may not have a denominator that is a power of 2.)

In continued fraction search we use doubling search to narrow down $r$ to an interval with endpoints $[a_0, a_1, \ldots, a_i, 2^j]$ and $[a_0, a_1, \ldots, a_i, 2^{j+1}]$ for some $j \geq 0$, and then use binary search to further locate $r$ in the interval with endpoints $[a_0, a_1, \ldots, a_i, k]$ and $[a_0, a_1, \ldots, a_i, k, 1]$. Since $r$ is guaranteed to be rational, this search must eventually terminate.

Once $r$ is determined, we can use another first-order formula to compute the $C, C'$ in Theorem 10.6.5.

## 10.7 Efficient computation of synchronized sequences

Suppose $f(n)$ is $(k, \ell)$-synchronized. How quickly can we compute $f(n)$?

**Theorem 10.7.1** *If $f(n)$ is $(k, \ell)$-synchronized, we can compute it in $O(\log n)$ time and space.*

*Proof* Since $f$ is $(k, \ell)$-synchronized, there is an automaton $M$ recognizing the language $L = \{ [0,0]^*(n, f(n))_{k,\ell} : n \geq 0 \}$. Given $n$, we can now easily create a DFA $M'$ of $O(\log n)$ states accepting those words over $(\Sigma_k \times \Sigma_k)^*$ where the first component is of the form $0^*(n)_k$ and the second component is arbitrary. Now, using the direct product construction, we can form a new DFA $M''$ for the intersection of these two languages. Now using any traversal algorithm for directed graphs, such as breadth-first search, we can look for a path from the initial state of $M''$ to any final state. Breadth-first search is particularly suited to our task, because we can maintain a queue of states to be explored further, and halt as soon as an accepting state in $M''$ is discovered. Such a path will be labeled with a base-$k$ representation of $n$ in the first component, and a base-$\ell$ representation of $f(n)$ in the second component.     □

**Example 10.7.2** Continuing the example of Section 10.5, let us compute $A(10)$ for the Thue-Morse sequence. First we create the DFA $M'$:

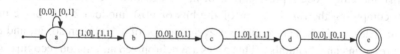

Then we form the DFA $M''$ by breadth-first search. Only reachable states are shown.

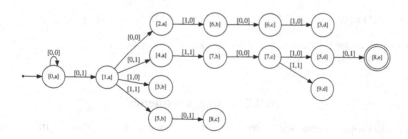

The unique accepting path

$$[0,a] \xrightarrow{[0,1]} [1,a] \xrightarrow{[0,1]} [4,a] \xrightarrow{[1,1]} [7,b] \xrightarrow{[0,0]} [7,c] \xrightarrow{[1,0]} [5,d] \xrightarrow{[0,1]} [8,e]$$

is labeled `001010` in the first component, and `111001` in the second component, showing that $A(10) = 57$.

With `Walnut` we can simply say, for example,

```
eval ap10 "$tmap(10,s)":
```

The resulting DFA will be a linear chain of nodes accepting exactly one word, which is the base-2 representation of 57.

## 10.8 Examples of synchronized functions

In this section we give a number of functions on automatic sequences that are synchronized.

### 10.8.1 Binary Gray code

A Gray code is a way of enumerating the natural numbers as binary words so that the representation of $n$ differs from that of $n + 1$ in exactly one bit position. In the most famous Gray code—binary reflected Gray code—given $g(n)$, the Gray code representation of $n$, we can find the representation of $n$ by computing the running sum of the bits of $g(n)$, modulo 2 [164]. We use two states, with $q_0$ representing an even number of 1 bits seen so far, and $q_1$ representing an odd number. This gives a synchronized automaton recognizing, in parallel, the base-2 expansions of the pairs $(g(n), n)$, depicted in Figure 10.9. To show that $(n, g(n))$ is 2-synchronized, we just need to switch the two labels on every transition. This gives an automaton of two states that we can call `gray.txt` and store in the `Automata Library` directory.

We can now prove that $g(n)$ has the desired property:

```
reg diffbyone {0,1} {0,1} "([0,0]|[1,1])*([0,1]|[1,0])
    ([0,0]|[1,1])*":
eval graycheck "An,x,y ($gray(n,x) & $gray(n+1,y))
    => $diffbyone(x,y)":
```

### 10.8.2 Propp's sequence

Recall Propp's sequence from Chapter 1: it is the unique strictly increasing function $s : \mathbb{N} \to \mathbb{N}$ for which $s(s(n)) = 3n$.

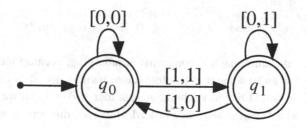

Figure 10.9 $(g(n), n)$ is 2-synchronized.

We can represent this sequence in a number of different ways. First, there is its range: $S = \{s(n) : n \geq 0\} = \{0, 2, 3, 6, 7, 8, 9, 12, 15, 18, \ldots\}$. This range $S$ forms a 3-automatic set, whose characteristic function is computed by the DFAO in Figure 10.10. In fact, a number $r$ appears in the range of $s$ if and only

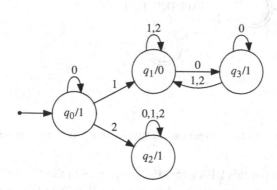

Figure 10.10 DFAO for the characteristic sequence of the range of Propp's function.

if $(r)_3$ starts with 2 or ends with 0, which we can check as follows:

```
morphism s "0->012 1->311 2->222 3->311":
morphism g "0->1 1->0 2->1 3->1":
promote BB s:
image PRO g BB:
reg proppr msd_3 "0*(2(0|1|2)*|(0|1|2)*0)":
eval proppchk0 "?msd_3 An PRO[n]=@1 <=> $proppr(n)":
```

However, this automaton is somewhat unsatisfying, because the range appears to throw away some useful information: namely, for each element $r$ of the range, we would like to know the $n$ such that $s(n) = r$. So we could represent $s(n)$ as a 3-regular sequence instead. However, this representation does not easily allow checking the identity $s(s(n)) = 3n$.

Perhaps the most useful representation for $s$ is as a 3-synchronized function. The automaton in Figure 10.11 provides this:

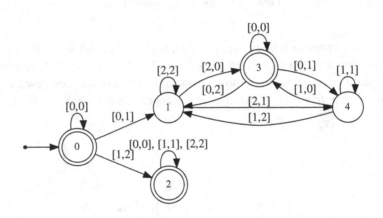

Figure 10.11 Synchronized DFA for Propp's function, base 3.

With the aid of this DFA (stored as `prop.txt` in the `Automata Library` of `Walnut`) we can prove that $s$ does indeed satisfy the identity $s(s(n)) = 3n$.

```
eval proppchk "?msd_3 An,x,y ($prop(n,x)&$prop(x,y)) => y=3*n":
```

We can also check that our DFAO for the range of $s$ was correct:

```
eval proppchk2 "?msd_3 An PRO[n]=@1 <=> Em $prop(m,n)":
```

Finally, we can verify yet another representation for $s$, namely

$$s(n) = \begin{cases} 0, & \text{if } n = 0; \\ n + 3^k, & \text{if } 3^k \le n < 2 \cdot 3^k \text{ for } k \ge 0; \\ 3(n - 3^k), & \text{if } 2 \cdot 3^k \le n < 3^{k+1} \text{ for } k \ge 0, \end{cases}$$

with the following Walnut code:

```
reg power3 msd_3 "0*10*":
def pow3n "?msd_3 $power3(x) & x<=n & ~Et $power3(t) &
   x<t & t<=n":
# x is the largest power of 3 that is <= n
eval proppchk3 "?msd_3 An,x (($pow3n(n,x)&n<2*x)=>$prop(n,n+x))
   | (($pow3n(n,x) & n>=2*x) => $prop(n,(3*n)-3*x))":
```

For more about this sequence, see [11].

This example illustrates one of the most useful aspects of $k$-synchronized sequences, in contrast with the larger class of $k$-regular sequences. For $k$-synchronized sequences, we can typically write a first-order statement to verify a particular property, whereas for $k$-regular sequences there is no general way to do this. Even a claim like "$\mathbf{x}[i] = 0$ for infinitely many $i$" is not checkable, in general, for $k$-regular sequences. See [231].

### 10.8.3 Distance between symbols

Consider an automatic sequence $(s_i)_{i \ge 0}$ and a symbol $a$. For each $n$ we can compute the position of the first occurrence of two $a$s exactly $n$ symbols apart. Let $d_a(n) = \min\{r : s_r = a = s_{n+r}\}$; this function is synchronized.

Let us compute this for the Thue-Morse sequence and $a = 1$:

```
def two1 "T[r]=@1 & T[n+r]=@1":
def two1min "$two1(n,r) & As s<r => ~$two1(n,s)":
```

The resulting automaton is depicted in Figure 10.12.

One advantage to the synchronized representation of a function is that we can easily verify guessed results about it. For example, some experimentation suggests the identities

$$d_1(4n + 3) = 2 - t_{n+1}$$
$$d_1(4n + 1) = d_1(8n + 1) = t_n + 1$$
$$d_1(8n + 5) = 2 - t_n,$$

and we can prove these as follows:

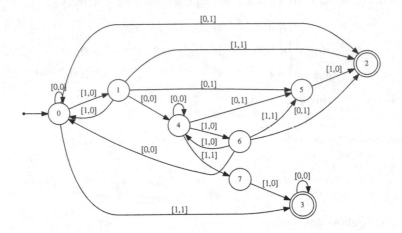

Figure 10.12 First occurrence of two 1s at distance *n* in **t**.

```
def test1 "An ($twolmin(4*n+3,1) <=> T[n+1]=@1) &
    ($twolmin(4*n+3,2) <=> T[n+1]=@0)":
def test2a "An ($twolmin(4*n+1,1) <=> T[n]=@0) &
    ($twolmin(4*n+1,2) <=> T[n]=@1)":
def test2b "An,r $twolmin(4*n+1,r) <=> $twolmin(8*n+1,r)":
def test3 "An ($twolmin(8*n+5,1) <=> T[n]=@1) &
    ($twolmin(8*n+5,2) <=> T[n]=@0)":
```

## 10.8.4 Separation

Let $w$ be a recurrent length-$n$ factor $w$ of a sequence **x**. Let $i_j(w)$ be the starting position of the $j$th occurrence of $w$ in **x**. Then $i_{j+1}(w) - i_j(w)$ is the distance between two consecutive occurrences of $w \in$ **x**. (There is also an interpretation of distance where the two consecutive occurrences are not allowed to overlap; we leave it to the reader to consider that one.)

We can consider the four quantities

$$S_1(n) = \min_{|w|=n} \min_j (i_{j+1}(w) - i_j(w)),$$

$$S_2(n) = \min_{|w|=n} \max_j (i_{j+1}(w) - i_j(w)),$$

$$S_3(n) = \max_{|w|=n} \min_j (i_{j+1}(w) - i_j(w)),$$

$$S_4(n) = \max_{|w|=n} \max_j (i_{j+1}(w) - i_j(w)).$$

Note that if **x** is not uniformly recurrent, then the functions $S_2$ and $S_4$ may not be well defined for all $n$. The function $S_1(n)$ was called the *repetitivity index* by Carpi and D'Alonzo [69]. The function $S_4(n)$ is the same as the separation bound $S(n)$ mentioned in Section 2.2.

**Theorem 10.8.1** *Suppose* **x** *is k-automatic. Then the functions* $S_1$ *and* $S_3$ *are k-synchronized, and if* **x** *is uniformly recurrent, so are* $S_2$ *and* $S_4$.

*Proof* For each of these four interpretations, $1 \leq i \leq 4$, we can easily write a first-order formula giving the value $t = S_i(n)$ for each corresponding $n$. □

Here is the Walnut code for the Thue-Morse sequence:

```
def tmfactoreq "At t<n => T[i+t]=T[j+t]":
def tmconsec "(k>j) & $tmfactoreq(i,j,n) & $tmfactoreq(i,k,n) &
    Al (j<l & l<k) => ~$tmfactoreq(i,l,n)":
def mindist "(Aj,k $tmconsec(i,j,k,n) => s+j<=k) &
    (Ej,k $tmconsec(i,j,k,n) & s+j=k)":
def maxdist "(Aj,k $tmconsec(i,j,k,n) => s+j>=k) &
    (Ej,k $tmconsec(i,j,k,n) & s+j=k)":
def s1 "(Ei $mindist(i,n,t)) & (Ai,s $mindist(i,n,s) => s>=t)":
def s2 "(Ei $maxdist(i,n,t)) & (Ai,s $maxdist(i,n,s) => s>=t)":
def s3 "(Ei $mindist(i,n,t)) & (Ai,s $mindist(i,n,s) => s<=t)":
def s4 "(Ei $maxdist(i,n,t)) & (Ai,s $maxdist(i,n,s) => s<=t)":
```

The first few values for the Thue-Morse sequence are as follows:

| $n$ | 1 | 2 | 3 | 4 | 5 | 6 | 7 | 8 | 9 | 10 | 11 | 12 | 13 |
|---|---|---|---|---|---|---|---|---|---|---|---|---|---|
| $S_1(n)$ | 1 | 2 | 3 | 4 | 6 | 6 | 8 | 8 | 12 | 12 | 12 | 12 | 16 |
| $S_2(n)$ | 3 | 4 | 8 | 8 | 16 | 16 | 16 | 16 | 32 | 32 | 32 | 32 | 32 |
| $S_3(n)$ | 1 | 4 | 4 | 8 | 8 | 16 | 16 | 16 | 16 | 32 | 32 | 32 | 32 |
| $S_4(n)$ | 3 | 8 | 9 | 18 | 18 | 36 | 36 | 36 | 36 | 72 | 72 | 72 | 72 |

*Exercise* 121 What do the formulas give when used on a non-recurrent automatic sequence, such as **sb**?

As another consequence, we can now prove a theorem about the asymptotic critical exponent of an automatic sequence. This concept was introduced in Section 2.2. The asymptotic critical exponent ace($\mathbf{x}$) of an infinite word is defined to be

$$\sup\{\alpha \; : \; \text{there exist arbitrarily long factors } w \text{ of } \mathbf{x} \text{ with } \exp(w) \geq \alpha\}.$$

**Theorem 10.8.2** *If* $\mathbf{x}$ *is a* $k$-*automatic sequence, then* ace($\mathbf{x}$) $> 1$.

*Proof* We saw in Theorem 10.8.1 that if $\mathbf{x}$ is $k$-automatic, then the function $S_1(n)$ is $k$-synchronized. By Theorem 10.6.1 (a), we have $S_1(n) = O(n)$. Hence there exists a constant $c$ such that for all sufficiently large $n$, there are two consecutive occurrences of some length-$n$ factor $z$ at distance $d$ from each other, with $d \leq cn$. So $n \geq d/c$. Let $w = w_n$ be a word of length at most $d + n$ with two distinct occurrences of $z$, one as prefix and one as suffix. Then

$$\exp(w) = |w|/\operatorname{per}(w) \geq (d + n)/d \geq (d + d/c)/d = 1 + 1/c > 1.$$

□

### 10.8.5 Initial nonrepetitive complexity

Subrahmonian Moothatu [368] introduced the following function, called the *initial nonrepetitive complexity*:

$$\textsc{Inc}_{\mathbf{x}}(n) = \max\{r \; : \; \mathbf{x}[i..i+n-1] \neq \mathbf{x}[j..j+n-1] \text{ for all } i, j \text{ with } 0 \leq i < j < r\},$$

the number of length-$n$ factors that occur in a prefix of $\mathbf{x}$ prior to the first occurrence of a repeated factor.

This function is synchronized for automatic sequences $\mathbf{x}$. For example, let us compute this for the Thue-Morse sequence.

```
def tmnr "Ai,j (i<j & j<r) => ~$tmfactoreq(i,j,n)":
def tminc "$tmnr(n,r) & As (s>r) => ~$tmnr(n,s)":
```

Nicholson and Rampersad [283] observed that $\textsc{Inc}_{\mathbf{t}}(n) = 3\cdot 2^k$ for $2^k < n \leq 2^{k+1}$ and $k \geq 0$. We can verify this as follows:

```
def incchk "An,x ($power2(x) & x<n & n<=2*x) => $tminc(n,3*x)":
```

*Exercise* 122 Guess and prove formulas for $\textsc{Inc}_{\mathbf{x}}(n)$ for some other infinite words $\mathbf{x}$.

### 10.8.6 Repeated factors

Closely related to initial nonrepetitive complexity is the *repeated factor function* $r_{\mathbf{x}}(n)$ introduced by Bugeaud and Kim [63]: $r_{\mathbf{x}}(n)$ denotes the length of the shortest prefix of **x** containing two (possibly overlapping) occurrences of some length-$n$ word.

This function is also $k$-synchronized for automatic sequences **x**. To see this, write a formula asserting that the prefix of length $s$ contains two occurrences of some length-$n$ factor:

$$\text{twofac}(n, s) := \exists i, j \, (i < j) \wedge (j + n \le s) \wedge \forall t \, \mathbf{x}[i + t] = \mathbf{x}[j + t].$$

Next, write a formula asserting that the prefix of length $r$ contains two occurrences of some length-$n$ factor, but the prefix of length $r - 1$ does not:

$$\text{kim}(n, r) := \text{twofac}(n, r) \wedge \neg \text{twofac}(n, r - 1).$$

When we carry this out for the Thue-Morse sequence, we get the DFA in Figure 10.13.

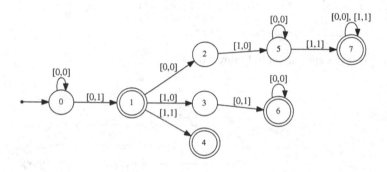

Figure 10.13 DFA for the repeated factor function of Bugeaud-Kim.

From this we can easily verify their result (p. 3284) that $r_t(2^n - m) = 5 \cdot 2^{n-1} - m$, if $0 \le m < 2^{n-1}$ and $n \ge 1$.

Hence we can show that $r_t(n) \ge (5/2)n$ for all $n$, and $r_t(n) = (5/2)n$ for $n = 2^i, i \ge 1$. Thus $\liminf_{n \to \infty} r_t(n)/n = 5/2$.

Similarly, we have $r_t(n) \le 4n - 3$ for $n \ge 2$ and $r_t(n) = 4n - 3$ infinitely often. Thus $\limsup_{n \to \infty} r_t(n)/n = 4$.

*Exercise* 123  Carry out the same computation for the variant where the two occurrences are not allowed to overlap.

### 10.8.7 Condensation

The *condensation function* $C_{\mathbf{x}}(n)$ for an infinite word $\mathbf{x}$ maps $n$ to the length of the shortest factor of $\mathbf{x}$ containing, as factors, all the length-$n$ factors of $\mathbf{x}$.

We can create a template expressing the synchronization of $C_{\mathbf{x}}(n)$, as follows:

CONTAINALL$(j, n, s) := \forall i$ OCCURS$(i, j, n, s)$

CONDENSE$(n, s) := (\exists j \text{ CONTAINALL}(j, n, s)) \wedge (\neg \exists k \text{ CONTAINALL}(k, n, s-1))$.

The first line creates CONTAINALL$(j, n, s)$, which asserts that $\mathbf{x}[j..j+s-1]$ contains all length-$n$ factors of $\mathbf{x}$.

The second line creates CONDENSE$(n, s)$, which asserts that there is some $j$ such that $\mathbf{x}[j..j+s-1]$ contains all length-$n$ factors of $\mathbf{x}$, but there is no $k$ such that $\mathbf{x}[k..k+s-2]$ contains all length-$n$ factors of $\mathbf{x}$.

When we instantiate this for the Thue-Morse sequence we get

```
def tmfactoreq "At t<n => T[i+t]=T[j+t]":
def tmoccurs "n<=s & Ek (k+n<=s) & $tmfactoreq(i,j+k,n)":
def tmcontainall "Ai $tmoccurs(i,j,n,s)":
def tmcondense "(Ej $tmcontainall(j,n,s)) &
   (~Ek $tmcontainall(k,n,s-1))":
```

This gives the automaton in Figure 10.14.

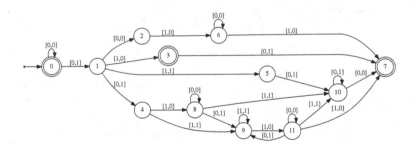

Figure 10.14 Synchronized DFA for the condensation function for **t**.

Goč, Henshall, and the author [169] showed that $C_{\mathbf{t}}(n)$ satisfies the formula

$$C_{\mathbf{t}}(n) = \begin{cases} 2, & \text{if } n = 1; \\ 5, & \text{if } n = 2; \\ 2^{j+2} + 2n - 2, & \text{if } n \geq 3 \text{ and } 2^j + 2 \leq n \leq 2^{j+1} + 1. \end{cases}$$

We can verify this formula for $n \geq 3$ as follows (letting the variable $k$ stand for $2^j$):

```
reg power2 msd_2 "0*10*":
eval checktmcond "An,k,s (n>=3 & $power2(k) & k+2<=n &
   n<=2*k+1 & $tmcondense(n,s)) => s+2=4*k+2*n":
```

## 10.8.8 Uniform recurrence

The counterpart to condensation is uniform recurrence. The *recurrence function* $R_x(n)$ is the smallest $s$ such that all length-$s$ factors of $x$ contain, as factors, all length-$n$ factors of $x$. Of course, this $s$ may not exist in general.

We can create a template expressing the synchronization of $R_x(n)$, as follows:

$$\text{CONTAINALL}(j, n, s) := \forall i \; \text{OCCURS}(i, j, n, s)$$

$$\text{RECUR}(n, s) := (\forall j \; \text{CONTAINALL}(j, n, s)) \wedge (\exists k \; \neg \text{CONTAINALL}(k, n, s - 1)).$$

The first line creates $\text{CONTAINALL}(j, n, s)$, which asserts that $x[j..j + s - 1]$ contains all length-$n$ factors of $x$.

The second line creates $\text{RECUR}(n, s)$, which asserts that for every $j$, the word $x[j..j + s - 1]$ contains all length-$n$ factors of $x$, and there is some $k$ such that $x[k..k + s - 2]$ fails to contains all length-$n$ factors of $x$.

When we instantiate this for the Thue-Morse sequence we get

```
def tmfactoreq "At t<n => T[i+t]=T[j+t]":
def tmoccurs "n<=s & Ek k+n<=s & $tmfactoreq(i,j+k,n)":
def tmcontainall "Ai $tmoccurs(i,j,n,s)":
def tmrecur "(Aj $tmcontainall(j,n,s)) &
   (Ek ~$tmcontainall(k,n,s-1))":
```

This gives the automaton in Figure 10.15. From this we can reprove a theorem of Morse and Hedlund [276, Thm. 8.2]:

**Theorem 10.8.3** *We have*

$$R_t(n) = \begin{cases} 3, & \text{if } n = 1; \\ 9, & \text{if } n = 2; \\ 9 \cdot 2^j + n - 1, & \text{if } n \geq 3 \text{ and } 2^j + 2 \leq n \leq 2^{j+1} + 1. \end{cases}$$

We can verify this formula for $n \geq 3$ as follows (letting the variable $k$ stand for $2^j$):

```
reg power2 msd_2 "0*10*":
eval checktmrecur "An,k,s (n>=3 & $power2(k) & k+2<=n
   & n<=2*k+1 & $tmrecur(n,s)) => s+1=9*k+n":
```

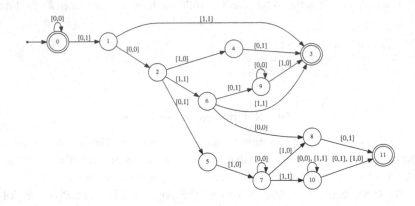

Figure 10.15 Recurrence for Thue-Morse.

which returns TRUE.

We can now use our bounds on synchronized sequences to prove the following result [109].

**Theorem 10.8.4** *If a k-automatic sequence* **x** *is uniformly recurrent, then it is linearly recurrent.*

*Proof* Suppose **x** is uniformly recurrent. In Section 10.8.4 we showed that the function $S_4(n)$, giving the maximum separation between two consecutive occurrences of a length-$n$ factor of **x**, is $k$-synchronized. Since **x** is uniformly recurrent, $S_4(n)$ is well defined. It then follows from Theorem 10.6.1 (a) that $S_4(n) = O(n)$. $\square$

Also see [130, 268, 270, 272].

Next, let us compute an expression for the recurrence function $R_\mathbf{r}(n)$ and recurrence quotient for the Rudin-Shapiro sequence **r**. Allouche and Bousquet-Mélou [8] gave the estimate $R_\mathbf{r}(n + 1) < 172n$ for $n \geq 1$. (Actually, their result was more general, as it applies to any "generalized" Rudin-Shapiro sequence.) We used our method to prove the following result:

**Theorem 10.8.5** *Let* $\mathbf{r} = (r(n))_{n\geq 0}$ *be the Rudin-Shapiro sequence. Then*

$$R_{\mathbf{r}}(n) = \begin{cases} 5, & \text{if } n = 1; \\ 19, & \text{if } n = 2; \\ 25, & \text{if } n = 3; \\ 40 \cdot 2^t + n - 1, & \text{if } n \geq 4 \text{ and } 2^t + 2 \leq n \leq 2^{t+1} + 1. \end{cases}$$

*Furthermore, the recurrence quotient*

$$\sup_{n\geq 1} \frac{R_{\mathbf{r}}(n)}{n}$$

*is equal to 41; it is not attained.*

**Proof** We use the following `Walnut` commands:

```
reg power2 msd_2 "0*10*":
def rsfaceq "At t<n => RS[i+t]=RS[j+t]":
def rsoccurs "n<=s & Ek k+n<=s & $rsfaceq(i,j+k,n)":
def rscontainall "Ai $rsoccurs(i,j,n,s)":
def rsrecur "(Aj $rscontainall(j,n,s)) &
    (Ek ~$rscontainall(k,n,s-1))":
```

The result is a synchronized automaton of 19 states. We can check the inequality with

```
def rsrecurchk "$rsrecur(1,5) & $rsrecur(2,19) & $rsrecur(3,25)
    & An,x (n>=4 & $power2(x) & x+2<=n & n<=2*x+1) =>
    $rsrecur(n, (40*x+n)-1)":
```

For the recurrence quotient, the local maximum is evidently achieved when $n = 2^r + 2$ for some $r \geq 1$; here it is equal to $(41 \cdot 2^r + 2)/(2^r + 2)$. As $r \to \infty$, this clearly approaches 41 from below. □

### 10.8.9 Starting position of first run of length $\geq n$

Given an automatic sequence $\mathbf{x}$ containing arbitrarily long runs of a single symbol, define $f_a(n)$ to be the starting position of the first run of $a$s of length $\geq n$. This function is synchronized. To see this, let us write a first-order formula for the pairs $(n, s)$ with $s = f_a(n)$.

$$\text{Run}(i, n) := \forall j \, (i \leq j \land j < i + n) \implies \mathbf{x}[j] = a$$
$$\text{FirstRun}(n) = \text{Run}(s, n) \land \forall t \, (t < s) => \neg \text{Run}(t, n).$$

Similarly, $g(n)$, the starting position of the first run of length $\geq n$ of any symbol, is also synchronized.

Let us compute $f_0(n)$ for the second-bit sequence **sb**, as follows:

```
def sbrun "Aj (i<=j & j<i+n) => SB[j]=@0":
def sbfirstrun "$sbrun(s,n) & At t<s => ~$sbrun(t,n)":
```

With this we can prove the following result for $f(n)$ in this case:

$$f(n) = \begin{cases} 0, & \text{if } n \leq 3; \\ 2^{k+2}, & \text{if } 2^k < n \leq 2^{k+1}, k \geq 1, n \geq 4. \end{cases}$$

```
eval sbruncheck "An,s $sbfirstrun(n,s) <=> ((n<=3 & s=0) |
   (Ex $power2(x) & n>=4 & x<n & n<=2*x & s=4*x))":
```

Recall that a *maximal run* is a sequence of consecutive symbols $x[i..i+n-1]$ all equal to $a$, where $x[i + n] \neq a$ and (if $i > 0$) $x[i - 1] \neq a$. We can prove a theorem about the distribution of the lengths of maximal runs. Basically, it says they are sparsely distributed.

**Theorem 10.8.6** *Let* $x$ *be a* $k$-*automatic sequence. There exists a constant* $C$ *such that for all* $i \geq 0$, *there are in* $x$ *at most* $C$ *different maximal run lengths* $\ell \in [k^i, k^{i+1})$.

*Proof* Let $f(i)$ be the number of different maximal run lengths lying in the interval $[k^i, k^{i+1})$.

For each different run length $t \in [k^i, k^{i+1})$ there exists a factor of $x$ of the form $ab^tc$ in $x$ with $a \neq b \neq c$. These different factors can only overlap, at most, at the endpoints $a, c$, so even with the most efficient "packing" of these factors together, the last such maximal run to appear in $x$ must appear at a starting position $p \geq (f(i) - 1)k^i$. On the other hand, a maximal run $b^t$ corresponds to some factor $ab^tc$ of length $t + 2$. Since, as we saw in Section 10.5, the appearance function is $k$-synchronized, Theorem 10.6.1 (a) shows that there exists a constant $c$ such that the first occurrence of such a maximal run is at a position $\leq c(t + 2)$. Hence $(f(i) - 1)k^i \leq p \leq c(t + 2) \leq c(k^{i+1} + 1)$. It follows that $f(i) \leq 1 + 2ck$. Taking $C = 1 + 2ck$, the result follows. $\quad\square$

**Corollary 10.8.7** *Let* $x$ *be a* $k$-*automatic sequence, and let* $\ell_1 < \ell_2 < \cdots$ *be the lengths of all maximal runs appearing in* $x$. *Then the base-*$k$ *representations of* $\{\ell_1, \ell_2, \ldots\}$ *can be written as a finite union of sets of the form* $uv^*w$.

*Proof* From Theorem 10.8.6 we know that the number of different maximal run lengths in the interval $[k^n, k^{n+1})$ is $O(1)$. Hence, letting $L$ be the language of base-$k$ representations of all these different maximal run lengths, the language $L$ contains at most a constant number of different words of each length: it is "slender". Furthermore, since there is a first-order formula for specifying that $n$ is the length of a maximal run, we know that $L$ is a regular language. By a theorem of [345, 370], a slender regular language is the union of a finite number of regular languages of the form $uv^*w$. □

*Exercise* 124 Deduce Eilenberg's gap theorem [133] from Corollary 10.8.7: if $S$ is a $k$-automatic set, and $t_S(n)$ is the $n$th smallest element of $S$, then either $t_S(n+1) - t_S(n)$ is bounded above by a constant, or $\limsup_{n\to\infty} t_S(n+1)/t_S(n) > 1$.

*Remark* 10.8.8 A small variation of the same proof works for any regular numeration system, such as the Fibonacci numeration system. In this case you have to replace $k^i$ with $F_i$, the $i$th Fibonacci number.

We can now apply the ideas of this section to the infinite fixed point

$$\mathbf{vn} = 001001100100111\cdots$$

of the morphism $0 \to 001$, $1 \to 1$. This sequence was previously studied by Allouche et al. [7], where the authors prove it is not 2-automatic. Their proof was somewhat involved, but with the bounds of Theorem 10.6.1, we can prove a stronger result rather easily.

**Theorem 10.8.9** *The sequence* **vn** *is not $k$-automatic for any base $k \geq 2$.*

*Proof* Suppose **vn** is $k$-automatic. The starting position of the first occurrence of a run of $n$ 1s would be $k$-synchronized and hence is $O(n)$. However, the first occurrence of $1^n$ appears at position $2^{n+1} - n - 1$, a contradiction. □

*Exercise* 125 Use the notion of synchronized sequence to prove the following result of Schlage-Puchta [338]: if an automatic sequence $(a_n)_{n\geq 0}$ has arbitrarily long runs, then there exists a constant $c > 0$ such that $a_n = a$ for $n \in [x, (1+c)x]$ and infinitely many $x$.

### 10.8.10 Separator length

Garel [161] introduced what she called *separator length:* the length $\ell$ of the shortest factor beginning at position $i$ of an aperiodic infinite word $\mathbf{x}$ that does not appear earlier in the sequence. Carpi and Maggi [70] proved this is $k$-synchronized. We can reprove this as follows:

$$\mathrm{garel}(i, \ell) := (\forall j\, (j < i) \implies \neg\mathrm{FACTOREQ}(i, j, \ell))$$
$$\wedge\, (\exists k\, (k < i) \wedge \mathrm{FACTOREQ}(i, k, \ell - 1)).$$

The first clause says that $\mathbf{x}[i..i + \ell - 1]$ does not appear earlier in $\mathbf{x}$, but $\mathbf{x}[i..i + \ell - 2]$ does. Let us carry this out for the Thue-Morse sequence:

```
def tmgarel "(Aj j<i => ~$tmfactoreq(i,j,1)) &
  (Ek k<i & $factoreq(i,k,1-1))":
```

This gives the automaton in Figure 10.16.

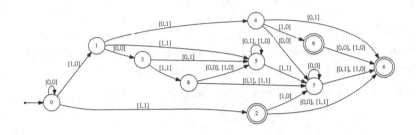

Figure 10.16 Automaton for `tmgarel`.

## 10.8.11 Palindrome separation

Let **x** be an infinite word with arbitrarily large palindromes. For each $n$ we can find the longest distance $d_{\mathbf{x}}(n)$ between two consecutive length-$n$ palindromes appearing in **x**, that is,

$$d_{\mathbf{x}}(n) = \max\{j-i \ : \ i < j \text{ and } \mathbf{x}[i..i+n-1] \text{ is a palindrome and } \mathbf{x}[j..j+n-1]$$
$$\text{is a palindrome and } \mathbf{x}[k..k+n-1] \text{ is not a palindrome for } i < k < j\}.$$

Let us carry this out for the Fibonacci word **f**.

```
def fibpal "?msd_fib (n>0) & At t<n => F[i+t] = F[i+n-1-t]":
def fibpaldist "?msd_fib Ei,j i<j & i+s=j & $fibpal(i,n) &
  $fibpal(j,n) & Ak (i<k & k<j) => ~$fibpal(k,n)":
def fibpalsep "?msd_fib $fibpaldist(n,s) & At t>s =>
  ~$fibpaldist(n,t)":
def fps "?msd_fib En $fibpalsep(n,s)":
```

With this we can prove that the maximum separation between palindromes in **f** is either $F_{3i+1}$ or $F_{3i+2}$ for $i \geq 0$. Furthermore, there is a 28-state synchronized automaton that computes this distance.

*Exercise* 126  Using this synchronized automaton, show that

$$d_{\mathbf{f}}(n) = \begin{cases} F_{3k+2}, & \text{if } n \text{ is even and } F_{3k} \le n \le F_{3k+2} - 2; \\ F_{3k+2}, & \text{if } F_{3k+2} - 1 \le n \le F_{3k+3} - 1; \\ F_{3k+1}, & \text{if } n \text{ is odd and } F_{3k+1} - 1 \le n \le F_{3k+2} - 2; \\ F_{3k-1}, & \text{if } n \text{ is odd and } F_{3k} \le n \le F_{3k+1} - 2. \end{cases}$$

### 10.8.12 Repetition words

Mignosi and Restivo [264] studied the following function: for each $i$, the length of the shortest prefix $w$ of $\mathbf{x}[i..\infty]$ for which either $w$ is a suffix of $\mathbf{x}[0..i - 1]$ or vice versa.

We can compute this for the Thue-Morse sequence as follows:

```
def tmrepe "(i>=n&$factoreq(i,i-n,n))|(n>i & $factoreq(0,n,i))":
def tmmig "(n>0)&$tmrepe(i,n)&Am (m>0&m<n) => ~$tmrepe(i,m)":
```

This gives the DFA in Figure 10.17. Also see [310].

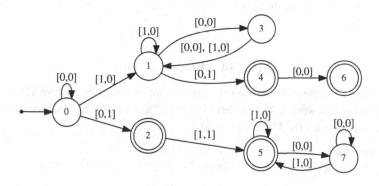

Figure 10.17 DFA for the repetition word synchronized function of Mignosi-Restivo.

### 10.8.13 Largest centered square

For each position $n$ of an infinite sequence $\mathbf{x}$ we can consider the order $f(n) = s$ of the largest (possibly empty) square centered at that position, that is,

$$\mathbf{x}[n - s..n - 1] = \mathbf{x}[n..n + s - 1].$$

This function is also synchronized. For the Fibonacci infinite word we can compute it as follows:

```
def fibcs "?msd_fib (n>=s) & $ffactoreq(n-s,n,s) &
   At (t>s & n>=t) => ~$ffactoreq(n-t,n,t)":
```

This gives the DFA in Figure 10.18.

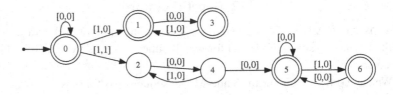

Figure 10.18 DFA for the synchronized function of largest centered square.

*Exercise* 127    Show that $f(n) = F_j$ for $F_j \leq n < F_{j+1} - 1$ and $j \geq 4$, and 0 otherwise.

### 10.8.14 Shortest square

Let ssqo($i$) be the order of the shortest nonempty square beginning at position $i$ of an infinite word **x**, or 0 if there is none. Then ssqo($i$) is synchronized. Let us compute it for the Fibonacci word:

```
# square of order n>=1 beginning at position i
def squareo "?msd_fib (n>=1) & At t<n => F[i+t]=F[i+t+n]":

# shortest nonzero square order beginning at position i
def ssqo "?msd_fib $squareo(i,n)&Am (m>0&m<n)=>~$squareo(i,m)":
```

Then the range of ssqo is $\{1, 2, 3, 5\}$ and there is a 6-state DFAO computing it.

### 10.8.15 Orders of squares beginning at a given position

Recall that in Exercise 56 we showed that the Thue-Morse sequence **t** has at most one nonempty square $xx$ beginning at every position. So, defining the function $f(i)$ to be the order of the longest square beginning at position $i$ (and allowing, contrary to the usual convention, a square to be empty), this means that $f(i)$ is a 2-synchronized function. We can obtain the automaton for it as follows:

```
def tmsquare "$tmfactoreq(i,i+n,n)":
def tmlongestsquare "$tmsquare(i,s)&At $tmsquare(i,t) => t<=s":
```

It is depicted in Figure 10.19.

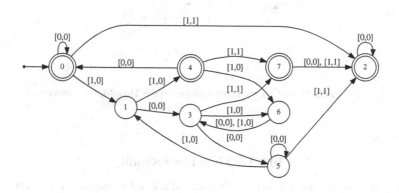

Figure 10.19 Synchronized function computing order of longest square in t beginning at a given position.

### 10.8.16 Longest palindromic suffix

Blondin Massé et al. [50] studied the longest palindromic suffix of $x[0..n-1]$ for a sequence $x$, in particular when $x = t$, the Thue-Morse sequence. If $x$ is automatic, then this length is synchronized.

We can construct a Walnut formula for this length, as follows:

```
def tmlps "(Ei $tmpal(i,s) & i+s=n) & (Aj,t ($tmpal(j,t) &
    j+t=n) => t<=s)":
```

The first part of the formula says that there is a length-$s$ palindrome ending at position $n-1$ and the second part says that every palindrome ending at position $n$ is of length $\leq s$. This gives a 17-state automaton.

Blondin Massé et al. were particularly interested in positions $n$ where the longest palindromic suffix of $x[0..n-1]$ appeared more than once in $x[0..n-1]$; they called them "lacunary". We can test this property for $n$ as follows:

```
def tmlops "Es $tmlps(n,s)&Ej (j+s+1<n) & $tmfactoreq(j,n-s,s)":
```

This gives a 10-state automaton recognizing the set of lacunary positions in Figure 10.20.

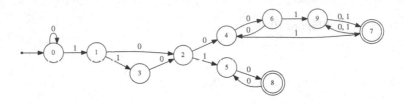

Figure 10.20 DFA for lacunary positions of the Thue-Morse sequence.

### 10.8.17 Thue irreducibility

Recall from Section 8.5.26 that Thue called a word **x** *irreducible* if every pair of consecutive occurrences of the same length-$n$ factor, say $x[i..i + n - 1]$ and $x[j..j + n - 1]$, with $i < j$, has at least two symbols separating the two occurrences, that is, satisfies the inequality $j \geq i+n+2$. In that section we constructed a DFAO $TI.txt$ that computes an irreducible word over a 4-letter alphabet. A natural question is to ask what this minimum separation, call it $f(n)$, looks like for different values of $n$. It is easy to see that $f(n)$ is synchronized, so we can compute it with Walnut. By examining the first few values we are led to the conjecture that $f(n) = 2^{k+1} - n$, if $2^k - 1 \leq n < 2^{k+1} - 1$, for $n \geq 2$ and $k \geq 1$. We verify this with $tiform$, which also returns TRUE.

```
def tifaceq "At t<n => TI[i+t]=TI[j+t]":
def tidist "Ai,j (n>=1 & i<j & $tifaceq(i,j,n)) => j>=i+n+d":
def timin "$tidist(d,n) & Ae e>d => ~$tidist(e,n)":
reg power2 msd_2 "0*10*":
eval tiform "An,x (n>=2 & $power2(x) & x>=2 & x<=n+1 & n<2*x-1)
   => $timin(2*x-n,n)":
```

### 10.8.18 The Mallows sequence

Recall the Mallows sequence $f(n)$ from Section 9.3. It is not hard to show that $f$ satisfies the identities $f(2^i + j) = 3 \cdot 2^{i-1} + j$ for $0 \leq j < 2^{i-1}$ and $f(3 \cdot 2^{i-1} + j) = 2^{i+1} + 2j$ for $0 \leq j < 2^{i-1}$ for $n \geq 2$. We can conclude that $f$ is 2-synchronized. In Walnut we can calculate it as follows:

```
reg power2 msd_2 "0*10*":
def mallows "At, j (n<=1 => s=n) & (n>=2 & $power2(t) & t<=n &
    2*t>n & n=t+j & 2*j<t) => 2*s = 3*t+2*j) & (($power2(t) &
    t<=n & 2*t>n & 2*n=3*t+2*j & 2*j<t) => s=2*t+2*j)":
```

### 10.8.19 Subword complexity

The material in this section is from [174].

Let $\rho_{\mathbf{x}}(n)$ denote the number of distinct length-$n$ factors of $\mathbf{x}$. Let us sketch a proof that this function is synchronized.[2] Here the proof is quite a bit harder than before.

Recall from Section 8.1.12 that we called a factor occurrence $\mathbf{x}[i..i + n - 1]$ novel if this is the first occurrence of the factor in $\mathbf{x}$. The crucial insight is the following: in every sequence of linear complexity, the starting positions of novel occurrences of factors are "clumped together" in a bounded number of contiguous blocks.

**Example 10.8.10** Consider the Thue-Morse sequence

$$\mathbf{t} = t_0 t_1 t_2 \cdots = 0110100110010110 \cdots .$$

The gray squares in the rows in Figure 10.21 depict the evolution of novel length-$n$ factors in the Thue-Morse sequence for $1 \leq n \leq 9$.

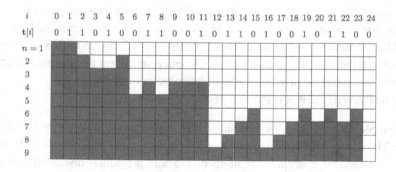

Figure 10.21 Evolution of novel factors of the Thue-Morse sequence.

**Theorem 10.8.11** *Let $\mathbf{x}$ be an infinite word. For $n \geq 1$, the number of contiguous blocks of starting occurrences of novel factors in row $n$ is at most* $\rho_{\mathbf{x}}(n) - \rho_{\mathbf{x}}(n - 1) + 1$.

---

[2] Material in this section is reprinted from [174] by permission from Springer Nature.

*Proof*  By induction on $n$. The base case is easy. Assume the claim is true for $n - 1$. We prove it for $n$.

Every position marking the start of a novel occurrence is still novel. Further, in every block except the first, we get novel occurrences at one position to the left of the beginning of the block. So if row $n - 1$ has $t$ contiguous blocks, then we get $t - 1$ novel occurrences at the beginning of each block, except the first.

The remaining $\rho_x(n) - \rho_x(n - 1) - (t - 1)$ novel occurrences could be, in the worst case, in their own individual contiguous blocks. Thus row $n$ has at most $t + \rho_x(n) - \rho_x(n - 1) - (t - 1) = \rho_x(n) - \rho_x(n - 1) + 1$ contiguous blocks.  □

**Corollary 10.8.12**  *If the sequence* x *has linear complexity (that is, $\rho_x(n) = O(n)$), then there is a constant C such that every row in the evolution of novel occurrences consists of at most C contiguous blocks.*

*Proof*  By a deep result of Cassaigne [71], we know that for every sequence of linear subword complexity (not just the $k$-automatic sequences), there exists a constant $C$ such that $\rho_x(n) - \rho_x(n - 1) \le C - 1$. Hence from our result, there are at most $C$ contiguous blocks in any row.  □

**Theorem 10.8.13**  *Let* x *be a $k$-automatic sequence. Then its subword complexity function $\rho_x(n)$ is $k$-synchronized.*

*Proof*  From Corollary 10.6.3 we know that $\rho_x(n) = O(n)$. Construct a DFA to accept $\{(n, m)_k : n \ge 0 \text{ and } m = \rho_x(n)\}$. There is a finite constant $C \ge 1$ such that the number of contiguous blocks of novel factors is bounded by $C$.

Use an automaton to nondeterministically "guess" the endpoints of every block and then verify that each factor of length $n$ starting at the positions inside blocks is a novel occurrence, while all other factors are not.

Finally, verify that $m$ is the sum of the sizes of the blocks.  □

**Example 10.8.14**  Let us first show that the subword complexity function for Thue-Morse has the property that $\rho_t(n + 1) - \rho_t(n) \le 4$ for all $n$. To do this, we need the concept of "right-special factor" previously discussed in Section 8.8.6: a finite factor $w$ of a binary sequence x is called *right-special* if both $w0$ and $w1$ appear in x. Then it is easy to see that $\rho_t(n+1) - \rho_t(n)$ is the number of right-special factors of length $n$.

To count these, we first make a formula for the property that the factor of t of length $n$ beginning at position $i$ is right-special:

$$\text{RtSpec}(i, n) = \exists j \; \text{FactorEq}(i, j, n) \wedge \mathbf{t}[i + n] \neq \mathbf{t}[j + n].$$

Next, we make a formula for the property that the factor of length $n$ beginning at position $i$ is novel:

$$\text{nf}(i,n) := \forall j\, (j < i) \implies \neg\text{FACTOREQ}(i,j,n).$$

Next, we make a formula for the property that the factor of length $n$ beginning at position $i$ is both novel and right-special:

$$\text{nrt}(i,n) := \text{nf}(i,n) \wedge \text{RTSPEC}(i,n).$$

Finally, we make a formula for the property that there exists some $n$ with 5 distinct right-special factors of length $n$:

$$\text{TMSPEC5}(i,n) := \exists n, i_1, i_2, i_3, i_4, i_5\, (i_1 < i_2) \wedge (i_2 < i_3) \wedge (i_3 < i_4) \wedge (i_4 < i_5)$$
$$\wedge\ \text{nrt}(i_1,n) \wedge \text{nrt}(i_2,n) \wedge \text{nrt}(i_3,n) \wedge \text{nrt}(i_4,n) \wedge \text{nrt}(i_5,n).$$

When we evaluate this with `Walnut`, it evaluates to false, so there are at most 4 special factors of every length.

So, from the arguments above we know that Thue-Morse novel factors are "clumped" into at most 5 contiguous blocks.

Suppose these clumps are the indices in $[a_1, b_1), [a_2, b_2), \dots, [a_5, b_5)$ for $0 = a_1 \le b_1, a_2 \le b_2, \dots, a_5 \le b_5$. (We allow $a_1 = b_1$, etc., because some of these 5 intervals could be empty.) Here is the formula $\text{TMsc}(n, r)$ asserting that the subword complexity of Thue-Morse for words of length $n$ is $r$:

$$\text{TMsc}(n,r) := \exists a_2, a_3, a_4, a_5, b_1, b_2, b_3, b_4, b_5 (b_1 \le a_2$$
$$\wedge\ a_2 \le b_2 \wedge b_2 \le a_3 \wedge a_3 \le b_3 \wedge b_3 \le a_4 \wedge a_4 \le b_4 \wedge b_4 \le a_5 \wedge a_5 \le b_5)$$
$$\wedge\ (\forall i\, (i < b_1) \implies \text{nf}(i,n)) \wedge (\forall i\, (a_2 \le i \wedge i < b_2) \implies \text{nf}(i,n))$$
$$\wedge\ (\forall i\, (a_3 \le i \wedge i < b_3) \implies \text{nf}(i,n)) \wedge (\forall i\, (a_4 \le i \wedge i < b_4) \implies \text{nf}(i,n))$$
$$\wedge\ (\forall i\, (a_5 \le i \wedge i < b_5) \implies \text{nf}(i,n)) \wedge (\forall i\, (i \ge b_1 \wedge i < a_2) \implies \neg\text{nf}(i,n))$$
$$\wedge\ (\forall i\, (i \ge b_2 \wedge i < a_3) \implies \neg\text{nf}(i,n)) \wedge (\forall i\, (i \ge b_3 \wedge i < a_4) \implies \neg\text{nf}(i,n))$$
$$\wedge\ (\forall i\, (i \ge b_4 \wedge i < a_5) \implies \neg\text{nf}(i,n)) \wedge (\forall i\, (i \ge b_5) \implies \neg\text{nf}(i,n))$$
$$\wedge\ r = b_1 + (b_2 - a_2) + (b_3 - a_3) + (b_4 - a_4) + (b_5 - a_5).$$

This formula asserts first that all indices inside the intervals correspond to the starting points of novel factors, and second that all indices outside the intervals do not correspond to the starting points of novel factors. When we evaluate this formula in `Walnut` (warning: it needs at least 16 gigs of RAM and runs for 100 seconds on a laptop), we get the automaton in Figure 10.22.

```
def nf "Aj j<i => ~$tmfactoreq(i,j,n)":
def tmsub "E a2,a3,a4,a5,b1,b2,b3,b4,b5 (b1<=a2&a2<=b2&b2<=a3
    &a3<=b3&b3<=a4&a4<=b4&b4<=a5&a5<=b5) &
    (Ai i<b1 => $nf(i,n)) & (Ai (a2<=i&i<b2) => $nf(i,n)) &
```

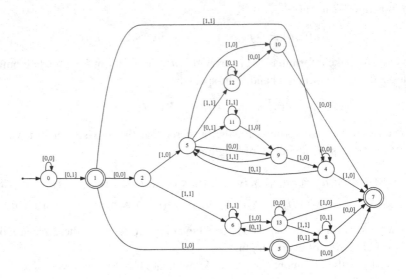

Figure 10.22 Synchronized automaton for Thue-Morse subword complexity.

```
(Ai (a3<=i&i<b3)=>$nf(i,n))&(Ai (a4<=i&i<b4) => $nf(i,n))&
(Ai (a5<=i&i<b5)=>$nf(i,n))&(Ai (i>=b1&i<a2) => ~$nf(i,n))&
(Ai (i>=b2&i<a3)=>~$nf(i,n))&(Ai (i>=b3&i<a4) => ~$nf(i,n))&
(Ai (i>=b4&i<a5)=>~$nf(i,n))&(Ai (i>=b5) => ~$nf(i,n))&
(s = b1+(b2-a2)+(b3-a3)+(b4-a4)+(b5-a5))":
```

Once we have the synchronized automaton, we can prove the formula (9.4) we conjectured for $\rho_t(n)$, as follows:

```
eval tmsubcheck "Ax,i,s,n (((n>=3&$power2(x)&n=x+i&i>=1
  & 2*i<=x&s+4=3*x+4*i)=>$tmsub(n,s)) & ((n>=3 & $power2(x)
  & 2*n=3*x+2*i&i>=1&2*i<=x&s+2=5*x+2*i) => $tmsub(n,s)))":
```

which evaluates to TRUE.

*Exercise* 128   Let **x** be an automatic sequence.

(a) Let $f(n)$ denote the length of the shortest nonempty factor ending at position $n$ of **x** that never occurred previously in **x**. Show that $f$ is synchronized.
(b) Let $g(n)$ denote the length of the longest factor ending at position $n$ that occurred previously in **x**. Show that $g$ is synchronized.

Compute both of these quantities for the Thue-Morse sequence **t**.

*Exercise* 129   One can define an analogue of subword complexity for two-dimensional arrays $\mathbf{X}$ indexed by the natural numbers: $\rho_{\mathbf{X}}(m, n)$ is the number of distinct $m \times n$ rectangular blocks appearing in $\mathbf{X}$.

- Prove an upper bound on the subword complexity of a $k$-automatic two-dimensional array (the number of distinct $m \times n$ blocks).
- Consider the array defined by $\mathbf{X}[i, j] = (t_i + t_j) \bmod 2$, where $(t_i)_{i \geq 0}$ is the Thue-Morse sequence. What is its subword complexity?

### 10.8.20  Critical exponents

A very useful theorem, which we will not prove here, is the following [335]:

**Theorem 10.8.15**   *There is an algorithm that, given a $k$-synchronized sequence $f(n)$, computes $\sup_{n \geq 1} f(n)/n$.*

As a result, we get the following:

**Theorem 10.8.16**   *The following aspects of $k$-regular sequences $\mathbf{x}$ are computable:*

*(a)  ce$(\mathbf{x})$, the critical exponent.*
*(b)  ice$(\mathbf{x})$, the initial critical exponent.*
*(c)  the recurrence constant for a uniformly recurrent $\mathbf{x}$.*

The algorithm for $\sup_{n \geq 1} f(n)/n$ has not yet been implemented in `Walnut`.

*Exercise* 130   Show that the following OEIS sequences are 2-synchronized:

- A006257, the Josephus sequence.
- A006165, the Arkin-Arney-Dewald-Ebel sequence.
- A035327.
- A055562, Bottomley's sequence.
- A079905.
- A080637.

Also show that A006166 is 3-synchronized.

## 10.9  First-order properties of synchronized sequences

Nearly all of the properties discussed in Chapter 8 for automatic sequences are *also* decidable for synchronized sequences. For example, we can decide if a $k$-synchronized sequence is squarefree.

As an illustration, consider the *ruler function* $r(n)$ defined by $r(n) = v_2(n+1)$, where $v_k(n)$ is the exponent of the largest power of $k$ dividing $n$; the first few terms are $01020103010\cdots$. We would like to show that $(r(n))_{n\geq 0}$ is square-free.

Unfortunately $r(n)$ is not synchronized, as it is bounded above by $\log_2 n$ and hence by Theorem 10.6.1 it would have to be $O(1)$, which it is not. Nevertheless, we can look at the image of $(r(n))_{n\geq 0}$ under the coding $i \to 2^i$. This gives us the sequence $121412181214121\cdots$ defined by $r'(n) = V_2(n+1)$, which is synchronized, as we saw in Section 10.2. We can then show that $(r'(n))_{n\geq 0}$ is squarefree, as follows:

```
reg v2 msd_2 msd_2 "([0,0]|[1,0])*[1,1][0,0]*":
def rp "$v2(n+1,s)":
eval rpsquare "Ei,n (n>=1) & At (t<n) => Es $rp(i+t,s) &
   $rp(i+t+n,s)":
```

*Exercise* 131  Is the sequence $(r(n))_{n\geq 0}$ mirror invariant?

*Exercise* 132  Create first-order formulas for the factor $x[i..i + n - 1]$ of a synchronized sequence **x** to be monotonically increasing (resp., strictly monotonically increasing).

## 10.10 Synchronized sequences in two bases

Walnut is able to handle synchronized sequences in two different bases. The restriction is that one can only do arithmetic on variables defined in the same numeration system.

As an example, consider the Hilbert curve HC from Section 2.4.20. This DFAO computes the $n$th move defining the curve, using the correspondence $U \leftrightarrow 0, R \leftrightarrow 1, D \leftrightarrow 2, L \leftrightarrow 3$.

Instead of the moves, we could consider the $x$-$y$ coordinates of the lattice points it traverses. It turns out (see [351]) this defines a $(4, 2, 2)$-synchronized function $(n, x_n, y_n)$ represented by a DFAO with 10 states, stored in the Word Automata directory under the name HS. The trick is that $n$ is represented in base 4, while $x_n$ and $y_n$ are represented in base 2.

We can then verify that HS does indeed trace out the sequence of coordinates as follows:

```
eval fn1 "An Ex,y HS[?msd_4 n][x][y]=@1":
# f(n) takes an ordered pair value for each n

eval fn2 "An Ex,y,xp,yp (HS[?msd_4 n][x][y]=@1 &
   HS[?msd_4 n][xp][yp]=@1) => (x=xp & y=yp)":
# f(n) takes only one value for each n
```

```
eval check_up "An (HC[?msd_4 n]=@0 <=> Ex,xp,y,yp
   HS[?msd_4 n][x][y]=@1 & HS[?msd_4 n+1][xp][yp]=@1 &
   xp=x & yp=y+1)":

eval check_right "An (HC[?msd_4 n]=@1 <=> Ex,xp,y,yp
   HS[?msd_4 n][x][y]=@1 & HS[?msd_4 n+1][xp][yp]=@1 & xp=x+1 & yp=y)":

eval check_down "An (HC[?msd_4 n]=@2 <=> Ex,xp,y,yp
   HS[?msd_4 n][x][y]=@1 & HS[?msd_4 n+1][xp][yp]=@1 & xp=x & yp+1=y)":

eval check_left "An (HC[?msd_4 n]=@3 <=> Ex,xp,y,yp
   HS[?msd_4 n][x][y]=@1 & HS[?msd_4 n+1][xp][yp]=@1 & xp+1=x & yp=y)":
```

and Walnut returns TRUE.

Finally, we can use Walnut to verify that every pair of natural numbers $(x, y)$ is hit, and hit only once, so our curve is indeed space-filling:

```
eval allhit "Ax,y En HS[?msd_4 n][x][y]=@1":
eval hitonce "An,np,x,y (HS[?msd_4 n][x][y]=@1 &
   HS[?msd_4 np][x][y]=@1) => (?msd_4 n=?msd_4 np)":
```

and Walnut returns TRUE once more.

*Exercise* 133 Carry out the same kind of analysis for Peano's spacefilling curve, using base 3.

Here is another example: recall that the Cantor numbers $(c(n))_{n \geq 0}$ are $(2, 3)$-synchronized; see Figure 10.6. We can verify with Walnut that the Cantor numbers have no *double arithmetic progressions* of size three: that is, no three indices $i, j, k$ in arithmetic progression such that the three integers $c(i), c(j), c(k)$ are also in arithmetic progression:

```
reg cs msd_2 msd_3 "([0,0]|[1,2])*":
eval doubleap "Ei,j,p,q,r (j>=1) & $cs(i,?msd_3 p) &
   $cs(i+j,?msd_3 q) & $cs(i+2*j,?msd_3 r) & ?msd_3 r+p=2*q":
```

and this returns FALSE. Notice that here, arithmetic on $i$ and $j$ is done in base 2, while arithmetic on $p, q, r$ is done in base 3.[3]

## 10.11 Fibonacci synchronization

We can talk about Fibonacci synchronization of a sequence $(a(n))_{n \geq 0}$ in analogy with base-$k$ synchronization.[4] Here both $n$ and $a(n)$ are expressed in Fibonacci representation, as discussed in Section 3.2.

---

[3] In fact, as we saw in Section 8.1.5, there are no three distinct elements of the Cantor sequence in arithmetic progression, no matter what the indices are. This example, therefore, is more instructive than consequential.

[4] Some material in this chapter is reprinted from [29] by permission from Springer Nature.

**Theorem 10.11.1** *Let* $\varphi = (1 + \sqrt{5})/2$, *the golden ratio, and let* **f** *be the Fibonacci word. The following functions are Fibonacci-synchronized:*

(a) $n \to \lfloor \varphi n \rfloor$.
(b) $n \to \lfloor \varphi^2 n \rfloor$.
(c) $n \to \lfloor n/\varphi \rfloor$.
(d) $n \to |\mathbf{f}[0..n-1]|_0$.
(e) $n \to |\mathbf{f}[0..n-1]|_1$.

*Proof* We start from the identities

$$[(n)_F 0]_F = \lfloor (n+1)\varphi \rfloor - 1$$
$$[(n)_F 00]_F = \lfloor (n+1)\varphi^2 \rfloor - 2$$

for $n \geq 0$, whose proof can be found, for example, in [314]. First we define a DFA shift that accepts two inputs in parallel if the second is the left shift of the first, with a 0 in the last position. Then we can construct synchronized DFAs for $\lfloor \varphi n \rfloor$ and $\lfloor \varphi^2 n \rfloor$ as follows:

```
reg shift {0,1} {0,1} "([0,0]|[0,1][1,1]*[1,0])*":
def phin "?msd_fib (s=0 & n=0) | Ex $shift(n-1,x) & s=x+1":
def phi2n "?msd_fib (s=0 & n=0) | Ex,y $shift(n-1,x) &
    $shift(x,y) & s=y+2":
```

with the automata depicted in Figure 10.23. Next, using the fact that $n/\varphi =$

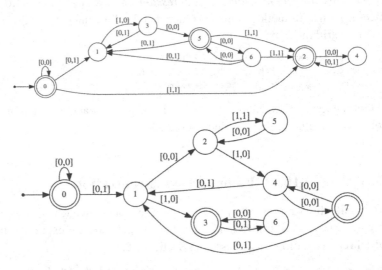

Figure 10.23 Synchronized Fibonacci automata for $\lfloor \varphi n \rfloor$ (top) and $\lfloor \varphi^2 n \rfloor$ (bottom).

$n\varphi - n$, we get a synchronized automaton for (c) as follows:

```
def noverphi "?msd_fib Et $phin(n,t) & s+n=t":
```

giving us the automaton in Figure 10.24.

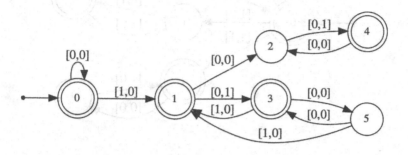

Figure 10.24 Synchronized Fibonacci automaton for $\lfloor n/\varphi \rfloor$.

Finally we have

$$\mathbf{f}[0..n-1]_0 = \sum_{0 \le i < n} \overline{\mathbf{f}[n]}$$

$$= \sum_{0 \le i < n} (\lfloor (i+2)/\varphi \rfloor - \lfloor (i+1)/\varphi \rfloor)$$

$$= \lfloor (n+1)/\varphi \rfloor,$$

which can be implemented as follows:

```
def fibpref0 "?msd_fib $noverphi(n+1,s)":
def fibpref1 "?msd_fib Eu $fibpref0(n,u) & n=s+u":
```

giving us the automata in Figure 10.25.                          □

The following table gives the first few values of the sequences of Theorem 10.11.1.

| $n$ | 0 | 1 | 2 | 3 | 4 | 5 | 6 | 7 | 8 | 9 | 10 | 11 |
|---|---|---|---|---|---|---|---|---|---|---|---|---|
| $\lfloor \varphi n \rfloor$ | 0 | 1 | 3 | 4 | 6 | 8 | 9 | 11 | 12 | 14 | 16 | 17 |
| $\lfloor \varphi^2 n \rfloor$ | 0 | 2 | 5 | 7 | 10 | 13 | 15 | 18 | 20 | 23 | 26 | 28 |
| $\lfloor n/\varphi \rfloor$ | 0 | 0 | 1 | 1 | 2 | 3 | 3 | 4 | 4 | 5 | 6 | 6 |
| $\lvert \mathbf{f}[0..n-1]\rvert_0$ | 0 | 1 | 1 | 2 | 3 | 3 | 4 | 4 | 5 | 6 | 6 | 7 |
| $\lvert \mathbf{f}[0..n-1]\rvert_1$ | 0 | 0 | 1 | 1 | 1 | 2 | 2 | 3 | 3 | 3 | 4 | 4 |

*Remark* 10.11.2   Sequences of the form $(\lfloor \alpha n \rfloor)_{n \ge 1}$ for irrational $\alpha$ are sometimes called Beatty sequences [32]. If $\alpha = \varphi$, we get the "lower Wythoff sequence", and if $\alpha = \varphi^2$, we get the "upper Wythoff sequence" [382].

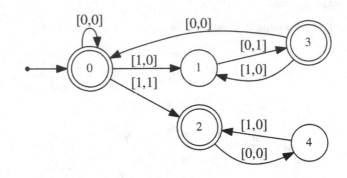

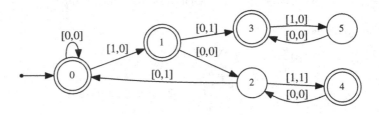

Figure 10.25 Synchronized automata for $|\mathbf{f}[0..n-1]|_0$ (top) and $|\mathbf{f}[0..n-1]|_1$ (bottom).

*Exercise* 134   Show that every $n \geq 1$ can be represented as one of $\lfloor \varphi r \rfloor$ or $\lfloor \varphi^2 s \rfloor$ for some $r, s$, but not both.

**Corollary 10.11.3**   *Let $\gamma \in \mathbb{Q}(\sqrt{5}) = \mathbb{Q}(\varphi)$ be positive. Then the sequence $(\lfloor \gamma n \rfloor)_{n \geq 0}$ is Fibonacci-synchronized.*

*Proof*   Write $\gamma = (a + b\varphi)/c$ for integers $a, b, c$ with $c$ positive.

First, note that for all real $x$ and integers $c \geq 1$ we have $\lfloor x/c \rfloor = \lfloor \frac{\lfloor x \rfloor}{c} \rfloor$. Let

$a, c$ be integers with $a, c$ positive. Then, writing $f(n) = \lfloor \varphi n \rfloor$, we have

$$\lfloor \gamma n \rfloor = \left\lfloor \left( \frac{a + b\varphi}{c} \right) n \right\rfloor = \left\lfloor \frac{an + \varphi bn}{c} \right\rfloor = \left\lfloor \frac{\lfloor an + \varphi bn \rfloor}{c} \right\rfloor$$
$$= \left\lfloor \frac{an + \lfloor \varphi bn \rfloor}{c} \right\rfloor = \left\lfloor \frac{an + f(bn)}{c} \right\rfloor.$$

Since $f(n)$ is synchronized, so is $f(bn)$. And hence so is $an + f(bn)$. And hence so is $\lfloor (an + f(bn))/c \rfloor$.

If $b$ is negative then we use the fact that $\lfloor -x \rfloor = -1 - \lfloor x \rfloor$ if $x \notin \mathbb{Z}$. □

Now we can use this material to prove a famous characterization of the sequences $A_n = \lfloor \varphi n \rfloor$ and $B_n = \lfloor \varphi^2 n \rfloor$ in terms of the so-called "mex" or minimal excludant function, due to [382]. Given a set $S \subsetneq \mathbb{N}$, we define $\text{mex}(S) = \min\{i \geq 0 : i \notin S\}$, the least natural number not in $S$, namely, that

$$A_n = \text{mex}\{A_i, B_i : 0 \leq i < n\}$$
$$B_n = A_n + n.$$

We can check this as follows:

```
def include "?msd_fib Ei i<n & ($phin(i,s) | $phi2n(i,s))":
# s appears in {A_i, B_i : 0 <= i < n }
def mex "?msd_fib (~$include(n,s)) & At t<s => $include(n,t)":
# s equals mex {A_i, B_i : 0 <= i < n }
eval fibmexcheck1 "?msd_fib An,s $mex(n,s) <=> $phin(n,s)":
eval fibmexcheck2 "?msd_fib An,s $phi2n(n,s) <=>
    (Et $phin(n,t) & s=t+n)":
```

Next, let us prove some recent conjectures of Don Reble about letters in 3-term arithmetic progressions in the infinite Fibonacci word $\mathbf{f} = (f_n)_{n \geq 0} = 01001001 \cdots$, which is sequence A003849 in the OEIS. Letting

$$\text{AP}_0 := \{n : \exists i \ \mathbf{f}[i] = \mathbf{f}[i + n] = \mathbf{f}[i + 2n] = 0\} = \{0, 2, 3, 4, 5, 6, 8, 9, 10, \ldots\}$$
$$\text{AP}_1 := \{n : \exists i \ \mathbf{f}[i] = \mathbf{f}[i + n] = \mathbf{f}[i + 2n] = 1\} = \{0, 3, 5, 8, 10, 13, 16, 18, \ldots\},$$

we can define the sets

$$R_1 := \text{AP}_0 \setminus \text{AP}_1 = \{2, 4, 6, 9, 11, 12, 15, 17, 19, 22, 23, 25, \ldots\}$$
$$R_2 := \mathbb{N} \setminus (\text{AP}_0 \cup \text{AP}_1) = \{1, 7, 14, 20, 27, 35, 41, 48, 54, \ldots\}$$
$$R_3 := \text{AP}_0 \cap \text{AP}_1 = \{0, 3, 5, 8, 10, 13, 16, 18, 21, 24, 26, \ldots\}.$$

Defining $r = 2$, $s = (\sqrt{5} - 1)/2$, $t = (1 + \sqrt{5})/2$, Reble conjectured that for

$x \geq 1$ we have

$$x + 1 \in R_1 \iff x \in A189377 = \{n + \lfloor sn/r \rfloor + \lfloor tn/r \rfloor : n \geq 1\}$$
$$x + 1 \in R_2 \iff x \in A189378 = \{n + \lfloor rn/s \rfloor + \lfloor tn/s \rfloor : n \geq 1\}$$
$$x + 1 \in R_3 \iff x \in A189379 = \{n + \lfloor rn/t \rfloor + \lfloor sn/t \rfloor : n \geq 1\}.$$

So we can prove all the Reble conjectures as follows. Here F is Walnut's way of representing the Fibonacci word **f**.

```
def ap0 "?msd_fib Ei F[i]=@0 & F[i]=F[i+n] & F[i]=F[i+2*n]":
def ap1 "?msd_fib Ei F[i]=@1 & F[i]=F[i+n] & F[i]=F[i+2*n]":

def r1 "?msd_fib $ap0(n) & ~$ap1(n)":
def r2 "?msd_fib ~$ap0(n) & ~$ap1(n)":
def r3 "?msd_fib $ap0(n) & $ap1(n)":

def fibsr "?msd_fib Er $phin(n,r) & s=(r-n)/2":
def fibtr "?msd_fib Er $phin(n,r) & s=r/2":
def fibrs "?msd_fib $phin(2*n,s)":
def fibts "?msd_fib Er $phin(n,r) & s=r+n":
def fibrt "?msd_fib Er $phin(2*n,r) & s=r-2*n":
def fibst "?msd_fib Er $phin(n,r) & s=2*n-(r+1)":

def a189377 "?msd_fib En,x,y $fibsr(n,x)&$fibtr(n,y)&z=n+x+y":
def a189378 "?msd_fib En,x,y $fibrs(n,x)&$fibts(n,y)&z=n+x+y":
def a189379 "?msd_fib En,x,y $fibrt(n,x)&$fibst(n,y)&z=n+x+y":

eval reble1 "?msd_fib Ax (x>=1) => ($r1(x+1)<=>$a189377(x))":
eval reble2 "?msd_fib Ax (x>=1) => ($r2(x+1)<=>$a189378(x))":
eval reble3 "?msd_fib Ax (x>=1) => ($r3(x+1)<=>$a189379(x))":
```

and Walnut returns TRUE for the last three.

The positions of the 1s in A003849 form sequence A003622, namely (as is well known) $\lfloor n\varphi^2 \rfloor - 1$, where $\varphi = (1 + \sqrt{5})/2$. We can easily prove this with Walnut, as follows.

```
eval pos1 "?msd_fib An (F[n]=@1) <=> (Er $phi2n(r,n+1))":
```

Now let's look at the possible distances between all occurrences of the 1s. This is the set

$$D_1 = \{n : \exists i \ \mathbf{f}[i] = \mathbf{f}[i + n] = 1\} = \{0, 2, 3, 5, 6, 7, 8, 10, 11, 13, 14, 15, 16, \ldots\},$$

which we can define in Walnut as follows:

```
def dist1 "?msd_fib Ei (F[i]=@1 & F[i+n]=@1)":
```

Notice that $D_1$ is not cofinite, which we can check as follows:

```
eval d1notcofinite "?msd_fib Am En (n>m & ~$dist1(n))":
```

The set $D_1$ is (up to the inclusion of 0) sequence A307295 in the OEIS. This latter sequence is defined in the OEIS to be A001950$(n/2 + 1)$ if $n$ is even, and A001950$((n + 1)/2) + 1$ if $n$ is odd, where A001950 is the sequence $\lfloor \varphi^2 n \rfloor$. We can prove the equality of these two sequences as follows:

```
def even "?msd_fib Em n=2*m":
def odd "?msd_fib Em n=2*m+1":
def a307295 "?msd_fib (Em $even(m) & $phi2n(m/2+1,n)) |
   (Em,r $odd(m) & $phi2n((m+1)/2,r) & n=r+1)":
eval chkdist1 "?msd_fib An (n>=1)=>($dist1(n) <=> $a307295(n))":
```

The complementary sequence of $D_1$ (that is, $\mathbb{N} \setminus D_1$) is

$$\overline{D_1} = \{1, 4, 9, 12, 17, 22, 25, \ldots\},$$

which is sequence A276885. There the formula $2\lfloor (n - 1)\varphi \rfloor + n$ is given for A276885, which we can prove as follows:

```
def altc "?msd_fib Em,r $phin(m-1,r) & n=2*r+m":
eval test276885 "?msd_fib An $dist1(n) <=> ~$altc(n)":
```

See, for example, [118].

R. J. Mathar conjectured (see A276885) that

$$\overline{D_1} = \{1\} \cup \text{A089910},$$

where A089910 $= \{n : \mathbf{f}[n - 1] = \mathbf{f}[n - 2]\}$. We can prove this as follows:

```
eval mathar "?msd_fib An (n>=2) => ($altc(n)<=>F[n-1]=F[n-2])":
```

*Exercise 135* Define $a(n) = \lfloor \varphi n \rfloor$, and $b(n) = \lfloor \varphi^2 n \rfloor$. Use Walnut to prove the following identities about the functions $a$ and $b$ from [67]:

   (a) $b(n) = a(a(n)) + 1$
   (b) $a(n) + b(n) = b(a(n)) + 1$
   (c) $a(b(n)) = b(a(n)) + 1$
   (d) $a(n) + b(n) = a(b(n))$
   (e) $b(b(n)) = a(b(a(n))) + 2$
   (f) $a(b(b(n))) = b(b(a(n))) + 3$

*Exercise 136* Suppose the Fibonacci representation of $n$ is $e_1 e_2 \cdots e_i$. Show that $|\mathbf{f}[0..n - 1]|_0 = [e_1 e_2 \cdots e_{i-1}]_F + e_i$.

*Exercise 137* Prove the following result. Hint: use Exercise 136. Let $h : \Sigma_2^* \to \Delta^*$ be an arbitrary morphism such that $h(01) \neq \epsilon$. Then $h(\mathbf{f})$ is an infinite Fibonacci-automatic word.

Theorem 10.6.1 also holds for Fibonacci-synchronized sequences. However, so far no analogue of Theorem 10.8.16 is known for these sequences. In practice, however, one can usually determine the critical exponent by determining the orders of rational powers slightly below the critical exponent; often they will be simple to describe.

*Open Question* 10.11.4　Prove the analogue of Theorem 10.8.16 for Fibonacci- and Tribonacci-synchronized sequences.

Similarly, we can look at the positions of the 0s in **f**. This forms sequence A022342, which, as is well known, is $(\lfloor n\varphi \rfloor - 1)_{n \geq 0}$. We can check this as follows:

```
def pos0 "?msd_fib F[n]=@0":
def check0 "?msd_fib An $pos0(n) <=> (Em,r n+1=m & $phin(r,m))":
```

Let us now examine the separator functions $S_1, S_2, S_3, S_4$ for the Fibonacci word **f**. Here are the first few values:

| $n$ | 1 | 2 | 3 | 4 | 5 | 6 | 7 | 8 | 9 | 10 | 11 | 12 | 13 |
|---|---|---|---|---|---|---|---|---|---|---|---|---|---|
| $S_1(n)$ | 1 | 2 | 2 | 3 | 3 | 3 | 5 | 5 | 5 | 5 | 5 | 8 | 8 |
| $S_2(n)$ | 2 | 3 | 3 | 5 | 5 | 5 | 8 | 8 | 8 | 8 | 8 | 13 | 13 |
| $S_3(n)$ | 2 | 3 | 5 | 5 | 8 | 8 | 8 | 13 | 13 | 13 | 13 | 13 | 21 |
| $S_4(n)$ | 3 | 5 | 8 | 8 | 13 | 13 | 13 | 21 | 21 | 21 | 21 | 21 | 34 |

These are all Fibonacci-synchronized functions. The Walnut code is given as follows:

```
def occursf "?msd_fib At t<n => F[i+t]=F[j+t]":
def consecf "?msd_fib k>j & $occursf(i,j,n) & $occursf(i,k,n) &
   Al (j<l & l<k) => ~$occursf(i,l,n)":
def mindistf "?msd_fib (Aj,k $consecf(i,j,k,n) => s+j <= k) &
   (Ej,k $consecf(i,j,k,n) & s+j = k)":
def maxdistf "?msd_fib (Aj,k $consecf(i,j,k,n) => s+j >= k) &
   (Ej,k $consecf(i,j,k,n) & s+j=k)":
def s1f "?msd_fib (Ei $mindistf(i,n,t))&(Ai,s $mindistf(i,n,s) => s>=t)":
def s2f "?msd_fib (Ei $maxdistf(i,n,t))&(Ai,s $maxdistf(i,n,s) => s>=t)":
def s3f "?msd_fib (Ei $mindistf(i,n,t))&(Ai,s $mindistf(i,n,s) => s<=t)":
def s4f "?msd_fib (Ei $maxdistf(i,n,t))&(Ai,s $maxdistf(i,n,s) => s<=t)":
```

*Exercise* 138　Find and prove explicit formulas for the functions $S_1, S_2, S_3, S_4$ for the Fibonacci word.

*Remark* 10.11.5　Corollary 10.11.3 can be generalized to all quadratic irrationals. See [195, 194] paper.

Finally, we obtain a result of Rampersad et al. [312] on balanced words:

**Theorem 10.11.6**　*Let* $\mathbf{x}_4 = 0210312013012031021301201302103\cdots$ *be the infinite word obtained from the Fibonacci word* **f** *by replacing all the* 0s with $(01)^\omega$, and all the 1s with $(23)^\omega$. Then $\mathbf{x}_4$ is a balanced word with critical exponent $1 + \varphi/2$, where $\varphi = (1 + \sqrt{5})/2$.

*Proof* There are a number of ways to do this. Perhaps the easiest is to use the "guessing" procedure outlined in Section 5.6 to obtain a candidate Fibonacci DFAO generating $\mathbf{x}_4$ and then verify it is correct. This 8-state DFAO X4.txt, in the Word Automata Library of Walnut, is provided in the default distribution of Walnut.

We can now make Fibonacci-synchronized DFAs for the positions of the $n$th 0 and $n$th 1 in $\mathbf{f}$, using the ideas presented earlier and check that X4 is defined as stated above.

```
def even "?msd_fib Em n=2*m":
def odd "?msd_fib Em n=2*m+1":
def pos0synch "?msd_fib Em $phin(n+1,m) & m=s+1":
def pos1synch "?msd_fib Em $phi2n(n+1,m) & m=s+1":
def checkx4 "?msd_fib As
    (X4[s]=@0 => En $pos0synch(n,s) & $even(n)) &
    (X4[s]=@1 => En $pos0synch(n,s) & $odd(n)) &
    (X4[s]=@2 => En $pos1synch(n,s) & $even(n)) &
    (X4[s]=@3 => En $pos1synch(n,s) & $odd(n))":
```

The fact that $\mathbf{x}_4$ so defined is balanced follows from a theorem of Hubert [205] (and, in another formulation, [179]). It remains to compute the critical exponent of $\mathbf{x}_4$.

First, we compute the periods $p$ such that a repetition with exponent $\geq 5/3$ and period $p$ occurs in $\mathbf{x}_4$:

```
eval periods_of_high_powers "?msd_fib Ei (p>=1) &
    (Aj (3*j<=2*p) => X4[i+j]=X4[i+j+p])";
```

The language recognized by the resulting automaton is $0^*1001000^*$; i.e., representations of numbers of the form $F_n + F_{n-3} = 2F_{n-1}$.

```
reg pows msd_fib "0*1001000*";
```

Next we compute pairs $(n, p)$ such that $\mathbf{x}_4$ has a factor of length $n + p$ with period $p$, and furthermore that factor cannot be extended to a longer factor of length $n + p + 1$ with the same period.

```
def maximal_reps "?msd_fib Ei (Aj (j<n) =>
    X4[i+j]=X4[i+j+p]) & (X4[i+n]!=X4[i+n+p])";
```

We now compute pairs $(n, p)$ where $p$ has to be of the form $0^*1001000^*$ and $n + p$ is the longest length of any factor having that period.

```
eval highest_powers "?msd_fib (p>=1) & $pows(p) &
    $maximal_reps(n,p) & (Am $maximal_reps(m,p) => m<=n)";
```

The output of this last command is an automaton accepting pairs $(n, p)$ having the form

$$[0,0]^*[0,1][1,0][0,0][1,1][0,0]([1,0][0,0])^*[0,0](\epsilon, [1,0]).$$

So when $p = 2F_{i-1}$ we see that $n = F_i - 2$. Thus, the maximal repetitions of "large exponent" in $\mathbf{x}_4$ have exponent of the form $1 + (F_i - 2)/(2F_{i-1})$, and this converges to $1 + \varphi/2$ from below. We conclude that $\mathbf{x}_4$ has critical exponent $1 + \varphi/2$.                                                                    □

For more work along these lines, see [29, 28].

## 10.12  Tribonacci-synchronized sequences

In this section we consider some Tribonacci-synchronized sequences. Recall that the Tribonacci word $\mathbf{tr} = \mathbf{tr}[0..\infty]$ is defined as the fixed point of the morphism $0 \to 01$, $1 \to 02$, and $2 \to 0$.

For $n \geq 1$, the sequence $A_n$ (resp., $B_n$, $C_n$) is defined to be one more than the position of the $n$th 0 (resp., 1, 2) in $\mathbf{tr}$. For $n \geq 0$, the sequence $D_n$ (resp., $E_n$, $F_n$) is defined to be $|\mathbf{tr}[0..n-1]|_0$ (resp., $|\mathbf{tr}[0..n-1]|_1$, $|\mathbf{tr}[0..n-1]|_2$). Here are the first few values of these sequences:

| OEIS | $n$ | 0 | 1 | 2 | 3 | 4 | 5 | 6 | 7 | 8 | 9 | 10 | 11 |
|------|-----|---|---|---|---|---|---|---|---|---|---|----|----|
| A003144 | $A_n$ | 0 | 1 | 3 | 5 | 7 | 8 | 10 | 12 | 14 | 16 | 18 | 20 |
| A003145 | $B_n$ | 0 | 2 | 6 | 9 | 13 | 15 | 19 | 22 | 26 | 30 | 33 | 37 |
| A003146 | $C_n$ | 0 | 4 | 11 | 17 | 24 | 28 | 35 | 41 | 48 | 55 | 61 | 68 |
| A276796 | $D_n$ | 0 | 1 | 1 | 2 | 2 | 3 | 3 | 4 | 5 | 5 | 6 | 6 |
| A276797 | $E_n$ | 0 | 0 | 1 | 1 | 1 | 1 | 2 | 2 | 2 | 3 | 3 | 3 |
| A276798 | $F_n$ | 0 | 0 | 0 | 0 | 1 | 1 | 1 | 1 | 1 | 1 | 1 | 2 |

To show that these sequences are synchronized, we use the fact that

$$A_n = [(n - 1)_T 0]_T + 1$$
$$B_n = [(n - 1)_T 00]_T + 2$$
$$C_n = [(n - 1)_T 000]_T + 4$$

whose proof can be found, for example, in [120, Theorem 13]. Based on this, we can create Walnut Tribonacci-synchronized formulas for each sequence, as follows:

```
def triba "?msd_trib (s=0&n=0) | Ex $shift(n-1,x) & s=x+1":
def tribb "?msd_trib (s=0&n=0) | Ex,y $shift(n-1,x) &
    $shift(x,y) & s=y+2":
```

```
def tribc "?msd_trib (s=0&n=0) | Ex,y,z $shift(n-1,x) &
   $shift(x,y) & $shift(y,z) & s=z+4":
def tribd "?msd_trib Et,u $triba(s,t)&$triba(s+1,u)&t<=n&n<u":
def tribe "?msd_trib Et,u $tribb(s,t)&$tribb(s+1,u)&t<=n&n<u":
def tribf "?msd_trib Et,u $tribc(s,t)&$tribc(s+1,u)&t<=n&n<u":
```

From this we can verify the following result of Duchêne and Rigo [125]:

$$A_n = \text{mex}\{A_i, B_i, C_i : 0 \le i < n\}$$

$$B_n = A_n + \text{mex}(B_i - A_i, C_i - B_i : 0 \le i < n)$$

$$C_n = A_n + B_n + n.$$

```
def tinclude1 "?msd_trib Ei i<n & ($triba(i,s) | $tribb(i,s)
   | $tribc(i,s))":
# s appears in {A_i, B_i, C_i : 0 <= i < n }
def tinclude2 "?msd_trib Ei i<n & ((Et,u $triba(i,t) &
   $tribb(i,u)&s+t=u) | (Et,u $tribb(i,t)&$tribc(i,u)&s+t=u))":
# s appears in {B_i-A_i, C_i-B_i : 0 <= i < n }
def tmex1 "?msd_trib (~$tinclude1(n,s)) & At t<s =>
   $tinclude1(n,t)":
# s = mex {A_i, B_i, C_i : 0 <= i < n }
def tmex2 "?msd_trib (~$tinclude2(n,s)) & At t<s =>
   $tinclude2(n,t)":
# s = mex{B_i - A_i, C_i - B_i : 0 <= i < n }
eval tribmexcheck1 "?msd_trib An,s $tmex1(n,s) <=>
   $triba(n,s)":
eval tribmexcheck2 "?msd_trib An,s,t,u ($tmex2(n,t) &
   $triba(n,s) & $tribb(n,u)) => u=s+t":
eval tribmexcheck3 "?msd_trib An,s,t,u ($triba(n,s) &
   $tribb(n,t) & $tribc(n,u)) => u=s+t+n":
```

## 10.13 Abelian properties

Some aspects of automatic sequences have abelian analogues. By "abelian" we mean that two words that are permutations of each other are considered equivalent. In other words, $x$ is equivalent to $w$ if $\psi(x) = \psi(w)$, where $\psi$ is the Parikh map of Section 2.1 that counts the number of occurrences of each symbol.

In general, we cannot handle abelian properties of factors using our methods based on first-order logic, because there is no general way to express a statement like

$$\psi(\mathbf{x}[i..i + n - 1]) = \psi(\mathbf{x}[j..j + n - 1])$$

in $FO(\mathbb{N}, +, V_k)$. In fact, there is no general way to count unbounded occurrences of symbols in $FO(\mathbb{N}, +, V_k)$ or its analogues. In the 2-automatic case, it is provable that the locations of abelian squares are, in general, first-order inexpressible [334, §5.2].

For some automatic sequences, however, as we have seen, the number of occurrences of any given letter in a length-$n$ prefix is synchronized. For these particular kinds of simple sequences, we can test and enumerate abelian properties of factors.

Here are the kinds of properties that interest us:

- orders and positions of abelian squares and cubes. Recall from Section 2.1 that an *abelian square* is a word of the form $xx'$ with $\psi(x) = \psi(x')$, and an *abelian cube* is a word of the form $xx'x''$ with $\psi(x) = \psi(x') = \psi(x'')$;
- number of distinct abelian squares and cubes occurring in an infinite word, or in its prefixes of length $n$;
- total number of occurrences of abelian squares and cubes occurring in an infinite word, or in its prefixes of length $n$;
- abelian complexity: the number of distinct length-$n$, where two factors that are permutations of each other are considered to be the same;
- the abelian analogue of being bordered;
- the abelian analogue of return words.

In this section, we show how to handle these abelian aspects for automatic sequences where the number of occurrences of each symbol is synchronized.

The material in this section is based on the papers [172, 127, 353]. For an overview of abelian properties, see [86, 305].

### 10.13.1 Synchronization of $\psi$ for Thue-Morse

As an example, consider the Thue-Morse sequence **t**. We start by showing that the function $n \to |\mathbf{t}[0..n-1]|_0$ counting the number of 0s in a length-$n$ prefix of **t** is synchronized.

To see this, observe that if $n$ is even, then the length-$n$ prefix of **t** has exactly $\frac{n}{2}$ 0s. If $n$ is odd, then this prefix has $\frac{n-1}{2}$ 0s, plus one more if $t_{n-1} = 0$. So we can define this synchronized function in Walnut as follows:

```
def tmpref0 "Er,t n=2*t+r & r<2 & (r=0 => s=t) & ((r=1 &
    T[n-1]=@1) => s=t) & ((r=1 & T[n-1]=@0) => s=t+1)":
```

This gives the 6-state automaton depicted in Figure 10.26.

Next, from this synchronized function we get a similar one for arbitrary factors: $(i, n) \to |\mathbf{t}[i..i+n-1]|_0$, and also one that counts 1s: $(i, n) \to |\mathbf{t}[i..i+n-1]|_1$.

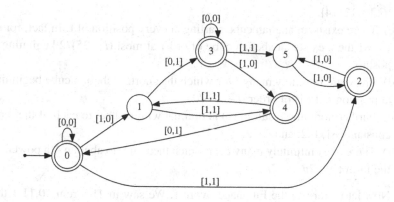

Figure 10.26 Synchronized DFA for Thue-Morse.

```
def tmfac0 "Et,u $tmpref0(i+n,t) & $tmpref0(i,u) & s+u=t":
def tmfac1 "Er $tmfac0(i,n,r) & n=r+s":
```

These automata have 34 states.

Next, from the DFA tmfac0 we can construct a DFA that on input $i, j, n$ tests whether $\psi(\mathbf{t}[i..i+n-1]) = \psi(\mathbf{t}[j..j+n-1])$. Of course, since $\mathbf{t}$ is a binary word, it suffices to check that $|\mathbf{t}[i..i+n-1]|_0 = |\mathbf{t}[j..j+n-1]|_0$.

```
def tmabelfaceq "Es $tmfac0(i,n,s) & $tmfac0(j,n,s)":
```

This automaton has 57 states.

### 10.13.2 Abelian squares and cubes

Now we can determine the orders of abelian squares and cubes in $\mathbf{t}$:

```
def tmabsquare "Ei $tmabelfaceq(i,i+n,n)":
def tmabcube "Ei $tmabelfaceq(i,i+n,n)&$tmabelfaceq(i,i+2*n,n)":
```

By examination of the resulting automaton, we see that there are abelian squares of all orders, and abelian cubes of even orders only.

*Exercise* 139 Prove the following more explicit versions of results of Avgustinovich et al. [23]:

(a) For all $i \geq 0$ there is an abelian square $\mathbf{t}[i..i+2n-1]$ with $n \in \{1, 2, 3, 5\}$.

(b) For all $i \geq 6$ there is an abelian square $\mathbf{t}[i - n..i + n - 1]$ with $n \in \{6, 10, 12, 14\}$.

(c) There exists an abelian cube starting at every position of $\mathbf{t}$. In fact, for all $i > 81$ there exists an abelian cube of order at most $(i + 25)/2$ beginning at position $i$.

(d) There are infinitely many $i$ for which the shortest abelian cube beginning at position $i$ of $\mathbf{t}$ is of order $(i + 25)/2$.

(e) Furthermore, the result in (c) is optimal with respect to each of the three constants $81, 1/2$, and $25/2$.

(f) There exist infinitely many $i$ for which there are no abelian 4th powers of the form $\mathbf{t}[i - 2n..i + 2n - 1]$.

Now let us turn to the Fibonacci word $\mathbf{f}$. We saw in Theorem 10.11.1 that the function $n \to |\mathbf{f}[0..n - 1]|_0$ is Fibonacci-synchronized. Hence the function $(i, n) \to |\mathbf{f}[i..i + n - 1]|_0$ is also synchronized:

```
def fibfac0 "?msd_fib Ex,y $fibpref0(i+n,x) & $fibpref0(i,y)
    & x=s+y":
```

This automaton has 22 states.

Next, from this DFAO we can construct a DFA that on input $i, j, n$ tests whether $\psi(\mathbf{f}[i..i + n - 1]) = \psi(\mathbf{f}[j..j + n - 1])$. Again, it suffices to check that $|\mathbf{f}[i..i + n - 1]|_0 = |\mathbf{f}[j..j + n - 1]|_0$.

```
def fibabelfaceq "?msd_fib Es $fibfac0(i,n,s)&$fibfac0(j,n,s)":
```

This automaton has 35 states.

Now we can show that $\mathbf{f}$ has abelian squares of all orders:

```
eval fibabelsq "?msd_fib An Ei $fibabelfaceq(i,i+n,n)":
```

Let us examine for which orders $\mathbf{f}$ has abelian cubes:

```
def fibabelcube "?msd_fib Ei $fibabelfaceq(i,i+n,n) &
    $fibabelfaceq(i,i+2*n,n)":
```

We get the automaton in Figure 10.27.

We can now prove the following special case of a theorem of Fici et al. [145].

**Theorem 10.13.1** *For $n \geq 1$, the Fibonacci word $\mathbf{f}$ has an abelian cube of order $n$ if and only if $\lfloor 3\varphi n \rfloor \neq 3\lfloor \varphi n \rfloor + 1$.*

*Proof* We use Walnut:

```
eval testcube "?msd_fib An (n>=1) => ($fibabelcube(n)
    <=> Es,t $phin(n,s) & $phin(3*n,t) & t!=3*s+1)":
```

and it returns TRUE.                                    □

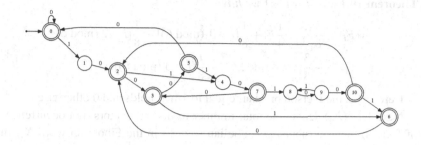

Figure 10.27 Orders of abelian cubes in **f**.

*Exercise* 140   What are the orders of the abelian 4th powers in **f**?

Cummings and Smyth [99] gave a closed form for $w(F_i)$, the total number of all occurrences of (nonempty) abelian squares in the Fibonacci words $X_i$. We can achieve this more generally for *any length-n prefix* of the infinite Fibonacci word **f** using the logical formula

$$(k > 0) \wedge (i + 2k \leq n) \wedge \text{ABELFACEQ}(i, i + k, k),$$

and the techniques of Section 9.8. Then we specialize to $n = F_i$ to get their result.

```
eval cummings n "?msd_fib k>0&i+2*k<=n&$fibabelfaceq(i,i+k,k)":
```

When we do, we get a linear representation of rank 127 that counts the total number $w(n)$ of occurrences of abelian squares in the prefix of length $n$ of the Fibonacci word. This can be minimized to a linear representation $(v, \gamma, w)$ of rank 34 that solves the more general problem.

To recover the Cummings-Smyth result, we compute the minimal polynomial of the matrix $\gamma(0)$ corresponding to the formula above. It is

$$X(X^6 - 1)(X^2 - X - 1)(X^2 - 3X - 1).$$

Let $\varphi = (1 + \sqrt{5})/2$ and $-1/\varphi$ be the zeros of $X^2 - X - 1$; then the zeros of $X^2 - 3X - 1$ are easily seen to be $\varphi^2$ and $1/\varphi^2$. This means that we can write $w(F_i)$ as a linear combination of $F_i$, $F_{i+1}$, $F_i^2$, $F_{i+1}^2$ and a periodic function of period 6. Solving from the data gives

**Theorem 10.13.2** *For $i \geq 1$ we have*

$$w(F_i) = \frac{1}{8}F_i^2 - \frac{1}{4}F_i + \frac{1}{8}[i \equiv 1 \ (\mathrm{mod}\ 6)] + \frac{1}{8}[i \equiv 2 \ (\mathrm{mod}\ 6)]$$
$$- \frac{3}{8}[i \equiv 4 \ (\mathrm{mod}\ 6)] + \frac{1}{8}[i \equiv 5 \ (\mathrm{mod}\ 6)].$$

Here $[P]$ is the Iverson bracket, equal to 1 if $P$ holds and 0 otherwise.

Next, let $h(F_n)$ denote the total number of distinct factors (not occurrences of factors) that are (nonempty) abelian squares in the Fibonacci word $X_n$. In this case we use the formula

$$(k \geq 1) \wedge (i + 2k \leq n) \wedge \text{ABELFACEQ}(i, i + k, k) \wedge \forall j < i \ \neg\text{FACTOREQ}(i, j, 2k),$$

which specifies that $\mathbf{f}[i..i + 2k - 1]$ is an abelian square that lies in the prefix $\mathbf{f}[0..n - 1]$ and furthermore never appeared earlier in $\mathbf{f}$.

```
eval fibtotabsq n "?msd_fib (k>=1) & (i+2*k<=n) &
    $fibabelfaceq(i,i+k,k) & Aj j<i => ~$ffactoreq(i,j,2*k)":
```

We get the minimal polynomial

$$X^2(X^6 - 1)(X^2 - 3X + 1)(X^2 - X - 1).$$

Using the same technique as above we get

**Theorem 10.13.3** *For $n \geq 2$ we have*

$$h(F_n) = \frac{1}{10}\Big((1 + \varphi^{-2})\varphi^n + (2 + \varphi)(-1/\varphi)^n + (\varphi - \frac{3}{2})\varphi^{2n} - (\varphi + \frac{1}{2})\varphi^{-2n}$$
$$- 3[n \equiv 0 \ (\mathrm{mod}\ 6)] - \frac{19}{2}[n \equiv 1 \ (\mathrm{mod}\ 6)] - \frac{11}{2}[n \equiv 2 \ (\mathrm{mod}\ 6)]$$
$$- 7[n \equiv 3 \ (\mathrm{mod}\ 6)] - \frac{31}{2}[n \equiv 4 \ (\mathrm{mod}\ 6)] - \frac{19}{2}[n \equiv 5 \ (\mathrm{mod}\ 6)]\Big).$$

For another new result, consider counting the total number $a(n)$ of distinct factors of length $2n$ of the infinite word $\mathbf{f}$ that are (nonempty) abelian squares. This function is rather erratic. Table 10.2 gives the first few values. We use the formula

```
eval fibabsqn n "?msd_fib (n>=1) & $fibabelfaceq(i,i+n,n) &
    Aj j<i => ~$ffactoreq(i,j,2*n)":
```

This gives us a linear representation of rank 50, which minimizes to one of rank 16.

**Theorem 10.13.4** $a(n) = 1$ *infinitely often and* $a(n) = 2n - 1$ *infinitely often.*

| $n$ | 1 | 2 | 3 | 4 | 5 | 6 | 7 | 8 | 9 | 10 | 11 | 12 | 13 | 14 | 15 |
|-----|---|---|---|---|---|---|---|---|---|----|----|----|----|----|----|
| $a(n)$ | 1 | 3 | 5 | 1 | 9 | 5 | 5 | 15 | 3 | 13 | 13 | 5 | 25 | 9 | 15 |

Table 10.2 *First few values of $a(n)$.*

*Proof* Let us show that $a(n) = 1$ iff $n = 1$ or $(n)_F = (100)^i 101$ for $i \geq 0$. For the first statement, we create a DFA accepting those $(n)_F$ for which $a(n) = 1$, via the formula

$$\forall i, j \; (\text{ABELFACEQ}(i, i + n, n) \wedge \text{ABELFACEQ}(j, j + n, n)) \implies \text{FACTOREQ}(i, j, 2n).$$

The resulting 6-state automaton accepts the set specified, as we can check here:

```
reg fas msd_fib "0*1|0*(100)*101":
def fibabchk "?msd_fib (n>=1) & Ai,j ($fibabelfaceq(i,i+n,n) &
  $fibabelfaceq(j,j+n,n)) => $ffactoreq(i,j,2*n)":
eval fibabsqtest "An $fibabchk(n) <=> $fas(n)":
```

For the second result, let us show that $a(n) = 2n - 1$ if $(n)_F = 10^i$ for $i \geq 0$. We first compute the minimal polynomial of the matrix $\gamma(0)$ of the linear representation; it is $X^2(X - 1)(X^2 - 3X + 1)$. This means that, for $n \geq 5$, we have $a(F_n) = c_1 + c_2(-1)^n + c_3\alpha^n + c_4\beta^n$ where, as usual, $\alpha = (1 + \sqrt{5})/2$ and $\beta = (1 - \sqrt{5})/2$. Solving for the constants, we determine that $a(F_n) = 2F_n - 1$ for $n \geq 2$, as desired. $\square$

Now let us turn to the Tribonacci word. Since we have already synchronized automata for counting the occurrences of letters in prefixes $|\mathbf{tr}[0..n-1]|_a$, $a \in \{0, 1, 2\}$ above (under the names `tribd`, `tribe`, `tribf`), we can now compute the analogous functions for factors:

```
def tribfac0 "?msd_trib Ex,y $tribd(i+n,x)&$tribd(i,y)&x=s+y":
def tribfac1 "?msd_trib Ex,y $tribe(i+n,x)&$tribe(i,y)&x=s+y":
def tribfac2 "?msd_trib Ex,y $tribf(i+n,x)&$tribf(i,y)&x=s+y":
```

From this we can get a DFA for determining whether the factor $\mathbf{tr}[i..i + n - 1]$ and $\mathbf{tr}[j..j + n - 1]$ are abelian equivalent:

```
def tribabelfaceq "?msd_trib Es,t $tribfac0(i,n,s) &
  $tribfac0(j,n,s) & $tribfac1(i,n,t) & $tribfac1(j,n,t)":
```

This DFA has 2613 states.

**Theorem 10.13.5**

*(a) There are abelian squares of all orders in* **tr**.

*(b) Furthermore, if we consider two abelian squares xx' and yy' to be the same if x is abelian equivalent to y, then every order has either one or two abelian squares. Both possibilities occur infinitely often.*

*Proof*

(a) In Walnut we write

```
def abelsquare "?msd_trib $tribabelfaceq(i,i+n,n)":
eval allorders "?msd_trib An Ei $abelsquare(i,n)":
```

which returns TRUE.

(b) The large number of states needed for the automaton abelsquare (that is, 830 states) forces us to check this in a rather roundabout way.

First, we define minabelsq$(i, n)$ to be true if $\mathbf{tr}[i..i + 2n - 1]$ is the first-occurring abelian square of order $n$, the one that minimizes $i$.

Next, we define abel2sq$(j, n)$ to be true if $\mathbf{tr}[j..j + 2n - 1]$ is an abelian square of order $n$, but one that is not equivalent to the one that occurs first.

Finally, we define abel3sq$(k, n)$ to be true if there exist $i$ and $j$ such that minabelsq$(i, n)$ and abel2sq$(j, n)$ hold, but $\mathbf{tr}[k..k + 2n - 1]$ is an abelian square not equivalent to either $\mathbf{tr}[i..i + 2n - 1]$ or $\mathbf{tr}[j..j + 2n - 1]$. We then show that abel3sq$(k, n)$ is never true.

```
def minabelsq "?msd_trib $abelsquare(i,n) & At t<i =>
   ~$abelsquare(t,n)":
def abel2sq "?msd_trib $abelsquare(j,n) & (Ei
   $minabelsq(i,n) & ~$tribabelfaceq(i,j,n))":
def abel3sq "?msd_trib Ei,j $minabelsq(i,n) & $abel2sq(j,n)
   & $abelsquare(k,n) & (~$tribabelfaceq(i,k,n))
   & (~$tribabelfaceq(j,k,n))":
eval no3square "?msd_trib Ak,n ~$abel3sq(k,n)":
```

Finally, we can determine for which orders there are 2 distinct abelian squares in **tr**, and show that there are infinitely many orders for which this holds, and also for which this does not hold.

```
def twosquares "?msd_trib Ej $abel2sq(j,n)":
eval inftwo "?msd_trib Am En (n>m) & $twosquares(n)":
eval infone "?msd_trib Am En (n>m) & ~$twosquares(n)":
```

The DFA for twosquares has 463 states, which suggests that there is probably no really simple description for the orders having two distinct abelian squares.

□

Let us now consider abelian cubes in **tr**. We write a formula for the existence of an abelian cube of order $n$ in **tr**.

```
def abelcube "?msd_trib Ei $tribabelfaceq(i,i+n,n) &
   $tribabelfaceq(i,i+2*n,n)":
```

The resulting Tribonacci automaton has 1169 states, which suggests that there is probably no simple way to describe these orders. Furthermore, the set of orders is both finite and co-finite: Normally, we would verify this last claim with `Walnut` code like the following:

```
eval abelcubeinf "?msd_trib Am En (n>m) & $abelcube(n)":
eval noabelcubeinf "?msd_trib Am En (n>m) & ~$abelcube(n)":
```

However, it runs out of space, even with 150 Gigs of storage. Instead, use breadth-first search in the automaton `abelcube` to discover that state 867 has a path to itself labeled 0, and is reachable from state 0 via a path labeled $110^{12}$. Furthermore state 867 goes to state 786 on input 1. Hence every $n$ with $(n)_T = 110^n$ for $n \geq 12$ is accepted, while every $n$ with $(n)_T = 110^n 1$ for $n \geq 12$ is rejected.

### 10.13.3 Abelian complexity

Now let us consider the abelian complexity of **t**, the number of distinct subwords, up to abelian equivalence of factors. The abelian complexity of **t** at $n = 2$ is 3, because of the 4 factors $00, 01, 10, 11$ the factors $01$ and $10$ are equivalent. We now show how to calculate it in general using our decision procedure.

We can create a DFA that asserts that $\mathbf{t}[i..i+n-1]$ is a novel occurrence of a length-$n$ factor with that Parikh vector, and obtain the linear representation for the number of such $i$:

```
eval tmabcomp n "Aj j<i => ~$tmabelfaceq(i,j,n)":
```

This gives us a linear representation of rank 16. We can minimize the resulting linear representation $(v, \gamma, w)$, obtaining

$$v = [1\,0\,0]; \qquad \gamma(0) = \begin{bmatrix} 1 & 0 & 0 \\ 0 & 0 & 1 \\ 0 & 0 & 1 \end{bmatrix}; \qquad \gamma(1) = \begin{bmatrix} 0 & 1 & 0 \\ 0 & 1 & 0 \\ 0 & 1 & 0 \end{bmatrix}; \qquad w = \begin{bmatrix} 1 \\ 2 \\ 3 \end{bmatrix}.$$

Now we can either use the "semigroup trick" described in Section 4.11, or we can just observe directly that any product of the form $\gamma(1x0)$ equals

$$\begin{bmatrix} 0 & 0 & 1 \\ 0 & 0 & 1 \\ 0 & 0 & 1 \end{bmatrix}$$

while any product of the form $\gamma(1x1)$ equals

$$\begin{bmatrix} 0 & 1 & 0 \\ 0 & 1 & 0 \\ 0 & 1 & 0 \end{bmatrix}.$$

Hence we have proved a result of [316]:

**Theorem 10.13.6** *The abelian complexity of the Thue-Morse sequence is* 1 *if* $n = 0$, 2 *if* $n \geq 1$ *is odd, and* 3 *if* $n \geq 2$ *is even.*

*Exercise* 141   Determine the abelian complexity of the Fibonacci word.

For the abelian complexity of the Tribonacci word, see [375, 353].

### 10.13.4 Abelian borders

A word $w$ is said to be *abelian bordered* if there are nonempty words $x, y, y', z$ such that $w = xy = y'z$ with $\psi(y) = \psi(y')$. For example, the English word researchers is abelian bordered but not bordered in the ordinary sense.

If the number of occurrences of letters in prefixes is synchronized, then we can determine which factors are abelian bordered. Let's do this for the Thue-Morse sequence:

```
def tmabelbord "j>=1 & j<n & Es $tmfac0(i,j,s) &
   $tmfac0((i+n)-j,j,s)":
   # T[i..i+n-1] has an abelian border of length j
def tmbord "j>=1 & j<n & $tmfactoreq(i,(i+n)-j,j)":
   # T[i..i+n-1] has an ordinary border of length j
def tmhasabelbord "Ej $tmabelbord(i,j,n)":
   # T[i..i+n-1] is abelian bordered
def tmhasbord "Ej $tmbord(i,j,n)":
   # T[i..i+n-1] is bordered in the ordinary sense
def tmabelunbord "Ei ~$tmhasabelbord(i,n)":
   # T has an abelian unbordered factor of length n
def abelbordnotbord "Ei $tmhasabelbord(i,n) & ~$tmhasbord(i,n)":
   # T has a length-n factor that is abelian bordered
   # but not bordered in the usual sense
```

The 12-state automaton tmabelunbord accepts those $n$ for which **t** has an abelian unbordered factor of length $n$. It appeared in [172].

The 23-state automaton abelbordnotbord accepts those $n$ for which there is a length-$n$ factor of **t** that is abelian bordered, but not bordered in the ordinary sense. It has a rather complicated structure!

For more about abelian borders, see [172].

### 10.13.5 Abelian return words

We studied (ordinary) return words in Section 8.8.1. There is an obvious generalization of this concept to the abelian case: $\mathbf{x}[i..i+n-1]$ is called an *abelian return* to $\mathbf{x}[j+m-1]$ if $\mathbf{x}[i..i+m-1]$ and $\mathbf{x}[i+n..i+m+n-1]$ are abelian equivalent to $\mathbf{x}[j..j+m-1]$, while $\mathbf{x}[t..t+m-1]$ is not equivalent to $\mathbf{x}[j..j+m-1]$ for $i < t < i+n$.

The formula asserting that $\mathbf{x}[i..i+n-1]$ is an abelian return to $\mathbf{x}[j..j+m-1]$ is then

$$\text{AbelFacEq}(i, j, m) \wedge \text{AbelFacEq}(i + n, j, m)$$
$$\wedge \; \forall t \, (i < t \wedge t < i + n) \implies \neg \text{AbelFacEq}(t, j, m).$$

Let us compute the abelian return words for the Fibonacci word $\mathbf{f}$:

```
def fibabelfaceq "?msd_fib Es $fibfac0(i,n,s)&$fibfac0(j,n,s)":
def fibabelret "?msd_fib n>=1 & $fibabelfaceq(i,j,m) &
$fibabelfaceq(i+n,j,m)&At (i<t&t<i+n)=>~$fibabelfaceq(t,j,m)":
```

Now let us count the number of abelian return words for each factor $\mathbf{f}[j..j + m - 1]$.

```
def fibnovelabelret j m "?msd_fib $fibabelret(i,j,m,n) &
    At ($fibabelret(t,j,m,n) & $fibabelfaceq(t,i,n)) => t>=i":
```

This gives a linear representation of rank 43 with four matrices corresponding to the bit-pairs $\{(0, 0), (0, 1), (1, 0), (1, 1)\}$. We can now use the "semigroup trick" to prove the following special case of a theorem of Puzynina and Zamboni [306]:

**Theorem 10.13.7**   *Every factor of* $\mathbf{f}$ *has either* 2 *or* 3 *abelian return words to it.*

For more about abelian return words, see [319, 311].

## 10.13.6 Prefix normality

A related property is prefix normality. We say that a finite binary word $x$ is *prefix normal* if, for all $n$, the prefix of length $n$ of $x$ contains at least as many 1s as every factor of length $n$. For example, 11010011001011001 is prefix normal. Let us determine which factors of Thue-Morse are prefix normal.

```
def tmprefixnormal "Aj,m,r,s (i<=j & j+m<=i+n & $tmfac1(i,m,r) &
    $tmfac1(j,m,s)) => r>=s":
def tmprefixnormallen "Ei $tmprefixnormal(i,n)":
```

The lengths of prefix-normal factors in Thue-Morse are therefore as given in Figure 10.28. This DFA accepts a finite set and the largest $n$ it accepts is $n = 17$. For more about prefix normality, see [65, 26, 51, 90].

*Exercise* 142   Recover the result of Kaboré and Kientéga [216] for the abelian complexity of the fixed point of $0 \to 012$, $1 \to 120$, and $2 \to 201$.

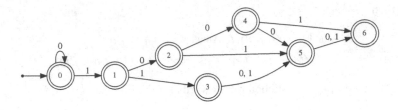

Figure 10.28 Lengths of prefix-normal factors in Thue-Morse.

## 10.14 Unsynchronized sequences

It is easy to construct "natural" examples of $k$-regular sequences that are unsynchronized. For example, define $f(n) = n/2^{v_2(n)}$ for $n \geq 1$, the "odd part" of $n$. It is easy to see that $f(n)$ is 2-regular, since it obeys the relations

$$f(2n) = f(n)$$
$$f(4n + 3) = 4f(2n + 1) - f(4n + 1)$$
$$f(8n + 1) = -2f(2n + 1) + 3f(4n + 1)$$
$$f(8n + 5) = 6f(2n + 1) - f(4n + 1).$$

**Theorem 10.14.1**    *$f(n)$ is not 2-synchronized.*

*Proof*    Suppose it were. Then $\{(n, f(n))_2 \ : \ n \geq 0\}$ would be recognized by some DFA $M$. Suppose $M$ has $t$ states and choose the word $z = [1,0]^t[0,1]^t$. It is easy to see that $z \in L(M)$. Now use the pumping lemma to write $z = uvw$ with $|uv| \leq t$ and $|v| \geq 1$. Pump with $i = 0$ to get $uw = [1,0]^{t-|v|}[0,1]^t$, which is easily seen to not be in $L(M)$, a contradiction.                                   □

Here are some other natural examples of unsynchronized functions associated with automatic sequences.

**Theorem 10.14.2**    *The characteristic sequence* $\mathbf{c} = 0110100010 \cdots$ *of the powers of 2 is 2-automatic, but the function* $U_{\mathbf{c}}(n)$ *counting the number of unbordered factors of* $\mathbf{c}$ *is not 2-synchronized.*

*Proof*    It is not hard to verify that $\mathbf{c}$ is 2-automatic and that $\mathbf{c}$ has exactly $r + 2$ unbordered factors of length $2^r + 1$, for $r \geq 2$—namely, the factors beginning at positions $2^i$ for $0 \le i \le r - 1$, and the factors beginning at positions $2^{r+1}$ and $3 \cdot 2^r$.

Suppose $U_c(n)$ is 2-synchronized. Then $U'(n)$, defined to be $U_c(n)$ if $n = 2^r + 1$, and 0 otherwise, is easily seen to be 2-synchronized also. From the observation in the previous paragraph, $U'(n)$ is neither $O(1)$ nor $\ge cn$ infinitely often, which contradicts Theorem 10.6.1. □

In [336], the authors proved the following result:

**Theorem 10.14.3** *The function counting the number of distinct palindromes in the prefix of length n of a k-automatic sequence is not always k-synchronized.*

*Proof* The proof is based on two infinite words, $\mathbf{a} = (a_i)_{i \ge 0}$ and $\mathbf{b} = (b_i)_{i \ge 0}$, defined as follows:

$$a_i = \begin{cases} (k \bmod 2) + 1, & \text{if there exists } k \text{ such that } 4^{k+1} - 4^k \le i \le 4^{k+1} + 4^k; \\ 0, & \text{otherwise.} \end{cases}$$

$$b_i = \begin{cases} (k \bmod 2) + 1, & \text{if there exists } k \text{ such that } 4^{k+1} - 4^k < i < 4^{k+1} + 4^k; \\ 0, & \text{otherwise.} \end{cases}$$

It is easy to see that $\mathbf{a}$ and $\mathbf{b}$ are 4-automatic.

We now compare the palindromes in $\mathbf{a}$ to those in $\mathbf{b}$. From the definition, every palindrome in either sequence is clearly in

$$0^* \cup 1^* \cup 2^* \cup 0^*1^*0^* \cup 0^*2^*0^*.$$

Since $\mathbf{a}$ has longer blocks of 1s and 2s than $\mathbf{b}$ does, there may be some palindromes of the form $1^i$ or $2^i$ that occur in a prefix of $\mathbf{a}$, but not the corresponding prefix of $\mathbf{b}$. Conversely, $\mathbf{b}$ may contain palindromes of the form $0^i$ that do not occur in the corresponding prefix of $\mathbf{a}$. The net difference, if any, is at most a constant.

The palindromes not of the form $a^i$, where $a \in \{0, 1, 2\}$, are of the form $0^i1^j0^i$ or $0^i2^j0^i$, and must be centered at a position that is a power of 4. It is not hard to see that if $\mathbf{a}[i..i + n - 1]$ is a novel palindrome occurrence of this form in $\mathbf{a}$, then $\mathbf{b}[i..i+n-1]$ is also a novel palindrome occurrence of this form.

On the other hand, for each $k \ge 1$, there are two palindromes that occur in $\mathbf{b}$ but not $\mathbf{a}$. The first is of the form $01^j0$ or $02^j0$, since the corresponding factor of $\mathbf{a}$ is either $1 \cdots 1$ or $2 \cdots 2$, and hence has been previously accounted for (as a palindrome of the form $1^*$ or $2^*$). Second, there is a factor of the form $0^*1^*0^*$ or $0^*2^*0^*$ in $\mathbf{b}$ which appears as $20^*1^*0^*$ or $10^*2^*0^*$ in $\mathbf{a}$ because the neighboring block of 1s or 2s is slightly wider in $\mathbf{a}$ and therefore slightly closer.

We conclude that the length-$n$ prefix of **b** has $2 \log_4 n + O(1)$ more palindromes than the length-$n$ prefix of **a**.

Now suppose, contrary to what we want to prove, that the number of palindromes in the prefix of length $n$ of a $k$-automatic sequence is $k$-synchronized. In particular, the sequence **a** (resp., **b**) is 4-automatic, so the number of palindromes in $\mathbf{a}[0..n-1]$ (resp., $\mathbf{b}[0..n-1]$) is 4-synchronized. By the closure properties of synchronized sequences, the number of palindromes in $\mathbf{b}[0..n-1]$ minus the number of palindromes in $\mathbf{a}[0..n-1]$ is 4-synchronized. But from above this difference is $2 \log_4 n + O(1)$, which by Theorem 10.6.1 cannot be 4-synchronized. This is a contradiction.                                                  □

*Exercise* 143    Show that the cyclic complexity (introduced in Section 9.11.15) of an automatic sequence need not be synchronized.

*Exercise* 144    Let $f(n)$ be the position of the $n$th 1 occurring in the period-doubling sequence **pd**, for $n \geq 0$. Show that $f(n)$ is not 2-synchronized.

*Exercise* 145    Let $g(n)$ be the position of the $n$th 1 occurring in the Rudin-Shapiro sequence **r**, for $n \geq 0$. Show that $g(n)$ is not 2-synchronized.

*Exercise* 146    Consider the sequence $(f(n))_{n\geq 0}$ defined in Example 9.2.3. Show that it is not 2-synchronized. Hint: use the pumping lemma.

*Exercise* 147    Consider the sequence $(h(n))_{n\geq 0}$ defined by $h(n) = 2^{s_2(n)}$. Show that $h$ is not 2-synchronized. Hint: use the pumping lemma.

## 10.15 How to guess a synchronized sequence

If you suspect that a sequence $(a(n))_{n\geq 0}$ is $k$-synchronized, then you can often deduce the DFAO recognizing the language $\{(n, a(n))_k \ : \ n \geq 0\}$ as follows: interpret pairs of digits $[a, b]$ as a single digit $ka + b$ in base $k^2$, and then use the guessing procedure described in Section 5.6.

Once a candidate automaton has been found, often its correctness can be proved using the techniques of this chapter.

As an example, consider the sequence **vtm** = 2102012101202102$\cdots$, the ternary variant of the Thue-Morse sequence. We can define the running sum of the sequence as follows: $f(n) = \sum_{0\leq i<n} \mathbf{vtm}[i]$. It turns out that this function is 2-synchronized! We can prove this as follows: first, we use the guessing procedure of Section 5.6 to find a candidate DFA for the synchronized automaton. It is displayed in Figure 10.29; let us call it rsvtm.txt and store it in the *Automata Library* directory of Walnut.

Its correctness can be proved in two steps: letting $g$ be the function computed

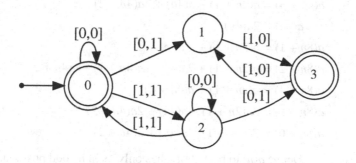

Figure 10.29 Synchronized automaton for the running sum of **vtm**.

by rsvtm, first check that $g(0) = 0$. Next, check that if $g(n) = x$, then $g(n+1) = x + $ **vtm**$[n]$. The truth of these two claims suffice to prove that $f = g$, as desired. We can carry out this proof in Walnut as follows:

```
eval checkrsv "$rsvtm(0,0) & An,x
    (((($rsvtm(n,x) & VTM[n]=@0) => $rsvtm(n+1,x)) &
    (($rsvtm(n,x) & VTM[n]=@1) => $rsvtm(n+1,x+1)) &
    (($rsvtm(n,x) & VTM[n]=@2) => $rsvtm(n+1,x+2)))
```

and this returns TRUE.

*Exercise* 148 Define $b(n) = \sum_{0 \le i \le n} t_i$, where $\mathbf{t} = t_0 t_1 t_2 \cdots$ is the Thue-Morse sequence. Guess a synchronized automaton for $b(n)$, and then verify its correctness by using Walnut to verify that $b(0) = 0$ and $b(n + 1) = b(n) + t_{n+1}$.

*Exercise* 149 Consider the sequence $(a(n))_{n \ge 0}$ defined by $a(n) = n$ for $n \le 2$, and for $n \ge 1$ we set

$$a(2n + 2) = \text{ the least natural number not in } \{a(0), a(1), \ldots, a(2n + 1)\},$$

and $a(2n + 1) = a(2n) + a(2n + 2)$. This is sequence A210770 in the OEIS. Guess a 2-synchronized automaton for this sequence and use it to verify the properties above. Also verify the following identities:

$$a(4n + 3) = a(2n + 1) - a(4n) + 2a(4n + 2)$$
$$a(8n) = 2a(4n)$$
$$a(8n + 1) = a(2n + 1) + 3a(4n)$$
$$a(8n + 2) = a(2n + 1) + 2a(4n) - a(4n + 1) + a(4n + 2)$$
$$a(8n + 4) = a(2n + 1) + a(4n + 2)$$
$$a(8n + 5) = 3a(2n + 1) - a(4n) + 2a(4n + 2)$$
$$a(8n + 6) = 2a(2n + 1) - a(4n) + a(4n + 2).$$

*Exercise* 150    Define $a(n)$ to be 1 if $(n)_2$ has only 1s in its odd positions (msd first, with most significant digit considered as position 1), and 0 otherwise. Define $b(n)$ to be $\sum_{0 \leq i \leq n} a(n)$, the summatory function of $(a(n))_{n \geq 0}$. Show that $b(n)$ is $(4, 2)$-synchronized.

# 11

# Additive number theory

Additive number theory is the study of the additive properties of integers.[1]

For example, Lagrange proved (1770) that every natural number is the sum of four squares [188]. In additive number theory, a subset $S \subseteq \mathbb{N}$ is called an *additive basis of order h* if every natural number can be written as a sum of at most $h$ members of $S$, not necessarily distinct. The set $S$ is called an *asymptotic additive basis of order h* if every *sufficiently large* natural number can be so expressed.

Quoting Nathanson [282, p. 7],

*"The central problem in additive number theory is to determine if a given set of integers is a basis of finite order."*

Let $S, T$ be sets. We define the *sumset* $S + T$ as follows:

$$S + T = \{s + t \ : \ s \in S, \ t \in T\},$$

and analogously for more than two terms.

Given an automatic set $S$, for each fixed $j$ we can easily construct first-order logical formulas asserting that every natural number (resp., every sufficiently large natural number) is the sum of $j$ terms of $S$, as follows:

$$\forall n \ \exists \ x_1, \ldots, x_j \ \chi_S(x_1) = 1 \ \wedge \ \cdots \ \wedge \chi_S(x_j) = 1$$
$$\wedge \ n = x_1 + \cdots + x_j$$
$$\exists m \ \forall n \geq m \ \exists \ x_1, \ldots, x_j \ \chi_S(x_1) = 1 \ \wedge \ \cdots \ \wedge \chi_S(x_j) = 1$$
$$\wedge \ n = x_1 + \cdots + x_j.$$

---

[1] Much of the material in this chapter is reprinted from [36] by permission from Springer Nature.

Similarly, we can obtain the analogous formulas where we demand that the summands be distinct:

$$\forall n \, \exists \, x_1 < \cdots < x_j \; \chi_S(x_1) = 1 \wedge \cdots \wedge \chi_S(x_j) = 1$$
$$\wedge \; n = x_1 + \cdots + x_j$$
$$\exists m \, \forall n \geq m \, \exists \, x_1 < \cdots < x_j \; \chi_S(x_1) = 1 \wedge \cdots \wedge \chi_S(x_j) = 1$$
$$\wedge \; n = x_1 + \cdots + x_j.$$

It follows that if $S$ is an automatic set, then the set of numbers representable as the sum of $j$ terms (resp., $j$ distinct terms) of $S$ is itself automatic.

In this chapter we look at some results based on these simple ideas and variations of them. This chapter is based on the papers [37, 35, 356, 308].

## 11.1 The evil and odious numbers

We start with some results about the "evil" and "odious" numbers, introduced in Section 10.2. Let $\mathbf{t} = t_0 t_1 t_2 \cdots$ be the Thue-Morse sequence. Recall that the evil numbers

$$\mathcal{E} = \{0, 3, 5, 6, 9, 10, 12, 15, 17, 18, 20, 23, 24, 27, 29, 30, \ldots\}$$

are those integers $n$ for which $t_n = 0$, and the odious numbers

$$O = \{1, 2, 4, 7, 8, 11, 13, 14, 16, 19, 21, 22, 25, 26, 28, 31, \ldots\}$$

are those integers $n$ for which $t_n = 1$. Using Theorem 6.6.1 and `Walnut`, we can investigate the additive properties of these numbers.

**Theorem 11.1.1** *A natural number is the sum of exactly two evil numbers iff it is neither 2, 4, nor of the form $2 \cdot 4^i - 1$ for $i \geq 0$.*

*Proof* It is trivial to write a first-order statement, with $n$ a free variable, that asserts that $n = i + j$ for $t_i = t_j = 0$. We can now translate this statement into `Walnut`. The translation is more or less straightforward:

```
def sum2e "E i,j n=i+j & T[i]=@0 & T[j]=@0":
```

which gives us the DFA in Figure 11.1.

A brief inspection shows the automaton rejects exactly the integers specified in the conclusion. Or we can check it as follows:

```
reg power4 msd_2 "0*1(00)*":
eval sum2echeck "An (n=2|n=4|(Ex $power4(x) & n+1=2*x))
   <=> ~$sum2e(n)":
```

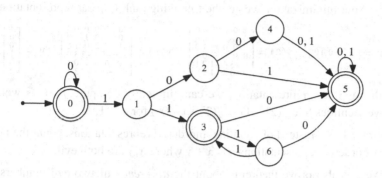

Figure 11.1 Automaton for sum of two evil numbers.

□

*Exercise 151* Show that a positive integer is the sum of exactly two odious numbers iff it is not of the form $2 \cdot 4^i - 1$ for $i \geq 0$.

However, the evil numbers form an asymptotic additive basis of order 3, as the following theorem shows. We can even demand that the summands be distinct.

**Theorem 11.1.2** *Every natural number $n > 10$ is the sum of 3 distinct evil numbers.*

*Proof* We run Walnut with the following commands:

```
def sum3de "E i,j,k i<j & j<k & n=i+j+k & T[i]=@0 & T[j]=@0 &
   T[k]=@0":
eval sum3decheck "An n>10 => $sum3de(n)":
```

and Walnut returns TRUE. □

*Exercise 152* Find and prove an analogous result for the sum of 3 distinct odious numbers.

Furthermore, we can prove results about the *number* of representations. For example, let us determine $f(n)$, the number of ways to write $n = x + y$, with $x \leq y$ and both $x$ and $y$ evil numbers. This corresponds to counting unordered representations.

```
eval evil2num n "Ey x<=y & T[x]=@0 & T[y]=@0 & n=x+y":
```

As a result, `Walnut` gives us a rank-14 linear representation for the function $f(n)$. After minimization, we get the following rank-6 linear representation:

$$v = [1\,0\,0\,0\,0\,0] \quad \gamma(0) = \begin{bmatrix} 1 & 0 & 0 & 0 & 0 & 0 \\ 0 & 0 & 1 & 0 & 0 & 0 \\ 0 & 0 & 0 & 0 & 1 & 0 \\ 0 & 0 & 0 & 0 & 0 & 1 \\ 0 & -3 & 4 & -1 & 0 & 1 \\ 0 & -3 & 3 & -1 & 0 & 2 \end{bmatrix} \quad \gamma(1) = \begin{bmatrix} 0 & 1 & 0 & 0 & 0 & 0 \\ 0 & 0 & 0 & 1 & 0 & 0 \\ 1 & -3 & 2 & 0 & 1 & 0 \\ 2 & -5 & 3 & -2 & 3 & 0 \\ -1 & 0 & 0 & 1 & 0 & 1 \\ 1 & -5 & 3 & -2 & 3 & 1 \end{bmatrix} \quad w = \begin{bmatrix} 1 \\ 0 \\ 0 \\ 1 \\ 0 \\ 2 \end{bmatrix}.$$

With this linear representation, we can efficiently compute $f(n)$, as well as prove identities like $f(2^n - 1) = \frac{1}{8}(2^n + (-2)^n)$ for $n \geq 1$.

*Exercise* 153   Instead of counting unordered representations, count the number of ordered representations $n = x + y$ where $x, y$ are both evil.

We can also prove theorems about the *difference* of two evil numbers, or two odious numbers. Consider the following two lemmas, which were recently proved using a case-based argument in a paper about discriminators [187]:

**Theorem 11.1.3**

(a) *Let $i \geq 3$ and $1 \leq m < 2^i - 3$. Then there exist two evil numbers $j, \ell$ with $0 \leq j < \ell \leq 2^i + 1$ such that $m = \ell - j$.*

(b) *Let $i \geq 1$ and $1 \leq m < 2^i$. Then there exist two odious numbers $j, \ell$ with $1 \leq j < \ell \leq 2^i$ such that $m = \ell - j$.*

We can construct alternative proofs of these facts using `Walnut`.

*Proof*   We write the following in `Walnut`:

```
reg power2 msd_2 "0*10*":
eval evildiff "A x,m ($power2(x) & x>=8 & m>=1 & m+3<x) =>
    (E j,l j<l & l<=x+1 & m+j=l & T[j]=@0 & T[l]=@0)":
eval odiousdiff "A x,m ($power2(x) & x>=2 & m>=1 & m<x) =>
    (E j,l  j>=1 & j<l & l<=x & m+j=l & T[j]=@1 & T[l]=@1)":
```

Notice that in order to enforce the requirement that we deal with $2^i$ for $i \geq 3$, we require that $x$ be a power of 2 and $x \geq 8$.

Both `Walnut` statements return TRUE.                               □


## 11.2 Other examples

We can prove analogous results for many other automatic sets. For example, consider the set $S = \{0, 3, 7, 12, 15, 24, 28, 31, 48, 51, 56, 60, 63, 96, 99, \ldots\}$ of natural numbers whose base-2 representation contains no maximal runs of length 1. Let us first test the assertion that $S$ forms an asymptotic additive basis of order 2:

```
reg noshortruns msd_2 "0*(000*|111*)*":
eval test2 "Em An n>m => Ex,y $noshortruns(x) & $noshortruns(y)
    & n=x+y":
```

Here `Walnut` returns FALSE.

Next, let's show that $S$ does form an asymptotic additive basis of order 3:

```
eval test3 "Em An n>m => Ex,y,z $noshortruns(x) &
    $noshortruns(y) & $noshortruns(z) & n=x+y+z":
```

This returns TRUE, so such an $m$ exists. Let us find it.

```
def representable "Ex,y,z $noshortruns(x) &
    $noshortruns(y) & $noshortruns(z) & n=x+y+z":
def bound "(~$representable(n)) & Am m>n => $representable(m)":
```

The automaton `bound` accepts the representation of exactly one integer, namely 44. Thus we have shown

**Theorem 11.2.1** *Every integer $n > 44$ is the sum of three elements of $S$.*

*Exercise* 154   Recall that a natural number is called a *Cantor number* if its base-3 representation contains no 1. Prove that every even number is the sum of two Cantor numbers.

*Exercise* 155   Consider the *alternate Cantor numbers*, which have no 2 in their base-3 expansion.

(a)  Show that every number is the sum of 2 alternate Cantor numbers.

(b)  Show that every number $\geq 7$ is the sum of 2 numbers that are not alternate Cantor numbers.

(c)  Show that infinitely many numbers are not the sum of an alternate Cantor number and a non-alternate Cantor number.

*Exercise* 156   Consider the set $T = \{0, 3, 12, 15, 48, 51, 60, 63, 192, 195, \ldots\}$ of natural numbers whose base-2 representation contains only maximal runs of even length. What multiples of 3 are represented by $T + T$?

*Exercise* 157   Let $S_3$ be the set of natural numbers that are representable as the sum of three squares.

(a)  Show that $S_3$ is 2-automatic. (You might have to consult a number theory book.)

(b)  Show that every natural number is both the sum and difference of two elements of $S_3$.

## 11.3 Summands from different sets

We can also combine summands from different sets, provided they are defined over the same numeration system. The *Rudin-Shapiro* numbers

$$3, 6, 11, 12, 13, 15, 19, 22, 24, 25, 26, 30, \ldots$$

are those $n$ for which the number of 11s occurring in the base-2 representation of $n$ is odd; they form sequence A022155 in the OEIS. We can describe the natural numbers representable as a sum of an odious number and a Rudin-Shapiro number.

**Theorem 11.3.1**   *Every natural number, except* $0, 1, 2, 3, 6, 9$, *is the sum of an odious number and a Rudin-Shapiro number.*

*Proof*   We use the Walnut commands

```
def trsum "E i,j n=i+j & T[i]=@1 & RS[j] = @1":
eval trsumchk "An $trsum(n) <=> ~(n<=3 | n=6 | n=9)":
```

and the result from Walnut is TRUE.                                    □

*Exercise* 158   Show every sufficiently large natural number is the sum of two Rudin-Shapiro numbers, two non-Rudin-Shapiro numbers, and the sum of a Rudin-Shapiro and non-Rudin-Shapiro number.

## 11.4 Wythoff sequences

Let $\varphi = (1 + \sqrt{5})/2$. Define

$$L = \{\lfloor \varphi n \rfloor : n \geq 1\}$$
$$U = \{\lfloor \varphi^2 n \rfloor : n \geq 1\},$$

the lower and upper Wythoff sets. Kawsumarng et al. [220] studied the additive properties of these sets. In particular, they characterized the sumsets $L + L$, $L + U$, $U + U$, $L + U + U$, and $U + U + U$. We can reproduce their results, and more, using our method.

Recall that in Section 10.11, we created synchronized formulas for $\lfloor \varphi n \rfloor$ and $\lfloor \varphi^2 n \rfloor$. From these we can construct logical formulas for the sets $L$ and $S$ as follows:

```
def lower "?msd_fib En n>=1 & $phin(n,s)":
def upper "?msd_fib En n>=1 & $phi2n(n,s)":
```

## Theorem 11.4.1

*(a)* $L + L = \mathbb{N} - \{0, 1, 3\}$.

*(b)* $L + U = \mathbb{N} - \{F_n - 1 : n \geq 1\}$.

*(c)* $L + U + U = \mathbb{N} - \{0, 1, 2, 3, 4, 6, 9\}$.

*(d)* $U + U + U = \mathbb{N} - \{0, 1, 2, 3, 4, 5, 7, 8, 10, 13, 18, 26\}$.

*(e)* $U + U$ *is recognized by the DFA in Figure 11.2.*

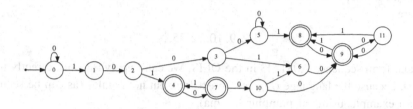

Figure 11.2 Fibonacci DFA for the sumset $U + U$.

*Proof* We use the following Walnut code:

```
def lplusl "?msd_fib Ea,b n=a+b & $lower(a) & $lower(b)":
eval lpluslcheck "?msd_fib An $lplusl(n) <=> (n>=4 | n=2)":

reg isfib msd_fib "0*10*":
def lplusu "?msd_fib Ea,b n=a+b & $lower(a) & $upper(b)":
eval lplusucheck "?msd_fib An $lplusu(n) <=> (~Ex $isfib(x)
   & n+1=x)":

def lplusuplusu "?msd_fib Ea,b,c n=a+b+c & $lower(a) &
   $upper(b) & $upper(c)":
eval lplusuplusucheck "?msd_fib An $lplusuplusu(n) <=>
   (n>=10 | n=5 | n=7 | n=8)":

def uplusuplusu "?msd_fib Ea,b,c n=a+b+c & $upper(a) &
   $upper(b) & $upper(c)":
eval uplusuplusucheck "?msd_fib An $uplusuplusu(n) <=>
   ~(n<=5 | n=7 | n=8 | n=10 | n=13 | n=18 | n=26)":

def uplusu "?msd_fib Ea,b n=a+b & $upper(a) & $upper(b)":
```

This provides proofs for assertions (a)–(e) of the theorem.  □

## 11.5 The method of over- and under-approximation

We can use automatic sequences to prove additive number theory results about sets $S$ that are not automatic. The idea is to *approximate* a non-automatic $S$ with a subset or superset $S'$ that *is* automatic. If we want to prove that $S$ forms an additive basis, then it suffices to show this for an automatic subset $S'$. Similarly, if we want to prove that $S$ is not an asymptotic additive basis, it suffices to prove this for an automatic superset $S'$.

For example, consider the "digitally balanced numbers" in base 2. This is the set $D = \{n : |(n)_2|_0 = |(n)_2|_1\}$, that is, the integers containing an equal number of 0s and 1s in their base-2 representation. The first few such numbers are

$$0, 2, 9, 10, 12, 35, \ldots$$

and form sequence A031443 in the OEIS. We can't apply `Walnut` directly to $D$, because the language $(D)_2$ is context-free, but not regular (as can be seen, for example, using the pumping lemma).

Let us prove that $D$ forms an asymptotic additive basis of order 3, by under-approximating it. One set that works is the integers of the form

$$0^*10(10 \cup 01 \cup 1100 \cup 0011)^* \cup 0^*1(10 \cup 01)^*0 \cup 0^*.$$

We can check this in `Walnut` as follows:

```
reg qq msd_2 "0*10(10|01|1100|0011)*|0*1(10|01)*0|0*":
def eqq "E x,y,z n=x+y+z & $qq(x) & $qq(y) & $qq(z)":
eval eqqtest "An n>=68 => $eqq(n)":
```

So every integer $\geq 68$ is the sum of three elements of $D$.

On the other hand, the digitally balanced numbers $D$ do not form an asymptotic additive basis of order 2. In order to see this, we need to *over-approximate* $D$. One set that works is

$$D' = \{n : |(n)_2| \text{ is even, but } n \text{ is not of the form } 2^k - 1\}.$$

Using `Walnut` we can prove this as follows:

```
reg even1 msd_2 "0*|0*1(0|1)((0|1)(0|1))*":
reg all1 msd_2 "0*11*":
def dprime "$even1(n) & ~$all1(n)":
def dprimesum "Ex,y $dprime(x) & $dprime(y) & n=x+y":
eval dprimesumchk "Am En n>m & ~$dprimesum(n)":
```

*Exercise* 159   Obtain analogous results for the set $\{n : |(n)_2|_0 > |(n)_2|_1\}$.

## 11.6 De Bruijn's problem

N. G. de Bruijn investigated the following problem. Consider the set

$$S = \{0, 1, 4, 5, 16, 17, 20, 21, 64, \ldots\}$$

which consists of those integers having only 0s and 1s in their base-4 representation. Then every element of $\mathbb{Z}$ can be represented uniquely as $s_1 - 2s_2$ for $s_1, s_2 \in S$, and this is also true of $7s_1 - 2s_2$. De Bruijn raised the question of characterizing those $(a, b)$ for which $as_1 - bs_2$ has this unique representation property.

For each specific $a$ and $b$, we can answer this question using Walnut. Because we are talking about representations of elements of $\mathbb{Z}$ and not $\mathbb{N}$, we have to check two different equalities. We use the following code:

```
reg deb msd_4 "(0|1)*":
def debr12 "?msd_4 (An Es,t $deb(s) & $deb(t) & n+2*t = s) &
    (An Es,t $deb(s) & $deb(t) & s+n = 2*t) &
    (As,t,sp,tp ($deb(s) & $deb(t) & $deb(sp) & $deb(tp) &
    s+2*tp = sp+2*t) => (s=sp & t=tp))":
def debr72 "?msd_4 (An Es,t $deb(s) & $deb(t) & n+2*t = 7*s) &
    (An Es,t $deb(s) & $deb(t) & 7*s+n = 2*t) &
    (As,t,sp,tp ($deb(s) & $deb(t) & $deb(sp) & $deb(tp) &
    7*s+2*tp = 7*sp+2*t) => (s=sp & t=tp))":
```

and Walnut returns TRUE for both. See [114, 115].

## 11.7 Frobenius numbers

Let $S$ be a nonempty set of natural numbers with $\gcd(S) = 1$. The *Frobenius number* $g(S)$ is defined to be the greatest integer $t$ such that $t$ *cannot* be written as a non-negative integer linear combination of elements of $S$. For example, $g(\{6, 9, 20\}) = 43$. For more about Frobenius numbers, see the book of Ramírez-Alfonsín [309].

Let $\mathbf{s} = (s_i)_{i \geq 0}$ be an increasing sequence of natural numbers such that $\gcd(s_i, s_{i+1}, \ldots) = 1$ for all $i \geq 0$. For $i \geq 0$ define $G_{\mathbf{s}}(i) = g(s_i, s_{i+1}, \ldots)$, the Frobenius number of a final segment of $\mathbf{s}$.

In some cases it is possible to use Walnut to calculate $G_{\mathbf{s}}$. Let us do this for the case of the evil and odious numbers, defined in Example 10.2.2.

**Theorem 11.7.1** *The function $G_e(n)$ is 2-synchronized.*

To prove this, we start with the following result.

**Lemma 11.7.2**   *If $n \geq 1$ can be written as the sum of four evil numbers $\geq m$, then $n$ can be written as the sum of one, two, or three evil numbers $\geq m$.*

*Proof*   This assertion can be phrased as a first-order formula, namely,

$$\forall m, n \; \mathrm{evil}_4(m, n) \implies \mathrm{evil}_{1,2,3}(m, n),$$

where

$$\mathrm{evil}_{1,2,3}(m, n) := \exists j, k, \ell \; t(j) = t(k) = t(\ell) = 0 \wedge j, k, \ell \geq m$$
$$\wedge \; (n = j \vee n = j + k \vee n = j + k + \ell)$$
$$\mathrm{evil}_4(m, n) := \exists i, j, k, \ell \; t(i) = t(j) = t(k) = t(\ell) = 0 \wedge i, j, k, \ell \geq m$$
$$\wedge \; n = i + j + k + \ell.$$

In Walnut this is:

```
def evil123rep "Ej,k,l T[j]=@0 & T[k]=@0 & T[l]=@0 &
   j>=m & k>=m & l>=m & (n=j | n=j+k | n=j+k+l)":

def evil4rep "Ei,j,k,l T[i]=@0 & T[j]=@0 & T[k]=@0 &
   T[l]=@0 & i >= m & j>=m & k>=m & l>=m & n=j+k+l+m":

eval evilcheck "Am,n $evil4rep(m,n) => $evil123rep(m,n)":
```

This returns TRUE, so the lemma is proved.                              □

**Lemma 11.7.3**   *Let $n \geq 1$ be a non-negative integer linear combination of evil numbers $\geq m$. Then $n$ can be written as the sum of either one, two, or three evil numbers $\geq m$.*

*Proof*   Let $n$ be written as a non-negative integer linear combination of evil numbers $\geq m$. Without loss of generality choose a representation for $n$ that minimizes $s$, the sum of the coefficients. If this sum is at least 4, we can write $n = u + v$ where $u$ is the sum of 4 evil numbers and $v$ is the sum of $n - 4$ evil numbers, all $\geq m$. But then by Lemma 11.7.2, we can write $u$ as the sum of 3 evil numbers $\geq m$, so $n$ is the sum of $n - 1$ evil numbers $\geq m$, a contradiction. So $s$ is no more than 3, as desired.                              □

We can now prove Theorem 11.7.1.

*Proof*   It suffices to give a first-order definition of $G_e(n)$. We can do this as follows:

```
def evilg "(Aj j>n => $evil123rep(2*m,j))&~$evil123rep(2*m,n)":
```

The reason why we use $2m$ and not $m$ is that evil123 is defined for elements of the sequence that are $\geq m$, while the $m$th element of the evil numbers is either $2m$ or $2m + 1$.

This gives a 58-state synchronized automaton computing $G_e(n)$. □

Now that we have a synchronized automaton, we can determine the asymptotic behavior of $G_e(n)$.

**Theorem 11.7.4** *We have $4m \leq G_e(m) \leq 6m + 7$ for all $m \geq 0$. These bounds are optimal, because they are attained for infinitely many m.*

*Proof* We run the following Walnut commands, which all evaluate to TRUE.

```
eval upperb "Am,n $evilg(m,n) => n<=6*m+7":
eval upperopt "Ai Em,n m>i & $evilg(m,n) & n=6*m+7":
eval lowerb "Am,n $evilg(m,n) => n>=4*m":
eval loweropt "Ai Em,n m>i & $evilg(m,n) & n=4*m":
```

□

**Corollary 11.7.5** *We have*

$$\inf_{i \geq 1} G_e(i)/i = 4 \qquad \sup_{i \geq 1} G_e(i)/i = 7$$

$$\liminf_{i \geq 1} G_e(i)/i = 4 \qquad \limsup_{i \geq 1} G_e(i)/i = 6.$$

The sequence $(G_e(i))_{i \geq 0}$ has a rather erratic behavior. In particular we can prove

**Theorem 11.7.6**

(a) *The difference $G_e(i + 1) - G_e(i)$ can be arbitrarily large.*

(b) *There are arbitrarily long blocks of indices on which $G_e(i)$ is constant.*

*Proof* We use the following Walnut code.

```
eval evilgdiff "Ai Ej,m,n1,n2 j>=i & $evilg(m,n1) &
    $evilg(m+1,n2) & n2=n1+j":
eval evalmonotone "Ai Ej,m,u j>=i & $evilg(m,u) &
    (At,v t>m & t<m+j & $evilg(t,v)) => u=v)":
```

Both return TRUE. □

*Exercise* 160 Carry out the same sort of analysis for the odious numbers.

For more about these ideas, see [350].

# 11.8 Counting number of representations

Using the ideas in Chapter 9, we can also use `Walnut` to count the number of representations of $n$ as a sum of members of some automatic set. In general, `Walnut` produces a linear representation for this function. In some cases this linear representation is enough to prove various properties of the number-of-representations function.

To illustrate this technique, let's start with the set $O$ of odious numbers. Recall that these are the numbers $\{1, 2, 4, 7, 8, 11, \ldots\}$ having an odd number of 1s in their base-2 representation.

**Theorem 11.8.1** *Let $T_5(n)$ be the number of representations of $n$ as the sum of 5 elements of $O$, where representations that just differ in the order of summands are counted as distinct. Then $T_5(2^n) > T_5(2^n + 1)$ for all sufficiently large $n$.*

*Proof* We start by creating a linear representation $(v, \gamma, w)$ for $T_5(n)$ with `Walnut`:

```
eval m5 n "n=a+b+c+d+e & T[a]=@1 & T[b]=@1 & T[c]=@1 &
    T[d]=@1 & T[e]=@1":
```

This creates a linear representation of rank 160 for $T_5(n)$. We then copy the `Maple` code for this linear representation from `Result/m5.mpl` and use the `linalg/minpoly` command of `Maple` to determine the minimal polynomial $f(X)$ of $\gamma(0)$, and then factor it. It is

$$X^4(X-1)(X-2)(X-4)(X-8)(X-16)(X+2)(X+4)(X+8)(X^2-8)(X^2-2X-16).$$

Note that the dominant zero is 16.

As we saw in Chapter 9, this means that $T_5(2^n)$ and $T_5(2^n + 1)$ are both linear combinations of the $n$th powers of the zeros of $f(X)$, so the same thing is true for their difference $d(n) := T_5(2^n) - T_5(2^n + 1)$. Using our linear representation we can evaluate $d(n)$ for 16 different values, solve the resulting linear system, and determine an exact expression for $d(n)$. When we do so, we discover that the coefficient of the dominant term $16^n$ is positive (in fact, it is $1/14039101440$). This means that $d(n)$ is eventually positive. □

Now let's move on to prove two remarkable theorems involving number of representations as sums of automatic sets.

The first is due to Lambek and Moser [233]. Later, other proofs were given by Dombi [122], Chen and Wang [82], Sándor [333], Lev [240], and Tang [371]. In addition to the set of odious number $O$ just mentioned, it involves its complement, the set of evil numbers $\mathcal{E}$.

**Theorem 11.8.2** *Let $R_\mathcal{E}(n)$ denote the number of representations of $n$ as the sum of two evil numbers, $x + y$, where $x < y$, and similarly $R_O(n)$ for the sum of two odious numbers. Then $R_\mathcal{E}(n) = R_O(n)$ for all $n \geq 0$.*

*Proof* We use `Walnut` to compute linear representations for these two functions:

```
eval re n "n=x+y & x<y & T[x]=@0 & T[y]=@0":
eval ro n "n=x+y & x<y & T[x]=@1 & T[y]=@1":
```

The resulting linear representations have rank 12. When we minimize them, we discover they minimize to exactly the same linear representation of rank 5. So the two enumeration functions are the same. □

Similarly, we can prove the following similar result, due to Chen and Wang [82].

**Theorem 11.8.3** *Define $t'_n$ as follows: $t'_0 = 1$, $t'_1 = 0$, and $t'_{2n} = 1 - t'_n$ and $t'_{2n+1} = t'_n$ for $n \geq 1$. Set*

$$C = \{n \geq 0 : t'_n = 0\} = \{1, 3, 4, 7, 9, 10, 12, 15, \ldots\};$$
$$D = \{n \geq 0 : t'_n = 1\} = \{0, 2, 5, 6, 8, 11, 13, 14, \ldots\}.$$

*Let $R_C(n)$ be the number of representations of $n$ as a sum $x + y$ of two elements of $C$, with $x \leq y$, and similarly for $R_D(n)$. Then $R_C(n) = R_D(n)$ for $n \geq 1$.*

The proof is quite similar to the result for the odious and evil numbers, with one minor complication. Since the equality holds only for $n \geq 1$, we actually produce the linear representations for $R_C(n+1)$ and $R_D(n+1)$ instead, and then minimize and compare them. For more details, see [354].

# 12

# Paperfolding sequences

Up to now our logical formulas have allowed us to state formulas concerning a single automatic sequence, or perhaps two at the same time (as in Section 8.9.3). In some cases, however, it's possible to use our approach to prove results about *infinitely* many sequences (even *uncountably* many sequences) at once!

This seems astounding at first glance, but the idea is simple: we parameterize a family $(X_p(n))_n$ of sequences with another sequence $p$. We then create a *single* DFAO that takes both a parameterization $p$ and a number $n$ as input, and computes $X_p(n)$.

In this chapter, we illustrate this idea for a celebrated family of sequences, the *paperfolding sequences*.[1]

Parts of this chapter appeared previously in [334] and [170].

## 12.1 The general idea

We previously discussed the regular paperfolding sequence in Section 2.4.9 of this book. Davis and Knuth [112] generalized this sequence by allowing the folds that we discussed before to be either right-hand over left, or vice versa. Let us recode the paperfolding sequences over the alphabet $\{1, -1\}$, to better match the existing literature. We often abbreviate $-1$ as $\overline{1}$.

During unfolding, we can read off the sequence of fold choices that we made, and encode it by letting 1 denote a hill and $\overline{1}$ a valley. Given a sequence of *unfolding instructions* $\mathbf{f} = f_0 f_1 f_2 \cdots$ over the alphabet $\{1, -1\}$, a paperfolding sequence $\mathbf{P_f} = p_1 p_2 p_3 \cdots$ is defined as the limit of the finite sequences

---

[1] Much of the material in this chapter is reprinted from [170] by permission from Springer Nature.

316

$\mathbf{P}_{f_0 \cdots f_i}$ defined by

$$\mathbf{P}_\epsilon = \epsilon$$
$$\mathbf{P}_{f_0 \cdots f_i} = \mathbf{P}_{f_0 \cdots f_{i-1}} \ f_i \ -(\mathbf{P}_{f_0 \cdots f_{i-1}})^R, \quad i \geq 0.$$

The *regular paperfolding sequence* then corresponds to the unfolding instructions $111 \cdots$. Notice that, by convention, paperfolding sequences are indexed starting at 1, and we never refer to $p_0$.

For example, if we choose the sequence of unfolding instructions $1\overline{1}\,1\overline{1} \cdots$, then the resulting paperfolding sequence is

$$1\overline{1}\,\overline{1}\,111\overline{1}\,\overline{1}\,1\overline{1}\,\overline{1}\,\overline{1}\,111\overline{1} \cdots.$$

Since there are uncountably many choices of unfolding instructions, this gives uncountably many distinct paperfolding sequences.

Dekking, Mendès France, and van der Poorten [119] observed that we can easily determine the paperfolding sequence $\mathbf{P}_{f_0 f_1 \cdots}$ from the sequence of *unfolding instructions* $(f_i)_{i \geq 0}$, as follows: write $n = 2^s \cdot r$, where $r$ is odd. Then

$$\mathbf{P}_{f_0 f_1 \cdots}[n] = \begin{cases} f_s, & \text{if } r \equiv 1 \ (\text{mod } 4); \\ -f_s, & \text{if } r \equiv 3 \ (\text{mod } 4). \end{cases} \qquad (12.1)$$

As Luke Schaeffer observed, this formula makes it possible to create a *single DFAO* that computes all of the paperfolding sequences *simultaneously*, provided we feed in enough unfolding instructions in parallel with the base-2 representation of $n$, starting with the *least significant digit*. More precisely, an input to the automaton is of the form

$$[f_0, e_0][f_1, e_1] \cdots [f_{t-1}, e_{t-1}]$$

and the result is $\mathbf{P}_{f_0 \cdots f_{t-1}}[n] \in \{1, -1\}$ where $n = \sum_{0 \leq i < t} e_i 2^i$, if $1 \leq n < 2^t$, and 0 otherwise. Notice that $t$ unfolding instructions provide exactly enough information to determine the first $2^t - 1$ terms of a paperfolding sequence, and $t$ bits are exactly what is needed to specify an index in the range $1 \leq n < 2^t$.

This adds a bit of subtlety: when we evaluate a formula involving terms of the paperfolding sequence, the result makes sense only if we have been provided sufficiently many terms of the unfolding instructions to access the terms of the sequence required. (One way around this would be to work with $\omega$-automata instead of ordinary automata, but Walnut has not implemented this yet.) This demands a certain amount of extra care in constructing the formulas to prove results.

The generalized paperfolding automaton is depicted in Figure 12.1. Here the symbol "*" is a "wildcard" that matches both 0 and 1. The output associated

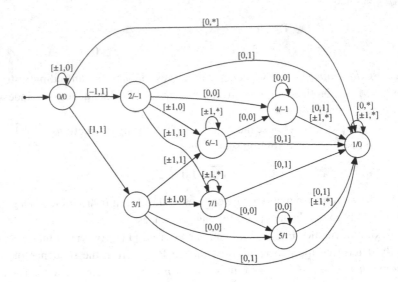

Figure 12.1 The paperfolding automaton for arbitrary unfolding instructions, lsd first.

with the input is contained in the last state reached. Notice there is no output associated with $n = 0$.

For example, suppose we use the unfolding instructions $1, 1, 1$. Then to compute $\mathbf{P}_{111}[6]$ for this sequence, we feed in $[1, 0][1, 1][1, 1]$ to the automaton. Here the first coordinates spell out the unfolding instructions $1, 1, 1$ and the second coordinates spell out $(6)_2$ in reverse order. The output is then $-1$.

If we index a paperfolding sequence at a position not specified by the number of nonzero unfolding instructions provided, then the automaton returns 0. We do allow 0's in the unfolding instructions, but only at the end of an input (corresponding to the most significant digits). If the unfolding instructions are not invalid (because, for example, there is a 1 or $-1$ after a 0), the automaton also returns 0.

With this automaton, we can use Walnut to reprove a number of old results about the set of all paperfolding sequences, and also some new ones.

To determine whether the index into a paperfolding sequence is valid, we can check if FOLD$[f][n]$ is nonzero. Another way is as follows. Using a regular expression, we can create an automaton linkf that takes a folding word $f$

and a number $x$ as input, and accepts if $x = 2^{|f|}$. Then the index $n$ is valid if $1 \le n < x$.

```
reg linkf {-1,0,1} {0,1} "([1,0]|[-1,0])*[0,1][0,0]*":
```

## 12.2 Appearance

One of the most useful results concerns the appearance function of the paper-folding sequences. Recall from Section 10.5 that this function $A_{\mathbf{P_f}}(n)$ measures the length of the shortest prefix of $\mathbf{P_f}$ that contains all the length-$n$ factors of $\mathbf{P_f}$. The fundamental result is as follows:

**Theorem 12.2.1** *We have*

$$A_{\mathbf{P_f}}(n) \le \begin{cases} 3, & \text{if } n = 1; \\ 7, & \text{if } n = 2; \\ 6 \cdot 2^h + n - 1, & \text{if } n \ge 3 \text{ and } h = \lceil \log_2 n \rceil. \end{cases}$$

*Furthermore, this upper bound is best possible, in the sense that for each $n$ there is a paperfolding sequence that achieves the listed bound.*

Proving this theorem guarantees that if we are trying to prove results about the factors that occur in $\mathbf{P_f}$, we can restrict our attention to $\mathbf{P}_x$ for some appropriate finite prefix $x$ of $\mathbf{f}$ that is relatively short.

*Proof* For $n \le 2$ we can check the result by hand. For $n \ge 3$ we can use Walnut to carry out the proof. We start by creating the automaton for the FACTOREQ formula for paperfolding sequences.

```
def pffactoreq "?lsd_2 Ex $linkf(f,x) & i+n<=x & j+n<=x &
   At (t<n) => FOLD[f][i+t]=FOLD[f][j+t]":
# 156 states
```

Next, we first create a synchronized automaton `tpc1` for the function $n \rightarrow 2^{\lceil \log_2 n \rceil}$, and test that for $n \ge 3$ the upper bound in the theorem holds:

```
reg power2 lsd_2 "0*10*":
def tpc1 "?lsd_2 $power2(x) & 2*n>x & n<=x":
# x = 2^{ceil(log_2 n)}

eval paperf_appearance "?lsd_2 Af,n,x,i,y ($linkf(f,x)
   & i>=1 & i+n<=x & n>=3 & $tpc1(n,y)) =>
   Ej (j<=6*y & $pffactoreq(f,i,j,n))":
```

The idea is that $f$ is a word of length $t$ giving unfolding instructions, $x = 2^t$, and $y = 2^{\lceil \log_2 n \rceil}$. Provided we have enough instructions (that is, provided

$i + n \leq x$) then for all $i \geq 1$, there exists $j \leq 6y$ such that the factors beginning at positions $i$ and $j$ coincide.

Similarly, we can show that for each $n \geq 3$, the bound $6 \cdot 2^h + n - 1$ is attained by some paperfolding sequence:

```
eval paperf_appearance2 "?lsd_2 An (n>=3) =>
    (Ef,y,x,i $linkf(f,x) & i>=1 & i+n<=x & $tpcl(n,y) &
    ~Ej j>=1 & j<=6*y-1 & j+n<=x & $pffactoreq(f,i,j,n))":
```

Both of these return TRUE, so the theorem is proved. □

The bound in Theorem 12.2.1 is best possible, as we have seen, but it is often somewhat clumsy to use. Instead we can use the following bound:

**Theorem 12.2.2** *For all paperfolding sequences f and $n \geq 1$, every factor of length n must occur starting at a position $j \leq 12n$.*

*Proof* We use the following Walnut code:

```
eval pf_weak_bound "?lsd_2 Af,n,x,i ($linkf(f,x) & i>=1 & i+n<=x
    & n>=1) => Ej (j>=1 & j<=12*n & $pffactoreq(f,i,j,n))":
```

and it returns TRUE. □

*Exercise* 161 Use Walnut to find a good upper bound on the recurrence function for the paperfolding sequences.

## 12.3 Powers in the paperfolding sequence

Prodinger and Urbanek [302] proved the following theorem, which we can reprove using our approach.

**Theorem 12.3.1** *If xx is a nonempty factor of any paperfolding sequence, then $|x| \in \{1, 3, 5\}$. Furthermore, every paperfolding sequence contains squares of orders $1, 3$, and $5$.*

*Proof* We use the following code to check to determine all possible orders of squares that appear in some paperfolding sequence.

```
eval paperf_square_orders "?lsd_2 Ef,i,x $linkf(f,x) & i>=1
    & n>=1 & i+2*n<=x & $pffactoreq(f,i,i+n,n)":
```

This gives us the automaton in Figure 12.2, and so the only orders of squares that occur in the paperfolding sequences are $1, 3$, and $5$.

Next we show that every infinite paperfolding sequence contains a square of order $1, 3$, and $5$. It suffices to show that every finite paperfolding sequence

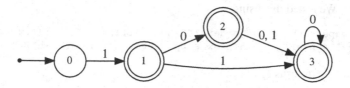

Figure 12.2 Orders of squares that appear in paperfolding sequences.

specified by an instruction sequence of length 6 has a square of each of these orders. This can be done just by computing all 64 paperfolding sequences. Or we can use `Walnut` as follows:

```
eval square2 "?lsd_2 Af,n ($linkf(f,64) & (n=1|n=3|n=5)) =>
  Ei (i>=1 & i+2*n<=64) & $pffactoreq(f,i,i+n,n)":
```

□

*Exercise* 162    Show that every infinite paperfolding sequence actually contains two distinct squares of order 1, four distinct squares of order 3, and two distinct squares of order 5.

Allouche and Bousquet-Mélou [9] showed that the only cubes in paperfolding sequences are 111 or $\overline{1}\,\overline{1}\,\overline{1}$, and that there are no $3^+$ powers in any paperfolding sequence. Let us now reprove these results.

**Theorem 12.3.2**    *The only cubes contained in any paperfolding sequence are* 111 *and* $\overline{1}\,\overline{1}\,\overline{1}$. *Furthermore, every infinite paperfolding sequence contains these cubes.*

*Proof*    For the first part, it suffices to determine the orders of cubes $xxx$ that can appear in any paperfolding sequence. We use the technique described above, modulo the change of condition:

$$\mathbf{P}_f[i..i + 2n - 1] = \mathbf{P}_f[i + n..i + 3n - 1].$$

In `Walnut` this is

```
eval paperf_cube_orders "?lsd_2 Ef,i,x $linkf(f,x) & i>=1 &
  n>=1 & i+3*n<=x & $pffactoreq(f,i,i+n,2*n)":
```

The output is an automaton of two states accepting only the order 1. The second part is proved as in the case of squares.    □

**Theorem 12.3.3**    *No paperfolding sequence contains a $3^+$-power.*

*Proof*    We tested this using

```
eval paperf_threeplus_orders "?lsd_2 Ef,i,x,n $linkf(f,x) &
    i>=1 & n>=1 & i+3*n+1<=x & $pffactoreq(f,i,i+n,2*n+1)":
```

and Walnut returns FALSE.                                              □

Allouche and Bousquet-Mélou [9] also studied the "almost-squares" in the paperfolding sequences; these are words of the form $wcw$, where $w$ is nonempty and $c$ is a single letter. They claimed that any such almost-square satisfies $|w| \in \{1, 2, 3, 4, 7\}$, but this is not quite correct. The correct statement, as proved in [217, Prop. 3], is that either $|w| \in \{2, 4\}$ or $|w| = 2^k - 1$ for some $k \geq 1$. Furthermore, there are almost-squares corresponding to all these orders. We can now reconfirm the corrected version of their results.

**Theorem 12.3.4**    *If $wcw$ is a factor of a paperfolding sequence, where $w$ is a word and $c$ is a single letter, then either $|w| \in \{2, 4\}$ or $|w| = 2^k - 1$ for some $k \geq 1$. Furthermore, for all $k \geq 1$, and all paperfolding sequences, and every $n \in \{2, 4\} \cup \{2^k - 1 : k \geq 1\}$, there is a factor of the form $wcw$ with $|w| = n$.*

*Proof*    We can verify the first claim with the methods above, computing those $n$ for which

$$\mathbf{P_f}[i..i + n - 1] = \mathbf{P_f}[i + n + 1..i + 2n].$$

We implemented this using

```
eval paperf_almost_squares "?lsd_2 Ef,i,x $linkf(f,x) & i>=1 &
    n>=1 & i+2*n+1<=x & $pffactoreq(f,i,i+n+1,n)":
```

and found the following five-state automaton:
Note that the $n$ accepted are precisely those with base-2 expansion 10, 100, and 11 $\cdots$ 1 (expressed msd-first).

The second statement is easily checked when $n = 2, 4$, so we focus on the case where $n = 2^k - 1$. In this case we let $y = 2^k$ and use the bound from Theorem 12.2.2. In Walnut we write

```
eval paperf_almost_squares2 "?lsd_2 Af,x,n,y ($linkf(f,x) &
    $power2(y) & n+1=y & x>=14*y) => Ei (i>=1 & i+2*n+2<=x &
    $pffactoreq(f,i,i+n+1,n))":
```

which returns true.                                                   □

*Exercise* 163    Determine the orders of overlaps that appear in paperfolding sequences.

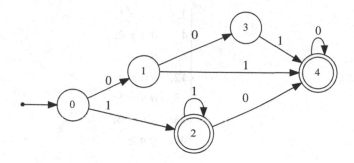

Figure 12.3 Orders of almost-squares in all paperfolding sequences, lsd first.

## 12.4 Palindromes

Let us determine the lengths of palindromes appearing in the paperfolding sequences. We can do this as follows:

```
def paperf_pal "?lsd_2 Ef,i,x $linkf(f,x) & n>=1 & i+n<x &
   At (t<n) => FOLD[f][i+t]=FOLD[f][(i+n)-(t+1)]":
```

The resulting automaton accepts only $\{1, 2, 3, 4, 5, 6, 7, 9, 11, 13\}$.

*Exercise* 164   Show that in fact every paperfolding sequence has palindromes of length $\{1, 2, 3, 4, 5, 6, 7, 9, 11, 13\}$ and no others. (It is possible to prove this with Walnut, or without it.)

## 12.5 Subword complexity

We can use Walnut to compute the subword complexity of the paperfolding sequences. This was done previously by Allouche [4]. It is, in fact, the same function for each such sequence:

**Theorem 12.5.1** *The subword complexity* $\rho_{\mathbf{P_t}}(n)$ *of a paperfolding sequence* *satisfies the following:*

$$\rho_{P_f}(n) = \begin{cases} 2, & \text{if } n = 1; \\ 4, & \text{if } n = 2; \\ 8, & \text{if } n = 3; \\ 12, & \text{if } n = 4; \\ 18, & \text{if } n = 5; \\ 23, & \text{if } n = 6; \\ 4n, & \text{if } n \geq 7. \end{cases}$$

*Proof* For $n \leq 7$ we can verify this by enumerating all the factors. From Example 10.8.14 we know that for an infinite word **x**, the difference $\rho_x(n + 1) - \rho_x(n)$ is the number of right-special factors of length $n$. Hence, we can handle the remaining cases by showing that the number of right-special factors of length $n$ is exactly 4 for all $n \geq 7$.

To do this, we create a formula asserting that the factor of length $n$ beginning at position $i$ is right-special and, furthermore, that this occurrence is novel (in the sense of Section 8.1.12). Here "right-special" has to be interpreted as applying to the finite prefix of the paperfolding sequence specified by the finite word **f**; a particular factor might be right-special for a long paperfolding sequence but not a short prefix of it.

We do this in Walnut as follows:

```
def pfrightspec "?lsd_2 i>=1 & Ej,x $linkf(f,x) & j>=1 &
   i+n<=x & j+n<=x & $pffactoreq(f,i,j,n) &
   FOLD[f][i+n] != FOLD[f][j+n]":

def pfnovel "?lsd_2 i>=1 & Ex $linkf(f,x) &
   Aj (i+n<=x & j+n<=x & j<i) => ~$pffactoreq(f,i,j,n)":

def pfnrs "?lsd_2 $pfrightspec(f,i,n) & $pfnovel(f,i,n)":
```

Once we have this, we assert that there are (i) at least four special factors of each length $n \geq 2$ and (ii) there are not more than four for $n \geq 7$.

```
def spec4 "?lsd_2 Af,n,x (n>=2 & $linkf(f,x) & 13*(n+1)<=x) =>
   Ei1,i2,i3,i4 1<=i1 & i1<i2 & i2<i3 & i3<i4 & $pfnrs(f,i1,n) &
   $pfnrs(f,i2,n) & $pfnrs(f,i3,n) & $pfnrs(f,i4,n)":

def spec5 "?lsd_2 ~Ef,n,i1,i2,i3,i4,i5 (n>=7) & 1<=i1 & i1<i2
   & i2<i3 & i3<i4 & i4<i5 & $pfnrs(f,i1,n) & $pfnrs(f,i2,n)
   & $pfnrs(f,i3,n) & $pfnrs(f,i4,n) & $pfnrs(f,i5,n)":
```

Both return TRUE, so the theorem about subword complexity is proved. Note that the condition $13(n + 1) \leq x$ in the first formula guarantees (by Theorem 12.2.2) that we have enough terms to guarantee that we do not misclassify a factor as not special, when it would be if we looked at a longer extension of the paperfolding sequence. □

## 12.6 Rampersad's conjecture

Narad Rampersad once conjectured that if **f** and **g** are two distinct infinite sequences of unfolding instructions, then the paperfolding sequences $\mathbf{P_f}$ and $\mathbf{P_g}$ have only finitely many common factors.

Since `Walnut` can only deal with finite prefixes of unfolding instructions, it seems difficult to express this precise statement in our logical language. Instead, we reformulate it in a stronger way that implies the desired result. The exact statement of this reformulation is admittedly based on experiments, but we can prove it rigorously with `Walnut`.

**Theorem 12.6.1** *For all finite sequences of paperfolding instructions f and g, if f differs from g in the k'th position, then* $\mathbf{P_f}$ *and* $\mathbf{P_g}$ *have no factors of length* $14 \cdot 2^k$ *in common.*

*Proof* Obviously we need an automaton that can compare two sequences of paperfolding instructions and determine where they differ. We can do this with a regular expression as follows:

```
reg compare {-1,0,1} {-1,0,1} lsd_2 "([1,1,0]|[-1,-1,0])*
    ([1,-1,1]|[-1,1,1])([1,1,0]|[1,-1,0]|[-1,1,0]|[-1,-1,0])*
    [0,0,0]*":
```

This automaton accepts the input $(f, g, y)$ if $y = 2^k$ and $k$ is the index of the first position where $f$ and $g$ differ.

Next we create formulas that assert that (i) no factor of the stated length appears in both paperfolding sequences, and (ii) if the bound is decreased by 1, then there is a factor in common.

```
def pfcomparefac "?lsd_2 At (t<n) => FOLD[f][i+t]=FOLD[g][j+t]":
    # checks if P(f)[i..i+n-1] = P(g)[j..j+n-1]
    # 580 states, 23596ms

eval ramp1 "?lsd_2 Af,g,x,y,i,j,n ($linkf(f,x) & $linkf(g,x) &
    $compare(f,g,y) & n=14*y & y>=1 & i>=1 & j>=1 & i+n<=x &
    j+n<=x) => ~$pfcomparefac(f,g,i,j,n)":
    # proves theorem

eval ramp2 "?lsd_2 Ax $power2(x) => (Ef,g,n,y,i,j $linkf(f,y) &
```

```
$linkf(g,y) & $compare(f,g,x) & n=14*x-1 & y>=1 &  i>=1 &
j>=1 & i+n<=y & j+n<=y & $pfcomparefac(f,g,i,j,n))":
# proves it's best possible for all k
```

Both return TRUE, so the proof is complete. □

Furthermore, we can determine those pairs of unfolding instructions that have the longest possible factors in common. The following command generates an automaton accepting the triples $f, g, x$ with $x = 2^k$ and a factor of length $14x - 1$ in common:

```
eval paperf_longest "?lsd_2 En,y,i,j $linkf(f,y) & $linkf(g,y) &
    $compare(f,g,x) & n=14*x-1 & i>=1 & j>=1 & i+n<=y & j+n<=y &
    $pfcomparefac(f,g,i,j,n)":
```

Recently, the author and G. Fici applied many of the same ideas in this chapter to prove theorems about uncountably many different Toeplitz sequences; see [149]. Can you find other applications of these ideas?

# 13

# A final word

In this book we have presented and studied the logical approach to automatic sequences, a powerful tool for doing combinatorics on words, using the Walnut system.

It is possible to go even further. For example, the system Pecan, developed by a team at the University of Illinois, permits computation with $\omega$-automata. This allows a more comprehensive logical theory where we can decide many properties of Sturmian words. For this exciting new development, see [289, 194].

We hope to add more to Walnut in the future. Five obvious capabilities that we plan to implement are as follows:

- being able to deal with bi-infinite sequences; that is, those with arbitrary integer indices, including negative numbers;
- more flexible handling of numeration systems based on other recurrences;
- the result of Cobham [91] that applying a uniform transducer to a $k$-automatic sequence results in another $k$-automatic sequence;
- an algorithm for determining the lim sup of a $k$-automatic relation [335]; and
- the results from Luke Schaeffer's thesis [334] on applying DFAOs to factors of an automatic sequence.

## 13.1 Limits to the approach

Nevertheless, there are some limits to what we can hope to do. For example, it does not seem possible to use this approach to study the abelian properties of arbitrary automatic sequences. In [334], Luke Schaeffer proved that the positions of abelian squares in the paperfolding sequence do not form an

327

automatic sequence, thus showing that there is not a first-order statement in $\langle \mathbb{N}, +, V_2 \rangle$ specifying these positions. To handle abelian squares in general, then, we would need a more powerful decidable logical system.

Other kinds of questions also do not seem susceptible to the methods described in this book. For example, Narayanan [281] studied, for each $k$, the smallest odd $n$ such that the length-$kn$ prefix of the Thue-Morse sequence $\mathbf{t}$ is a $k$-antipower. Although we can express this assertion as a first-order statement for each individual $k$, it does not seem possible to do so for all $k$ in one formula (because of the multiplication).

Along the same lines, Currie and Johnson [103] defined a word to be *level* if every letter occurs with the same frequency as every other letter, $\pm 1$. However, it does not seem possible to express the assertion that $\mathbf{x}[i..i + n - 1]$ is level in $\langle \mathbb{N}, +, V_k \rangle$, because it involves counting.

For some numeration systems $S$, we can even prove that there is no corresponding adder, and hence $S$ is not a regular numeration system (in our notion specified in Section 6.4). For example, consider the greedy numeration system associated with the sequence $1, 3, 7, 15, \ldots$, that is, $(2^n - 1)_{n \geq 1}$. The digits are $\{0, 1, 2\}$ and the rule is that a 2 must be followed by all 0s. If this system were regular, then those $n$ having a 2 in their representation would form an automatic set. However, the set of such $n$ corresponds to the 1s in the fixed point of $0 \to 001, 1 \to 1$, which we proved in Section 10.8.9 to be not automatic.

As another example of a result we do not seem to be able to prove using the logical approach, consider the classic theorem of Mignosi et al. [265] about the Fibonacci word $\mathbf{f}$:

**Theorem 13.1.1**  *For all $\epsilon > 0$ there exists an integer $m$ such that for all $n \geq m$, the prefix $\mathbf{f}[0..n - 1]$ has a suffix that is a $(\varphi^2 - \epsilon)$-power.*

Even in the following more explicit version, it does not seem possible to prove this using our method:

**Theorem 13.1.2**  *For all $n \geq F_{2i-1} - F_i$ the prefix $\mathbf{f}[0..n - 1]$ has a suffix of exponent $\geq (F_{i+1} - 1)/F_{i-1}$.*

Here the issue seems to be that it is not possible to express both $F_{2i}$ and $F_i$ simultaneously.

As another example of something I do not know how to phrase in our first-order language, consider the following result of Currie and Visentin [106]: for all $n \geq 1$ the Fibonacci word $\mathbf{f}$ has a prefix of length $F_{4n-1} - 1$ that is an abelian $L_{2n-1}$ power.

Similarly, there does not seem to be a way to express the assertion that a sequence contains abelian powers of unbounded exponent. This is in contrast to the case of ordinary powers, as discussed in Section 8.5.15.

We encourage readers to try to develop decision methods for some of these difficult properties.

# References

[1]  M. H. Albert and S. Linton. A practical algorithm for reducing non-deterministic finite state automata. Technical Report OUCS-2004-11, University of Otago, 2004.

[2]  G. Allouche, J.-P. Allouche, and J. Shallit. Kolams indiens, dessins sur le sable aux îles Vanuatu, courbe de Sierpiński, et morphismes de monoïde. *Ann. Inst. Fourier (Grenoble)* **56** (2006), 2115–2130.

[3]  J.-P. Allouche. Automates finis en théorie des nombres. *Exposition. Math.* **5** (1987), 239–266.

[4]  J.-P. Allouche. The number of factors in a paperfolding sequence. *Bull. Austral. Math. Soc.* **46** (1992), 23–32.

[5]  J.-P. Allouche, D. Astoorian, J. Randall, and J. Shallit. Morphisms, squarefree strings, and the Tower of Hanoi puzzle. *Amer. Math. Monthly* **101** (1994), 651–658.

[6]  J.-P. Allouche, M. Baake, J. Cassaigne, and D. Damanik. Palindrome complexity. *Theoret. Comput. Sci.* **292** (2003), 9–31.

[7]  J.-P. Allouche, J. Bétréma, and J. Shallit. Sur des points fixes de morphismes du monoïde libre. *RAIRO Inform. Théor. App.* **23** (1989), 235–249.

[8]  J.-P. Allouche and M. Bousquet-Mélou. Canonical positions for the factors in the paperfolding sequences. *Theoret. Comput. Sci.* **129** (1994), 263–278.

[9]  J.-P. Allouche and M. Bousquet-Mélou. Facteurs des suites de Rudin-Shapiro généralisées. *Bull. Belgian Math. Soc.* **1** (1994), 145–164.

[10]  J.-P. Allouche, J. Currie, and J. Shallit. Extremal infinite overlap-free binary words. *Electron. J. Combin.* **5** (1998), R27.

[11]  J.-P. Allouche, N. Rampersad, and J. Shallit. On integer sequences whose first iterates are linear. *Aequationes Math.* **69** (2005), 114–127.

[12]  J.-P. Allouche, N. Rampersad, and J. Shallit. Periodicity, repetitions, and orbits of an automatic sequence. *Theoret. Comput. Sci.* **410** (2009), 2795–2803.

[13]  J.-P. Allouche and A. Sapir. Restricted Towers of Hanoi and morphisms. In C. De Felice and A. Restivo, editors, *DLT 2005*, Vol. 3572 of *Lecture Notes in Computer Science*, pp. 1–10. Springer-Verlag, 2005.

[14]  J.-P. Allouche and J. O. Shallit. The ring of *k*-regular sequences. *Theoret. Comput. Sci.* **98** (1992), 163–197.

[15] J.-P. Allouche and J. Shallit. The ubiquitous Prouhet-Thue-Morse sequence. In C. Ding, T. Helleseth, and H. Niederreiter, editors, *Sequences and Their Applications, Proceedings of SETA '98*, pp. 1–16. Springer-Verlag, 1999.

[16] J.-P. Allouche and J. Shallit. *Automatic Sequences: Theory, Applications, Generalizations*. Cambridge University Press, 2003.

[17] J.-P. Allouche and J. O. Shallit. The ring of $k$-regular sequences, II. *Theoret. Comput. Sci.* **307** (2003), 3–29.

[18] J.-P. Allouche, J. Shallit, and R. Yassawi. How to prove that a sequence is not automatic. Arxiv preprint arXiv:2104.13072 [math.NT], available at `arxiv.org/abs/2104.13072`, 2021.

[19] A. Apostolico and V. E. Brimkov. Fibonacci arrays and their two-dimensional repetitions. *Theoret. Comput. Sci.* **237** (2000), 263–273.

[20] F. Ardila. The coefficients of a Fibonacci power series. *Fibonacci Quart.* **42** (2004), 202–204.

[21] P. Arnoux and G. Rauzy. Représentation géométrique de suites de complexité $2n + 1$. *Bull. Soc. Math. France* **119** (1991), 199–215.

[22] Y. H. Au, C. Drexler-Lemire, and J. Shallit. Notes and note pairs in Nørgård's infinity series. *J. Math. Music* **11** (2017), 1–19.

[23] S. Avgustinovich, J. Karhumäki, and S. Puzynina. On abelian versions of critical factorization theorem. *RAIRO Inform. Théor. App.* **46** (2012), 3–15.

[24] G. Badkobeh, G. Fici, and Z. Lipták. On the number of closed factors in a word. In A.-H. Dediu, E. Formenti, C. Martín-Vide, and B. Truthe, editors, *Language and Automata Theory and Applications, LATA 2015*, Vol. 8977 of *Lecture Notes in Computer Science*, pp. 381–390. Springer-Verlag, 2015.

[25] G. Badkobeh and P. Ochem. Avoiding conjugacy classes on the 5-letter alphabet. *RAIRO Inform. Théor. App.* **54** (2020), Paper 2.

[26] P. Balister and S. Gerke. The asymptotic number of prefix normal words. *Theoret. Comput. Sci.* **784** (2019), 75–80.

[27] A. R. Baranwal. Decision algorithms for Ostrowski-automatic sequences. Master's thesis, University of Waterloo, School of Computer Science, 2020.

[28] A. R. Baranwal, L. Schaeffer, and J. Shallit. Ostrowski-automatic sequences: theory and applications. *Theoret. Comput. Sci.* **858** (2021), 122–142.

[29] A. R. Baranwal and J. Shallit. Critical exponent of infinite balanced words via the Pell number system. In R. Mercaş and D. Reidenbach, editors, *WORDS 2019*, Vol. 11682 of *Lecture Notes in Computer Science*, pp. 80–92. Springer-Verlag, 2019.

[30] P. T. Bateman, C. G. Jockusch, and A. R. Woods. Decidability and undecidability of theories with a predicate for the primes. *J. Symbolic Logic* **58** (1993), 672–687.

[31] L. E. Baum and M. M. Sweet. Continued fractions of algebraic power series in characteristic 2. *Ann. Math.* **103** (1976), 593–610.

[32] S. Beatty. Problem 3173. *Amer. Math. Monthly* **33** (1926), 159. Solution, **34** (1927), 159–160.

[33] J. Bell, É. Charlier, A. Fraenkel, and M. Rigo. A decision problem for ultimately periodic sets in non-standard numeration systems. *Internat. J. Algebra Comput.* **19** (2009), 809–839.

[34] J. P. Bell, M. Coons, and K. G. Hare. The minimal growth of a $k$-regular sequence. *Bull. Austral. Math. Soc.* **90** (2014), 195–203.

[35] J. Bell, K. Hare, and J. Shallit. When is an automatic set an additive basis? *Proc. Amer. Math. Soc. Ser. B* **5** (2018), 50–63.

[36] J. Bell, T. F. Lidbetter, and J. Shallit. Additive number theory via approximation by regular languages. In M. Hoshi and S. Seki, editors, *DLT 2018*, Vol. 11088 of *Lecture Notes in Computer Science*, pp. 121–132. Springer-Verlag, 2018.

[37] J. Bell, T. F. Lidbetter, and J. Shallit. Additive number theory via approximation by regular languages. *Internat. J. Found. Comp. Sci.* **31** (2020), 667–687.

[38] J. P. Bell and B. W. Madill. Iterative algebras. *Algebr. Represent. Theory* **18** (2015), 1533–1546.

[39] J. P. Bell and J. Shallit. Lie complexity of words. Arxiv preprint arXiv:2102.03821 [cs.FL], available at arxiv.org/abs/2102.03821, 2021.

[40] J. Bellissard, A. Bovier, and J.-M. Ghez. Spectral properties of a tight binding Hamiltonian with period doubling potential. *Commun. Math. Phys.* **135** (1991), 379–399.

[41] E. R. Berlekamp, J. H. Conway, and R. K. Guy. *Winning Ways for Your Mathematical Plays*, Vol. 1. Academic Press, 1982.

[42] J. Berstel. Sur les mots sans carré définis par un morphisme. In H. A. Maurer, editor, *Proc. 6th Int'l Conf. on Automata, Languages, and Programming (ICALP)*, Vol. 71 of *Lecture Notes in Computer Science*, pp. 16–25. Springer-Verlag, 1979.

[43] J. Berstel. Mots de Fibonacci. *Séminaire d'Informatique Théorique, LITP* **6-7** (1980–81), 57–78.

[44] J. Berstel. Fibonacci words—a survey. In G. Rozenberg and A. Salomaa, editors, *The Book of L*, pp. 13–27. Springer-Verlag, 1986.

[45] J. Berstel. Axel Thue's work on repetitions in words. In P. Leroux and C. Reutenauer, editors, *Séries Formelles et Combinatoire Algébrique*, Vol. 11 of *Publications du LaCim*, pp. 65–80. Université du Québec à Montréal, 1992.

[46] J. Berstel, A. Lauve, C. Reutenauer, and F. V. Saliola. *Combinatorics on Words: Christoffel Words and Repetitions in Words*, Vol. 27 of *CRM Monograph Series*. Amer. Math. Soc., 2009.

[47] J. Berstel and C. Reutenauer. *Noncommutative Rational Series With Applications*, Vol. 137 of *Encyclopedia of Mathematics and Its Applications*. Cambridge University Press, 2011.

[48] A. Bès. A survey of arithmetical definability. *Bull. Belgian Math. Soc.* (2001), 1–54. Supplementary volume, M. Crabbé, F. Point, and C. Michaux, eds., *A Tribute to Maurice Boffa*.

[49] V. D. Blondel, J. Theys, and A. A. Vladimirov. An elementary counterexample to the finiteness conjecture. *SIAM J. Matrix Anal. Appl.* **24** (2003), 963–970.

[50] A. Blondin Massé, S. Brlek, A. Garon, and S. Labbé. Combinatorial properties of $f$-palindromes in the Thue-Morse sequence. *Pure Math. Appl.* **19**(2-3) (2008), 39–52.

[51] A. Blondin Massé, J. de Carufel, A. Goupil, M. Lapointe, E. Nadeau, and E. Vandomme. Leaf realization problem, caterpillar graphs and prefix normal words. *Theoret. Comput. Sci.* **732** (2018), 1–13.

[52] A. Borchert and N. Rampersad. Words with many palindrome pair factors. *Electron. J. Combin.* **22** (2015), #P4.23 (electronic). Available at tinyurl.com/2p87wsrz.

[53] S. Brlek. Enumeration of factors in the Thue-Morse word. *Disc. Appl. Math.* **24** (1989), 83–96.

[54] S. Brown, N. Rampersad, J. Shallit, and T. Vasiga. Squares and overlaps in the Thue-Morse sequence and some variants. *RAIRO Inform. Théor. App.* **40** (2006), 473–484.

[55] V. Bruyère and G. Hansel. Bertrand numeration systems and recognizability. *Theoret. Comput. Sci.* **181** (1997), 17–43.

[56] V. Bruyère, G. Hansel, C. Michaux, and R. Villemaire. Logic and $p$-recognizable sets of integers. *Bull. Belgian Math. Soc.* **1** (1994), 191–238. Corrigendum, *Bull. Belg. Math. Soc.* **1** (1994), 577.

[57] M. Bucci, A. de Luca, and A. De Luca. Rich and periodic-like words. In V. Diekert and D. Nowotka, editors, *Developments in Language Theory, DLT 2009*, Vol. 5583 of *Lecture Notes in Computer Science*, pp. 145–155. Springer-Verlag, 2009.

[58] M. Bucci, A. De Luca, and G. Fici. Enumeration and structure of trapezoidal words. *Theoret. Comput. Sci.* **468** (2013), 12–22.

[59] M. Bucci, A. De Luca, A. Glen, and L. Q. Zamboni. A new characteristic property of rich words. *Theoret. Comput. Sci.* **410** (2009), 2860–2863.

[60] M. Bucci, A. De Luca, and L. Q. Zamboni. Reversible Christoffel factorizations. *Theoret. Comput. Sci.* **495** (2013), 17–24.

[61] J. R. Büchi. Weak secord-order arithmetic and finite automata. *Z. Math. Logik Grundlagen Math.* **6** (1960), 66–92. Reprinted in S. Mac Lane and D. Siefkes, eds., *The Collected Works of J. Richard Büchi*, Springer-Verlag, 1990, pp. 398–424.

[62] J. R. Büchi. On a decision method in restricted second order arithmetic. In *Logic, Methodology and Philosophy of Science (Proc. 1960 Internat. Congr.)*, pp. 1–11. Stanford University Press, 1962.

[63] Y. Bugeaud and D. H. Kim. A new complexity function, repetitions in Sturmian words, and irrationality exponents of Sturmian numbers. *Trans. Amer. Math. Soc.* **371** (2019), 3281–3308.

[64] Y. Bugeaud, D. Krieger, and J. Shallit. Morphic and automatic words: maximal blocks and diophantine approximation. *Acta Arith.* **149** (2011), 181–199.

[65] P. Burcsi, G. Fici, Z. Lipták, F. Ruskey, and J. Sawada. On prefix normal words and prefix normal forms. *Theoret. Comput. Sci.* **659** (2017), 1–13.

[66] L. Carlitz. Fibonacci representations. *Fibonacci Quart.* **6** (1968), 193–220.

[67] L. Carlitz, R. Scoville, and V. E. Hoggatt, Jr. Fibonacci representations. *Fibonacci Quart.* **10** (1972), 1–28. Addendum, **10** (1972), 527–530.

[68] L. Carlitz, R. Scoville, and V. E. Hoggatt, Jr. Fibonacci representations of higher order. *Fibonacci Quart.* **10** (1972), 43–69,94.

[69] A. Carpi and V. D'Alonzo. On the repetitivity index of infinite words. *Internat. J. Algebra Comput.* **19** (2009), 145–158.

[70] A. Carpi and C. Maggi. On synchronized sequences and their separators. *RAIRO Inform. Théor. App.* **35** (2001), 513–524.

[71] J. Cassaigne. Special factors of sequences with linear subword complexity. In J. Dassow, G. Rozenberg, and A. Salomaa, editors, *Developments in Language Theory II*, pp. 25–34. World Scientific, 1996.

[72] J. Cassaigne. Sequences with grouped factors. In *Developments in Language Theory III*, pp. 211–222. Aristotle University of Thessaloniki, 1998.

[73] A. Černý. Lyndon factorization of generalized words of Thue. *Discrete Math. & Theoret. Comput. Sci.* **5** (2002), 17–46.

[74] É. Charlier. First-order logic and numeration systems. In V. Berthé and M. Rigo, editors, *Sequences, Groups, and Number Theory*, pp. 89–141. Birkhäuser, 2018.

[75] É. Charlier, A. Massuir, M. Rigo, and E. Rowland. Ultimate periodicity problem for linear numeration systems. Arxiv preprint arXiv:2007.08147 [cs.DM], available at arxiv.org/abs/2007.08147, 2020.

[76] É. Charlier, N. Rampersad, M. Rigo, and L. Waxweiler. The minimal automaton recognizing $m\mathbb{N}$ in a linear numeration system. *INTEGERS—Elect. J. Comb. Numb. Theory* **11B** (2011), #A4 (electronic).

[77] É. Charlier, N. Rampersad, and J. Shallit. Enumeration and decidable properties of automatic sequences. In G. Mauri and A. Leporati, editors, *Developments in Language Theory, 15th International Conference, DLT 2011*, Vol. 6795 of *Lecture Notes in Computer Science*, pp. 165–179. Springer-Verlag, 2011.

[78] É. Charlier, N. Rampersad, and J. Shallit. Enumeration and decidable properties of automatic sequences. *Internat. J. Found. Comp. Sci.* **23** (2012), 1035–1066.

[79] Z. Chase. A new upper bound for separating words. Arxiv preprint arXiv:2007.12097 [math.CO], available at arxiv.org/abs/2007.12097, 2020.

[80] Z. Chase. Separating words and trace reconstruction. In *STOC 2021*, pp. 21–31. ACM, 2021.

[81] N. Chekhova, P. Hubert, and A. Messaoudi. Propriétés combinatoires, ergodiques et arithmétiques de la substitution de Tribonacci. *J. Théorie Nombres Bordeaux* **13** (2001), 371–394.

[82] Y.-G. Chen and B. Wang. On additive properties of two special sequences. *Acta Arith.* **110** (2003), 299–303.

[83] J. Chen and Z.-X. Wen. On the abelian complexity of generalized Thue-Morse sequences. *Theoret. Comput. Sci.* **780** (2019), 66–73.

[84] C. Choffrut, A. Malcher, C. Mereghetti, and B. Palano. First-order logics: some characterizations and closure properties. *Acta Inform.* **49** (2012), 225–248.

[85] S. Chow and T. Slattery. On Fibonacci partitions. *J. Number Theory* **225** (2021), 310–326.

[86] M. Christodoulakis and M. Christou. Abelian concepts in strings: a review. In J. Holub, B. W. Watson, and J. Žd'árek, editors, *Festschrift for Bořivoj Melichar*, pp. 19–45. Czech Technical University, 2012.

[87] M. Christou, M. Crochemore, and C. S. Iliopoulos. Quasiperiodicities in Fibonacci strings. *Ars Combin.* **129** (2016), 211–225.

[88] W.-F. Chuan. Symmetric Fibonacci words. *Fibonacci Quart.* **31** (1993), 251–255.

[89] A. Church. An unsolvable problem of elementary number theory. *Amer. J. Math.* **58** (1936), 345–363.

[90] F. Cicalese, Z. Lipták, and M. Rossi. On infinite prefix normal words. *Theoret. Comput. Sci.* **859** (2021), 134–148.

[91] A. Cobham. Uniform tag sequences. *Math. Systems Theory* **6** (1972), 164–192.

[92] A. Condon. The complexity of the max word problem and the power of one-way interactive proof systems. *Comput. Complexity* **3** (1993), 292–305.

[93] M. Coons. Regular sequences and the joint spectral radius. *Internat. J. Found. Comp. Sci.* **28** (2017), 135–140.

[94] M. Coons and L. Spiegelhofer. Number theoretic aspects of regular sequences. In V. Berthé and M. Rigo, editors, *Sequences, Groups, and Number Theory*, Trends in Mathematics, pp. 37–87. Springer-Verlag, 2018.

[95] E. M. Coven and G. A. Hedlund. Sequences with minimal block growth. *Math. Systems Theory* **7** (1973), 138–153.

[96] M. Crochemore. An optimal algorithm for computing the repetitions in a word. *Inform. Process. Lett.* **12** (1981), 244–250.

[97] M. Crochemore, F. Mignosi, and A. Restivo. Automata and forbidden words. *Inform. Process. Lett.* **67** (1998), 111–117.

[98] L. J. Cummings, D. Moore, and J. Karhumäki. Borders of Fibonacci strings. *J. Combin. Math. Combin. Comput.* **20** (1996), 81–87.

[99] L. J. Cummings and W. F. Smyth. Weak repetitions in strings. *J. Combin. Math. Combin. Comput.* **24** (1997), 33–48.

[100] R. Cummings, J. Shallit, and P. Staadecker. Mesosome avoidance. Arxiv preprint arXiv:2107.13813 [cs.DM], available at arxiv.org/abs/2107.13813, 2021.

[101] J. Currie. Lexicographically least words in the orbit closure of the Rudin-Shapiro word. *Theoret. Comput. Sci.* **41** (2011), 4742–4746.

[102] J. Currie, T. Harju, P. Ochem, and N. Rampersad. Some further results on square-free arithmetic progressions in infinite words. *Theoret. Comput. Sci.* **799** (2019), 140–148.

[103] J. D. Currie and J. T. Johnson. There are level ternary circular square-free words of length $n$ for $n \neq 5, 7, 9, 10, 14, 17$. Arxiv preprint arXiv:2005.06235 [math.CO], available at arxiv.org/abs/2005.06235, 2020.

[104] J. Currie, N. Rampersad, and J. Shallit. Binary words containing infinitely many overlaps. *Electron. J. Combin.* **13** (2006), #R82 (electronic).

[105] J. D. Currie and K. Saari. Least periods of factors of infinite words. *RAIRO Inform. Théor. App.* **43** (2009), 165–178.

[106] J. Currie and T. Visentin. On abelian 2-avoidable binary patterns. *Acta Inform.* **43** (2007), 521–533.

[107] F. D'Alessandro. A combinatorial problem on trapezoidal words. *Theoret. Comput. Sci.* **273** (2002), 11–33.

[108] D. Damanik. Local symmetries in the period-doubling sequence. *Disc. Appl. Math.* **100** (2000), 115–121.

[109] D. Damanik and D. Lenz. Substitution dynamical systems: Characterization of linear repetitivity and applications. *J. Math. Anal. Appl.* **321** (2006), 766–780.

[110] S. Davies. State complexity of reversals of deterministic finite automata with output. In C. Câmpeanu, editor, *CIAA 2018*, Vol. 10977 of *Lecture Notes in Computer Science*, pp. 133–145. Springer-Verlag, 2018.

[111] M. Davis. A computer program for Presburger's algorithm. In *Summaries of Talks Presented at the Summer Institute for Symbolic Logic*, pp. 215–233. Institute for Defense Analysis, Princeton, NJ, 1957. Reprinted in J. Siemann and G. Wrightson, eds., *Automation of Reasoning—Classical Papers on Computational Logic 1957–1966*, Vol. 1, Springer, 1983, pp. 41–48.

[112] C. Davis and D. E. Knuth. Number representations and dragon curves–I, II. *J. Recreational Math.* **3** (1970), 66–81, 133–149.

[113] R. A. Dean. A sequence without repeats on $x, x^{-1}, y, y^{-1}$. *Amer. Math. Monthly* **72** (1965), 383–385.

[114] N. G. de Bruijn. On bases for the set of integers. *Publ. Math. (Debrecen)* **1** (1950), 232–242.

[115] N. G. de Bruijn. Some direct decompositions of the set of integers. *Math. Comp.* **18** (1964), 537–546.

[116] C. Defant. Anti-power prefixes of the Thue-Morse word. *Electron. J. Combin.* **24**(1) (2017), #P1.32 (electronic). Available at tinyurl.com/mvv2zxpv.

[117] F. Dejean. Sur un théorème de Thue. *J. Combin. Theory. Ser. A* **13** (1972), 90–99.

[118] F. M. Dekking. The Frobenius problem for homomorphic embeddings of languages into the integers. *Theoret. Comput. Sci.* **732** (2018), 73–79.

[119] F. M. Dekking, M. Mendès France, and A. J. van der Poorten. Folds! *Math. Intelligencer* **4** (1982), 130–138, 173–181, 190–195. Erratum, **5** (1983), 5.

[120] F. M. Dekking, J. Shallit, and N. J. A. Sloane. Queens in exile: non-attacking queens on infinite chess boards. *Electron. J. Combin.* **27** (2020), #P1.52 (electronic).

[121] E. D. Demaine, S. Eisenstat, J. Shallit, and D. A. Wilson. Remarks on separating words. In M. Holzer, M. Kutrib, and G. Pighizzini, editors, *Descriptional Complexity of Formal Systems, 13th International Workshop, DCFS 2011*, Vol. 6808 of *Lecture Notes in Computer Science*, pp. 147–157. Springer-Verlag, 2011.

[122] G. Dombi. Additive properties of certain sets. *Acta Arith.* **103** (2002), 137–146.

[123] X. Droubay. Palindromes in the Fibonacci word. *Inform. Process. Lett.* **55** (1995), 217–221.

[124] X. Droubay, J. Justin, and G. Pirillo. Episturmian words and some constructions of de Luca and Rauzy. *Theoret. Comput. Sci.* **255** (2001), 539–553.

[125] E. Duchêne and M. Rigo. A morphic approach to combinatorial games: the Tribonacci case. *RAIRO Inform. Théor. App.* **42** (2008), 375–393.

[126] C. F. Du, H. Mousavi, E. Rowland, L. Schaeffer, and J. Shallit. Decision algorithms for Fibonacci-automatic words, II: Related sequences and avoidability. *Theoret. Comput. Sci.* **657** (2017), 146–162.

[127] C. F. Du, H. Mousavi, L. Schaeffer, and J. Shallit. Decision algorithms for Fibonacci-automatic words III: Enumeration and abelian properties. *Internat. J. Found. Comp. Sci.* **27** (2016), 943–963.

[128] A. Durand-Gasselin and P. Habermehl. On the use of non-deterministic automata for Presburger arithmetic. In P. Gastin and F. Laroussinie, editors, *CONCUR 2010*, Vol. 6269 of *Lecture Notes in Computer Science*, pp. 373–387. Springer-Verlag, 2010.

[129] F. Durand. A characterization of substitutive sequences using return words. *Discrete Math.* **179** (1998), 89–101.

[130] F. Durand. Decidability of uniform recurrence of morphic sequences. *Internat. J. Found. Comp. Sci.* **24** (2013), 123–146.

[131] F. Durand. Decidability of the HD0L ultimate periodicity problem. *RAIRO Inform. Théor. App.* **47** (2013), 201–214.

[132] J. P. Duval. Factorizing words over an ordered alphabet. *J. Algorithms* **4** (1983), 363–381.

[133] S. Eilenberg. *Automata, Languages, and Machines*, Vol. A. Academic Press, 1974.

[134] C. C. Elgot. Decision problems of finite automata design and related arithmetics. *Trans. Amer. Math. Soc.* **98** (1961), 21–51.

[135] J. Endrullis, C. Grabmayer, D. Hendriks, and H. Zantema. The degree of squares is an atom. In F. Manea and D. Nowotka, editors, *Proc. WORDS 2015*, Vol. 9304 of *Lecture Notes in Computer Science*, pp. 109–121. Springer-Verlag, 2015.

[136] J. Endrullis, D. Hendriks, and J. W. Klop. Degrees of streams. *INTEGERS— Elect. J. Comb. Numb. Theory* **11B** (2011), A6 (electronic).

[137] J. Endrullis, D. Hendriks, and J. W. Klop. Streams are forever. *Bull. European Assoc. Theor. Comput. Sci.*, No. 109, (2013), 70–106.

[138] J. Endrullis, J. W. Klop, A. Saarela, and M. Whiteland. Degrees of transducibility. In F. Manea and D. Nowotka, editors, *Proc. WORDS 2015*, Vol. 9304 of *Lecture Notes in Computer Science*, pp. 1–13. Springer-Verlag, 2015.

[139] P. Erdős. Some unsolved problems. *Magyar Tud. Akad. Mat. Kutató Int. Közl.* **6** (1961), 221–254.

[140] M. Euwe. Mengentheoretische Betrachtungen über das Schachspiel. *Proc. Konin. Akad. Wetenschappen, Amsterdam* **32** (1929), 633–642.

[141] G. Everest, A. van der Poorten, I. Shparlinski, and T. Ward. *Recurrence Sequences*, Vol. 104 of *Mathematical Surveys and Monographs*. Amer. Math. Soc., 2003.

[142] I. Fagnot. Sur les facteurs des mots automatiques. *Theoret. Comput. Sci.* **172** (1997), 67–89.

[143] J. Ferrante and C. W. Rackoff. A decision procedure for the first order theory of real addition with order. *SIAM J. Comput.* **4** (1975), 69–76.

[144] J. Ferrante and C. W. Rackoff. *The Computational Complexity of Logical Theories*, Vol. 718 of *Lecture Notes in Mathematics*. Springer-Verlag, 1979.

[145] G. Fici, A. Langiu, T. Lecroq, A. Lefebvre, F. Mignosi, J. Peltomäki, and É. Prieur-Gaston. Abelian powers and repetitions in Sturmian words. *Theoret. Comput. Sci.* **635** (2016), 16–34.

[146] G. Fici, M. Postic, and M. Silva. Abelian antipowers in infinite words. *Adv. in Appl. Math.* **108** (2019), 67–78.

[147] G. Fici, A. Restivo, M. Silva, and L. Q. Zamboni. Anti-powers in infinite words. Arxiv preprint arXiv:1606.02868 [cs.DM], available at `arxiv.org/abs/1606.02868`, 2016.

[148] G. Fici, A. Restivo, M. Silva, and L. Q. Zamboni. Anti-powers in infinite words. *J. Combin. Theory. Ser. A* **157** (2018), 109–119.

[149] G. Fici and J. Shallit. Properties of a class of Toeplitz words. Arxiv preprint arXiv:2112.12125 [cs.FL], available at `arxiv.org/abs/2112.12125`, 2021.

[150] G. Fici and L. Q. Zamboni. On the least number of palindromes contained in an infinite word. *Theoret. Comput. Sci.* **481** (2013), 1–8.

338                                    *References*

[151]  M. J. Fischer and M. O. Rabin. Super-exponential complexity of Presburger arithmetic. In R. M. Karp, editor, *Complexity of Computation*, Vol. 7 of *SIAM-AMS Proceedings*, pp. 27–42. Amer. Math. Soc., 1974.

[152]  L. Fleischer and J. Shallit. Words avoiding reversed factors, revisited. Arxiv preprint arXiv:1911.11704 [cs.FL], available at arxiv.org/abs/1911.11704, 2019.

[153]  L. Fleischer and J. Shallit. Automata, palindromes, and reversed subwords. *J. Automata, Languages, and Combinatorics* **26** (2021), 221–253.

[154]  M. Forsyth, A. Jayakumar, J. Peltomäki, and J. Shallit. Remarks on privileged words. *Internat. J. Found. Comp. Sci.* **27** (2016), 431–442.

[155]  A. S. Fraenkel. Systems of numeration. *Amer. Math. Monthly* **92** (1985), 105–114.

[156]  A. S. Fraenkel and J. Simpson. The exact number of squares in Fibonacci words. *Theoret. Comput. Sci.* **218** (1999), 95–106. Corrigendum, **547** (2014), 122.

[157]  C. Frougny. Representations of numbers and finite automata. *Math. Systems Theory* **25** (1992), 37–60.

[158]  C. Frougny and B. Solomyak. On representation of integers in linear numeration systems. In M. Pollicott and K. Schmidt, editors, *Ergodic Theory of $\mathbb{Z}^d$ Actions (Warwick, 1993–1994)*, Vol. 228 of *London Mathematical Society Lecture Note Series*, pp. 345–368. Cambridge University Press, 1996.

[159]  D. Gabric, J. Shallit, and X. F. Zhong. Avoidance of split overlaps. *Discrete Math.* **344** (2021), 112176.

[160]  G. Gamard, P. Ochem, G. Richomme, and P. Séébold. Avoidability of circular formulas. *Theoret. Comput. Sci.* **726** (2018), 1–4.

[161]  E. Garel. Séparateurs dans les mots infinis engendrés par morphismes. *Theoret. Comput. Sci.* **180** (1997), 81–113.

[162]  P. Gawrychowski, D. Krieger, N. Rampersad, and J. Shallit. Finding the growth rate of a regular or context-free language in polynomial time. *Internat. J. Found. Comp. Sci.* **21** (2010), 597–618.

[163]  J. Geldenhuys, B. van der Merwe, and L. van Zijl. Reducing nondeterministic finite automata with SAT solvers. In A. Yli-Jyrä, A. Kornai, J. Sakarovitch, and B. Watson, editors, *FSMNLP: International Workshop on Finite-State Methods and Natural Language Processing, 8th International Workshop*, Vol. 6062 of *Lecture Notes in Artificial Intelligence*, pp. 81–92. Springer-Verlag, 2010.

[164]  E. Gilbert. Gray codes and paths on the *n*-cube. *Bell System Tech. J.* **37** (1958), 815–826.

[165]  A. Glen. Powers in a class of *a*-strict episturmian words. *Theoret. Comput. Sci.* **380** (2007), 330–354.

[166]  A. Glen, J. Justin, S. Widmer, and L. Q. Zamboni. Palindromic richness. *European J. Combin.* **30** (2009), 510–531.

[167]  A. Glen, F. Levé, and G. Richomme. Quasiperiodic and Lyndon episturmian words. *Theoret. Comput. Sci.* **409** (2008), 578–600.

[168]  D. Goč, D. Henshall, and J. Shallit. Automatic theorem-proving in combinatorics on words. In N. Moreira and R. Reis, editors, *Implementation and Application of Automata—17th International Conference, CIAA 2012*, Vol. 7381 of *Lecture Notes in Computer Science*, pp. 180–191. Springer-Verlag, 2012.

[169] D. Goč, D. Henshall, and J. Shallit. Automatic theorem-proving in combinatorics on words. *Internat. J. Found. Comp. Sci.* **24** (2013), 781–798.

[170] D. Goč, H. Mousavi, L. Schaeffer, and J. Shallit. A new approach to the paperfolding sequences. In A. Beckmann et al., editors, *Computability in Europe, CIE 2015*, Vol. 9136 of *Lecture Notes in Computer Science*, pp. 34–43. Springer-Verlag, 2015.

[171] D. Goč, H. Mousavi, and J. Shallit. On the number of unbordered factors. In A. H. Dediu, C. Martín-Vide, and B. Truthe, editors, *Languages and Automata Theory and Applications—7th International Conference, LATA 2013*, Vol. 7810 of *Lecture Notes in Computer Science*, pp. 299–310. Springer-Verlag, 2013.

[172] D. Goč, N. Rampersad, M. Rigo, and P. Salimov. On the number of abelian bordered words (with an example of automatic theorem-proving). *Internat. J. Found. Comp. Sci.* **25** (2014), 1097–1110.

[173] D. Goč, K. Saari, and J. Shallit. Primitive words and Lyndon words in automatic and linearly recurrent sequences. In A. H. Dediu, C. Martín-Vide, and B. Truthe, editors, *Languages and Automata Theory and Applications—7th International Conference, LATA 2013*, Vol. 7810 of *Lecture Notes in Computer Science*, pp. 311–322. Springer-Verlag, 2013.

[174] D. Goč, L. Schaeffer, and J. Shallit. Subword complexity and $k$-synchronization. In M.-P. Béal and O. Carton, editors, *DLT 2013*, Vol. 7907 of *Lecture Notes in Computer Science*, pp. 252–263. Springer-Verlag, 2013.

[175] D. Goč and J. Shallit. Least periods of $k$-automatic sequences. Arxiv preprint arXiv:1207.5450 [cs.FL], available at `arxiv.org/abs/1207.5450`, 2012.

[176] M. J. E. Golay. Multi-slit spectrometry. *J. Optical Soc. Amer.* **39** (1949), 437–444.

[177] M. J. E. Golay. Static multislit spectrometry and its application to the panoramic display of infrared spectra. *J. Optical Soc. Amer.* **41** (1951), 468–472.

[178] P. Goralčík and V. Koubek. On discerning words by automata. In L. Kott, editor, *Proc. 13th Int'l Conf. on Automata, Languages, and Programming (ICALP)*, Vol. 226 of *Lecture Notes in Computer Science*, pp. 116–122. Springer-Verlag, 1986.

[179] R. L. Graham. Covering the positive integers by disjoint sets of the form $\{[n\alpha + \beta] : n = 1, 2, \ldots\}$. *J. Combin. Theory. Ser. A* **15** (1973), 354–358.

[180] D. Gries. Describing an algorithm by Hopcroft. *Acta Inform.* **2** (1973), 97–109.

[181] J. Guckenheimer. On the bifurcation of maps of the interval. *Inventiones Math.* **39** (1977), 165–178.

[182] F. Guépin, C. Haase, and J. Worrell. On the existential theories of Büchi arithmetic and linear $p$-adic fields. In *34th Annual ACM/IEEE Symposium on Logic in Computer Science (LICS)*, pp. 1–10. IEEE Computer Society, 2019.

[183] C. Haase. A survival guide to Presburger arithmetic. *ACM SIGLOG News* **5**(3) (2018), 67–82.

[184] C. Haase. Approaching arithmetic theories with finite-state automata. In A. Leporati et al., editors, *LATA 2020*, Vol. 12038 of *Lecture Notes in Computer Science*, pp. 33–43. Springer-Verlag, 2020.

[185] C. Haase and J. Różycki. On the expressiveness of Büchi arithmetic. In S. Kiefer and C. Tasson, editors, *Foundations of Software Science and Computation Structures, FOSSACS 2021*, Vol. 12650 of *Lecture Notes in Computer Science*, pp. 310–323. Springer-Verlag, 2021.

[186] T. C. Hales. Formal proof. *Notices Amer. Math. Soc.* **55**(11) (2008), 1370–1380.

[187] S. Haque and J. Shallit. Discriminators and $k$-regular sequences. *INTEGERS— Elect. J. Comb. Numb. Theory* **16** (2016), #A76 (electronic). Available at tinyurl.com/4277ph96.

[188] G. H. Hardy and E. M. Wright. *An Introduction to the Theory of Numbers.* Oxford University Press, 5th edition, 1985.

[189] T. Harju. Disposability in square-free words. *Theoret. Comput. Sci.* **862** (2021), 155–159.

[190] T. Harju. Avoiding square-free words on free groups. Arxiv preprint arXiv:2104.06837 [math.CO], available at arxiv.org/abs/2104.06837, 2021.

[191] T. Harju and T. Kärki. On the number of frames of binary words. *Theoret. Comput. Sci.* **412** (2011), 5276–5284.

[192] T. Harju and M. Linna. On the periodicity of morphisms on free monoids. *RAIRO Inform. Théor. App.* **20** (1986), 47–54.

[193] M. J. H. Heule and O. Kullmann. The science of brute force. *Comm. ACM* **60**(8) (2017), 70–79.

[194] P. Hieronymi, D. Ma, R. Oei Ma, L. Schaeffer, C. Schulz, and J. Shallit. Decidability for Sturmian words. Arxiv preprint arXiv:2102.08207 [cs.LO], available at arxiv.org/abs/2102.08207, 2021.

[195] P. Hieronymi and A. Terry, Jr. Ostrowski numeration systems, addition, and finite automata. *Notre Dame J. Formal Logic* **59** (2018), 215–232.

[196] D. Hilbert. Über die stetige Abbildung einer Linie auf ein Flächenstück. *Math. Annalen* **38** (1891), 459–460.

[197] A. M. Hinz, S. Klavžar, U. Milutinović, and C. Petr. *The Tower of Hanoi—Myths and Maths.* Birkhäuser, 2013.

[198] B. Hodgson. Décidabilité par automate fini. *Ann. Sci. Math. Québec* **7** (1983), 39–57.

[199] T. Høholdt, H. E. Jensen, and J. Justesen. Aperiodic correlations and the merit factor of a class of binary sequences. *IEEE Trans. Inform. Theory* **31** (1985), 549–552.

[200] J. Honkala. A decision method for the recognizability of sets defined by number systems. *RAIRO Inform. Théor. App.* **20** (1986), 395–403.

[201] J. Honkala. Quasi-universal $k$-regular sequences. *Theoret. Comput. Sci.* **891** (2021), 84–89.

[202] J. E. Hopcroft. An $n \log n$ algorithm for minimizing the states in a finite automaton. In Z. Kohavi, editor, *The Theory of Machines and Computation*, pp. 189–196. Academic Press, New York, 1971.

[203] J. E. Hopcroft and J. D. Ullman. *Introduction to Automata Theory, Languages, and Computation.* Addison-Wesley, 1979.

[204] Y.-k. Huang and Z.-y. Wen. The number of fractional powers in the Fibonacci word. Arxiv preprint arXiv:1811.11444 [math.DS], available at arxiv.org/abs/1811.11444, 2018.

[205] P. Hubert. Suites équilibrées. *Theoret. Comput. Sci.* **242** (2000), 91–108.

[206] T. I, S. Inenaga, H. Bannai, and M. Takeda. Counting and verifying maximal palindromes. In E. Chavez and S. Lonardi, editors, *String Processing and Information Retrieval – 17th International Symposium, SPIRE 2010*, Vol. 6393 of *Lecture Notes in Computer Science*, pp. 135–146. Springer-Verlag, 2010.

[207] A. Ido and G. Melançon. Lyndon factorization of the Thue-Morse word and its relatives. *Discrete Math. & Theoret. Comput. Sci.* 1 (1997), 43–52.

[208] L. Ilie and S. Yu. Reducing NFAs by invariant equivalences. *Theoret. Comput. Sci.* 306 (2003), 373–390.

[209] L. Ilie, G. Novarro, and S. Yu. On NFA reductions. In J. Karhumäki, H. Maurer, G. Păun, and G. Rozenberg, editors, *Theory is Forever*, Vol. 3113 of *Lecture Notes in Computer Science*, pp. 112–124. Springer-Verlag, 2004.

[210] C. S. Iliopoulos, D. Moore, and W. F. Smyth. A characterization of the squares in a Fibonacci string. *Theoret. Comput. Sci.* 172 (1997), 281–291.

[211] G. Jacob. Décidabilité de la finitude des demi-groupes de matrices. In *Theoretical Computer Science*, Vol. 48 of *Lecture Notes in Computer Science*, pp. 259–269. Springer-Verlag, 1977.

[212] G. Jacob. Un algorithme calculant le cardinal, fini ou infini, des demi-groupes de matrices. *Theoret. Comput. Sci.* 5 (1977/78), 183–204.

[213] G. Jacob. La finitude des représentations linéaires des semi-groupes est décidable. *J. Algebra* 52 (1978), 437–459.

[214] K. Jacobs. *Invitation to Mathematics*. Princeton University Press, 1992.

[215] T. Jiang and B. Ravikumar. NFA minimization problems are hard. *SIAM J. Comput.* 22 (1993), 1117–1141.

[216] I. Kaboré and B. Kientéga. Abelian complexity of Thue-Morse word over a ternary alphabet. In S. Brlek, F. Dolce, C. Reutenauer, and É. Vandomme, editors, *WORDS 2017*, Vol. 10432 of *Lecture Notes in Computer Science*, pp. 132–143. Springer-Verlag, 2017.

[217] J.-Y. Kao, N. Rampersad, J. Shallit, and M. Silva. Words avoiding repetitions in arithmetic progressions. *Theoret. Comput. Sci.* 391 (2008), 126–137.

[218] C. S. Kaplan and J. Shallit. A frameless 2-coloring of the plane lattice. *Math. Mag.* 94 (2021), 353–360.

[219] J. Karhumäki. On cube-free $\omega$-words generated by binary morphisms. *Disc. Appl. Math.* 5 (1983), 279–297.

[220] S. Kawsumarng, T. Khemaratchatakumthorn, P. Noppakaew, and P. Pongsriiam. Sumsets associated with Wythoff sequences and Fibonacci numbers. *Period. Math. Hung.* 82 (2021), 98–113.

[221] J. Kellendonk, D. Lenz, and J. Savinien. A characterization of subshifts with bounded powers. *Discrete Math.* 313 (2013), 2881–2894.

[222] D. Kempa and N. Prezza. At the roots of dictionary compression: string attractors. In *STOC'18 Proceedings*, pp. 827–840. ACM Press, 2018.

[223] F. Klaedtke. Bounds on the automata size for Presburger arithmetic. *ACM Trans. Comput. Logic* 9(2) (2008), Article 11.

[224] S. Klavžar and S. Shpectorov. Asymptotic number of isometric generalized Fibonacci cubes. *European J. Combin.* 33 (2012), 220–226.

[225] D. E. Knuth, J. Morris, and V. Pratt. Fast pattern matching in strings. *SIAM J. Comput.* 6 (1977), 323–350.

[226] T. Knuutila. Re-describing an algorithm by Hopcroft. *Theoret. Comput. Sci.* **250** (2001), 333–363.

[227] T. Kociumaka, G. Navarro, and N. Prezza. Towards a definitive measure of repetitiveness. In Y. Kohayakawa and F. K. Miyazawa, editors, *LATIN 2020*, Vol. 12118 of *Lecture Notes in Computer Science*, pp. 207–219. Springer-Verlag, 2020.

[228] B. Konev and A. Lisitsa. A SAT attack on the Erdős discrepancy problem. Arxiv preprint arXiv:1402.2184 [cs.DM], available at arxiv.org/abs/1402.2184, 2014.

[229] C. Krawchuk and N. Rampersad. Cyclic complexity of some infinite words and generalizations. *INTEGERS—Elect. J. Comb. Numb. Theory* **18A** (2018), #A12 (electronic). Available at tinyurl.com/mr2k2cbw.

[230] T. J. P. Krebs. A more reasonable proof of Cobham's theorem. *Internat. J. Found. Comp. Sci.* **32** (2021), 203–207.

[231] D. Krenn and J. Shallit. Decidability and *k*-regular sequences. *Theoret. Comput. Sci.* **907** (2022), 34–44.

[232] K. Kutsukake, T. Matsumoto, Y. Nakashima, S. Inenaga, H. Bannai, and M. Takeda. On repetitiveness measures of Thue-Morse words. In C. Boucher and S. V. Thankachan, editors, *SPIRE 2020*, Vol. 12303 of *Lecture Notes in Computer Science*, pp. 213–220. Springer-Verlag, 2020.

[233] J. Lambek and L. Moser. On some two way classifications of integers. *Canad. Math. Bull.* **2** (1959), 85–89.

[234] B. M. Landman and A. Robertson. *Ramsey Theory on the Integers*, Vol. 73 of *Student Mathematical Library*. Amer. Math. Soc., 2015.

[235] B. Lando. Periodicity and ultimate periodicity of D0L systems. *Theoret. Comput. Sci.* **82** (1991), 19–33.

[236] J. Leech. A problem on strings of beads. *Math. Gazette* **41** (1957), 277–278.

[237] S. Lehr. Sums and rational multiples of *q*–automatic sequences are *q*–automatic. *Theoret. Comput. Sci.* **108** (1993), 385–391.

[238] C. G. Lekkerkerker. Voorstelling van natuurlijke getallen door een som van getallen van Fibonacci. *Simon Stevin* **29** (1952), 190–195.

[239] J. Leroux. A polynomial time Presburger criterion and synthesis for number decision diagrams. In *20th IEEE Symposium on Logic in Computer Science (LICS 2005)*, pp. 147–156. IEEE Press, 2005.

[240] V. F. Lev. Reconstructing integer sets from their representation functions. *Electron. J. Combin.* **11**(1) (2004), #R78.

[241] F. Levé and G. Richomme. Quasiperiodic infinite words: some answers. *Bull. European Assoc. Theor. Comput. Sci.*, No. 84, (2004), 128–138.

[242] F. Levé and G. Richomme. Quasiperiodic Sturmian words and morphisms. *Theoret. Comput. Sci.* **372** (2007), 15–25.

[243] F. Levé and G. Richomme. On quasiperiodic morphisms. In J. Karhumäki, A. Lepistö, and L. Zamboni, editors, *Proc. WORDS 2013*, Vol. 8079 of *Lecture Notes in Computer Science*, pp. 181–192. Springer-Verlag, 2013.

[244] M. Linna. On periodic ω-sequences obtained by iterating morphisms. *Ann. Univ. Turku. Ser. A I* **186** (1984), 64–71.

[245] M. Lothaire. *Combinatorics on Words*, Vol. 17 of *Encyclopedia of Mathematics and Its Applications*. Addison-Wesley, 1983.

[246] M. Lothaire. *Algebraic Combinatorics on Words*, Vol. 90 of *Encyclopedia of Mathematics and Its Applications*. Cambridge University Press, 2002.

[247] A. de Luca. On the combinatorics of finite words. *Theoret. Comput. Sci.* **218** (1999), 13–39.

[248] A. de Luca, A. Glen, and L. Q. Zamboni. Rich, Sturmian, and trapezoidal words. *Theoret. Comput. Sci.* **407** (2008), 569–573.

[249] A. de Luca and L. Mione. On bispecial factors of the Thue-Morse word. *Inform. Process. Lett.* **49** (1994), 179–183.

[250] A. de Luca and S. Varricchio. Some combinatorial properties of the Thue-Morse sequence and a problem in semigroups. *Theoret. Comput. Sci.* **63** (1989), 333–348.

[251] S. Luchinin and S. Puzynina. Symmetry groups of infinite words. In N. Moreira and R. Reis, editors, *DLT 2021*, Vol. 12811 of *Lecture Notes in Computer Science*, pp. 267–278. Springer-Verlag, 2021.

[252] R. C. Lyndon and M. P. Schützenberger. The equation $a^M = b^N c^P$ in a free group. *Michigan Math. J.* **9** (1962), 289–298.

[253] J. Malitz. *Introduction to Mathematical Logic*. Springer-Verlag, 1979.

[254] A. Mandel and I. Simon. On finite semigroups of matrices. *Theoret. Comput. Sci.* **5** (1977/78), 101–111.

[255] S. Mantaci, A. Restivo, G. Romana, G. Rosone, and M. Sciortino. String attractors and combinatorics on words. In *ICTCS 2019*, Vol. 2504 of *CEUR Workshop Proceedings*, pp. 57–71, 2019. Available at ceur-ws.org/Vol-2504/paper8.pdf.

[256] S. Mantaci, A. Restivo, G. Romana, G. Rosone, and M. Sciortino. A combinatorial view on string attractors. *Theoret. Comput. Sci.* **850** (2021), 236–248.

[257] S. Marcus. Symmetry phenomena in infinite words, with biological, philosophical and aesthetic relevance. *Symmetry: Culture and Science* **14/15** (2003-2004), 477–487.

[258] V. Marsault and J. Sakarovitch. Ultimate periodicity of *b*-recognisable sets: A quasilinear procedure. In M. P. Béal and O. Carton, editors, *Developments in Language Theory, 17th International Conference, DLT 2013*, Vol. 7907 of *Lecture Notes in Computer Science*, pp. 362–373. Springer-Verlag, 2013.

[259] Y. V. Matiyasevich. *Hilbert's Tenth Problem*. The MIT Press, 1993.

[260] G. Melançon. Lyndon factorization of infinite words. In C. Puech and R. Reischuk, editors, *STACS 96, 13th Annual Symposium on Theoretical Aspects of Computer Science*, Vol. 1046 of *Lecture Notes in Computer Science*, pp. 147–154. Springer-Verlag, 1996.

[261] G. Melançon. Lyndon word. In M. Hazewinkel, editor, *Encyclopedia of Mathematics*. Springer-Verlag, 2001.

[262] R. Mercaş, P. Ochem, A. V. Samsonov, and A. M. Shur. Binary patterns in binary cube-free words: avoidability and growth. *RAIRO Inform. Théor. App.* **48** (2014), 369–389.

[263] F. Mignosi and G. Pirillo. Repetitions in the Fibonacci infinite word. *RAIRO Inform. Théor. App.* **26** (1992), 199–204.

[264] F. Mignosi and A. Restivo. Characteristic Sturmian words are extremal for the critical factorization theorem. *Theoret. Comput. Sci.* **454** (2012), 199–205.

[265] F. Mignosi, A. Restivo, and S. Salemi. Periodicity and the golden ratio. *Theoret. Comput. Sci.* **204** (1998), 153–167.

[266] F. Mignosi, A. Restivo, and M. Sciortino. Words and forbidden factors. *Theoret. Comput. Sci.* **273** (2002), 99–117.

[267] M. Milosevic and N. Rampersad. Squarefree words with interior disposable factors. *Theoret. Comput. Sci.* **863** (2021), 120–126.

[268] I. Mitrofanov. On uniform recurrence of HD0L systems. Arxiv preprint arXiv:1111.1999 [math.CO], available at arxiv.org/abs/1111.1999, 2011.

[269] I. Mitrofanov. A proof for the decidability of HD0L ultimate periodicity. Arxiv preprint arXiv:1110.4780 [math.CO], available at arxiv.org/abs/1110.4780, 2011.

[270] I. Mitrofanov. On uniform recurrence of morphic sequences. Arxiv preprint arXiv:1412.5066 [math.CO], available at arxiv.org/abs/1412.5066, 2014.

[271] I. Mitrofanov. Periodicity of morphic words. *J. Math. Sci.* **206** (2015), 679–687.

[272] I. Mitrofanov. On almost periodicity of morphic sequences. *Doklady Math.* **93** (2016), 207–210.

[273] L. Mol and N. Rampersad. Lengths of extremal square-free ternary words. Arxiv preprint arXiv:2001.11763 [math.CO], available at arxiv.org/abs/2001.11763, 2020.

[274] L. Mol, N. Rampersad, and J. Shallit. Extremal overlap-free and extremal $\beta$-free binary words. Arxiv preprint arXiv:2006.10152 [math.CO], available at arxiv.org/abs/2006.10152, 2020.

[275] M. Morse. Recurrent geodesics on a surface of negative curvature. *Trans. Amer. Math. Soc.* **22** (1921), 84–100.

[276] M. Morse and G. A. Hedlund. Symbolic dynamics. *Amer. J. Math.* **60** (1938), 815–866.

[277] M. Morse and G. A. Hedlund. Symbolic dynamics II. Sturmian trajectories. *Amer. J. Math.* **62** (1940), 1–42.

[278] H. Mousavi. Automatic theorem proving in Walnut. Arxiv preprint arXiv:1603.06017 [cs.FL], available at arxiv.org/abs/1603.06017, 2016.

[279] H. Mousavi, L. Schaeffer, and J. Shallit. Decision algorithms for Fibonacci-automatic words, I: basic results. *RAIRO Inform. Théor. App.* **50** (2016), 39–66.

[280] H. Mousavi and J. Shallit. Mechanical proofs of properties of the Tribonacci word. In F. Manea and D. Nowotka, editors, *Proc. WORDS 2015*, Vol. 9304 of *Lecture Notes in Computer Science*, pp. 1–21. Springer-Verlag, 2015.

[281] S. Narayanan. Functions on antipower prefix lengths of the Thue-Morse word. *Discrete Math.* **343** (2020), 111675.

[282] M. B. Nathanson. *Additive Number Theory: The Classical Bases.* Springer-Verlag, 1996.

[283] J. Nicholson and N. Rampersad. Non-repetitive complexity of infinite words. *Disc. Appl. Math.* **208** (2016), 114–122.

[284] F. Nicolas and Yu. Pritykin. On uniformly recurrent morphic sequences. *Internat. J. Found. Comp. Sci.* **20** (2009), 919–940.

[285] J. Reyes Noche. On Stewart's choral sequence. *Gibón* **8**(1) (2008), 1–5.

[286] J. Reyes Noche. Generalized choral sequences. *Matimyás Matematika* **31** (2008), 25–28.

[287] J. Reyes Noche. On generalized choral sequences. *Gibón* **9** (2011), 51–69.

[288] P. Ochem, N. Rampersad, and J. Shallit. Avoiding approximate squares. *Internat. J. Found. Comp. Sci.* **19** (2008), 633–648.

[289] R. Oei, D. Ma, C. Schulz, and P. Hieronymi. Pecan: An automated theorem prover for automatic sequences using Büchi automata. Arxiv preprint arXiv:2102.01727 [cs.LO], available at arxiv.org/abs/2102.01727, 2021.

[290] A. Ostrowski. Bemerkungen zur Theorie der Diophantischen Approximationen. *Abh. Math. Sem. Hamburg* **1** (1922), 77–98,250–251. Reprinted in *Collected Mathematical Papers*, Vol. 3, pp. 57–80.

[291] H. Pandey, V. K. Singh, and A. Pandey. A new NFA reduction algorithm for state minimization problem. *Internat. J. Appl. Info. Sys.* **8** (2015), 27–30.

[292] J.-J. Pansiot. A propos d'une conjecture de F. Dejean sur les répétitions dans les mots. *Disc. Appl. Math.* **7** (1984), 297–311.

[293] J.-J. Pansiot. Decidability of periodicity for infinite words. *RAIRO Inform. Théor. App.* **20** (1986), 43–46.

[294] E. Parker and S. Chatterjee. An automata-theoretic algorithm for counting solutions to Presburger formulas. In E. Duesterwald, editor, *CC 2004*, Vol. 2985 of *Lecture Notes in Computer Science*, pp. 104–119. Springer-Verlag, 2004.

[295] J. Peltomäki. Introducing privileged words: privileged complexity of Sturmian words. *Theoret. Comput. Sci.* **500** (2013), 57–67.

[296] J. Peltomäki. Privileged factors in the Thue-Morse word—a comparison of privileged words and palindromes. *Disc. Appl. Math.* **193** (2015), 187–199.

[297] D. Perrin and J.-E. Pin. *Infinite Words: Automata, Semigroups, Logic and Games*, Vol. 141 of *Pure and Applied Mathematics*. Elsevier, 2004.

[298] M. Petkovšek, H. S. Wilf, and D. Zeilberger. $A = B$. A. K. Peters, 1996.

[299] A. J. van der Poorten and J. O. Shallit. Folded continued fractions. *J. Number Theory* **40** (1992), 237–250.

[300] M. Presburger. Über die Volständigkeit eines gewissen Systems der Arithmetik ganzer Zahlen, in welchem die Addition als einzige Operation hervortritt. In *Sparawozdanie z I Kongresu Matematyków Krajów Slowianskich*, pp. 92–101, 395. Sklad Glówny, Warsaw, 1929.

[301] M. Presburger. On the completeness of a certain system of arithmetic of whole numbers in which addition occurs as the only operation. *Hist. Phil. Logic* **12** (1991), 225–233.

[302] H. Prodinger and F. J. Urbanek. Infinite 0–1-sequences without long adjacent identical blocks. *Discrete Math.* **28** (1979), 277–289.

[303] E. Prouhet. Mémoire sur quelques relations entre les puissances des nombres. *C. R. Acad. Sci. Paris* **33** (1851), 225.

[304] B. P. Przybocki. Lengths of irreducible and delicate words. Arxiv preprint arXiv:2108.06646 [math.CO], available at arxiv.org/abs/2108.06646, 2021.

[305] S. Puzynina. Abelian properties of words. In R. Mercaş and D. Reidenbach, editors, *WORDS 2019*, Vol. 11682 of *Lecture Notes in Computer Science*, pp. 28–45. Springer-Verlag, 2019.

[306] S. Puzynina and L. Q. Zamboni. Abelian returns in Sturmian words. *J. Combin. Theory. Ser. A* **120** (2013), 390–408.

[307] A. Rajasekaran, N. Rampersad, and J. Shallit. Overpals, underlaps, and underpals. In S. Brlek, F. Dolce, C. Reutenauer, and É. Vandomme, editors, *WORDS 2017*, Vol. 10432 of *Lecture Notes in Computer Science*, pp. 17–29. Springer-Verlag, 2017.

[308] A. Rajasekaran, J. Shallit, and T. Smith. Additive number theory via automata theory. *Theoret. Comput. Sci.* **64** (2020), 542–567.

[309] J. L. Ramírez-Alfonsín. *The Diophantine Frobenius Problem*. Oxford University Press, 2005.

[310] N. Rampersad. The periodic complexity function of the Thue-Morse word, the Rudin-Shapiro word, and the period-doubling word. Arxiv preprint arXiv:2112.04416 [math.CO], available at arxiv.org/abs/2112.04416, 2021.

[311] N. Rampersad, M. Rigo, and P. Salimov. A note on abelian returns in rotation words. *Theoret. Comput. Sci.* **528** (2014), 101–107.

[312] N. Rampersad, J. Shallit, and É. Vandomme. Critical exponents of balanced words. *Theoret. Comput. Sci.* **777** (2019), 454–463.

[313] N. Rampersad, J. Shallit, and M.-w. Wang. Avoiding large squares in infinite binary words. *Theoret. Comput. Sci.* **339** (2005), 19–34.

[314] D. Reble. Zeckendorf vs. Wythoff representations: comments on A007895. Manuscript available at oeis.org/A007895/a007895.pdf, 2008.

[315] S. Riasat. Powers and anti-powers in binary words. Master's thesis, University of Waterloo, Waterloo, Ontario, Canada, 2019. Available at tinyurl.com/2pbzumf6.

[316] G. Richomme, K. Saari, and L. Q. Zamboni. Abelian complexity in minimal subshifts. *J. London Math. Soc.* **83** (2011), 79–95.

[317] M. Rigo. *Formal Languages, Automata and Numeration Systems 1: Introduction to Combinatorics on Words*. Wiley, 2014.

[318] M. Rigo. *Formal Languages, Automata and Numeration Systems 2: Applications to Recognizability and Decidability*. Wiley, 2014.

[319] M. Rigo, P. Salimov, and E. Vandomme. Some properties of abelian return words. *J. Integer Sequences* **16** (2013), Article 13.2.5 (electronic). Available at cs.uwaterloo.ca/journals/JIS/VOL16/Rigo/rigo3.html.

[320] M. Rigo and L. Waxweiler. A note on syndeticity, recognizable sets and Cobham's theorem. *Bull. European Assoc. Theor. Comput. Sci.*, No. 88, (2006), 169–173.

[321] N. Robbins. Fibonacci partitions. *Fibonacci Quart.* **34** (1996), 306–313.

[322] J. M. Robson. Separating strings with small automata. *Inform. Process. Lett.* **30** (1989), 209–214.

[323] J. M. Robson. Separating words with machines and groups. *RAIRO Inform. Théor. App.* **30** (1996), 81–86.

[324] E. Rowland and J. Shallit. *k*-automatic sets of rational numbers. In A. H. Dediu and C. Martín-Vide, editors, *Languages and Automata Theory and Applications—6th International Conference, LATA 2012*, Vol. 7183 of *Lecture Notes in Computer Science*, pp. 490–501. Springer-Verlag, 2012.

[325] E. Rowland and J. Shallit. Automatic sets of rational numbers. *Internat. J. Found. Comp. Sci.* **26** (2015), 343–365.

[326] A. Roy and H. Straubing. Definability of languages by generalized first-order formulas over (ℕ, +). *SIAM J. Comput.* **37** (2007), 502–521.

[327] W. Rudin. Some theorems on Fourier coefficients. *Proc. Amer. Math. Soc.* **10** (1959), 855–859.

[328] K. Saari. Periods of factors of the Fibonacci word. In *WORDS 07*, 2007.

[329] O. Salon. Suites automatiques à multi-indices. In *Séminaire de Théorie des Nombres de Bordeaux*, pp. 4.01–4.27, 1986-1987.

[330] O. Salon. Suites automatiques à multi-indices et algébricité. *C. R. Acad. Sci. Paris* **305** (1987), 501–504.

[331] O. Salon. Quelles tuiles! (pavages apériodiques du plan et automates bidimensionnels). *Séminaire de Théorie des Nombres de Bordeaux* **1** (1989), 1–25.

[332] O. Salon. *Propriétés arithmétiques des automates multidimensionnels.* PhD thesis, Université Bordeaux I, 1989.

[333] C. Sándor. Partitions of natural numbers and their representation functions. *INTEGERS—Elect. J. Comb. Numb. Theory* **4** (2004), #A18.

[334] L. Schaeffer. Deciding properties of automatic sequences. Master's thesis, School of Computer Science, University of Waterloo, 2013.

[335] L. Schaeffer and J. Shallit. The critical exponent is computable for automatic sequences. *Internat. J. Found. Comp. Sci.* **23** (2012), 1611–1626.

[336] L. Schaeffer and J. Shallit. Closed, palindromic, rich, privileged, trapezoidal, and balanced words in automatic sequences. *Electron. J. Combin.* **23**(1) (2016), #P1.25 (electronic).

[337] L. Schaeffer and J. Shallit. String attractors for automatic sequences. Arxiv preprint arXiv:2012.06840 [cs.FL], available at arxiv.org/abs/2012.06840, 2021.

[338] J.-C. Schlage-Puchta. A criterion for non-automaticity of sequences. *J. Integer Sequences* **6** (2003), Article 03.3.8 (electronic). Available at tinyurl.com/5ppysyct.

[339] S. Schmitz. Complexity hierarchies beyond elementary. *ACM Trans. Comput. Theory* **8**(1) (2016), Article 3.

[340] T. Schüle. *Verification of Infinite State Systems Using Presburger Arithmetic.* PhD thesis, Fachbereich Informatik, Technischen Universität Kaiserslautern, 2007.

[341] N. Schweikardt. Arithmetic, first-order logic, and counting quantifiers. *ACM Trans. Comput. Logic* **6** (2005), 634–671.

[342] P. Séébold. *Propriétés combinatoires des mots infinis engendrés par certains morphismes (Thèse de 3e cycle).* PhD thesis, Université P. et M. Curie, Institut de Programmation, Paris, 1985.

[343] P. Séébold. Lyndon factorization of the Prouhet words. *Theoret. Comput. Sci.* **307** (2003), 179–197.

[344] J. O. Shallit. Simple continued fractions for some irrational numbers. *J. Number Theory* **11** (1979), 209–217.

[345] J. O. Shallit. Numeration systems, linear recurrences, and regular sets. *Inform. Comput.* **113** (1994), 331–347.

[346] J. Shallit. *A Second Course in Formal Languages and Automata Theory.* Cambridge University Press, 2009.

[347] J. Shallit. The critical exponent is computable for automatic sequences. In P. Ambrož, S. Holub, and Z. Masáková, editors, *WORDS 2011, 8th International Conference*, pp. 231–239. Elect. Proc. Theor. Comput. Sci., 2011. Revised version, with L. Schaeffer, available at `arxiv.org/abs/1104.2303v2`.

[348] J. Shallit. Enumeration and automatic sequences. *Pure Math. Appl.* **25** (2015), 96–106.

[349] J. Shallit. Subword complexity of the Fibonacci-Thue-Morse sequence: the proof of Dekking's conjecture. *Indag. Math.* **32** (2021), 729–735.

[350] J. Shallit. Frobenius numbers and automatic sequences. Arxiv preprint arXiv:2103.10904 [math.NT], available at `arxiv.org/abs/2103.10904`, 2021.

[351] J. Shallit. Hilbert's spacefilling curve described by automatic, regular, and synchronized sequences. Arxiv preprint arXiv:2106.01062 [cs.FL], available at `arxiv.org/abs/2106.01062`, 2021.

[352] J. Shallit. Robbins and Ardila meet Berstel. *Inform. Process. Lett.* **167** (2021), 106081.

[353] J. Shallit. Abelian complexity and synchronization. *INTEGERS—Elect. J. Comb. Numb. Theory* **21** (2021), #A36 (electronic). Available at `tinyurl.com/36ba7eza`.

[354] J. Shallit. Additive number theory via automata and logic. Arxiv preprint arXiv:2112.13627 [math.NT], available at `arxiv.org/abs/2112.13627`, 2021.

[355] J. Shallit. Synchronized sequences. In T. Lecroq and S. Puzynina, editors, *WORDS 2021*, Vol. 12847 of *Lecture Notes in Computer Science*, pp. 1–19. Springer-Verlag, 2021.

[356] J. Shallit. Sumsets of Wythoff sequences, Fibonacci representation, and beyond. *Period. Math. Hung.* **84** (2022), 37–46.

[357] J. Shallit. Note on a Fibonacci parity sequence. Arxiv preprint arXiv:2203.10504 [cs.FL]. Available at `arxiv.org/abs/2203.10504`, 2022.

[358] J. O. Shallit and M.-w. Wang. Weakly self-avoiding words and a construction of Friedman. *Electron. J. Combin.* **8**(1) (2001), N2 (electronic), `tinyurl.com/bmhsns56`

[359] J. Shallit and R. Zarifi. Circular critical exponents for Thue–Morse factors. *RAIRO Inform. Théor. App.* **53** (2019), 37–49.

[360] H. S. Shapiro. Extremal problems for polynomials and power series. Master's thesis, MIT, 1952.

[361] A. M. Shur. Combinatorial complexity of rational languages. *Diskretn. Anal. Issled. Oper., Ser. 1* **12**(2) (2005), 78–99. In Russian.

[362] A. Shur. Growth properties of power-free languages. *Comput. Sci. Rev.* **6** (2012), 187–208.

[363] M. Sipser. *Introduction to the Theory of Computation*. Cengage Learning, 3rd edition, 2013.

[364] R. Siromoney, L. Mathew, V. Dare, and K. Subramanian. Infinite Lyndon words. *Inform. Process. Lett.* **50** (1994), 101–104.

[365] N. J. A. Sloane et al. The On-Line Encyclopedia of Integer Sequences, 2022. Available at `oeis.org`.

[366] D. Sprunger, W. Tune, J. Endrullis, and L. S. Moss. Eigenvalues and transduction of morphic sequences. In A. M. Shur and M. V. Volkov, editors, *Developments in Language Theory, 18th International Conference, DLT 2014*, Vol. 8633 of *Lecture Notes in Computer Science*, pp. 239–251. Springer-Verlag, 2014.

[367] I. Stewart. *How to Cut a Cake: And Other Mathematical Conundrums*. Cambridge University Press, 2006.

[368] T. K. Subrahmonian Moothatu. Eulerian entropy and non-repetitive subword complexity. *Theoret. Comput. Sci.* **420** (2012), 80–88.

[369] Z. Sun and A. Winterhof. On the maximum order complexity of the Thue-Morse and Rudin-Shapiro sequence. *Uniform. Distrib. Theory* **14** (2019), 33–42.

[370] A. Szilard, S. Yu, K. Zhang, and J. O. Shallit. Characterizing regular languages with polynomial densities. In I. M. Havel and V. Koubek, editors, *Proc. 17th Symposium, Mathematical Foundations of Computer Science 1992*, Vol. 629 of *Lecture Notes in Computer Science*, pp. 494–503. Springer-Verlag, 1992.

[371] M. Tang. Partitions of the set of natural numbers and their representation functions. *Discrete Math.* **308** (2008), 2614–2616.

[372] B. Tan and Z.-Y. Wen. Some properties of the Tribonacci sequence. *European J. Combin.* **28** (2007), 1703–1719.

[373] A. Thue. Über unendliche Zeichenreihen. *Norske vid. Selsk. Skr. Mat. Nat. Kl.* **7** (1906), 1–22. Reprinted in *Selected Mathematical Papers of Axel Thue*, T. Nagell, editor, Universitetsforlaget, Oslo, 1977, pp. 139–158.

[374] A. Thue. Über die gegenseitige Lage gleicher Teile gewisser Zeichenreihen. *Norske vid. Selsk. Skr. Mat. Nat. Kl.* **1** (1912), 1–67. Reprinted in *Selected Mathematical Papers of Axel Thue*, T. Nagell, editor, Universitetsforlaget, Oslo, 1977, pp. 413–478.

[375] O. Turek. Abelian complexity function of the Tribonacci word. *J. Integer Sequences* **18** (2015), Article 15.3.4 (electronic). Available at tinyurl.com/mr2xuv3p.

[376] S. Vajda. *Fibonacci and Lucas Numbers, and the Golden Section: Theory and Applications*. Dover, 2007.

[377] A. Valmari. Fast brief practical DFA minimization. *Inform. Process. Lett.* **112** (2012), 213–217.

[378] A. Wah and H. Picciotto. *Algebra: Themes, Tools, Concepts*. Creative Publications, Mountain View, CA, 1994. Available at tinyurl.com/bdpbt6m6.

[379] T. White. On the coefficients of a recursion relation for the Fibonacci partition function. *Fibonacci Quart.* **24** (1986), 133–137.

[380] S. Widmer. Permutation complexity of the Thue-Morse word. *Adv. in Appl. Math.* **47** (2011), 309–329.

[381] H. Wilf. What is an answer? *Amer. Math. Monthly* **89** (1982), 289–292.

[382] W. A. Wythoff. A modification of the game of nim. *Nieuw Archief voor Wiskunde* **7** (1907), 199–202.

[383] E. Zeckendorf. Représentation des nombres naturels par une somme de nombres de Fibonacci ou de nombres de Lucas. *Bull. Soc. Roy. Liège* **41** (1972), 179–182.

# Index

Printed in the United States
by Baker & Taylor Publisher Services